From Pariah to Patriot

John G. Gagliardo

From Pariah to Patriot

THE CHANGING IMAGE

OF THE GERMAN PEASANT

1770-1840

THE UNIVERSITY PRESS OF KENTUCKY

Standard Book Number 8131-1187-0
Library of Congress Catalog Card Number 72-80091

COPYRIGHT © 1969 BY THE UNIVERSITY PRESS OF KENTUCKY

A statewide cooperative scholarly publishing agency serving Berea College,
Centre College of Kentucky, Eastern Kentucky University, Kentucky State
College, Morehead State University, Murray State University, University
of Kentucky, University of Louisville, and Western Kentucky University.
Editorial and Sales Offices: Lexington, Kentucky 40506

To the memory of my father,

my first and best teacher

Contents

Preface

In the social history of the western world in the last two hundred years, few trends are as arresting as the gradual rise of the lower orders of society to a position of prominence in the planning of governments. It was once thought that the French Revolution alone had inaugurated the era of popular political ideology in Europe, and that it alone had begun the implementation of the idea of political equality through the concept of universal citizenship. It is now generally acknowledged, however, that while the revolution remains of inestimable importance in the development of democratic ideology, some of the roots of egalitarian political ideas can be found as early as the mid-eighteenth century in both the theory and the practice of enlightened absolutism.

One important facet of the development of egalitarianism in both a social and a political sense, and one which well illustrates the progress of social leveling under the old regime before the revolution, is the gradual abolition of serfdom in many countries of Europe. In many territories of Germany, for example, the final abolition of serfdom in the first decades of the nineteenth century was merely the ultimate step of a series begun in the early years of the eighteenth century. But wherever the formal progress of social egalitarianism can be confirmed through legal innovations or structural changes in government, the progress of some sort of egalitarian ideology can also be confirmed. This study is an attempt to describe and to analyze the development of one aspect of such an ideology in Germany—the complex of opinions concerning the peasant and his place in society which accompanied agrarian reform in its most active years, roughly from 1770 to about 1840.

German agrarian reforms themselves—that is, the actual legal and administrative aspects of reform—have been studied by numerous scholars in Germany and elsewhere for a long time, and there exists a fairly detailed and comprehensive body of literature on the subject. But a survey of the public literature accompanying this series of reforms has never been undertaken and scholars have remained largely silent on one of the most dramatic and significant concomitants of agrarian reform—the genesis and growth of a remarkable new image of the peasant. An understanding of the nature of this image and of the reasons for its growth is essential not only to a comprehension of the public support for agrarian reform, but above all to the explanation of the public acceptance of the idea of the peasant as a full-fledged citizen. The liberation of the German peasant involved much more than institutional and legal changes; it involved freedom from the tyranny and oppression of a hostile and contemptuous public opinion.

At first glance, one is tempted to regard the rapid development of laudatory opinions concerning the peasant as merely the more or less natural outgrowth of a desire on the part of agrarian reformers to advance their goals. But further study makes it clear that the literature of this period was not often concerned with agriculture or the peasants in themselves, but rather with the peasants as parts of an entire social system. It also becomes apparent that the writers and commentators, no matter how abstract or timeless their specific arguments may have been, were themselves deeply involved in contemporary social questions. No matter how narrowly defined, therefore, reform literature cannot be seen as an internally coherent and systematic attempt to secure one or another reform, but must be regarded in its relationship to the whole picture of German public life in a period of vast social, economic, and political changes. By the year 1840, throughout every category of German publications in which they were mentioned, agriculture and the peasant had assumed a social importance far greater than was necessary merely to prove the advisability of reform. The transformation of the peasant in the public mind from the status of a creature almost less than human to that of a paragon of German national virtue is a phenomenon which transects the entire range of German social development in the years 1770-1840.

Because of the scarcity of works in English dealing in any way with the European and, specifically, the German peasantry, any work on this subject becomes peculiarly susceptible to certain misinterpretations stemming from the perhaps wholly understandable but nonetheless misplaced desire on the part of the reader to make a single book provide answers to a range of questions which an entire shelf of books could scarcely begin to cover. A general outline of the intentions (and nonintentions) of this study will perhaps obviate some of the disappointments.

Broadly speaking, it is here intended, first, to describe the changing image of the German peasant from a social pariah to a patriotic citizen of his fatherland. In the course of less than a century the peasant came to be considered as one who contributed special qualities and performed special duties of singular importance for his society. The second intention is to explain the development of this conception, or image, by relating the specific characteristics attributed to the peasant (as well as the increasingly numerous and valuable social functions he was supposed to perform) to the private and public concerns of German life as seen by those who wrote about him.

With this limited scope, the study does not attempt to address directly the problem of the concrete influence of this progressively developing image on actual agrarian reform or on the transformation of the objective conditions of peasant life. These changes are important for present purposes only insofar as they may have constituted an influence on the thoughts of those who devoted attention to the peasant and his problems generally. With few exceptions, therefore, actual alterations in agrarian relationships are included in the main body of the work only when they are essential to an understanding of the opinions of any given individual or group of individuals. Otherwise, they are relegated to a background chapter (chapter I), which is designed to provide minimum circumstantial context for the study.

The emphasis on opinion has certain other implications as well. Since opinions on matters of general public concern do not generally spring up, change, or disappear overnight, the chronological limits of a study dealing with such opinions can only be approximate and, if particular dates are actually used, even somewhat arbitrary. In this work, 1770 stands only to represent the beginning of a decade in which public discussion of agrarian issues and the peasant, as evident from the literature of the time, became quantitatively greater and qualitatively more intense than in preceding decades. Similarly, 1840 is used to represent the approximate point by which all the important and characteristic features of the new peasant image had become more or less fully developed and fixed as a conceptual type. The year 1848, which especially for those versed in German history might seem to be a more logical terminus, in fact merely demonstrates, in the argumentation surrounding the revolutions of that year and the Frankfurt Parliament, that the new image had already achieved maturity; from the standpoint of the development of the image itself, 1848 is of no special significance.

It is no part of the purpose of this book to judge the objective validity of the opinions which constitute the primary evidence for the essay. Thus, for example, it is not really important here whether peasants actually were more pious (or wiser, better natured, or physically stronger) than city folk, as they were commonly said to be; it is important that they were commonly held to be so, and it is important to know why it was necessary or desirable for those who thought so to hold and make known such opinions, regardless of their correspondence, or lack of it, to reality. Again, whether the success of Prussian arms against Napoleon in 1813 and following years was actually due to the participation of a "new" peasant in the Prussian army (or, for that matter, the whole question of just how successful Prussian arms actually were) is of little importance to the central object of the book. What is important is that numbers of writers and publicists thought or said that the campaigns against Napoleon were highly successful, that this success was in significant measure the proof of the peasant's civic virtue, and that the whole affair was a reason for his further social advancement. It is above all to the point that his participation in the wars had demonstrable effects on the picture formed of him at that time and later.

Acknowledgments

I would like to express my gratitude to several persons whose help has made this study possible. I am greatly indebted to the late Professor Hajo Holborn of Yale University, for I have benefited enormously from his painstaking criticism and the profundity of his knowledge of German history. His recent death has saddened and made poorer the community of European historians on both sides of the Atlantic. I would also like to thank Professor Leonard Krieger, now of Columbia University, for his numerous suggestions and Professor Oswald Backus of the University of Kansas, who was kind enough to read the manuscript and to make a number of helpful comments and criticisms.

I gratefully acknowledge my debt to the staffs of the Sterling Memorial Library at Yale University, Watson Library at the University of Kansas, Converse Memorial Library at Amherst College, and the library of the University of Illinois at Chicago Circle—and especially to the members of the Interlibrary Loans Departments of all four institutions—for their assistance in procuring research materials for this work.

Chapter III of this book appeared, with a few minor changes, under the title: "Moralism, Rural Ideology, and the German Peasant in the Late Eighteenth Century," in *Agricultural History*, XLII, 2 (April 1968), 79-102. My thanks go to the Agricultural History Society for permission to reprint this article in its present amended form.

Finally, many others have helped me in their own ways. Deming and Jane Sherman and Duncan and Marjorie McDougall are but a few of the many people whose importance to this work is greater than they know.

Boston University   JOHN G. GAGLIARDO

Part One

The Background

1 The German Agrarian Scene, 1770-1840

Throughout the period covered by this study, the various states and territories of Germany were predominantly oriented towards the land. The agricultural character of the German scene was reflected in virtually every aspect of collective activity, and in that sense the years from 1770 to 1840 represent a relatively static period. Within this time considerable progress within the agriculturally oriented society was made and developments which in a later period were to turn many Germans away from the soil were proceeding apace, but the overwhelming importance of agriculture in Germany was not appreciably attenuated in this interval. Agriculture produced more wealth and directly employed more people than any other sector of the economy. The peasantry gained its objective importance from these hard facts, which were as well recognized among contemporaries in that time as among historians today. Still, the position occupied by the peasant within the agricultural order did change, and drastically so, in this seventy-year period; indeed, the entire structure of society underwent a transformation of considerable magnitude.

Yet the alteration in the peasant's position did not come through what he was able to do for himself in the direction of improvement. For various reasons—his illiteracy, his parochialism, his aversion to innovation and, most important, his legally, politically, and economically inferior position in the social order—the peasant was almost entirely incapable of undertaking systematic measures for his own betterment. Amelioration had to come from sources outside the peasantry itself, from more influential individuals and groups who had become convinced that the conditions of agrarian life had to be reformed.

In attempting to survey the background of agrarian conditions which obtained in Germany in the years 1770-1840, it is scarcely necessary to go any further into the past than the end of the Thirty Years' War.[1] Whatever strides Germany may have made towards the preconditions of a "modern" economy before 1618 were certainly obliterated by the recurrent catastrophes of that war. The foundations of large-scale domestic and international trade, the remarkable vigor of sixteenth-century urban life, and the concomitant increase in agricultural production—all were given a nearly mortal blow by the savage warfare which raged across Germany in the first half of the seventeenth century. If signs of a certain decay were already beginning to appear on the prosperous German scene by 1600, the war turned a slow decline into a precipitous collapse: total population in the German *Reichsgebiet* fell by perhaps as much as forty percent, from twenty to twelve million; many cities and towns lost as much as ninety percent of their 1618 population; the area of cultivated agricultural land decreased in approximately the same proportion as population; and the number of farm animals decreased by a greater percentage than that of population. The harsh necessities and austerity which descended upon all sectors of the ravaged German economy after the war made impossible the economic self-development of a relatively prosperous peasant class. In this sense, the war contributed in a major way to add the characteristics of real impoverishment and excessive coarseness of life to the social stigma already attached to the peasantry as the lowest social class.

Much of the economic history of Germany from the Peace of Westphalia in 1648 until the end of the eighteenth century was bound up with the gradual reestablishment of the agricultural conditions and level of production which obtained prior to 1618. Traffic in foodstuffs and manufactured articles was small, due to decreased buying power and to political barriers between German states. But within the various territories themselves an effort was made to improve commercial possibilities through construction

[1] The general material for this chapter was taken largely from Wilhelm Abel, *Geschichte der deutschen Landwirtschaft* (Stuttgart, 1962); Heinrich Bechtel, *Wirtschaftsgeschichte Deutschlands*, 3 vols. (Munich, 1951-1956); Theodor von der Goltz, *Geschichte der deutschen Landwirtschaft*, 2 vols. (Stuttgart and Berlin, 1902-1903); Georg Friedrich Knapp, *Die Bauernbefreiung und der Ursprung der Landarbeiter in den älteren Theilen Preussens*, 2 vols. (Leipzig, 1887); Friedrich K. Lütge, *Deutsche Sozial- und Wirtschaftsgeschichte*, 2d ed. (Berlin, 1960), and *Geschichte der deutschen Agrarverfassung* (Stuttgart, 1963); Hans Motteck, *Wirtschaftsgeschichte Deutschlands: ein Grundriss*, vol. I (Berlin, 1957); and August Sartorius von Waltershausen, *Deutsche Wirtschaftgeschichte, 1815-1914* (Jena, 1920).

and improvement of roads and bridges, more efficient use of waterways, and construction of canals. In the rural areas, many peasant holdings operated at a marginal level even in good years, and were often heavily indebted in bad years. The usual source of rural capital, the noble landlord, was frequently as financially embarrassed as were his peasants. Some efforts were made by German rulers to remedy this situation of capital starvation. Frederick II of Prussia, for example, established the credit institutes known as *Landschaften,* which consisted of a pooling of noble estates, on which members could borrow up to two-thirds the value of their estates. But rural credit remained a very serious problem for the entire eighteenth century.[2] In any case, the peasant cultivator benefited at most only very little and very indirectly from these credit schemes.

In Prussia and many other states, mercantilist policies were adopted in order to encourage the development of manufactures, and to make the sovereign political state as far as possible also sovereign in the economic sphere. In most respects, these policies were typical of those of other European states of this time: discouragement of imports, especially of manufactured and luxury goods; encouragement of exports; and the granting of state subsidies or exemptions or monopolies to foster the growth of essential industries. As many mercantilist tricks were exploited by German princes as the German scene would allow, usually (even in Prussia) with indifferent success. Agriculture probably did better under state encouragement than any other major sector of the economy. This was especially true in Prussia, where both Frederick William I and Frederick II regarded agriculture as their special ward. When required, they remitted taxes of landowners and peasants, distributed free seed from government warehouses to insolvent peasants, and at one time even hitched cavalry horses to the plow to help in cultivation.

It is important to remember, however, that in Germany vigorous programs of economic reconstruction prosecuted under the aegis of the state nearly always presupposed the imposition of a social discipline which, practically speaking, had the effect of excluding very much social mobility. As far as the peasantry

[2] See below, 46-50.

was concerned, this meant that for the late seventeenth century and most of the eighteenth, it was not only objective postwar economic conditions but also state policy itself which worked against the possibilities of the peasantry as a group or as individuals evolving towards a significantly greater prosperity and an enhanced reputation in society. Legal improvements which might have helped the peasantry, but which might also have had an adverse effect upon peasants' performance as agricultural producers, or which could create widespread resentment among landowning nobles, were regarded at the highest levels in the state for much of this period as inimical to the collective interest.

It was not until the Stein-Hardenberg period of reform, 1807-1821, that the first major change to affect the German economy since the Thirty Years' War occurred. This reform was carried out only in Prussia, of course, but most other German states, insofar as they had not already entered upon one or another path of reform, followed the Prussian example during or shortly after this period. The specific effects of these reforms on the peasant will be covered below; suffice it here to point out that the general effects for Germany as a whole meant the emancipation of the peasant from subjection to his lord, peasant proprietorship of land, the opening of noble lands to purchase by non-nobles, and access to middle-class professions and vocations for members of the nobility. These measures were intended among other things to provide middle-class capital for agricultural undertakings, and they accomplished their goal rather too well. Even before the Wars of Liberation against Napoleon, there was a great rush by the middle class to buy land, and after the temporary lull occasioned by the war, it turned into a speculative stampede. The desertion of land by newly-freed peasant proprietors who could not maintain a viable farm economy simply because they were inadequately prepared to do so, the drying-up of a number of markets in foreign countries due to the improvement of their own agricultural production, and the inability of landlords to get credit for making improvements—all tended to make large amounts of land available for sale at relatively low prices.

In 1821, the bottom fell out of the land market: land prices crashed, grain prices sank to new lows, and many already mortgaged lands had to be sold for new debts. It has been estimated that in eastern Prussia as many as eighty percent of the noble owners of small estates lost their property during this crisis, which lasted for a full decade. In many instances, the crisis was harder on the market-oriented lords of the larger estates than it was on the peasants, who for the most part still bought and sold in local markets. On the other hand, under these conditions, only very large estates could produce cheaply enough to make a sufficient profit, and the growth of larger units of agricultural production continued throughout this period; peasant-owned acreage increased very little. In many German states, agrarian reform was slowed considerably by these bad years in the face of the failure of large numbers of emancipated peasants to keep their heads above water financially. Even Prussia, the reform leader, experienced a reaction to agrarian social legislation, the threads of which were not again picked up until after the revolutionary events of 1848.

Immediately after 1830, the economic situation of agriculture improved. A series of poor harvests raised grain prices, and land values climbed. The beneficial effects of the *Zollverein,* or German Customs Union, which had become a virtually national institution in 1834, began to be felt in agriculture as trade movement to the cities increased. Until 1840, then, no important sudden changes in the agricultural economy occurred. The total effect of the many profound changes which touched agriculture on the German economy as a whole was one of freeing it from virtually feudal restrictions of many kinds; in a land which was soon to embark on a phenomenal commercial and industrial boom, freedom in the essential sector of agriculture was a fundamental precondition of the rapid development of manufacturing and commercial pursuits.

For those who expected economic freedom to convert the bewildered peasantry into a large, sturdy, and economically independent yeomanry, however, the three decades after the end of the Napoleonic wars were a progressive disappointment. The attitudes of reformers and social theorists of this period clearly reflect chagrin and concern over the increasingly obvious fact that a servile and dependent peasantry had not been changed by the magic wand of legal and economic freedom into a large group of stalwart landed proprietors. What they saw instead was the rapid proliferation of a landless proletariat which had neither the rooted stability of the old servile peasantry nor the bourgeois virtues of the independent peasant landowner.

Accompanying the general improvement of the German economy in the eighteenth and early nineteenth centuries was a series of more or less technical reforms and improvements within the agricultural sector specifically. These improvements were commonly based upon the example and precept of both the Dutch and the English "agricultural revolution," and insofar as they were instituted in any systematic way, they usually depended upon the sponsorship of the governments and rulers of the various German states. Where both were reasonably interested and energetic, as in Prussia under Frederick II, much more was accomplished than in areas where constant prodding from the state and an organizational framework adapted to reform policies did not exist.

In the second half of the eighteenth century, the most consistently sought goal of agricultural reform was probably crop rotation. This would have put an end to the three-field system by a scientific alternation of crops, eliminating the necessity of leaving one-third of the land in fallow at every planting. The practicability of crop rotation was seriously compromised by the unavailability of proper amounts of fertilizer for the land; even though crop alternation exhausted the soil less than the cultivation of the same crop year after year, organic elements still had to be artificially restored. Stimulants such as gypsum were sometimes used, but their expense and lack of general availability made widespread application impossible. Under the circumstances, increased production of manure was the only answer, and numerous essays and articles were devoted to the necessity for an increase in the number of animals and for better stabling and feeding procedures, which would facilitate the collection of dung.

These reforms were obviously related, therefore, and presupposed still other changes in the agricultural system. Frederick II of Prussia saw quite clearly that partition of the common pasture among the peasants who used it would result in better pasture care, which would in turn make it possible for each peasant to keep more animals. He implemented this reform on some of his own domains, with modest success, and recommended it to private nobles as well, only a few of whom were much interested. In theory it was only a step from partition of common lands to the joining of the scattered and noncontiguous strips of farm land of individual peasants. Frederick again hastened to carry this out, but dissatisfactions, quarrels, and complaints were so frequent that even on his domains it was largely a failure—and was almost uniformly unsuccessful on private lands. Other German princes, with a very few exceptions, were rewarded with even less positive results.

If the primary goal of agricultural reformers in the late eighteenth century was crop rotation, their primary achievement lay elsewhere—in the increased cultivation of products to be used as fodder for animals. This was not a modest achievement, for more fodder meant more animals and better feeding, which meant more dung for fertilizer, and this in turn meant more and better field crops. Clover, turnips, and other herbs were the fodder crops most in question here; but the potato gained prominence as chief crop toward the end of the century. The advantage of the potato over clover lay in the fact that it was good for human as well as animal consumption. It ultimately revolutionized the staple consumption of the German lower classes. With greater possibilities for stock raising thus created, more attention could also be given to animal husbandry and the improvement of breeds. Some rulers, for mercantilistic reasons chiefly, began to encourage specialized dairy farming, and in doing so contributed to increase the size and quality of herds. For the average peasant, however, most of this activity was virtually meaningless; more important to him were the few minor improvements in agricultural implements which occurred towards the end of the century.

The nineteenth century to 1840 witnessed no fundamentally new directions in the reform and improvement of methods and practices of agriculture. Peasant liberations of 1807 and subsequent years and the conferral of proprietorship did not immediately bring about the adoption of the three-field system except in certain areas of great urban growth, where rapidly increasing demand forced an early conversion to crop rotation and the fullest possible utilization of the land. In general, however, it was not until the 1830s and 1840s that unified holdings began to predominate. Some areas deliberately retained the three-field system: in Saxony, for example, where sheep raising formed an important part of the economy, the three-field system permitted extensive areas of pasture for the sheep to exist (on the fallow) without the necessity of permanently removing large areas of land from field crop cultivation. By the middle of the nineteenth century, however, the three-field system was very clearly on its way out elsewhere in Germany. The next important agricultural change was the application of science and the products of the new industry to the age-old problem of winning food from the land.

However, no immense economic change in the position of the peasantry took place as a result of agricultural reforms during this period. In 1840, as in the mid-eighteenth century, it was still the size of an individual's lands which tended to determine his wealth. Agricultural innovations were usually expensive; they required capital, and normally only the man who already disposed over fairly large lands could afford them. The small proprietor—the peasant—was hurt in the application of reforms to his own land not only because of his ignorance of the great potential of innovation, but also because he could not afford it. And because he could not afford it, his productivity per unit of land fell relative to that of the large landowner; his competitive position therefore suffered both absolutely and relatively. For the numerous theorists and reformers who looked to technical agricultural improvements as the guarantor of the independence of a free and proprietary peasantry, it became a gloomy truth in the 1820s and 1830s that the few peasants who managed to improve their economic position by introducing "scientific" farming of one sort or another were more than offset by the much larger number whose competitive position was disastrously affected by the greater ability of their wealthier noble or bourgeois landowning neighbors to make use of the new techniques.

The effects of the Thirty Years' War, so catastrophic for the German economy as a whole and for agriculture in particular, were also felt in the area of the status of the peasant, the man who worked the land. It must suffice here to say that the war worsened still further the personal and real relationships of the peasant class, which had only in some areas begun to improve its position since the great Peasants' War of 1525-1526. At the end of hostilities of the Thirty Years' War, what peasants remained on the land were utterly dependent on their lords for the buildings, equipment, and seed needed to pursue their occupation; and lords often took this opportunity to subject peasants to harsher conditions of tenure than had previously obtained. More than ever, the peasant became incapable of influencing his own social destiny.

There was never complete uniformity in the status of peasants in Germany as a whole; status varied from one area to another and even within the same area. But one can at least attempt to describe what elements went into the making of various status categories. At least two criteria must be employed to judge the condition of the peasant in the eighteenth century. The first refers to his personal legal status, the other to the rights of tenure he had on his land. Frequently related in characteristic combinations, they were never necessarily so, and must be considered as almost entirely distinct.

With regard, first, to his personal status, the peasant was either free, servile *(untertänig),* or in thralldom *(leibeigen).* A free peasant had all the legal freedom assigned to any free commoner. His obligations extended only to services, dues, or fees owed as ground rent on the land he farmed. He was free to leave his land, except for contractual agreements he may have made to the contrary, and his obligations to the landlord ceased when he left the land.

A servile peasant, on the other hand, had an inherent personal tie to his lord which was expressed in a number of different ways. He normally had to perform various kinds of services and make certain kinds of payments as obligations arising from his servitude;

and his family, which inherited his servile status, also had to perform certain tasks around the manor house or farm. The servile peasant was bound to the soil—he could neither leave the farm at will, nor marry without his lord's consent. The lord, for his part, could not remove the peasant and his family from the land, and he was obligated to help the peasant in time of need. Usually this peasant held land from his lord, but not always; if so, he owed not only the services and fees which belonged to his servile status, but also any services or dues which rested on the land as rent. A free peasant could become servile by accepting land from a lord on whose lands this constitution prevailed, unless specific reservation of his free status was agreed upon. How well or ill the servile peasant fared depended, of course, upon how large his total obligations were, how strictly they were enforced, and on the character of his lord.

The peasant in thralldom had virtually disappeared in Germany by the eighteenth century. The chief characteristics of peasants so classified were two: first, they were completely bound to the person of the lord, as much his goods and chattels as any buildings or farm implements or animals, and could be sold or otherwise alienated by him at any time; second, they had literally no legal rights, no legal personality, and could not acquire property of any sort, real or personal, for themselves. What they had and kept was theirs only on the sufferance of the lord. They represented, then, serfdom of the lowest order. As stated above, however, there were very few actual *Leibeigenen* left in Germany by the time of the beginning of this study, and the characteristics mentioned above as earmarks of their status were usually mitigated to a considerable degree in actual practice.

By the eighteenth century, a better yardstick for the measurement of the overall material condition of the peasantry was classification by right of tenure, or *Besitzrecht*. Six categories, with a few variations, comprehended virtually all peasants in Germany: 1) the independent proprietor; 2) the *Erbpacht-* and *Erbzinsleute;* 3) the *erbliche Lassiten;* 4) the *unerbliche Lassiten;* 5) the *Zeitpächter;* and, finally, 6) the peasant with precarious tenure. The independent proprietor owned his land free of all rents and dues, and owed only public taxes. Of these, there were very few, mostly in northwestern Germany. Secondly, the *Erb-pacht-* and *Erbzinsleute,* while not owners of their land, could bequeath it to an heir of their own choosing; and, character-istically, if they were servile, their obligations arising out of that servility were restricted to small commemorative payments on specified occasions. Thirdly, the *erbliche Lassiten* also possessed the right to bequeath their land, but the choice of the heir, as long as it remained within the peasant's family, was reserved to the lord from whom the land was held. Also, unlike the *Erbpacht-* and *Erbzinsleute,* the *erbliche Lassiten* could not mortgage or sell their usufruct in the land without the consent of the owner. A sharp line must be drawn to separate this category and the ones above from those which follow. This distinction is based on the heritability of land, and is justified because of the relative freedom in disposition of the land which these peasants possessed. In the judgment of contemporaries as in that of later historians, the vigor and interest of the peasant who could make an investment in land that he knew would remain in the family were greater than for the man who knew that the fruits of his work might be lost to the family or even to himself because he could not bequeath it.

The fourth category, then, that of the *unerbliche Lassiten,* refers to persons who could not bequeath their land, although they were normally permitted to express a preference as to its future occupant. Whether or not the preference was honored was, however, entirely in the lord's hands. The length of the usufruct enjoyed by these peasants was indefinite, but was characteristically for their own lifetime. *Zeitpächter* were lessees to whom the usufruct of land was granted for a certain specified period of time. The presence of a written contract stipulating the exact conditions of the tenure was a distinguishing char-acteristic of this group. Finally, the least favorable right of tenure, which actually was the lack of any right at all, granted usufruct of a piece of land for an undetermined period, but could be terminated at any time by the owner. It appears that very few peasants had this sort of tenure, and it may be that it was roughly coextensive, as a category, with that of the real *Leibei-genen* spoken of above.

In spite of the variety of combinations possible, recent research has demonstrated the existence of five large areas of Germany in which more or less "typical" agrarian constitutions appear to have prevailed; it is difficult to generalize more than that.[3] It is likely, however, that most peasants in Germany in the later eighteenth century enjoyed some form of hereditary tenure, while ordinary servility was the rule in personal legal status. Again, however, it should be emphasized that from a practical point of view the economic well-being of any peasant depended less upon his position within these formal sets of relationships than upon the number and nature of the dues, fees, and services actually required of him. Labor services in particular could be much more of a burden than the payments the peasant had to make, for they could interrupt his work on his own land at critical points; and it is this fact which explains the repeated requests of peasants and of agricultural reformers for commutation of services into payments in cash or kind. Labor services were spoken of as limited *(gemessen)* or unlimited *(ungemessen)*, according to whether the number and time of services were fixed and definite, or left entirely to the pleasure of the lord. Services in the latter category were of course the more onerous, and many appeals were directed to rulers by peasants performing these services, asking that they be defined and fixed.

These differences in peasant status are important to an understanding of reform sentiment and of attitudes towards the peasantry. In terms both of standard of living and of participation in community affairs, the free peasant proprietor of northwestern Germany seems to have provided a model of sorts for many reformers. But the various other stages also provided more realistic alternatives for short term reform; in the later eighteenth century, in a period when even the most sanguine reformer could hardly envision a totally free and proprietary peasantry, it was often enough merely to suggest improvements that would move the peasant one step higher in his rights of tenure or in the manner in which his servile obligations were to be fulfilled. On the other hand, it is not always possible to determine exactly

---

[3] See the highly original contributions of Friedrich K. Lütge, summarized in his *Deutsche Sozial- und Wirtschaftsgeschichte*, 108-19.

what contemporaries meant when they talked about "peasants" in general, precisely because the actual conditions of peasant life and the level of their personal culture varied so much.

If the status of peasants in Germany varied from one area to another, it was also true that this status in some areas changed in the course of the eighteenth century. Reforms were attempted in various areas throughout the century, some of which succeeded, some of which did not. For the sake of brevity, and because it showed at once the most initiative and the greatest variety of reforms, Prussia may be considered as the chief example for reform policy. The first major steps were those taken to abolish *Leibeigenschaft,* a term which at this time in Prussia meant simply nonhereditary rights of tenure. Decrees of 1718, 1719, and 1723 abolished *Leibeigenschaft* in this broader sense on the royal domains in East Prussia, Lithuania, and Eastern Pomerania, and granted peasants the right to sell their land, with the approval of the provincial Domains-Chamber which leased and supervised the domains. These decrees were slowly put into effect, and in following years King Frederick William I strove to regulate and fix the labor-service requirements, and generally also to lessen them.

The next major reform undertaken on the domains occurred in East Prussia and Lithuania, in 1763, when Frederick II forbade the royal officials who leased his domains to make use of *Gesinde-zwangsdienst,* the right to require services from the families of servile peasants. This order, together with the earlier reforms, in effect abolished hereditary personal servitude. A retreat from this position was suggested by an edict of 1773, but most provincial officials responsible for implementing the decree ignored it because of their feeling that it undermined and contradicted not only the decree of 1763, but also a later one of 1767, which had actually abolished all those services arising out of servitude alone. In 1804, another royal order formally restated the position of 1763. Meanwhile, in 1777, hereditary tenure was granted to all other domains peasants in the monarchy, although it was not until 1790 that it was determined that the royal domains-lessee was to choose which of the children of a peasant was to inherit the land from his father. Correspondingly, *Gesindezwangsdienst* was abolished for the domains in the rest of the monarchy between 1799 and 1805.

The last reform on the domains before the great reforms of 1807 and after concerned the redemption of the labor-service obligations of peasants. By a series of laws beginning in 1799, domains peasants all over the monarchy were given the opportunity to redeem certain of their services. In Pomerania, Neumark, and Brandenburg, peasants who redeemed such services were to become full owners of their land upon payment of a certain fixed sum beyond the redemption fees, known as *Einkaufsgeld.* Later legislation extended the possibility of ownership of land to peasants in East and West Prussia and Lithuania, which carried with it obligatory redemption of services. By the time of the agrarian reform law of 1807, then, the position of the domains peasants was a very good one; they were in all cases the hereditary occupants of their lands, and in some cases real proprietors; hereditary servitude was abolished; and the peasant was to a large extent free of services. But it was not the position of the domains peasants which made the reform legislation of 1807 necessary; the condition of peasants under private nobles had not kept pace with that of domains peasants, and while the Prussian kings made numerous attempts during the century to improve the lot of private peasants, both by specific legislation and by their own example, in dealing with nobles they had to proceed cautiously, and therefore accomplished little.

Both Frederick William I and Frederick II were comparatively successful in preventing physical mistreatment of peasants *(Bauernschinden),* and Frederick II succeeded in asserting the right of *Leibeigenen* in Pomerania and West Prussia, the worst areas of the monarchy, to the ownership of their goods and chattels *(mobilia).* But in spite of many other plans and attempts, the conspiracy of his own officials, most of whom were themselves noble landowners, resulted in a bloc of passive resistance to further reform, and Frederick had the continually frustrating experience of seeing the execution of his plans fail from a deliberate lack of enthusiasm on the part of his administrators.

In consequence, the lot of the private peasant at the end of the century varied in few essentials from what it had been at the beginning.

Reform projects in other German states followed much the same pattern as that of Prussia, with some differences. In the Danish-ruled duchies of Schleswig and Holstein, noble landowners themselves abolished personal servitude, which was to disappear, by stages, over an eight-year period beginning in 1797; labor services were also abolished and hereditary tenure introduced. In Bavaria, the enlightened Electors Max Joseph III and Karl Theodor worked to commute labor services of private peasants into cash payments, an arrangement which had existed on the domains in Bavaria since the end of the seventeenth century. Karl Friedrich of Baden abolished servitude on his domains in 1783—which meant the end of servitude in all of Baden, practically speaking, since only he had peasants who were servile. Dues of servility were abolished, but not labor services. Finally, in Hanover and a number of other smaller states, successful efforts were made to commute all services arising from servitude into cash payments. This was begun in Hanover in 1753, and was virtually completed there by the 1790s.

Reforms in the agrarian constitution of Prussia, as well as those that had been undertaken in Schleswig and Holstein, were praised in much of the agrarian publicistic literature of the late eighteenth century, and these reforms probably helped to stimulate reform sentiment in other German states. But even if the lot of some of the most heavily oppressed peasants was eased somewhat, the most basic problems of the agrarian constitution had not been dealt with anywhere to any major extent by the end of the eighteenth century. The occasion for more thorough reform came more quickly than many statesmen had supposed it would, for the collapse of Prussia in the battles of Jena and Auerstädt in 1806 and the subsequent occupation of much of Germany by Napoleon's armies forced a rapid reappraisal in Prussia of the administration of the state and of the sources of vitality and power of the monarchy. Under the tutelage of Baron vom Stein and later Prince Hardenberg, Prussia moved rapidly to reform herself in both areas.

With respect to agriculture and the peasant, the first important Prussian reform was contained in an edict of October 9, 1807. By this document, all class restrictions on the purchase of land were abolished; the acquisition of servile status by whatever means was prohibited; all peasants who possessed hereditary rights in their land, together with their families, were declared immediately free; and it was declared that all servitude was to be abolished as of St. Martin's Day (November 11) 1810. An edict of October 28, 1807, extended the abolition of servitude to the domains, where *all* peasants were declared free as of June 1, 1808. All peasants with hereditary tenure were permitted, subject to some restrictions, to mortgage and sell their land—which meant really only the sale of the occupancy of the land and the rental obligations attached to it.

Domains peasants in East and West Prussia and Lithuania were compelled to become full owners of their land, or else leave it, by a royal order of July 27, 1808. A rather complicated procedure was involved, by which the peasant was given the opportunity to buy his land from the monarch for a sum equal to about fifteen times the value of his total yearly obligations, with one-quarter of the latter total to remain on the land as a permanent public tax. He had nearly twenty-five years in which to pay the amount of the purchase price, and by whatever means he chose. Peasants who did not wish to remain on the land were to have their land auctioned off, and were to be paid the auction price, less costs; the new owner then became subject to the provisions of the law as outlined above.

In following years, the government attacked the problem of converting mere tenure into proprietorship for private peasants. By edict of September 14, 1811, all private peasants excepting those with the best rights of tenure (meaning the *Erbpacht-* and *Erbzinsleute,* essentially) were given the opportunity to become proprietors simply by giving up to their lord one-half or one-third of the land they occupied, depending on what sort of tenure they had: nonhereditary tenants gave up more than the hereditary. The provisions of this edict were not to go into force for four years after all conditions had been agreed upon by both lords and peasants. Because of the confusion of the Wars of

Liberation, few agreements were immediately made, and before even these could be implemented, grumbling and dissatisfaction on the part of the district estates *(Kreisstände)* and many individual landowners had forced the convocation of a national representative assembly to debate the problems arising out of the law of 1811. A special commission was created to make changes in the law, and the results of the deliberations were taken up in the declaration of May 29, 1816. The "crisis mentality" of the pre-Liberation period was already visibly waning, and conservative opposition to further reform showed up in this declaration; in general, it restated the provisions of the law of 1811, but considerably restricted the number of persons who could actually become proprietors by excluding peasants whose lands were by themselves too small to support a family, those who had no draught animals, and so forth. In the absence of the willingness of statesmen to push through any social guarantees for the livelihood of peasants (who, though they had become proprietors, would quite obviously be at the very margin of economic independence), the declaration of 1816, though not notably benevolent in intent, was yet beneficial in its effects. By preventing such peasants from becoming proprietors, it probably also prevented them from a ruination which proprietorship eventually brought even to many of their substantially better-off fellows who did gain ownership of their land.

With two laws of June 7, 1821, the great period of agrarian reform in Prussia came to an end. The first of these was designed to give the possibility of free proprietorship to those peasants who had been excluded by earlier legislation because of their favorable rights of tenure—chiefly the *Erbpacht-* and *Erbzinsleute.* It provided for the permanent redemption of all services and payments if either lord or peasant were interested, although it excluded from this possibility peasants who did not have a full team of draught animals.[4] The second law provided for the partition of village common lands in certain cases among the peasants who had rights to the use of the lands. Applied in a

---

[4] The stipulation concerning draught animals was a sensible one in many respects, for if a peasant had none, his chances of making good as an independent proprietor were poor; he simply could not cultivate as much or as well as the man who had one animal or a team.

large number of places, it was frequently accompanied by consolidation of the strip-fields of the peasants, and was quite effective in creating better agricultural conditions for some areas.

After 1821, and before 1848, further laws relating to consolidation of fields, partition of common lands, and minor regulations of provisions contained in earlier laws were passed; but in general, agrarian legislation for a number of years failed to follow through on original commitments to the peasantry as a whole. While legislation provided some peasants who already possessed sufficient means with the opportunity to develop their farms far beyond the limits imposed by the old system, it also exposed large numbers to the impersonal flux of the market, with few attempts to provide safeguards against bankruptcy or to set up a viable credit system for temporarily embarrassed peasants. Furthermore, it should not be assumed that the changes described above occurred all at once; and it would not be correct to paint a picture in which all peasants appeared to be either full proprietors or completely free of their old service requirements. Such was not the case at any time within the period of this study.

In other states of Germany, the abolition of *Leibeigenschaft* and of personal servitude was introduced somewhat more slowly than in Prussia, in general, and for the most part later. In the Rhenish Confederation, during the Napoleonic hegemony, however, some liberalization of agrarian relationships occurred under the aegis of the various Rhenish princes. Since conditions in these areas had not generally been as unfavorable to the peasant as in many other regions of Germany before the Napoleonic conquest, it was in the abolition of patrimonial jurisdiction and of hunting rights that the greatest practical effect of reform in these few years was to be found. As a rule, dues and services to the lord were not done away with. On the other hand, some serfs were freed, and many of the beneficial reforms of this period were preserved in the Restoration. Elsewhere, personal servitude of all types was abolished by decree in Bavaria in 1808, in Nassau in 1812, and in Waldeck in 1814. The new constitutions of various states provided for the abolition of servitude or confirmed its abolition where that was already the case. Among the most important states in which this occurred were Württemberg

(1817), Bavaria (1818), Baden (1818), Hesse-Darmstadt (1820), Coburg-Gotha (1821), and Kurhessen (1831). An edict of 1820 in both Grand Duchies of Mecklenburg had abolished *Leibeigen-schaft,* but at the same time swept away the traditional rights of tenure of previously servile peasants. In many of these states, the granting of hereditary tenures to peasants and the abolition of labor services came only in the second half of the nineteenth century. In many states west of the Elbe, governments were considerably less loath to grant independent tenures than was the Prussian government. The scarcity of great entrepreneurial estates and the prevalence of a large number of small farms in the western and southwestern areas led rather to overpopulation than to labor shortage, which was the great fear of landlord-entrepreneurs in the east; correspondingly, the desire to keep peasants dependent on the landlord was much greater east of the Elbe than west of it.

In spite of the very real progress represented by the agrarian legislation of the first quarter of the nineteenth century, however, there was a bad side to the new conditions. The newly-created peasant landowner now had no lord to assist him in time of need, and the responsibility for the support of himself and his family rested squarely on his own shoulders. A substantial number of peasants could not meet the challenge, and were forced to sell their land. Buyers of land included other peasants, but for the most part it was the large estates which absorbed those peasant lands which had to be given up. In most of Germany, the peasant felt it degrading to sell his land, and therefore many peasants whose lands were too small fully to support themselves and their families hired themselves out for labor in their spare time to peasants who had more land than they could farm by them-selves, or to the owners of the great market-oriented estates. In East and West Prussia, however, it was considered neither degrading nor disadvantageous to sell one's lands, and this attitude was not unusual all over central northern Germany, where large estates were common. Peasants who sold out either lived in the village off the proceeds of the sale, migrated to the cities, or became permanent agricultural laborers on the large estates.

The last years with which this study is concerned were therefore in some measure uneasy ones; the transformation of social relationships which came in the train of the agrarian legislation of the first decades of the nineteenth century worked certain changes which the reformers responsible for the changes had not foreseen. The greatest of these changes was the creation of an agricultural proletariat out of landless peasants or of those whose holdings were too small to provide an adequate income, the interests of whom varied in many important respects from those of the owners of viable peasant farms. East-Elbian Germany became virtually devoid of independent peasant farms, and those peasants who, according to the intent of the reformers, were supposed to become owners of their farms instead either left the land and contributed significantly to the rapid growth of cities such as Berlin, or sank to the position of agricultural day-laborers with no land and extremely low wages. In this development, which Franz Schnabel has called "a mass proletarianization such as Germany had nowhere known prior to the World War and the period of inflation,"[5] western Prussia and indeed many parts of western and southern Germany presented a strong contrast to the northeast, for in these areas, where there was no substantial number of lords engaged in entrepreneurial farming, the small, economically independent peasant succeeded in maintaining himself better. This "proletarianization," however, presented terrific problems to many liberal-minded social thinkers of this period, who believed in economic freedom and the virtues of independence, and who saw the surest guarantee of developing political liberalism and constitutionalism in the existence of a large, free peasantry. The social literature of these years, insofar as it relates to the peasantry, clearly reflects the tension between this liberal ideal and its failure to develop into a reality.

The reactionary spirit of the 1830s and 1840s prevented both the Germanic Confederation and the various individual German governments, but especially that of Prussia where the problem was most difficult, from coming to grips with this growing social issue. The troubles of the uprooted peasants, the agricultural

[5] Franz Schnabel, *Deutsche Geschichte im neunzehnten Jahrhundert*, vol. II, 2d ed. (Munich, 1949), 293.

laborers, ignored by those who were in the best position to help them, joined with the problems of another class of disinherited workers, the artisans of the cities, to present themselves forcibly to the public consciousness for a solution in the German Revolution of 1848. In fact, however, the developed debates of 1848 serve to illustrate that nearly all of the major changes which Germany experienced in the late eighteenth and the early nineteenth centuries had long been such as to increase the amount of attention paid to the peasant by the men who thought about the needs, the problems, and the future of German society as a whole. Some of these changes have been discussed in this chapter; it now remains, in the rest of the book, to explore in detail precisely how public attitudes and opinions towards the peasantry were also transformed and developed in consequence of the pressures and problems stemming from rapidly changing conditions in politics, economics, and society.

2 The Beginnings of Reform Sentiment

The appearance of the peasant or concern for him in German public literature did not by any means have its origin in the last decades of the eighteenth century. He had a place of sorts in the literature of the German Middle Ages, although in that age it is difficult to assign to his appearance any significance beyond the unexciting fact that he and his class were made to form the great and scarcely differentiated matrix in which the deeds of kings and nobles and important events in state and church were supposed to stand out as gems. Medieval chroniclers and others were aware of the peasant, but in their writings he was normally the subject of comment only when some great disaster such as plague, flood, or exceptionally serious crop failure befell him. Attention to his problems was minimal; he and his fellows formed usually at best simply the overwhelming majority of souls which God had created on earth for that time, and at worst, upon occasion, an outright annoyance to the privileged classes which perforce had to do with him.[1]

A particularly conspicuous exception to the inattention shown to peasant problems in medieval German writings was the poem *Meier Helmbrecht,* which appeared in the middle of the thirteenth century. Written by a man calling himself "Wernher the Gardner," the poem concerns itself with a peasant's son who, against his father's wishes, ran off to join a band of robbers and after a career of debauchery and crime, was finally maimed and put to death by some of his outraged victims. Particularly striking is the "healthy peasant self-consciousness," as one writer has put it, which emerges in the beginning of the poem.[2] Warning his son not to run away, the old peasant enjoins him to stay with the plow, as he himself had done, for in so doing he would fulfill a sufficient usefulness. The proud and regal lady as well as the king and the haughty gentleman all owed their positions and well-being to the peasant's industry: when the peasant deserts him, the gentleman's arrogance will collapse miserably.[3] Such an appearance of humble folk in medieval literature was not common, and the particular sort of praise which the peasant class received in this poem was almost unique.

The advent of printing in western Europe made possible the dissemination of pamphlets, brochures, and various other kinds of literature on an increasingly larger scale. The peasant found his way into this literature, but in no sense as an object of considerable or steady attention. The excitement attendant on the Peasants' War of 1525 and its immediate consequences loosed on the German public a veritable flood of literature concerned with the peasant. For the first time in these writings, the man who had interest, and who could read, could get close to the real problems of the peasant and see the beginnings not only of an outlook sympathetic to the peasant, but also of a clear effort to offer solutions for its problems, however feeble and eventually unsuccessful that effort might have been. After the terrible reprisals against the peasants, the desire of nobles and princes affected by the war to normalize relationships and the concomitant unequivocal defeat of all hope for reform resulted in a rapid slackening of peasant literature, which fell off to a trickle in a short time.[4]

It is true, however, that in spite of Luther's condemnation of the Peasants' War and the consequent disillusionment of many peasants with his movement, Protestantism in general reinforced at least among clerics a long Christian tradition of public concern for the plight of the poor and humble of this earth. A vast homiletic literature from the sixteenth and subsequent centuries testifies to the real concern of ecclesiastical persons that the peasant not be forgotten as a man who ought to be able to enjoy the spiritual dignity of his "Christian liberty." Nor was this

[1] For a discussion of the peasant in the literature of the German Middle Ages, see especially Fritz Martini, *Das Bauerntum im deutschen Schrifttum, von den Anfängen bis zum 16. Jahrhundert* (Halle, 1944).

[2] Johannes Bühler, *Der deutsche Bauer im Wandel der Zeiten* (Cologne, 1938), 32.

[3] Wernher der Gartenaere, *Meier Helmbrecht*, ed. Wolfgang Schütz (Berlin, 1957), 51.

[4] For further treatment of this period, see K. Uhrig, "Der Bauer in der Publizistik der Reformation bis zum Ausgang des Bauernkrieges," *Archiv für Reformationsgeschichte*, CXXIX-CXXX, Heft 1-2 (1936), 70-125; CXXXI-CXXXII, Heft 3-4 (1936), 165-225.

sentiment restricted to Protestants, of course; the Catholic Reformation in many cases produced a similar rededication among priests and others to the problems of the downtrodden orders of society, which, as with Protestant preachers, was manifested in chastisement of lords for harsh treatment of peasants, in generalized injunctions to observe the principles of Christian charity, and in the utilization of appropriate parables such as that of the laborers in the vineyard.[5] But while much of this continuing concern was undoubtedly genuine, much of it was just as undoubtedly pure cant, put into sermons with the regularity and monotony of an "amen."

For about the next century after the Peasants' War, in any case, there were but sporadic eruptions of peasant sentiment, centering usually around particularly grave local conditions involving peasant obligations. Any sympathy for the peasants and any solutions offered for their betterment were usually restricted by the specific circumstances of a particular local situation. Of the relatively few nontechnical writings which in one way or another concerned themselves with the peasant after 1525, Grimmelshausen's *Der abenteuerliche Simplicissimus* (1669) ranks high in importance. Much of this story was based on the author's own experiences in the later years of the Thirty Years' War; the narrative deals with a young boy who is thrust into a life of adventure when carried off to war by a band of marauding soldiers. His restless life during and after the war gives him no peace, and after numerous adventures in various parts of the world, he finally settles down among his books for a life of meditation and repentance. The realistic descriptions of the ravages of war in peasant districts might be cited as indicative of an awareness of the peasant's circumstances in Germany, seen from a humanistic rather than a political standpoint. Grimmelshausen's own recognition of the importance of the peasant class was expressed in a song sung by the young hero just before he is carried off:

[5] Robert Kann, *A Study in Austrian Intellectual History: From Late Baroque to Romanticism* (New York, 1960), for example, discusses the attitudes of Abraham a Sancta Clara, one of the great preaching figures of the later seventeenth-century Catholic church in Austria, towards the various social classes, including the peasantry, and demonstrates his real compassion for the daily tribulations of the peasant. See especially 71-72.

Du sehr verachter Bauernstand
Bist doch der erste in dem Land;
Kein Mann dich gnugsam preisen kann
Wenn er dich nur recht siehet an.

Wie stünd es jetztund um die Welt,
Hätt' Adam nicht gebaut das Feld!
Mit Hacken nährt sich anfangs der,
Von dem die Fürsten kommen her.

Drum bist du billig hoch zu ehrn,
Weil du uns alle tust ernährn;
Natur, die liebt dich selber auch,
Gott segnet deinen Bauernbrauch.[6]

Oh peasant race, how much despised,
Yet greatly are you to be prized.
No man your praises can excel
If only he regard you well.

How little would the world now yield
If Adam had not tilled the field!
With spade and hoe he dug the earth
From which our princes have their worth.

All honour, then, to your employ
By which all men their lives enjoy.
Nature herself your labour loves
And God your handiwork approves.

Such praise was highly unusual for the time; generally speaking, the attitude of nobles and burghers towards the peasant class after 1525 was an even more condescending one than it had been before. After the Peasants' War of 1525, the depressed condition of the peasantry worsened still further, and the virtual enslavement which it underwent in many areas of Germany carried with it not only a lowering of material well-being, but also a loss of self-respect, which resulted in a coarseness and crudity of morals and customs. The decline of the peasant way of life and of agriculture after 1525, and the effective strangulation of the spirit of initiative among the peasants has been described in some detail by Johannes Janssen, who has also

---

[6] Hans Jakob Christoffel von Grimmelshausen, *Der abenteuerliche Simplicissimus* (Bonn, 1948), 30. Some verses of the song have been omitted here. The translation is from *The Adventures of a Simpleton*, trans. Walter Wallich (New York, 1963), 5.

presented evidence of the general contempt for the peasantry on the part of the upper classes following the Peasants' War.[7]

Whatever development of contemptuous attitudes towards the peasantry may have occurred before 1525 was greatly strengthened by the results of the Peasants' War. "The members of the upper classes in Germany," one historian has written, "gradually accustomed themselves to look down on the peasant with a certain contempt. His often clumsy manner, his coarse forms in daily intercourse with others, his frequently unrestrained greed in the enjoyment of the pleasures of his existence, the lack of cleanliness in his clothing and his living habits, among other things, called forth the scorn of the knights, who laid great weight upon outer distinction. He [was looked on] generally as dirty and stupid."[8] The boorish peasant, betrayed and deceived on every hand, is a familiar figure in the *Lustspielen* of Hans Sachs, and in this sense he may be said to represent the typical peasant as seen by the higher estates of his day.[9] Johannes Bühler, too, speaking of the time following the Peasants' War, has cited a little rhyme common among the gentlemen of the day:

> Der Bauer ist an Ochsen statt,
> Nur dass er keine Hörner hat.[10]

> The peasant could take the ox's place,
> Had he but horns above his face.

Nor did these upper-class attitudes change fundamentally for the next two centuries or so: an author of the 1680s affirmed that "Peasants are indeed human beings, but somewhat more unpolished and coarser than others. If one considers their customs and behavior, a polite man is easily distinguished from a peasant. To a peasant belongs the flail in his hand and a cudgel at his side, a mattock on his shoulder and a manure-fork at his door. Their loathsome customs are known to everyone, as well in speech as in behavior." Peasants reminded this commentator of dried fish:

---

[7] Johannes Janssen, *History of the German People at the Close of the Middle Ages,* trans. M. A. Mitchell and A. M. Christie, 16 vols. (London, 1896-1910), vol. XV, Chapter 4, *passim.*

[8] Heinrich Gerdes, *Geschichte des deutschen Bauernstandes* (Leipzig, 1910), 1-2.

[9] *Ibid.,* 2.

[10] Bühler, *Der deutsche Bauer,* 44.

both were at their best when "gently beaten and well pounded."[11] Johannes Bühler cites a Bavarian jurist of the early eighteenth century, who expressed the accepted superiority of the upper classes over the peasants in the following words: "The coarse peasant folk is not usually cited at the *Landtag,* and indeed rightly so, for the peasants stand between the unreasoning beast and man."[12] Such a statement is certainly too extreme to be taken as representative of all upper-class opinion on the subject, but as late as 1774, descriptions of the material conditions of the peasant's existence in many places indicate that his life-style might well have placed him close to the animal: the Württemberg constitutional theorist Johann Jakob Moser, for example, commented in a work published in that year that in many places in Germany and Austria peasants lived "in a kind of slavery. . . . Often they are not as well off as cattle elsewhere."[13]

In any case, it is undoubtedly true that class differences tended to become greater rather than smaller from the Reformation through much of the eighteenth century. Writing of the development of bourgeois attitudes, Karl Lamprecht has said that in the eighteenth century the separation between classes had progressed so far that the peasant was no longer an object of curiosity to the city man, "even as something strange"; furthermore, the new culture of the eighteenth century in Germany concerned itself literarily almost not at all with the peasant—for to treat even the resident of the small city in poetic fashion was not considered permissible.[14]   Johann Christoph Gottsched, for example, in a critique of the poetic art of 1751 urged contemporaries not to use German peasants and shepherds as models for their poems. The rural inhabitants, he said, possessed far too few amenities to please the artist, for most of them were poor, oppressed, and harassed; they were seldom the owners of their own homes, and

11 Quoted in Gustav Freytag, *Bilder aus der deutschen Vergangenheit,* 7th ed., 4 vols. (Leipzig, 1873-1882), III, 439, 442, from *Des Neunhaeutigen und Haimbuechenen schlimmen Baurenstands und Wandels Entdeckte Ubel- Sitten- und Lasterprob von Veroandro aus Wahrburg* (1684).

12 Bühler, *Der deutsche Bauer,* 44.

13 Johann Jakob Moser, *Von der Teutschen Unterthanen Rechten und Pflichten* (Frankfurt am Main and Leipzig, 1774), 96.

14 Karl Lamprecht, *Deutsche Geschichte,* 4th ed., 12 vols. in 16 (Freiburg and Berlin, 1904-1911), vol. VIII, part 1, p. 219.

had to pay so much in dues and taxes that they could scarcely keep body and soul together.[15]

Such opinions were partly a function of sharper differences in the educational levels of the various strata of the middle class. Karl Biedermann has pointed out that the bourgeois "elite" of education moved forward with unusual rapidity in the eighteenth century "in consequence of the heightened tempo in the movement of ideas," whereas the lower bourgeois strata, and above all the rural population, had either stood still or had followed the same course of development much more slowly. This resulted in a steadily widening cleavage between these groups with respect to education and the social attitudes which went with it.[16] Even at the end of the eighteenth century, contemptuous references to the peasant could be found in many urban places—as in the sophisticated north German cities, for example, where peasants were collectively and disdainfully called "Jan van Moor."[17] By the time at which this study begins, a little recognition of the intolerable condition of the peasantry and of the duty to reform that condition had developed among writers of various kinds in Germany, as elsewhere in western Europe. But that for the most part the peasant was at the beginning of this period still treated by most of the members of the upper classes with disdain, or, more commonly, was simply ignored, seems indisputable in spite of occasional notable exceptions.

One fact was inescapable, however, even for those who held the peasant as a human being in contempt; and that was that the overwhelming majority of Germans derived their livelihood, directly or indirectly, from agriculture. Even if the peasant merited little consideration as an individual, therefore, his importance as the chief caretaker of the most important single sector of the German economy was undeniable. The search for the beginnings of an awakening interest in the peasant therefore leads back to an upsurge of interest in agriculture itself, which came as a necessity in the wake of the Thirty Years' War. That

[15] Johann Christoph Gottsched, *Versuch einer kritischen Dichtkunst* (Leipzig, 1751), 582.
[16] Karl Biedermann, *Deutschland im achtzehnten Jahrhundert*, 2 vols. (Leipzig, 1880), II, 1140.
[17] Gerdes, *Geschichte*, 2.

war had so decimated the peasant population and had laid waste such great tracts of arable land in many parts of Germany that attention to agricultural production became a matter of utmost concern not only to individual landowners and agriculturists, but also to rulers, for whom it was an affair of immediate political importance.

A considerable economic literature quickly grew up around the central problem of agricultural rehabilitation. One type of such literature, the so-called *Hausväterliteratur,* included technical suggestions about crops, techniques, and the systematic ordering of the entire farm economy, intended primarily for the owners of landed estates. For most of the seventeenth and eighteenth centuries, this broadly technical literature was little concerned with the peasant, the man who actually worked the land, although occasional exceptions can be noted. A widely read and frequently reprinted work by Johannes Coler, a preacher in Brandenburg and Pomerania, for example, openly appealed to peasant readers and admonished all who read his work not to hold the peasant in contempt: if they looked into their own ancestry, said Coler, they would surely find peasant forebears somewhere—for, after all, "when Adam delved and Eve span, who was then the gentleman?"[18] This literature had many other distinguished representatives, especially in the later seventeenth and very early eighteenth centuries,[19] but gradually gave way to a much more highly specialized technical literature dealing with specific facets of agriculture as the eighteenth-century "agricultural revolution" gained force.

Much more important, for present purposes, was the growth of another, more general and public literature, in which the problems of agriculture were dealt with as but one part of the more general concern for the strengthening of the state through

---

18 von der Goltz, *Geschichte der deutschen Landwirtschaft,* I, 298.

19 Among the more important and better-known agricultural tracts of this type, the following might be mentioned: Wolf Helmhard Freiherr von Hohberg, *Georgica curiosa aucta* (Nürnberg, 1687); Franz Philipp bei Rhein, *Francisci Philippi Florini Oeconomus prudens et legalis continuatus oder Grosser Herren Stands und Adelichen Haus Vatter* (Nürnberg, 1702); Johann Jakob Agricola, *Schauplatz des allgemeinen Haushaltens* (Nördlingen, 1676); and Andreas Glorez von Maehren, *Vollstaendige Haus- und Landbibliothek* (Regensburg, 1699-1700).

the improvement of the economy as a whole. This literature was voluminous in both the seventeenth and the eighteenth centuries, and was associated with the rise of the so-called Cameralists, a group of officials, administrators, and professors who served the rulers of the various German states as fiscal and organizational experts during this period. Cameralism, as their general viewpoint is called, took its name from the treasury (*Kammer*) of the ruling prince; it has often been called simply the German brand of mercantilism, in that its goal was that of using state power to stimulate the economy and thereby create a larger tax base from which the ruler could draw increasingly greater revenues.[20]

Among the economic objects of the Cameralists' attention, agriculture had a very prominent place. This was so not only because agriculture directly employed a majority of the subjects of nearly every German ruler, but also because the landlocked character of many German states reduced somewhat the relative importance of certain other economic sectors such as overseas commerce (which was becoming steadily more important for the mercantilists of the great states of western Europe, by contrast). The peasant had a central importance in the Cameralist emphasis on agriculture not only because he, after all, was the human agent who coaxed food from the land, but also because the peasantry was supposed to supply the population increase which was one of the most earnestly solicited goals of German rulers after the Thirty Years' War. The sometime Austrian and Bavarian official Johann Joachim Becher (1625-1682), for example, strongly urged measures to promote population increase in his *Politischer Discurs von den eigentlichen Ursachen des Auff- und Abnehmens der Staedte Laender und Republicken* (Frankfurt, 1668) and while he noted that all classes in a state were necessary to the full flowering of the economy, he emphasized that the peasantry

[20] Albion W. Small, *The Cameralists: The Pioneers of German Social Polity* (Chicago and London, 1909), is the best English language study of Cameralism. In addition to Small's work, a more recent treatment of Austrian Cameralists, whose influence in Germany was strong throughout the period, has appeared: Louise Sommer, *Die österreichischen Kameralisten*, 2 vols. (Vienna, 1920-1925). Perhaps the most comprehensive bibliography of Cameralist writings is Edward Baumstark, *Kameralistische Encyclopädie: Handbuch der Kameralwissenschaften und ihrer Literatur* (Heidelberg and Leipzig, 1835).

was the most numerous and important of the directly productive classes. Another important seventeenth-century Cameralist, Veit Ludwig von Seckendorff (1626-1692), who occupied official positions in the Duchies of Gotha and Sachsenzeitz, also laid great weight on population growth, and did not disguise his opinion that peasants and artisans, "particularly [those] who work for the daily necessities," formed the best class. Agriculture was the basis for any increase in population, and von Seckendorff expressed himself in favor of the preservation of peasant lands and against the imposition of new fees or taxes on existing peasant lands.[21]

Even with this increased attention to agriculture and to the peasant, however, there was very little thought of any basic social change as a factor in increasing production; if the famous Christian Thomasius (1655-1728), professor in the Prussian university at Halle and a friend of the lower classes, could easily speak of the agricultural occupation as the "oldest, most noble, and most innocent art" in his *Cautelae circa praecognita jurisprudentiae* (1710), the philosopher Samuel Pufendorff (1631-1694) could just as easily ascribe the origins of personal servitude among the peasantry to free contract rather than to subjection by force, and could fail to find anything really objectionable to servitude on legal, moral, or economic grounds.[22] It was not really the business of the Cameralists, as servants of the absolute princes of the German states, to question or suggest reforms in the established political and social order; they were, at most, to improve techniques and make minor rearrangements within that order, and among the important Cameralists of the earlier eighteenth century—Julius Bernhard von Rohr, Julius Christoph Dithmar, Georg Heinrich Zincke, to mention but a few—there was little suggestion that real improvement in basic agricultural practices would eventually have to involve fundamental changes in the social basis of agriculture itself. As early as 1729, it is true, Simon Peter Gasser, sometime Chamber-Councillor, War- and Domains-Councillor, and professor of Cameralistics at Halle,

---

[21] Wilhelm Roscher, *Geschichte der National-Oekonomik in Deutschland* (Munich, 1874), 238-52.
[22] *Ibid.*, 307, 345.

realized that peasants were too heavily taxed in comparison to the rich cities, and suggested vaguely that forced labor services and a low level of agricultural production seemed somehow to be connected. But he did not pursue this idea, and generally rejected a lessening of peasant dues and fees.[23]

The second half of the eighteenth century witnessed if anything an increase in attention to agriculture among prominent Cameralists, as well as the beginning of somewhat more radical approaches to the problem of how to improve it. This was due perhaps partly to Physiocratic influences among German officials after the early 1760s; but probably to a much greater extent, it stemmed from the rapidly developing scientific approach to problems of cultivation and animal husbandry associated with the "agricultural revolution." The possibilities of sharply increased agricultural production, fortified by perhaps overpublicized examples from England and Holland, led fiscal-minded German mercantilists to consider with care whether German agriculture might not be made susceptible to the same reforming influences which were apparently being employed with such great success elsewhere.

Typical of this orientation were the writings of Johann Heinrich Gottlob von Justi (1720-1771), one of the most influential and prolific Cameralists of the century. Born in northern Germany, Justi was trained as a lawyer at Wittenberg, and his first positions were legal ones. Having spent some time as a legal advisor to the duchess of Sachsen-Eisenach, he moved to Vienna near the middle of the century, and was soon appointed to a professorship in the Collegium Theresianum in that city. He offered lectures in Cameralistics, and was at one time specifically commanded to address himself to the subject of mining. In pursuing this study, he apparently met with the opposition of some powerful vested interests, for he abruptly returned to northern Germany, where he appeared for brief periods of time in Mansfeld, Leipzig, and Göttingen. In Göttingen, he became *Polizei-Director* and a lecturer on Cameralistics at the university in the late 1750s. Following this, he occupied an official position in the Danish government, but left it to move to Altona, then to Hamburg. Still later,

23 *Ibid.*, 375-76.

he moved to Berlin, where he was an official in Prussian service until he became involved in a quarrel with creditors and favor-seekers, was arrested, and ultimately ended his life in confinement at Küstrin while negotiating for his release.[24]

To restrict Justi for present purposes to his thoughts on agriculture is in a certain sense unjust, since these form but part of a rather formidable system of Cameralistics. But his opinions may be regarded as typical of the later eighteenth-century Cameralist orientation towards agriculture. At the base of Justi's thought was the principle that "the prosperity of a country, and the power and happiness of a state, relate chiefly to the complete cultivation of the earth and the flowering condition of agriculture. The population, the entire food supply, manufactures, and even commercial enterprises rest on the prosperity of agriculture as on their firm and immovable base."[25] He deplored the condition of agriculture in Germany and in his writing advocated a more complete and perfect cultivation of the land. In doing so, he did not restrict himself to well-intentioned generalities, but suggested particular reforms and numerous technical innovations designed to improve the productive capacity of the land. The model to which he commonly referred in these writings was England, inasmuch as the English pioneered in the introduction of reforms beneficial to agriculture. He suggested the gradual abolition of the village as the sole form of organized rural habitation, and recommended that the peasants live, scattered, on their own lands—a radical change which presupposed consolidation of the peasants' lands and the abolition of the common rights of grazing and of driving stock across one another's lands.

Justi showed a grave concern for the lot of the peasant cultivator himself, and he found personal servitude and lack of hereditary tenure particularly objectionable. On the principle that self-interest was the only motive of diligence, Justi concluded that only peasants who owned their land would contribute optimally to the improvement of agricultural production. He sought to show that the utility derived by lords from the servitude of their

24 Small, *The Cameralists*, 286-91.
25 Johann Heinrich Gottlob von Justi, *Oeconomische Schriften über die wichtigsten, Gegenstände der Stadt- und Landwirthschaft*, 2 vols. (Berlin and Leipzig, 1760), II, 205-206.

peasants was very small, and he recommended that a levy be imposed on all lands not actually inhabited by their owner, with the stipulation that the owner himself must pay the tax; this scheme, which did not involve the invasion of the rights of property and person, would none the less soon enough result in increased peasant ownership of land. The elimination of peasant labor services would accompany this gradual transfer of proprietorship.[26]

Any praise which Justi may have given the peasant was not without qualification, for he saw in him a neglectfulness and a disposition to laziness which he regarded as virtually incurable by virtue of his lack of education and opportunities. But in no way was this a sufficient excuse for oppressing him: "That class of men who engage in agriculture, upon whom . . . the power and prosperity of the state, yes! one can say the well-being of all other estates and classes of the folk depends, deserves neither oppression nor contempt."[27] With this statement, which caught up the essence of much Cameralist thought on this point, as well as the public philosophy of not a few German rulers of the eighteenth century, Justi helped to set the stage for that sympathetic frame of mind on the part of governments in many German states which was a necessary ingredient in the realization of actual agrarian reform. Furthermore, a generation of writers and philosophers brought up in the traditions of a strong agricultural emphasis in much Cameralist economic thought could scarcely fail to feel concerned about the land and the people who lived on it and worked it. In these ways, the Cameralists participated in an important way in the formation of the ideas of those men who concerned themselves with the peasant for many years after 1770, even though, in their capacity as administrative technocrats, whose functions were confined to and by the governmental and social order under which they lived, they could not really work for the basic politico-economic changes which many of them by 1770 had begun to feel were necessary to give agriculture, and eventually also commerce and manufacturing, a substantial boost.

[26] *Ibid.*, II, 222-23.
[27] *Ibid.*, II, 227.

In their frequent glorification of agriculture as the foundation of a nation's welfare, Cameralists in the later eighteenth century were joined by the disciples of the French Physiocratic school. Sometimes, in fact, their agreement on this point has led later observers to conclude that Cameralism tended to merge with Physiocracy to some considerable extent. But while it is true that some German officials in the last third of the century or so were in fact Physiocrats, there is a fundamental difference between Cameralism and Physiocracy; it is important to signalize this difference in order to make clear that Physiocracy contributed to the formation of a new image of the peasant in Germany in its own special way, independent of Cameralism.

The fundamental distinction between the two may be stated as follows: the Physiocrat held that the extractive industries (agriculture, fishing, and mining, essentially) were the only sources of a "pure product," the only sources of the actual increase of real wealth; manufacturing merely changed the form of produce (i.e., raw material), and commerce merely transported it from one place to another. The statistical and "scientific" work of the French Physiocrats (Quesnay, Dupont de Nemours, Mercier de la Rivière, to mention only the most important) from the 1750s on had purported to demonstrate that any absolute increase in wealth as represented by manufacturing and commerce was in fact possible only on the basis of prior increases in the amount of raw materials extracted from nature. If, therefore, one were concerned to increase the wealth of a state, one had to pay attention chiefly to the extractive industries, of which agriculture was clearly the most important. It also followed that public taxes, if they were to be levied accurately and according to the real wealth of the country, ought to fall only on the produce of the extractive industries. This was the famous Physiocratic *impôt unique*, the burden of which to producers would be made up by corresponding increases in the selling price of their produce.[28]

By contrast, the Cameralist could not really accept the principle that the forces of nature, i.e., the extractive industries, were the

28 The "primary producers," that is, did not shoulder the actual tax burden alone; the assumption was that the price of their produce to the consumer would include an amount sufficient to guarantee a roughly equal distribution of the tax burden throughout the population.

only source of real wealth—and therefore also of public revenue. His job was to encourage prosperity through productivity wherever possible, and to create or increase sources of revenue for the state by levying taxes (or conferring exemptions) wherever these presently appeared most advantageous. His plans thus included crafts, industries, and commercial undertakings as well as agriculture. The relatively strong emphasis on agriculture as a source of wealth in Cameralist writings had little to do with any philosophical conviction about the ultimate sources of wealth, but was merely a result of a realistic appraisal of what was at that time apparently the greatest source of wealth in the German states. The dogmatic positions on free trade in grains and on other points taken up by most Physiocrats were not adopted by Cameralists, whose position on these issues was by no means consistent. For the Cameralist, the existing social and political order of his state was always the point of departure for his economic recommendations—which commonly prevented the emphasis on complete freedom for the peasant cultivator which was a fundamental premise of the Physiocratic system. By contrast, the framework of Physiocracy, as seen by its adherents, was entirely "scientific," in that it was bound to the principle of economic "laws of nature"; if these could not be implemented within the complex of presently existing social institutions, then the latter should be changed to conform to the former.[29]

German Physiocracy was almost entirely derivative from the theoretical works of the great French *économistes,* who far overshadowed their German disciples in both originality and output. Yet it was in Germany, not France, that the only practical attempt was ever made to implement in a systematic way a complete and doctrinally orthodox Physiocratic economic system. This was possible because of the "conversion" of Margrave Karl Friedrich of Baden, whose interest in political economics was well known in Germany, and who conducted a lengthy and detailed correspondence with the elder Mirabeau and Dupont de Nemours in France concerning the principles of their system. The court of the Margrave became the center of German Physiocracy, and

---

[29] As suggested by one of the leading German Physiocrats, Johann August Schlettwein, cited in Roscher, *Geschichte der National-Oekonomik,* 488-89.

Karl Friedrich attracted a number of the most important German Physiocrats to his civil service, among them Johann August Schlettwein (in 1763) and Johann Georg Schlosser (in 1773). It was Schlettwein who was chiefly responsible for the *impôt unique* and other Physiocratic measures actually put into force in some small sections of Baden. The utter failure of this tax and indeed of the system qua system put an end to doctrinaire implementation of the abstract principles of Physiocracy; but it could not obscure the very real progress which resulted from some of the individual reforms associated with the attempt. To judge from the literature of the time, not only the novelty of the doctrine itself, but also the bold attempt to put it into practice created considerable interest (and not a small amount of disputation) in Germany. Physiocrats in numerous German territories put pen to paper to propound their theories or to defend them against their critics. The vehicles for their points of view varied from the belligerent essays of the Swiss philosopher and reformer Isaak Iselin through the thoughtful and precise speculations of Schlettwein's economic tracts to the literary didacticism of Johann Heinrich Merck, who on more than one occasion in the pages of *Der teutsche Merkur* used fictional stories to persuade his audience.

Again, it was initially not so much the peasant himself who became the focus of favorable attention as a consequence of Physiocratic ideas, but rather agriculture as an occupation, as the source of the most essential social products. Isaak Iselin, for example, was fond of reminding merchants and traders that whereas a body politic could certainly do without the fine arts and all other luxuries which depended on trade and manufacturing for their existence, no state could long survive without a prosperous agricultural base. Furthermore, said he, it was quite conceivable that a state could attain a very considerable degree of well-being under agricultural pursuits alone, which were in any case the noblest occupation of man and the work determined for him by God Himself.[30] As a corollary, it was therefore neces-

---

[30] Isaak Iselin, *Vermischte Schriften*, 2 vols. (Zürich, 1770), II, 224-25. For a sketch of Iselin's life and work, see *Biographie universelle, ancienne et moderne*, 85 vols. (Paris, 1811-1862), XXI, 287-88.

sary in any state which laid a claim to be well governed that the improvement of agriculture must always precede that of other parts of the economy, which clearly depended on the primary production of the land.[31] Other Physiocratic writings took similar delight in ridiculing the perversity of mercantilist policies, which sought the most rapid possible increase of commercial and manufacturing activity—too often at the expense of agriculture. Production and traffic in luxury items for export was a source of special annoyance to Physiocrats, and led to strong recommendations that allocation of large amounts of money and manpower for such purposes be discouraged, since they did not contribute to an increase in the number of rich farmers who had a surplus capital for reinvestment in the land.[32] Princes, after all, it was said, should never forget that it is the earth which is the sole source of wealth, and that agriculture alone increases wealth.[33]

Whatever their considerable differences may have been in reasons and in method, however, Physiocrats and Cameralists were united in their desire to increase production from the land. In this desire, they were joined also by numerous noble landlords who, for less theoretical reasons, were concerned with specific methods for improving cultivation. As Leonard Krieger has pointed out, Prussian bureaucrats in the later years of Frederick II's reign showed many evidences of certain kinds of liberal economic sentiment.[34] As landowners themselves, they were representative of a considerable body of landed proprietors in Prussia and elsewhere, for whom a visibly increasing demand for foodstuffs meant an opportunity to take advantage of capitalistic agricultural enterprise, with all the particular technical reforms it suggested, if only on a modest scale. Their receptivity to liberal economic ideas, such as it was, was by no means always an indication of a general social or political liberalism, but rather a measure of their estimation of the pragmatic worth of such ideas in terms of cash value.

[31] Cited in Johann Georg Schlosser, *Kleine Schriften*, 6 vols. in 3 (Basel, 1780-1793), I, 224-25.

[32] "Die allgemeinsten oekonomischen Regierungs-Maximen eines Agricultur-Staates," *Leipziger Magazin zur Naturgeschichte und Oekonomie*, Drittes Stük (1786), 347.

[33] *Ibid.*, 324.

[34] Leonard Krieger, *The German Idea of Freedom: History of a Political Tradition* (Boston, 1957), 26.

Reforms, in any case, were an essential part of the plans of all these groups. They differed widely on the kinds and the degree of reform desired; but it became increasingly obvious, as time went on, that reform proposals designed to increase agricultural production were not always compatible with the social and political constitution under which agrarian work was then done; and it also became clear to many writers that the modest reforms they proposed would ultimately also involve more radical reform if they were not to fail of their effect. It is essential to survey the main directions of this reform literature because, first, it demonstrates that a major part of the interest in the peasant among important official and educated circles in Germany in the last two decades or so before the French Revolution was involved with the importance of the peasant as producer; and secondly, because the nature and degree of this interest in the peasant, and thus the image of the peasant itself, changed as a result of the constantly broadening and deepening perception of what reforms were necessary to make of the peasant the most efficient producer. That is, it was to an important extent from the reforms and reform ideas stimulated by this picture of the peasant as producer that it became possible and even necessary for a new social image of the peasant to be created.

The first category of reforms proposed to change the circumstances of the peasant's existence comprises a group of complaints and suggestions designed to eliminate or lessen certain harassments which prevented the peasant from deriving as much produce from his land as he might. This category includes the greatest imaginable variety of particular proposals, of which only a few of the most common need be indicated here. Perhaps the most often-raised complaint was directed against the damage done to the peasant's farm by the ravages of the hunt, an everyday amusement of the princes and the nobility. A poem of the early 1770s by Leopold von Goekingk, the editor of the *Journal von und für Deutschland,* painted a sad picture of the desperation of a poor peasant whose fields and meadows were trampled by his "gracious prince" in the course of a wild hunt; who, the peasant wondered, would now pay the taxes to the prince which were to have been raised by the peasant from the very crops which the prince was just now ruining?[35] Gottfried August Bürger, the Göttingen poet, found the same theme an apt one, and in two pointed poems damned the noble hunting-privilege *(Jagdgerechtigkeit)* very effectively. In the first, published in 1776 and entitled "The Peasant to His Most Serene Tyrant," he expressed the view that no prince had the right to destroy the property of others, and that just as surely as the sweat spilled behind plow and harrow was the peasant's own, so also was the bread it ultimately brought forth from the earth. The validity of rulership of princes thus careless of their subjects' rights was nakedly questioned by the defiant peasant:

> Ha! You would be my lord by right of God?
> God deals out blessings; you only steal!
> You're not of God, you tyrant![36]

The other poem, of 1786, entitled "The Wild Hunter," described in detail the vicious trampling of peasants' crops, the scattering of their stock, and the bodily damage done to the persons of the peasants by a count and his hunting retinue; it then recounted with relish the later death of the count and his punishment in the afterlife, which consisted in being pursued in all eternity through hell by the devil himself. The cruel count thus became a horrible example for all princes who, while seeking satisfaction for their greedy desires, "spare neither Creator nor creation."[37]

Somewhat more prosaic, but also more analytic, was an article of 1787 in August Ludwig Schlözer's *Staats-Anzeigen,* which was especially concerned to highlight the absurd contradictions in the *Jagdgerechtigkeit*: "Here a large family of people goes hungry; and there 20 deer fatten themselves in order to be hunted *parforce.*" Where the *parforce* hunt was used, a small army of dogs, horses, and servants, and a considerable number of "dilettantes"

---

[35] Leopold Ferdinand Günther von Goekingk, "Die Parforcejagd" (1771?), in *Deutsche Literatur: Sammlung literarischer Kunst- und Kulturdenkmäler in Entwicklungsreihen,* Reihe politische Dichtung, I (Leipzig, 1930), 50-53.

[36] Gottfried August Bürger, "Der Bauer an seinen durchlauchtigen Tyrannen" (1776), *Sämmtliche Werke* (Göttingen, 1844), I, 84.

[37] Bürger, "Der wilde Jäger" (1786), *ibid.,* I, 313-22.

took the field, trampling crops everywhere. The peasant whose crops were ruined, of course, was the one who paid for all this equipage; and even if he were compensated for the damage, which happened seldom enough (and then, with luck, he might get one thaler for every twenty thalers' damage), he, the taxpayer, after all, also paid his own compensation! The amount of land put back for hunting preserves was so large that it forced peasants to become poachers, the author complained; from this stage of criminality, they moved on down the scale until they met sorry ends as highway robbers. The author of this article—purported to be a count—saw, like the poet Bürger, a potentially gruesome punishment for these great lords of the hunt in the hereafter: if there were such a thing as the transmigration of souls, they would become themselves the prey, the horses, or even—the peasants![38] While no specific solutions were offered for the correction of this abuse of hunting privileges, the reform was clearly implied in the nature of the abuse itself.

In the same general category of abuses were complaints about the economic inefficiency of military policy concerning the use of peasants in the army. The dangers to cultivation inherent in immobilizing peasants as producers by keeping them in the army for long periods of time (fifteen or twenty years in some cases) was a frequent source of irritation to those whose primary concern was a prosperous economy.[39] The prince who retained peasants as soldiers for years and years, instead of discharging them when hostilities were ended or when they were wounded, avowed one writer, "loses through [such a policy] his best peasants and finally retains cripples whom he cannot feed himself, [and] who

---

[38] Graf von ...., "Vom Misbrauch der Jagd," *Staats-Anzeigen*, X (1787), 139, 141-44, 148.

[39] It was considerations such as these which in fact influenced many European states to take a substantial portion of their standing armies from the ranks of criminals and the unemployed—which were often enough synonymous. In view of a general labor shortage in Germany throughout the eighteenth century (a result of population losses in the Thirty Years' War) it is probably true that German princes had to rely much more than did other European sovereigns on conscription from peasants who were fully employed otherwise. The absurd vanity of scores of sovereign German princelings in maintaining armies for prestige and show worsened the situation still further by raising the numerical ratio of soldiery to civilian populace for Germany as a whole over that of other states in Europe.

either are a burden to others or, to his disgrace, must beg their way through the world."[40] This was, of course, to some extent at the same time a complaint against the institution of the standing army itself; this fact was realized quite clearly, as evidenced by one writer who recommended a "national army," consisting of men trained and ready to leave the plow when called to arms for some emergency, but until then able to expend their efforts in constructive economic activity.[41]

Arbitrary and cruel physical treatment of peasants on the part of landlords, carelessness in supervising their cultivation, and general and needless insensitivity to the economic needs of the peasant were attacked in Cameralist, Physiocratic, and other writings too often to require particular citation. These kinds of abuses were the subject of legislation in many German states far back into the eighteenth century, although enforcement of decrees against *Bauernschinden* (physical cruelty), for example, was often ineffective. Again, various attempts were made in many German states to secure better justice for the peasant, with widely varying degrees of success. Some of this legal reform was prompted by the hope that peasants would help the state to fulfill its desire to help them as a class by going to court against miscreant landlords when their rights (as then defined) were invaded. Court costs were reduced in many cases, processes shortened, and measures taken to protect peasants from unscrupulous lawyers who frequently urged peasants into lawsuits in which they had no real case, in order then to charge them exorbitant fees for legal services.

That these efforts to provide legal resort for the peasant without an undue strain on his purse had not been uniformly successful is proved by numerous complaints and suggestions made in this period for the improvement of the peasant's legal relationships. To one not familiar with the extreme willingness of the peasant to hop off to court at the slightest provocation, attempts to instruct the peasant in the rudiments of the legal process might seem of minor importance indeed; but the time and money lost

[40] Friedrich Carl von Moser, "Bauren-Politik und Bauren-Weisheit," *Patriotisches Archiv für Deutschland,* VII (1787), 428. Hereafter cited as *Patriotisches Archiv* (Moser).

[41] Georg Christian Oeder, *Bedenken über die Frage: Wie dem Bauernstande Freyheit und Eigenthum in den Ländern, wo ihm beydes fehlet, verschaffet werden könne?* (Frankfurt and Leipzig, 1769), 39-40.

to him through his ignorance constituted a real burden. Thus a proposal such as that of the Osnabrück official, historian, and literary man-of-all-work, Justus Möser, that a short, clear, and easily readable legal handbook for the peasant be prepared, was designed to spare the peasant various kinds of unpleasantness and expense. Ideally, the publication of the book would be supervised by the state, and would contain information on what sorts of cases ought to be taken to court and what sorts not, what procedures were involved in various steps of litigation, and so forth.[42] The importance assigned to putting this kind of information in the hands of peasants is further evidenced by the inclusion of legal advice in "farmer's almanacs" which began sprouting forth in large numbers in this time. Typical of the advice contained in these almanacs were the recommendations of R. Z. Becker, who admonished peasants to avoid court suits whenever possible, to love and understand their enemies, and to compromise wherever feasible, on the cozy principle that "A skinny settlement is better than a fat suit." But general hints on legal procedure were included for those who felt that their rights had seriously been invaded.[43]

Part of the problem of the inaccessibility of justice to the peasant was his difficulty in understanding laws, legal documents, and court verdicts. The use of foreign words and phrases (mostly Latin) and the formal and complex chancellery style in which legal documents were drawn up led to proposals that in the future the language of the people be employed by officials, in order that common folk might understand the real substance of issues before the court.[44] Peasant ignorance in matters such as these was taken advantage of by lawyers, who were generally hated and despised by the common people. A poem of the late 1780s by the "*Wandsbecker Bote*," Matthias Claudius, gave vent to the suspicion which attached to the lawyer. A peasant in the poem thanked God that he was a peasant and not a lawyer,

---

[42] Justus Möser, "Vorschlag zu einer Praktika für das Landvolk," *Sämtliche Werke: historisch-kritische Ausgabe in 14 Bänden,* ed. Ludwig Schirmeyer, 9 vols. to date (Oldenburg and Berlin, 1943-1965), V, 134-37.

[43] Rudolph Z. Becker, *Noth- und Hülfs-Büchlein für Bauersleute,* 3d ed. (Gotha and Leipzig, 1789), 397-404.

[44] "Von der einzigen unfehlbaren Methode die Processe zu verhüten," *Archiv für den Menschen und Bürger in allen Verhältnissen,* II (1781), 10.

doubted the honesty of the members of the legal profession, and preferred his manure-carrying to a life of bitter quarreling: with his soil and his manure, he philosophized, the peasant makes something out of nothing, while the lawyer makes nothing out of something![45] Hatred of lawyers was in some instances shared by rulers (Frederick William I of Prussia being a prime example) and, as suggested earlier, state officials were sometimes cautioned to be on the lookout for shyster lawyers operating among the peasants. At another level, some amelioration might have been expected had the suggestion of Justus Möser been followed, that noble landlords should appoint and pay a capable and honest lawyer to represent and advise their peasants when they fell into litigation. The lord himself might help, too, by advising the lawyers, since he was presumably an expert in the troubles of the peasants.[46]

Apart from these "major" harassments affecting the peasant's efficiency as cultivator, there were myriads of lesser ones which it is scarcely necessary to examine. They vary from the economic burden of almsgiving to rural beggars (which sometimes equaled the amount of money a peasant spent on his own family, but which was made virtually necessary by the propensity of refused beggars to burn down the peasants' houses, crops, or outbuildings)[47] to the plethora of public holidays, most of them religious, which kept the peasant from working and earning a decent living.[48] Taken together, all criticisms and complaints of this nature were little more than pot-shots at abuses and inconveniences which, regarded from the standpoint of the overall condition of the peasant's economy, were more obvious than of real importance.

Of a more fundamental nature was another kind of reform

[45] Matthias Claudius, "Der Bauer, nach geendigtem Prozess," *Matthias Claudius Werke*, 2 vols. (Dresden, n.d.), I, 549.

[46] Möser, "Also soll jeder Gutsherr seine Leibeignen vor Gerichte vertreten und den Zwangsdienst mildern," *Sämtliche Werke*, VII, 285-86.

[47] "Über das Betteln auf dem platten Lande und in kleinen Städten," *Berlinische Monatsschrift*, IX (January-June 1787), 6-8.

[48] F. C. von Moser, "Bauren-Politik und Bauren-Weisheit," *Patriotisches Archiv* (Moser), VII (1787), *passim*. This could be a page taken from the reform book of Joseph II of Austria (1765-1790) who, partly for the reason suggested here but also as part of a general attack on the politics of the Catholic church, drastically reduced the calendar of religious holidays.

literature, which sought on a broader basis to provide solutions for more permanent problems of agricultural cultivation. The pragmatic economic character of the problems raised in this category was still stronger than in the former: an unusually large amount of literature, for example, was devoted to the problems of credit, debt, and bankruptcy among the rural population. The marginal farming of many peasants, low legal limits to their capacity to borrow, and a lack of lending capital in rural areas— all these factors could throw hundreds of thousands of peasants into debt and even bankruptcy in the event of a less than average harvest in any one year. In consequence, peasants might have to leave the land or take on crushing burdens of outside work in order to maintain their farms. Solutions to the problem of indebtedness would therefore benefit not only the country as a whole by keeping land in cultivation, but also the peasant himself, who could continue to cultivate his land rather than begging his way through the world.

The issue was thus presented to the German public not only as an economic problem, but as a human one as well. A poem by Johann Anton Leisewitz in 1775 painted a poignant picture of the misery of a peasant and his wife whose only bed was to be impounded for debts; their only comfort lay in the fact that no human agency, at least, could take their immortality from them.[49] Justus Möser also employed an emotional description of the eviction of a peasant family from its land in order to illustrate the misfortune which could befall the peasant through no fault of his own, since debt was as often due to unavoidable circumstance as to laziness or poor management.[50] No one devoted more attention to the problems of credit and debt among the peasantry than Möser. His particularly great interest in this facet of the peasant's economy stemmed from his highly original views on the importance of the independent peasantry in German history and in his own time as well. It would not be fair to say that he was uninterested in increasing the total social product of agriculture, but it is undoubtedly true that he would wish for

---

[49] Johann Anton Leisewitz, "Die Pfandung" (1775), *Sämmtliche Schriften* (Braunschweig, 1838), 3-5.

[50] Möser, "Die Abmeierung, eine Erzählung," *Sämtliche Werke*, V, 100-102.

only as much increase as was commensurate with a large and reasonably prosperous community of peasant proprietors.[51] His interest in debt must be seen in this light; his own area, Westphalia, was full of peasants who possessed personal freedom, and who thus had no claim to help from their landlords in bad times. circumstances depend to a peculiarly great degree upon the Their preservation as cultivators therefore could under some determinations regulating the availability of credit and the contracting and discharge of debt.

An exposition of all of Möser's proposals would involve more detail than their importance here merits; but some indication of their variety will make it clear how many kinds of considerations had to enter into any permanent resolutions of this complicated issue. He sought to shame creditors into lower rates of interest,[52] and to make farm equipment unattachable, so that creditors could not force peasants to work for them with the same equipment the peasants had just bought with the credit extended.[53] He proposed to restrict the amount of credit a peasant could receive to the amount of profit he could derive from his land in three or four average years.[54] In general, he attempted to find methods of amortizing debts which benefited peasants as much as possible while not damaging creditors; if the latter became disaffected, they might refuse to extend any credit—with disastrous results for the peasant. Möser's favorite scheme for the discharge of indebtedness, a plan called *Todbau*, provided that the peasant turn over to his creditors a certain portion of his land, all revenues from which would go to the creditors until all debts were paid. The chief advantage of this scheme lay in the fact that no lien would attach to any part of the property the peasant himself still farmed.[55] All of these suggestions, together

[51] Thus, for example, Möser would not approve huge capitalistic agricultural units which involved only a few actual proprietors and a mass of agricultural day laborers.

[52] Möser, "Memorial eines geringen Kötters, den Verkauf fetter Ländereien betreffend," *Sämtliche Werke*, VIII, 58-59.

[53] Möser, "Ein grosser Kredit ist dem Eigenbehörigen nur zum Verderb, und hat er leider jetzt mehr Kredit als ein Freier," *ibid.*, VIII, 156-57.

[54] Möser, "Gedanken über die Mittel, den übermässigen Schulden der Untertanen zu wehren," *ibid.*, IV, 119-29.

[55] Möser, "Vorschlag zur Erleichterung der hofgesessenen Schuldner," *ibid.*, V, 93-96.

with a number of ideas for streamlining the administration of debtor-creditor relations, were deliberately designed to preserve both peasant proprietors and their sources of credit.

If Möser was chiefly concerned with free and independent proprietors, there were others whose purview was broader. One writer, Christian August Wichmann, called for proprietors and tenants to regard their relationship as a "company undertaking," in which gains and losses would be shared. An important part of this consisted in varying ground rents according to the yield of the crop—which would spare the peasant in a bad year, and benefit the landlord in a good one—and in allowing the lessee to subtract from the gross yearly income on which the rent levy would be made an amount equivalent to the permanent improvements he had made in land or buildings.[56] A fascinating governmental institution for the forestalling of debt and the extension of capital credit for agricultural undertakings was described by Christoph Meiners, a historian and professor at Göttingen. The Count of Lippe-Detmold had overseen the establishment of three state-supervised funds, one of which gave money away gratuitously as aid to peasants who had suffered extensive damage to their farms through no fault of their own, or who had no money for improvements deemed necessary to their continued existence on the land; a second fund was to loan out money to poorer peasants for improvements, at a low rate of interest (a maximum of three percent) and with convenient repayment terms. A third fund, finally, was to consist of private moneys from individuals who received a four percent return on their capital, and this money could be borrowed by anyone at five percent interest. In view of prevailing usurious interest rates, Meiners was understandably impressed with this plan, and recommended general imitation.[57] One fertile mind suggested insurance companies as a

---

[56] Christian August Wichmann, "Zufällige Betrachtung über die Pachterbankerotte," *Leipziger Magazin,* Erstes Stük (1782), 83-86.

[57] Christoph Meiners, "Nachricht von mehrern vortrefflichen Einrichtungen . . . in der Grafschaft Lippe-Detmold," *Göttingisches Historisches Magazin,* II (1788), 577-93. Interest rates varied from place to place in Germany, and from year to year, but for the rural areas, and more especially for peasants, they were almost uniformly high. Justus Möser mentioned 20 percent per annum in Westphalia, which was probably about average for Germany, though quite high in comparison with rates in western Europe as a whole. Möser, "Memorial eines geringen Kötters," *Sämtliche Werke,* VIII, 58-59.

method of protecting peasants from the financial effects of weather damage to their crops, and thus from the necessity of going into debt at all. Membership in such companies could be legally required or merely recommended, and insurance rates would vary according to the crops insured, the prevailing market price, and so forth.[58] There is no indication, however, that crop insurance was anywhere set on foot in Germany in the eighteenth century.[59]

Finally, and fairly obviously, if debt was seen as a function of a set of special circumstances rather than as a permanent and necessary state of affairs, then government itself might be expected to make the most apparent concession which lay within its power, and remit part or all of a peasant's taxes, just to keep him on his feet. Frederick II, after all, having foreseen the ravages his wars would bring to peasant lands, had remitted or reduced taxes, and was duly praised for it.[60] In the absence of special funds assuring credit for the peasant who had become impecunious due to natural disasters, it was asked, why could other princes not take a page from Frederick's book and remit taxes for a greater or lesser period of time?[61] Or even revise the general tax structure of their states so that the tax load on peasants would be lightened permanently, allowing them to stay out of debt in bad years and to have surplus capital for reinvestment in good years?[62]

All the concern so far demonstrated about the conditions of the peasant's life and work had as its goal the correction of particular abuses or circumstances which tended to hinder the ability of

[58] "Vorschlag und Entwurf zu Errichtung einer Wetter-Schadens-Versicherungs-gesellschaft," *Archiv für den Menschen und Bürger*, III (1781), 216-28.

[59] The idea may well have been adopted from fire insurance "collectives" which were not uncommon in Germany, especially in cities, in the eighteenth century. Lütge states, but without examples, that insurance against death of livestock existed in the eighteenth century, but that hail insurance appears to have come only in the nineteenth century. Friedrich K. Lütge, *Deutsche Sozial- und Wirtschaftsgeschichte*, 344-45.

[60] [Johann Caspar Riesbeck], *Briefe eines reisenden Franzosen über Deutschland: an seinen Bruder zu Paris*, 2 vols. (n.p., n.d.), II, 101.

[61] C. A. Wichmann, "Über die natürlichsten Mittel, dem Landmanne die Stall-fütterung zu erleichtern," *Leipziger Magazin*, Zweites Stük (1784), 213-14.

[62] "Die allgemeinsten oekonomischen Regierungs-Maximen," *ibid.*, Drittes Stük (1786), 327-40.

the peasant to produce a social surplus under an existing agrarian constitution. Complaints about aristocratic hunting privileges, the inefficiency of peasant conscription for military establishments, the improvement of justice, and even the intense interest in improving the mechanics of debtor-creditor relations and the availability of rural capital were based upon an implicit acceptance of an old order, and not one of the suggestions so far made involved more than a slight rearrangement of pieces in the confused puzzle of the agrarian *status quo.* On the other hand, it had been realized for many years before this time that the utilization of agricultural land under conditions inherited from the Middle Ages was in many respects highly inefficient. From the *Hausväter* and early Cameralists of the seventeenth century through the later Cameralists, experimental economists, and Physiocrats of the eighteenth, a flood of criticisms of the three-field system, compulsory planting, common lands, and other facets of traditional agricultural practice had achieved some concrete results in the legislation of a number of German territories, notably in Prussia, where consolidation of lands and partition of village commons was a major step towards rationalization of primary production. Without yet affecting the relationship of the peasant class to other classes of society, this type of criticism did imply major changes in land distribution among the peasantry itself.

Related to these major issues, and just as important for the peasant cultivator, was the question of what constituted the socially most desirable farm size. In the debate over this question, which became a really major issue only after 1800, population theorists in this time tended to carry the day. Recognizing the necessity for farms larger than could support merely marginal existence for a peasant family, they were none the less chiefly concerned to prevent the growth of oversized farms and rich peasants. The reason was simple: a large farm split into three or four medium-sized farms could support more families. These, while not rich, could be at least relatively well off, would pay more in dues and taxes, and would provide a larger body of consumers for the products of the crafts and industries. Furthermore, it was avowed, rich farmers could afford the luxury of letting their poorer land lie unused while they cultivated only the better fields, whereas peasants of medium income had to use all their land; consequently, the total production from a number of small farms was certain to be greater than that of a single farm on the same area of land. The economical habits of the medium-sized peasant would make of both him and his sons, no matter in what occupation they might be employed, more industrious craftsmen, better manufacturers, and more useful citizens altogether than affluent peasants and their sons.[63] If this argument was not sufficiently convincing, one could always find refuge in pious assurances that since rich peasants lacked appreciation of finer things, and thus didn't know how to make proper use of their riches in any case, excessive prosperity merely led to unhappiness and to the denial of the plow which had made the peasant rich in the first place.[64]

It was possible to regulate the size of land holdings by graduated land taxes, of course—as was indeed suggested by one observer, who felt that such a measure would result in the creation of a large number of medium-sized farms.[65] But more commonly proposed was the abolition of laws which stipulated the indivisibility of peasant lands. Such laws, once felt necessary to prevent overfragmentation of peasant farms, also had the effect of unnecessarily preserving over-large farms, and therefore also preventing marginally small farms from acquiring enough more land to make them viable and independent agricultural units. The optimal size of the individual peasant farm was thus at this time commonly taken to be the amount of land which could be farmed completely by the individual occupant without the necessity of any forced labor services.[66] Such considerations moved one

[63] [I. F. Autenrieth, and others], *Die uneingeschränkte Vertrennung der Bauern-Güter, oder Bauern-Lehen, wird in höchster Gegenwart Seiner Herzoglichen Durchlaucht, des regierenden Herrn Herzogs Carl, zu Wirtemberg und Töck etc. unter dem Vorsiz I. F. Autenrieth . . . öffentlich verteidiget werden, . . . 1779* (Stuttgart, 1779), 34-36.

[64] "Über den Zustand der Bauern in KurBraunschweig etc.," *Staats-Anzeigen,* IX (1786), 362-63.

[65] [Riesbeck], *Briefe eines reisenden Franzosen,* I, 116.

[66] [Oeder], *Bedenken,* 8. This suggested to Oeder, as to many other commentators, the desirability of partitioning the lords' domains, which were almost always worked by forced labor, into individual tenures for peasants. According to Oeder's estimate, the amount of land reserved for domain in the later decades of the

group of reformers, led by Jakob Friedrich Autenrieth, a Württemberg official and professor of Cameralistics at the Ducal Academy there, to hold a public debate in the presence of the Duke of Württemberg in order to show that prevailing land distribution "hinders the population in many ways, . . . puts the most troublesome fetters on the peasant, this so useful citizen of the state, sets limits to his diligence, and [is responsible for the fact] that the highest possible multitude of products from the fields, the best part of the national wealth, is not achieved." What these men sought was freedom for the peasant to partition his lands as he pleased; how much land he retained was his own affair. Merchants and craftsmen, they pointed out (erroneously), were not restricted in their occupations, and the peasant should not be in his, either: "Freedom is the soul of all industries!"[67]

As the last quotation might suggest, the demand for a measure of free choice for the peasant in matters affecting the amount of land he cultivated was only one facet of a generally growing desire to expand the realm in which the peasant might exercise his individual initiative. Behind much of this sentiment lay one of the most important and influential philosophical discoveries (or rediscoveries) of the eighteenth century, the principle of self-interest, or *amour propre,* as the motive power of human action. This idea was emphatically not the brain-child of Adam Smith, even in the realm of political economy, although it was undoubtedly given its most coherent and influential formulation by him.[68] Hints of it can be found in seventeenth-century mercantilism, and more than mere hints in philosophical oddities such as Bernard Mandeville's *Fable of the Bees,* in the works of Richard Cantillon, David Hume, and a number of other writers of the eighteenth century in the field of economics. Among German Cameralists, one need look no further than von Justi to find the conviction that hard work and purposeful application were functions of self-interest and nothing else. *Amour propre* was used to justify numerous specific proposals aimed at the realization of

eighteenth century comprised about one-quarter of all land under cultivation in Germany (14-15).

[67] [Autenrieth and others], *Die uneingeschränkte Vertrennung,* 30-31, 44-45.

[68] A full discussion of Smith's influence in Germany is included below in Chapter V.

the general goal of increased production and better distribution of agricultural goods. Free trade in grains, as advocated by Justus Möser and a number of others in this period, presupposed the freedom of the peasant to sell wherever he could get the best price.[69] Freedom for the peasant to plant whatever crops he wished, and could get the best prices for, was another oft-repeated demand, which struck at the base of the three-field system, and again was a method not only of improving the peasant's income, but of developing his initiative and providing society with a variety of products not possible under the restrictions inherent in the three-field system.[70] The abolition of forced labor services, whether as part of the ground rent or as a function of personal servitude, was demanded by some few reformers for the same reasons, although in these years this particular reform proposal was not as common as it was to be later. The same hands that did labor service for someone else would do much more if they were working for their possessor, this argument ran, and it was only in the freedom of a peasant to dispose of his own time and "In the enjoyment of the immediate fruits of his assiduity [that he] learns to know the worth of time."[71]

All of these insights could and did occur in many instances as piecemeal suggestions intended to be integrated into the old, still essentially feudal, agrarian order. But really systematic thinkers on the subject of agricultural improvement gradually came to the realization that a haphazard incorporation of particular reforms into the old system would merely result in glaring inconsistencies, and that attempts to balance these off would require so much time and effort, and so much tortuous compro-

---

[69] Möser, "Vorschlag, wie die Teuerung des Korns am besten auszuweichen," *Sämtliche Werke,* V, 27-35; and "Gedanken über die Getreidesperre, an die Deutschen," V, 44-51. It should be remarked that Möser's proposal, typical of many other individuals and especially characteristic of him, had the consumer rather than the producer in mind, since he was particularly concerned to prevent inflation of grain prices. On the other hand, it is true that the peasant was a consumer as well as a producer, and that free grain trade made it possible for peasants to sell grain surpluses which under unfree conditions might have been impossible to get rid of at anything more than sacrifice prices. Free trade thus also prevented deflation of prices, and would theoretically result in the much-prized "middle price" of eighteenth-century economists.

[70] C. A. Wichmann, "Zufällige Betrachtung," *Leipziger Magazin,* Erstes Stük (1782), 55-56. See also, "Die allgemeinsten oekonomischen Regierungs-Maximen," Drittes Stük (1786), 353.

[71] [Oeder], *Bedenken,* 31-33.

mise, that the effects of the reform themselves would be virtually lost. It was a consequence of this realization that the decades before the French Revolution witnessed a growth of the sentiment that agrarian Germany could not take full advantage of technical reforms until the system of land tenure itself and the relationship of the peasant to the land were changed in fundamental ways.

The directions taken by this sentiment were two: the first was towards hereditary tenure for peasants; the second, towards emancipation from personal servitude. The two were closely related by reason of their common affirmation of the principle of self-interest, and were therefore often lumped together in reform literature. J. H. G. von Justi, it will be recalled, had early reached the conclusion that servitude and insecure tenure were fundamentally involved in the depressed condition of German agriculture. It was the principle of self-interest which underlay von Justi's criticisms, and which tied one to the other: thus when another author spoke of the necessity for the "rightful" owners of the land (the peasants who actually worked it) to be secure in their ownership of both land and *mobilia*, because security of property was the foundation of the state economic order, he was referring to the willingness of the peasant to invest time and money in his own farm.[72] If the peasant had only a time-lease, or occupied the land merely on sufferance, he would be loath to exert himself to make improvements whose benefits might be enjoyed by others. The same principle held for the lifetime lease, since he could not be sure that his sons would inherit the improvements both he and they had made during his lifetime. Hereditary tenure, the guarantee of the right of the peasant to permanent tenure on his land and to choose his successor on the farm, satisfied the demands of self-interest by conferring on the peasant what amounted to quasi-ownership of his land.

But there was another side to this coin: granted that hereditary tenure meant that the lord could not expel from his land either the peasant or the heirs chosen by him for any but legal reasons, the question still remained of whether the peasant ought to be free to *leave* the land, to go somewhere else or take up some

---

[72] "Die allgemeinsten ökonomischen Regierungs-Maximen," *Leipziger Magazin*, Drittes Stük (1786), 326-27.

other occupation. A positive answer was certainly implied in the proposal for "full civic freedom" made by Georg Christian Oeder, a native of Schleswig, who served as professor in Copenhagen and in various official capacities in the Danish government, including the post of *Finanzrath* on the Danish Agricultural Commission. Oeder defined civic freedom as the freedom of every individual to increase and enjoy his own prosperity to the best of his ability and by any means compatible with the situation in the society under whose protection he lived.[73] Oeder was one of those who had proposed the abolition of forced labor services —and one might expect that the connection which almost everywhere existed between labor service and personal servitude might have been enough to account for Oeder's belief that servitude must be abolished. But in fact he separated the two, and appears to have condemned servitude for its restrictions on the movement of the individual in economic society generally, not merely because it restricted his productive capacity as a peasant.[74] Generally speaking, although Oeder's view would constitute an exception, hereditary tenure, or the security of the peasant in the use of his land, was an item of higher priority, at least for those commentators whose interests were largely economic, than was the abolition of servitude. This is probably explicable in terms of the rural labor shortage. As suggested above, a large proportion of the forced labor services in Germany were performed as part of the peasants' personal obligations to their lords rather than as part of their real obligations, or ground rent. There was therefore a certain fear among Cameralists and private landlords, especially, that the abolition of servitude, carrying with it the end of forced cultivation of the lords' domains, would mean a sharp drop in the total production of agricultural goods and a serious blow to the economic position of the lords.[75]

In spite of reservations expressed by economic thinkers about aspects of proposals made for reform, it is clear that by the end

[73] [Oeder], *Bedenken*, 48.

[74] These were not unconnected, however, in the sense that a peasant who didn't like his work, and who could do well something else he enjoyed more, would bring benefit to himself and to the rest of society by leaving his land to someone who would farm it better because he enjoyed it more.

[75] Even though cash compensation for the abolished services would be paid to landlords, according to virtually all proposals, the fear was that the wages demanded by free labor for the same work would greatly reduce profit margins.

of the 1780s a large measure of at least passive agreement concerning the most essential directions of agricultural reform had been achieved. The disjointed proposals of an earlier time for the correction of this or that abuse or hindrance to the peasant's economy did not indeed disappear, and may even have increased in number; but the strongly empirical judgments of the Cameralists and the somewhat more rationalistic conclusions of the Physiocrats had by 1789 reduced the problem of the increase of agricultural production to a few fundamental premises. The most important of these, and the ones most commonly agreed upon among them, were that the peasant must become at least a quasi-proprietor, and that he must be legally free.

But now a basic contradiction arose, one for which a resolution was demanded if indeed these reform proposals were ever to be made reality by state legislation. The qualities necessary in a peasant who was to dispose freely of his own person, his family, his land and all the equipment thereon; the qualities necessary in a peasant who was to be a free man and a proprietor; in short, the qualities necessary for the implementation of that personal initiative which economists had come to feel was essential to the progress of agriculture—these simply did not exist in the person of the peasant as he was conceived by the overwhelming majority of the educated and the politically responsible classes in Germany in the eighteenth century. The attitude that the peasant was as much beast as man; that he was constitutionally stupid, or vicious, or both; that he had the mind of a child who could never grow up—these and other similarly condescending views constituted a tremendous obstacle to the realization of basic reform. If that class of men called peasantry was incapable *by nature* of performing the tasks which the proposed reforms would place upon it, then there was obviously no point to the reforms themselves. What this means is that the realization of reforms designed to improve the economic position of the peasant depended not merely upon the ability of reformers to convince the proper classes of society of the technical excellence of their reform plans, but also upon the development of a new image of the peasant—an image which was adequate to the social performance presupposed by the reform plans and hopes.

Part Two

The Quickening Interest

3 The Origins of the Moral Image

The creation of positive and favorable characteristics for the peasant, or, as contemporaries might rather have put it, the "discovery" of them, was a process inseparable from the major intellectual currents and changes of eighteenth-century Germany. Political theories, whether absolutist or corporative-representative, the religious reawakening known as Pietism, the antirationalistic moralism of the reaction to the Enlightenment, and, of course, the Enlightenment itself—all these and other less clear and distinguishable thought lines crossed the peasant issue time and time again, weaving a complex pattern of mutual intersections. As an example, it has already been demonstrated that the peasant first became a focus of attention in Germany in the eighteenth century to a large extent because of his connection with agriculture and in his capacity as a primary producer; this was the result of the systematization of economic thought which had its roots in the economic needs of the modern dynastic state, and which expressed itself in Germany as Cameralism and, later in the period, also in Physiocracy. But Cameralists and Physiocrats could be Pietists as well; they could be moralists as well as administrators; and princes could be enlightened humanitarians as well as despots and tyrants. Any one man, in other words, could and usually did owe his ideas to more than one source.

Economic thought has been accounted of peculiar importance for the beginnings of the social rehabilitation of the peasant because, first, of the pragmatic nature of its interest in him, which largely accounts for the awakening concern for the peasantry in governmental circles; and, second, because of the nature of the consequences drawn from that interest, which manifested themselves as concrete and specific reform proposals. But it must be emphasized that the meaning of agriculture for society as seen by contemporaries was by no means restricted to its economic importance, even though the strongest emphasis in the prerevolutionary period was placed on that consideration. Agriculture as a facet of the economy was of course important for the goods it produced; but it was also important as a way of life, and because of the kind of man produced by that life. The Physiocrats were of course rabid on the subject of agriculture and its significance for society, and far outstripped less doctrinaire economists in singing its praises: "One learns . . . gradually to recognize that agriculture is the mother of the human race, and consequently the source of all wonderworks of the human wit, all industry of the human understanding, and generally of all the knowledge which the understanding has acquired for itself, which it has raised to sciences, and which it propagates upon descendants from generation to generation." Further, according to this source, agriculture is responsible for the existence and continuity of society and law, as well as for the preservation of the magisterial authority and the political power through which society and law are administered.[1]

But agriculture fulfilled the role suggested above, that of guarantor of social integrity, through the specific influences it exercised on human beings. This was the sense of the Swiss H. C. Hirzel's remark that agriculture was the moral foundation and the training ground of *all* virtue and utility,[2] and is the sentiment which lay behind the oft-repeated praise of agriculture as the foundation of civilized life. Even political or statist literature, not normally given to judgments of this kind, appeared to see advantages in the agricultural life: in addition to occasional references to the peasants as the strongest and best soldiers,[3] one may find evidence of a deeper affinity perceived to exist between agricultural life and the military arts.[4] The common denominator in this connection was the suggestion of manliness or masculinity, raw strength and stamina, which the agricultural occupation fostered in the peasant—insights which will crop up again in discussions yet to come. Scattered references by economists to the industry and diligence of the peasant, closely related to the foregoing, may also be found, but these are more than balanced by cold-eyed

[1] "Die allgemeinsten oekonomischen Regierungs-Maximen," *Leipziger Magazin,* Drittes Stük (1786), 318-19.
[2] H. C. Hirzel, *Die Wirthschaft eines philosophischen Bauers* (Zürich, 1761).
[3] [Oeder], *Bedenken,* 39.
[4] C. C. F. Hüpeden, "Zur Charakteristik von NiederHessen," *Staats-Anzeigen,* X (1787), 160.

assessments of the generally lazy disposition of the peasantry.[5]

In addition to the above judgments, infrequently encountered, some statist literature contained moral judgments. Political writings of this particular kind, together with moralist literature of various complexions, was of much more importance in the development of a positive picture of the personality of the peasant as a type than was most statist literature, however. Here, by way of defining "moralist literature," the peasant was placed in the service of various conceptions of social morality as an example with which to reproach the upper strata of German society, or of human society in general, for impiety and irreligion, superciliousness, overrefinement, pride, greed, dishonesty, and a host of other sins, crimes, and errors. A survey of the qualities most commonly attributed to the peasant will not only clarify the sources and directions of the moral convictions which called the association into being, but also will indicate something of the ideas which combined to give the peasant for the first time, if only as a type, an increasingly distinct and ultimately characteristic personality.

Probably no characteristic of the peasant was more often singled out for praise than his piety. The number of poems and other literary expressions which purported to demonstrate the sincere dependence of the peasant on his religion was very large. Rhapsodizing on the theme of the peasant's humble piety was

[5] See above, p. 36, where Justi comments on this. An even better example is a lengthy essay of the 1790s by Christian Garve, professor of philosophy at Leipzig and a philosophical popularizer of some repute in Germany. In this work, Garve rudely dismissed much contemporary eulogy of the peasant as poetic nonsense, doubted the prevalence of pure morals and customs among peasants, and assessed the average peasant as lazy, suspicious, and ignorant. On the other hand, he emphasized that such characteristics frequently arose from circumstances over which the peasants had little control, and defended some aspects of their suspiciousness against the reforming zeal of theoretical agriculturists. Christian Garve, "Über den Charakter der Bauern und ihr Verhältniss gegen die Gutsherrn und gegen die Regierung," *Vermischte Aufsätze* (Breslau, 1796), 1-228. All this raises an interesting point of propaganda technique: for those who were interested in drawing a good character for the peasant, it appeared desirable to paint him as extremely industrious; but for those who were trying to make out a good case for reform, it seemed necessary to bring out the peasant's ignorance and disinclination to work under then-existing conditions. A compromise position was represented by the formula that the peasant was by nature industrious, was lazy under the present unreformed agrarian constitution, but would give expression to his true diligence if given the opportunity through educational or other reforms.

nowhere more common than among the members of the Göttingen *Hainbund* (Sylvan League) a poetic circle established in 1772 by admirers of the poet and literary factotum Friedrich Gottlieb Klopstock. Johann Heinrich Voss, onetime editor of the *Göttinger Musenalmanach* and one of the better known members of the circle, specialized in idyls, a genre which had lately become popular; but while in these he pointed up the good qualities of peasant life, his own plebeian background (he was the son of a manumitted peasant) kept him from making of it an Arcadian shepherd's paradise, and in such poems as "The Happy Peasant" and "Peasant Happiness," he emphasized mostly the contentment of a life whose simplicity was due to an unswerving and unquestioning piety.[6] Another of the circle, Ludwig Hölty, whose forte was the ballad, but who also dabbled in songs of love, friendship, and nature, compared the advice given by an old peasant to his son,

> Üb' immer Treu und Redlichkeit
> Bis an dein kühles Grab,
> Und weiche keinen Finger breit
> Von Gottes wegen ab!

> Be always loyal and honest
> Until you're in your grave,
> And deviate not a finger's breadth
> From God's own Word and Way!

with the destructive and vicious life of the hated bailiff, who oppressed the peasant with satanic delight, or the Junker who, ignoring all injunctions to Christian charity, carelessly consumed even the widow's small possessions.[7]

Poems and songs written for the peasant, whether in light, folksy dialect, as was the habit of Matthias Claudius, or with scarcely veiled and heavyhanded didacticism, as with Friedrich Wilhelm Gleim, show a constant recurrence of this theme of piety, and were doubtless intended to instruct as well as to glorify. A typical effort by Gleim, entitled "Song of the Peasant," made

[6] Johann Heinrich Voss, "Der frohe Bauer" and "Baurenglück," *Sämtliche Gedichte*, 7 vols. (Königsberg, 1802), IV, 104, 109.
[7] L. H. C. Hölty, "Der alte Landmann an seinen Sohn," *Gedichte von Ludwig Heinrich Christoph Hölty* (Hamburg, 1783), 30-34.

the point that the peasant's supreme loyalty was always to God by putting in a peasant's mouth the impressive statement that he would gladly serve both God and king, "and true to both, but first to Him."[8] Humility and thankfulness for God's gifts, together with honesty—all external signs of the pious disposition—were other facets of the peasant's religious dependence which were seldom missed in rural poetics.[9]

The source of this agrarian piety was commonly assumed to be the peasant's occupation itself; as one writer put it, the uncertain production of agriculture from year to year fostered in the peasant a true humility and a sense of his dependence upon factors over which he had no control—the weather no doubt being a prime example—and therefore brought him to a deeply felt appreciation of nature's God.[10] Doubtless the inexplicable machinations of the grandees to whose mere whim he was often subject (as in the senseless destruction of the *parforce* hunt, or eviction from land for reasons having nothing to do with his own performance) also had something to do with the refuge he sought in religion and the promises of another, better world. The peasant, after all, was as convinced as Johann Christian Schubart that it was in "the sweat of [his] brow" that he was intended to eat his bread, "not with tears, not with heartache and grief"; that his creator had made him "for joy, for thanks and hymns, . . . not . . . for an estate where it should be [worse] for [him] than for the cattle which [he] feeds."[11] But there was an obvious discrepancy between what was supposed to be and what actually was, and this discrepancy must not only have deepened the peasant's dependence on religion as an answer to this riddle, but in doing so also have provided proof to others of an already-existing piety.

Justus Möser was probably thinking along both these lines

---

[8] Friedrich Wilhelm Gleim, "Lied des Bauers," *Sämmtliche Schriften von Friedrich Wilhelm Gleim,* neue verbesserte Auflage, 4 vols. (Leipzig, 1802-1803), IV, 9.

[9] Two good examples are Christian Friedrich Daniel Schubart, "Der Bauer in der Ernte" (1786) and "Der Bauer im Winter" (1786), *Des Patrioten: Gesammelte Schriften und Schicksale,* 8 vols. (Stuttgart, 1839-1840), IV, 214, 291-92.

[10] "Säze, welche allgemeine Evidenzen für alle Berufe in der menschlichen Gesellschaft zu seyn scheinen," *Archiv für den Menschen und Bürger,* V (1782), 9-10. The author of this article may well have been Johann August Schlettwein, the editor of this journal and an important German Physiocrat.

[11] Johann Christian Schubart, "Hutung, Trift und Brache; die grösten Gebrechen und die Pest der Landwirthschaft," *Leipziger Magazin,* Viertes Stük (1782), 424.

when he contrasted the superficiality of the townsman with the depth of the peasant in matters of religion. He wrote that religion in rural areas was "quite naturally" much stronger than in cities, and expressed his conviction that even if the "finer world" debated and disputed all religion out of existence, the needs of the peasant would always bring it back again.[12] And it is precisely here that the piety of the peasant becomes a tool in the hands of a moral philosophy. For Möser's phrase "finer world" was merely his personal expression for the vanguard of the Enlightenment in Germany, the religious skeptics, deists, and atheists, whose attacks on religious dogma, the divine inspiration of the Bible, and the validity of morality based on scripture were seen by the essentially orthodox Möser as an attempt to dissolve the very moral bonds which held society together. It was not just Pietism and the devotees of the extreme forms of inner spirituality who found in the peasant a refuge against rationalistic religious skepticism, but also the orthodox churches, both Protestant and Catholic. How it came about that the peasant could be used against this new skepticism is probably in the first instance related to empirical observations such as those upon which Möser's judgment may have been based, specifically, that the incidence of enlightened or skeptical religious ideas in the rural areas was in fact very small. While the chief reasons for this lay, of course, in the illiteracy, poverty, and relative intellectual inaccessibility of the peasantry, it is fully understandable that the defenders of traditional Christianity would prefer to find its causes in something more positive and edifying than sheer ignorance; thus, to some extent at least, their discovery of the "natural" propensity of the peasant to be pious, stemming from his occupation and his "natural" environment. This kind of solution was further reinforced by a tendency to describe the peasant as "realistic," particularly in comparison with the townsman, who was surrounded by the creations of his own arts and crafts, and who therefore saw not the real world, but only pictures and representations of it.[13] If the peasant was realistic, then, by extension, so was his

---

[12] Möser, "Eine Bauren-Theodicee," *Sämtliche Werke*, IX, 211-12.
[13] "Säze, welche allgemeine Evidenzen . . . zu seyn scheinen," *Archiv für den Menschen und Bürger*, (1782), 8.

piety. Not the townsman, seduced by the abstractions of the Enlightenment and its rational skepticism, but the peasant who lived in a real world had the conception of God which more nearly approached the truth. Fantasy, as one writer put it, like femininity, was after all more characteristic of the commercial nation than of the peasant nation, whose spirit was masculine and realistic.[14]

From the reality of his contacts with the land and with nature in general came another characteristic of the peasant: his natural wisdom. As early as 1732, the famous Swiss doctor and poet Albrecht von Haller in his well-known poem *"Die Alpen"* had protested against the ideals of an overrefined social culture, and had used Alpine shepherds as an example of essential human qualities missing in and yet held in contempt by contemporary society. One of these qualities was certainly that of measured wisdom and judgment based on experience—as shown in Haller's description of an ancient shepherd:

> Bald aber spricht ein Greis, von dessen grauen Haaren
> Sein angenehm Gespräch ein neu Gewichte nimmt.
> Die Vorwelt sah ihn schon, die Last von hundert Jahren
> Hat seinen Geist gestärkt und nur den Leib gekrümnt.
> Er ist ein Beispiel noch von unsern Heldenahnen,
> In deren Arm der Blitz und Gott im Herzen war.

> But soon there speaks an old man, whose grey hair
> Lends new weight to his pleasant words.
> An earlier world had known him, and the burden of his
> hundred years
> Has strengthened his spirit and bowed only his body.
> He is an example still of our heroic ancestors
> Whose arms were filled with lightning, whose hearts
> were filled with God.

Similarly, in speaking of a village leader, Haller wrote:

> Er ist des Dorfes Rat, sein Ausspruch macht sie sicher,
> Und die Erfahrenheit dient ihm vor Tausend Bücher.[15]

14 Schlosser, *Kleine Schriften*, II, 250-51.
15 Albrecht von Haller, "Die Alpen" (1732), in *Deutsche Literatur: Sammlung literarischer Kunst- und Kulturdenkmäler in Entwicklungsreihen*, Reihe Aufklärung, IV (Leipzig, 1931), 318.

He is advisor to the village, his judgment makes it secure,
And experience is more useful to him than a thousand books.

The value of experience in a real environment lay not in logically demonstrable principles of behavior which could be deliberately formalized into a system. Far from it: the peasant, as Möser said, was ruled by "Passion, this noble gift of God," which "leads [man] more surely than the most enlightened reason."[16] "The peasant," after all, "follows a long experience, or a venerable prejudice, and it is dangerous to disturb him."[17] The Bavarian writer Lorenz Westenrieder, who was very strongly influenced by Möser, made the same point when talking about the inadvisability of forcing certain types of agricultural reform on the peasant; the peasant knows by instinct what crops are most proper for his land, and he had best be left to himself: "Finally the learned gentlemen return from their frenzy, or are set straight by others, and the result is commonly this, that the simple peasant was right."[18] Against the prevailing view that the peasant was ignorant and even stupid, it was therefore argued that his knowledge was merely of a different (and perhaps better) kind than that which was commonly appreciated. The peasant was a complete empiricist, with nothing of the metaphysician in him; and his knowledge required no books because it was fixed in custom. The poet Gleim expressed this quite clearly when he wrote:

Es steckt manch' edles Blut in kleinen Bauernhütten,
Das noch den alten Brauch und Art der alten Sitten
Nicht gänzlich abgelegt.

Much noble blood is hid away in small peasant huts,
Which has not yet entirely put aside the usage and method
Of old customs.

And, he added for the benefit of those who thought the peasant

[16] Möser, "Schreiben einer Mutter an einen philosophischen Kinderlehrer," *Sämtliche Werke*, V, 262.

[17] Justus Möser, *Osnabrückische Geschichte*, 3d ed., 2 vols. (Berlin and Stettin, 1819-1824), I, 96.

[18] [Lorenz Westenrieder], "Gedanken über die Verbesserung der Landescultur in Baiern," *Beyträge zur vaterländischen Historie, Geographie, Statistik und Landwirthschaft, samt einer Uebersicht der schönen Literatur*, I (1788), 193-94.

stupid merely because he kept his mouth shut, the peasants now as in the days of old were indeed in wretched circumstances, but, like their forefathers, were men of keen wits, who "think much, say little."[19]

In these glorifications of natural wisdom and the reliance of the peasant on his own experience and the teachings of tradition, there was an obvious and deliberate attempt to decry the value of abstract knowledge and, more important, abstract reasoning. Nowhere is the anti-Enlightenment impulse behind the discovery of these peasant virtues clearer than in these attempts to place traditional values and the method by which they were attained in sharp contrast to the moral and social theorizing of the eighteenth-century *philosophes.* The sneers directed at "learned gentlemen" and "encyclopedists" by Möser, Westenrieder, and many others like them indicate not only a fundamental disagreement with the conclusions reached by much enlightened philosophy, and the social order towards which they tended, but also a recognition of the dependence of those conclusions upon certain epistemological and methodological assumptions. The destruction or denigration of the latter on the part of these moralists was therefore a root-and-branch attack on the whole body of enlightened thought.

But something positive was made out of this negative stance, of course. Just as his strong and simple piety suggested a social role for the peasant in the protection or preservation of religion, so also did this natural wisdom now suggest a role for him as the representative and guarantor of methods and conclusions relative to right conduct. It was again Möser who emphasized this educational function of the peasant, when he contrived a story of a ruler who was so impressed with the strength, honesty, and candor of the peasants in his principality that he instituted reforms in his court to produce the same qualities in his courtiers. "And," commented Möser, "the whole court was educated in such a way that the man at court became almost completely equal to the man on the land. But they could not entirely equal him, because he sat in the lap of Mother Nature and took the best

---

[19] Gleim, "Der Tanz auf dem Lande," *Sämmtliche Schriften,* II, 359.

teachings right out of her mouth."[20] This popular theme of the corrupt prince at the feet of the peasant was again illustrated in a supposedly true story related by Friedrich Carl von Moser: a debauched German prince became lost during a hunt, and eventually found himself in the hut of an old peasant. Ignorant of the prince's identity, the old man engaged him in a conversation about the depraved life the former was leading at court. He spelled out the abuses of the court and their bad effects on the country, but concluded forgivingly that the prince was still very young and would undoubtedly see the error of his ways when he grew older. Considerably sobered by this discussion, the prince returned to court and immediately abolished many bad practices.[21]

As strong a motif as the peasant's piety and his wisdom, but closely related to them, was that of the goodness and simplicity of the peasant's life. In this literature, frugality, poverty, and even the uniformity of the peasant's existence were raised to the level of virtues and appropriately praised. Some of this sentiment probably stemmed from a view of rural life which was mere imitation of a very long tradition of pastoral prose and poetry. In this sense, the publication of rural idyls fits quite well with the eighteenth-century fashion of taking long walks or vacations in the country, dressing whole courts in the idealized costumes of shepherds and shepherdesses, and toasting "natural men" such as a Jean-Jacques Rousseau was conceived to be. But a substantial part of it included more than mere rhapsody, more than artificial descriptions of the joys and beauties of nature. When Haller in his *"Die Alpen"* described the benefits of rural life, he not only gave vent to a lofty appreciation of natural physical settings, but also took considerable pains to contrast rural life with urban, and to damn the latter with acid comment: in the country, he said, was peace of soul, far from the smoke and the vain trifles of the city; here, an active life strengthened the forces of the body, and here there was no loafing idleness to "swell the belly."[22] Later, Ludwig Hölty in his poem *"Das Landleben"* referred in the same con-

[20] Möser, "Wie ein Vater seinen Sohn auf eine neue Weise erzog," *Sämtliche Werke*, VI, 213.

[21] Friedrich Carl von Moser, *Gesammelte moralische und politische Schriften*, 2 vols. (Frankfurt am Main, 1763-64), II, 23.

[22] von Haller, "Die Alpen," in *Deutsche Literatur*, Reihe Aufklärung, IV, 315.

temptuous way to the "counting-house" and the "cushions" of city folk;[23] and F. W. Gleim contrasted the simple and healthy diet of the long-lived peasant with the rich foods and the delicacies consumed by kings who toppled early into their graves.[24]

What is involved in these and many other similar writings is an unmistakable reaction to luxury, high life, and, most important, to the moral degeneracy and social corruption to which they were thought to give rise. The extent to which such sentiments before the French Revolution were derived directly from particular social critics such as Rousseau is uncertain, but is probably rather small.[25] Much more important, it would appear, were the objective economic and social conditions which underlay even Rousseau's criticisms. These conditions cannot be dealt with here in any detail, but broadly speaking they pertain to the growth of surplus capital in European society, most of which was concentrated in the cities, through acquisitive activities of trade and commerce, and, in Germany especially, at the princely courts, through taxation and so forth. Small centers of conspicuous consumption grew up, which were all the more obvious because of their scarcity and their isolation; and with them grew up various manufacturing enterprises and services to relieve the rich of their excess money. The vast expenditures of petty German courts on entertainment and various kinds of luxury in their competition with one another (and with Versailles), and the vanity of rich burghers in imitating the life-style of the court nobility, caused great worry not only among the puritanical strains of religious zealots, but also among governmental officials of the mercantilist stripe and some sections of the nobility and burghers who were envious of their richer fellows.

The connection of simplicity of life-style with piety and natural wisdom should be obvious: the pious man, in the first place, avoids greed and gluttony, works hard, practices charity, and

---

23 Hölty, "Das Landleben," *Gedichte,* 9.
24 Gleim, "Der Bauer," *Sämmtliche Schriften,* I, 52-53.
25 The question of Rousseau's influence is a very complex one; there is no doubt that some of his works were fairly well known in Germany at this time—and this is especially true of his *Émile* and the *Nouvelle Héloïse.* But without very detailed research, one can only confirm a certain parallelism between Rousseau's views on such things as reason, emotion, morality, rural and city life, education, and luxury and those of many German contemporaries.

avoids, in general, all debilitating and wasteful pleasures. Natural wisdom (or "passion") is his infallible guide in choosing the specific actions which accord with piety. And, invariably, these result in a simple life. Behind all of these, of course, is his occupation, which, in the case of the peasant, even in the absence of piety and wisdom, makes him honest—if for no other reason than that, unlike the city craftsman, he cannot cheat his customer by hidden shoddy workmanship: he merely loses income when he only half-finishes his work.[26] Finally, to complete the cycle, the simple life the peasant leads gives him no temptation or opportunity to be impious and, if one can believe a noted educator of the time, his capacity to learn (and therefore to increase his wisdom) is enlarged because, being uncorrupted, he had few waste thoughts and entrenched wrong or fantastic ideas.[27]

Class antagonisms of some kinds sharpened considerably in consequence of growing economic distinctions; and certainly the growing antagonism between the German bourgeoisie and the nobility so well documented and described by Johanna Schultze[28] was one important manifestation of these widening social rifts. But just as important, though perhaps less obvious, was the tendency of the middle class to cut itself away from the rural aegis under which it had once grown up, and which it had closely approached once again in many German areas during and after the Thirty Years' War. A consistent theme of moralist literature was that all class antagonisms must be softened; but many felt that the onus lay with the cities, since it was they which had introduced material luxury and a kind of "cosmopolitanism" as status symbols to separate themselves from the peasantry (and, incidentally, from the nobility also). Not entirely untypical was the accusation of one writer that city folk deliberately opposed attempts to raise the level of the peasant's education partly out

---

[26] "Säze, welche allgemeine Evidenzen . . . zu seyn scheinen," *Archiv für den Menschen und Bürger*, V (1782), 8.

[27] Rudolph Z. Becker, "Versuch über die Aufklärung des Landmannes," *Der teutsche Merkur* (August 1785), 120-21.

[28] Throughout her book, *Die Auseinandersetzung zwischen Adel und Bürgertum in den deutschen Zeitschriften der letzten drei Jahrzehnte des 18. Jahrhunderts, 1773-1806* (Berlin, 1925).

of fear of losing a distinction they imagined they enjoyed "by virtue of the dignity of their domicile in the city"—a superiority before which they felt the peasants should tremble with awe.[29]

Given the above image of the peasant, as it was gradually yet coherently developed in moralistic literature of various kinds, and given the rather dissolute picture drawn of the other social classes, it is not surprising that some attention was paid to the discrepancy between the intrinsic worth of the peasant and the contempt in which he and his occupation were generally held in public opinion. Haller was especially bitter on this point, and took particular care to praise his Alpine shepherd community, with an implied slap at the rest of society, as one in which "no distinction prevails which haughtiness has invented, / which makes virtue subject and vice noble."[30] A society which made the virtuous peasant a "subject" and the vice-ridden burgher patrician or blooded aristocrat a "noble" was precisely the point at issue here; it was handled in an unusual way by the Physiocrat Johann Heinrich Merck in the pages of *Der teutsche Merkur* in 1778. Merck invented a story in which, of all people, a minister-of-state gave up his luxurious life in the city in order to become a peasant with a relatively small farm. Mr. Oheim, as this improbable character was called, had always found it difficult to rid himself of the idea that all great men were necessarily well-educated and pushed a pen for a living. Having made the decision to become a peasant, however, he saw clearly that this opinion was wrong, and that small-scale, independent farming was the "most worthy occupation of an honorable man" who wished to see what his own diligence and understanding could accomplish, and who wanted to escape the bonds of uniformity.[31] The usual platitudes of happy family life and the advantages of the outdoor life were of course included. The story was purported to have been written by a city man, a visitor to Oheim's farm, who concluded at the end of his story that his own life was very distasteful in

---

[29] "Die allgemeinsten oekonomischen Regierungs-Maximen," *Leipziger Magazin*, Dritten Stük (1786), 349.

[30] von Haller, "Die Alpen," in *Deutsche Literatur*, Reihe Aufklärung, IV, 312.

[31] By a blithely unnoticed contradiction, however, it was of course precisely the "uniformity" of rural life which Merck appeared most to praise. What *he* had in mind may well have had to do with real uniforms.

comparison with that of Oheim, and who was bemused by the fact that he found so little envy of the upper classes among the peasants.[32]

Still more pointed was Merck's next effort in the *Merkur* the following year. Entitled "A Country Marriage," this story again compared city people with peasants, and found them lacking. Here, a rural official informed his city friends that his son intended to become a peasant. Justifying this desire, the official praised God that in the country, at least, useful occupations were not regarded as vile, and that all men who assisted in the production of the food necessary for life were accustomed to live in a condition of equality. Merck reiterated that not all of society consisted of men who put words on paper, and suggested that a peasant could do with utility what a nobleman often did with disastrous results—manage a farm. Finally, as the official in the story put it, so many people from the peasant class were going over into the classes of those who "want to nibble at the public treasury," that it must be considered a useful thing for others to enter the "natural class" as compensation.[33]

Merck's stories suggested recognition of a point which is important enough to insist upon again, namely, the interdependence of the proposals for agricultural reform based on cognizance of the economic importance of agriculture, on the one hand, and the reassessment of the peasant's character based on the moral qualities said to be produced in him by his occupation, on the other. An indifference to the peasant, or contempt for him, could scarcely

[32] Johann Heinrich Merck "Geschichte des Herrn Oheims," *Der teutsche Merkur* (January 1778), 47; (February 1778), 169-70; (October 1778), 28. Also, "Beschluss des Schreibens worinn die Geschichte des Herrn Oheims enthalten ist" (December 1778), 239.

[33] Merck, "Eine Landhochzeit," *ibid.* (December 1779), 193-207. The practice of drawing sharp contrasts between city and rural life in favor of the latter was particularly common in the numerous (but for the most part short-lived) village newspapers of the last decades of this century. It has been suggested that in this kind of literature, at least, damnation of urban life was less an object in itself than a way of destroying a tendency of the peasant to imagine the city as a kind of paradise where he could escape the toil and drudgery of peasant life—a way, in other words, of making him more content with his own lot and less inclined to forsake his fields for the very dubious prospect of a better life in the town. Ernst Grathoff, *Deutsche Bauern- und Dorfzeitungen des 18. Jahrhunderts: ein Beitrag zur Geschichte des Bauerntums, der öffentlichen Meinung und des Zeitungswesens* (Würzburg, 1937), 82-83.

fail to be reflected in an indifference or contempt for his occupation, and in fact sometimes stemmed from it. It was therefore much to the advantage of the political economists to contribute their efforts to establishing a personality for the peasant which would create a favorable climate for reform; and in fact, many of the most laudatory comments about the moral excellence of the peasant were made by such economists, and especially by the Physiocrats. Correspondingly, the moralists had a strong stake in the progress of agricultural reform, since it was necessary to abolish oppression of the peasant if he were not to develop the qualities of a slave, the very reverse of those for which he was praised.

Some combination or degree of personal freedom and proprietorship were nearly always regarded as essential to the full development of those moral qualities which agriculture in the absence of artificial hindrances tended to confer upon the peasant. If, as one author pointed out, the peasantry in spite of its social importance was still held in contempt among Germans because it still had much of the servile in it,[34] then the answer to this lay in the abolition of the conditions which fostered servility. Justus Möser, a moralist of no uncertain convictions, illustrates by his own tendency to ignore unfree peasants in his discussions that his high estimate of the personal qualities of the peasantry stemmed almost exclusively from his impressions of the free proprietors so common in Westphalia.[35] For many writers, the solid and upright peasant whom they described and applauded in their

[34] "Bauer," *Oeconomische Encyclopädie, oder allgemeines System der Land-Haus- und Staats-Wirthschaft, in alphabetischer Ordnung; aus dem Französischen übersetzt, und mit Anmerkungen und Zusätzen vermehrt . . .*, III (Berlin, 1774), 766.

[35] Thus in one writing concerning the influence of the people on legislation, Möser brought into his consideration none among the peasantry but those who were property owners. Möser, "Von dem Einflusse der Bevölkerung auf die Gesetzgebung," *Sämtliche Werke*, V, 11-22. On the other hand, in an article presumably written by Möser for Schlözer's *Staats-Anzeigen*, he defended servitude in Westphalia as neither harsh nor oppressive. Möser (?), "Leibeigenschaft in Westfalen," *Staats-Anzeigen*, III (1783), 406-15. One might therefore be justified in concluding that for Möser formal freedom was not absolutely essential to the makeup of a good peasant, and that the degree of oppressiveness of his servitude was of more importance than the fact of servitude itself. That is, the actual or effective freedom of the peasant, whether legally confirmed or not, was the important element in Möser's view of the peasant character.

works was as much or more of a thing yet to be realized as were the agricultural reforms of the economists; and in this fact, of course, lies the most essential connection of their different approaches to the peasant—the support each derived from the other. But it remains to be seen just how much further into the arena of reform either or both of these approaches carried the men who used them in this time.

It must be said at the outset that agreement on the necessity for agricultural reform did not, for the men involved, imply a basic change in the social constitution of the old regime. In spite of the reforms proposed by those of them who had concluded that the peasant must be freed and given disposition of the land he farmed, there was in this period almost no hint that such measures would mean any profound social changes. Most of them looked upon all agrarian reform as the amelioration of the conditions of a certain class within itself, which would not affect the external or formal class organization and relationships in their society; yet they preached, in the midst of a highly and rigidly stratified and hierarchical society, something which they called "equality." At first glance, this appears to be a flat contradiction, representing an almost witless obtuseness. But in fact the meaning of this equality can be satisfactorily explained by a brief consideration of the broader social views of which it was a part.

Justus Möser's attitudes are of a certain paradigmatic importance here; his conclusions were not merely representative of the general direction of thought of many others on social questions, but were also directly cited with considerable frequency by other writers in the last three decades of the century. Möser's view of society and its organization was influenced chiefly by two facts: his training as a lawyer, and the series of official positions he occupied in his native principality, the bishopric of Osnabrück.[36] In his life and work, Möser had contact with all strata of the population of Osnabrück, from peasants to nobles and princes. From the problems of government and his everyday experience

[36] Möser was Secretary of the Noble Estates from 1742 until 1747; *advocatus patriae* of the government of the Bishopric, representing the government's interests before all foreign and domestic powers, from 1747 until 1762; and in 1762, when Osnabrück fell to the House of Braunschweig-Lüneburg (George III of England), he was appointed by George to a position comparable to regent, which he held until his retirement in 1783. He died in 1794.

he developed a concept of society in which all classes played different but essentially equal roles. By their organic cooperation, which assumed the necessity of each class for the work of the whole, each class protected and advanced the others mutually. Society, like law itself, was a product of evolution, and both embodied the lessons of historical experience. The necessity of the existence of different classes was for Möser proved both by history and by the actual functions divided among them, so that a "class" was in fact little more than a group of men who performed the same general social function.

It is true, however, that Möser assigned to land and to the people who worked it a very special functional importance. One of his favorite metaphors was that the history of a state was like that of a "commercial company,"[37] which he elaborated to mean, specifically, that units of land were like shares in a joint-stock company.[38] Land ownership was indeed the basic fact of society, around which men and institutions revolved: "The history of Germany," he once wrote, "has, in my estimation, an entirely new direction to hope for if we follow the common landowners, as the true constituents of the nation, through all their changes; make from them the body and regard the great and small servants of this nation as bad or good accidents [*Zufälle*] of the body."[39] So important was private ownership of land to Möser that in an essay addressed to the German Emperor he once proposed that laws be made for estates *(Stände)*, whose distinction from one another would be based on criteria of ownership: at the top, actual owners of farm land; next, owners of city property; third, hereditary tenants of land; and last, those who neither owned land nor had hereditary tenure of it. The prestige associated with each would decline from the first to the last category, for "Rank is solely and uniquely bound to property."[40]

With his concern for land, Möser thus tended to regard all who did not belong to the class of peasants, herders, and hunters as "the waste or the chaff of the human race." The refined portion of mankind, the cities and the courts, he called the "flower bed"

---

[37] Möser, *Osnabrückische Geschichte,* II, iv.
[38] Möser, "Der Bauerhof als eine Aktie betrachtet," *Sämtliche Werke,* VI, 255-70.
[39] Möser, *Osnabrückische Geschichte,* I, xi.
[40] Möser, "Gesetze müssen für Stände gemacht werden," *Sämtliche Werke,* IX, 344-45.

of nature, while the open country was the grainfield; in order that both might grow best, they should be kept strictly separate. "The only abuse we moralists have to fear and to ward off," he admonished, "is this: that the flowers occupy more room than belongs to them."[41] Certainly he was not an advocate of an "open society," in which men from different social backgrounds would mix freely; far from it: he feared mutual corruption of function through mixing of classes, and was particularly concerned that the peasant not become "citified." Class separation and sharp delineation of function were Möser's goals, and these were in the first instance tied to his belief in the social importance of the peasantry.

Evidences of Möser's thoroughly conservative position on the social implications of his defense of the peasant can be seen in a number of statements. While he lauded the "first and golden" period of German history (from earliest times to the fall of Charlemagne's empire) precisely because every individual farm was occupied by a free warrior-owner, deplored the ensuing subjection and oppression of the peasant, and spoke approvingly of the efforts of the peasant *Bundschuh* to protect the traditional concept and reality of landed property,[42] he also defended the view that servitude arose out of needs clearly recognized on all sides,[43] and asserted the social necessity of peasant dues and fees.[44] So Möser sought, in effect, a balance of interests within the state, where "interest" was represented in a definite class. He put himself up as a defender of the peasant largely in order to chastise and correct "those who do not differentiate the duties [of society], and do not diligently honor in the peasant that which belongs to his vocation and to his class,"[45] because the peasants themselves had no spokesman to defend their interests. And it should be emphasized that what Möser strove for was not *preference* for the peasant, but merely *honor* for him in that "which belongs to his vocation and to his class."

[41] Möser, "Antwort an Amalien," *ibid.*, VII, 40-43.
[42] Möser, *Osnabrückische Geschichte*, I, xii-xviii.
[43] Möser, "Kurze Geschichte der Bauerhöfe," *Sämtliche Werke,* IV, 269-76.
[44] Möser, "Der Meier mit der Sündflut," *ibid.*, IX, 51-53.
[45] Möser, "Schreiben eines Frauenzimmers vom Lande an die Frau . . . in der Hauptstadt," *ibid.*, V, 79-80.

What did this actually imply to Möser by way of change? Apparently it meant little more than a change of attitude towards the peasant class, the supplanting of contempt by "honor." Möser castigated in no uncertain terms the common attitude that one could not associate with peasants without losing one's dignity,[46] and in story after story he pointed to the honorable services which the peasant rendered to society and to the state. But only in a negative sense did he ever put himself on record for any kind of formal legal change to implement his idea of increased social honor for the peasant: this was expressed in his opposition to a proposal for a sumptuary ordinance which would have required the peasant to wear drab clothing because of his supposed inferiority to other classes.[47] Unwilling though he was to change the status of the peasant class in its relationship to other classes, Möser's notion of an appeal to the conscience of other classes on behalf of the peasant might at least lead to the establishment of a rapport between classes which could result in an atmosphere of good will conducive to the introduction of practical reforms which did belong to the peasant's vocation and class.

While Möser's special approach to social problems in general and to the peasantry in particular was singular, and unusual for its time, many of his conclusions were typical of a brand of corporatistic (and chiefly aristocratic) thought which had arisen in Germany in the eighteenth century as a reaction to the social implications of the progress of absolutism. When Möser only half-facetiously suggested a new *Reichsrecht* based on legislation for "estates" rather than "subjects," he was mounting an attack on the tendencies of the absolute state to "level off" social classes in the sense of reducing all persons in the state, of whatever class, to a position of common subjection to the sovereign. The word "subject" implied no distinction between persons. Against this idea and reality, traditional German liberties, as Möser interpreted them, demanded a stratified and differentiated society which guaranteed the functional efficiency of each stratum in its own

---

[46] Möser, "Die Spinnstube," *ibid.,* IV, 50.
[47] Möser, "Antwort auf verschiedene Vorschläge wegen einer Kleiderordnung," *ibid.,* IV, 130-31.

distinctive work. Also, the universalist criteria which the absolute state tended to use in choosing for positions of administrative responsibility persons of whatever social background who possessed the qualities and technical knowledge necessary to perform the increasingly complex tasks of government, especially in the fiscal realm, was to Möser evidence of the breakdown of the old (and to him valid) concept of *Libertät*, which carried with it the strongest connotations of corporate rights and privileges.

Möser's defense of the peasantry was thoroughly consistent with his defense of corporate rights in general; he demanded for the peasant a full recognition of the equality of the peasantry as one corporate group among others in the community. To ask something less would be inconsistent with his total view of society, which depended for its workability upon the mutual respect of all estates. He demanded for the peasant the honor which was appropriate to the special function in society of his class, a function which Möser saw not only as an economic one, but also as a moral one. Finally, Möser's notion of equality had nothing to do with equality of persons; it was restricted entirely to the equal necessity of classes, or estates, as he defined them. And in this sense, his praise of the peasantry was part and parcel of the assertion of an entire social and political philosophy—a philosophy which he saw directly endangered by the political theory and practice and the social implications of absolutism.

This principle of the organization of society as a cooperation of classes or estates of equal necessity, however distinguished from one another by privileges or symbols establishing status rank, was of considerable currency in Germany before the revolutionary period; it was taken up not only by aristocrats, but also by the representatives of various other corporate groups which had particular interests to defend and which therefore sought to establish the validity of a conception of organic political and social equilibrium against the claims of any force to emerge in a clearly dominant role. Given the direction of German constitutional history from the Reformation on, tending steadily towards the *de facto* sovereignty of the absolute prince in most German territories, however, it was normally the threat from the political center which caused most worry, i.e., the possibility of a total destruction of the estates principle by the progress of absolutism.[48]

Another source of the defense of the principle that the peasantry as a class had a just claim to social honor lay in the religious reawakening known as Pietism. Pietism was essentially a reaction among German Protestants against the rigid forms and the scholastic orthodoxy characteristic of the Lutheran church after the great reforming period of the sixteenth century. By the third quarter of the seventeenth century, the dry dogmas and formulas of this church failed to satisfy the religious yearnings of many people in a Germany which had just been through the horrors and insecurities of the Thirty Years' War. Through the works of such figures as Philipp Jakob Spener and August Hermann Francke, the concept and practice of a more emotional Christianity was set afoot, a Christianity which emphasized immediate and individual religious experience, and which was signalized externally by a turn towards exemplary Christian behavior involving, among other things, philanthropic and missionary activity.

The movement had a special concern for the common man; this was partly a result of its own strong emphasis on the priesthood of all believers, and partly a result of the acceptance it found among simple people who saw in it a legitimization of their uncomplicated but heartfelt piety. Through the organization of actual religious communities as well as in the establishment of schools at the most elementary level, the common man, and particularly the peasant, was drawn into an especially close association with Pietism. So marked was its plebeian orientation, in fact, that its orthodox opponents used this, in a time of generally increasing social antagonisms, as a target of their scorn for the entire movement. In its effect on society as a whole, however, Pietism achieved more through its conversion and influence upon members of the upper classes. These were its organizers and its diffusers, after all, and there were numbers of them; apart from those who were thoroughly versed in the basic body of Pietist writings and who followed Pietist practices as an important part of their everyday lives, there were many

---

[48] On this subject see Krieger, *The German Idea of Freedom*, especially 71-80.

more within the bodies of the orthodox Protestant churches, both Lutheran and Reformed, who were touched by one or another aspect of Pietist teaching.

Among the political publicists of Pietist bent who had wide reading audiences in Germany in the later eighteenth century, the Württemberg official Friedrich Carl von Moser is of some importance. In such works as *Der Herr und der Diener* (1759) and *Doctor Leidemit* (1783), he attempted to show how the reduction of social antagonisms could be achieved through the constant practice of brotherly love and the exercise of the understanding which accompanied such love. Moser's interest in the peasant stemmed both from the official's concern for the producing class and from the Pietist's concern for the moral elevation of his brothers-in-Christ. What must be noted here is that for Moser, as for Möser, the social implications of his attention to the peasant were strictly confined to the realm of personal attitude, and were never translated into recommendations for structural change in the class organization of society as it then existed. To honor and even to admire the peasant meant, for Moser, that he should be treated as a human being with rights equal to those of other human beings, but it did not mean, to borrow a phrase from Edmund Burke, that he had equal rights to equal things. He did not believe in any kind of formal social egalitarianism.

The explanation of this unwillingness to reform social institutions may be found partly in the tendencies of Pietism itself. It need scarcely be insisted that Pietism, in common with all Christian sects, affirmed the religious equality of all men before God. A typical Pietist statement on this point was that of the Saxon agriculturist Johann Christian Schubart, who favored the extension of human rights to the peasant, "who, if . . . the Holy Scripture does not lie, is established by God Himself just as the princes, and without whom the rest would starve. These people, however, are looked upon as if they had different bodies, different souls, different blood from those to whom a prince (also a mortal human like others) has given rank and title."[49] But that these

[49] J. C. Schubart, "Nachtrag zur Schrift: Hutung, Trift und Brache; die grösten Gebrechen und die Pest der Landwirthschaft. Ein ernstes Wort von Herrn Hofrat Schubart," *Leipziger Magazin*, Zweites Stük (1783), 129-30. Schubart served in the Prussian army as a young man, then for a time became an official in a Masonic

kinds of "rights" implied no revolutionary social equality may be seen from the utterances of numerous Pietist leaders from the very beginning of the movement. Philipp Jakob Spener had declared that "God had, in his wisdom, separated the classes in certain orders—some to be rulers, others, subjects, some lords, others servants and so forth. These differences are not merely in name, but they carry with them certain offices and responsibilities."[50] Other leaders, including the influential Count Zinzendorf in the mid-eighteenth century, expressed their conviction of the necessity of social classes, not only because of God's ordinance but also because all offered the possibility of being serviceable to the community. Gerhard Kaiser in his recent study of Pietism and its connections with the patriotic awakening in Germany has suggested that this Pietist view of the nature of human society as a diverse complex of interacting individuals and classes was derived from a particularly complete acceptance of Luther's doctrine of the "calling."[51] If so, it would not be far-fetched to understand commentators on peasant affairs such as Moser and Schubart as men whose interest in technical agrarian reform was in part, at least, a logical outgrowth of the idea that a man must be given the greatest possible opportunity to perform fully the duties of his calling. Similarly, the failure to pursue this to the point of actual changes in the social order was due to a fear that such changes would lead to a confusion of the duties, responsibilities, and insignia which properly pertained to each calling, and therefore ultimately to a confusion or mixing of the callings themselves. Their belief in the calling obligated them not to attempt anything which might lead men astray from the occupations to which God had called them; but it also obligated them to create a climate of opinion in which every man was honored for doing well what his calling demanded. It thus appears

---

organization, and still later occupied the position of *Hofrat* in Hesse. He retired to an estate in Saxony, which he bought with his wife's money, and there established a model farm, one of the most widely known in Germany. His experiments with clover brought him to the attention of Joseph II of Austria, who conferred nobility upon him with the epithet "von Kleefeld"—Schubart of the Clover-field.

[50] Cited in Koppel S. Pinson, *Pietism as a Factor in the Rise of German Nationalism* (New York, 1934), 109.

[51] Gerhard Kaiser, *Pietismus und Patriotismus im literarischen Deutschland: ein Beitrag zum Problem der Säkularisation* (Wiesbaden, 1961), Chapter 7, *passim*.

thoroughly characteristic that Moser, for example, would combat a "pride of place" which failed to recognize the value of callings other than one's own, rather than propose a social equality of the peasant with the prince, and that he would advocate the foundation of a National Hall of Patriots, where the likenesses of all who had contributed significantly to the growth of the "inner forces" of the country would be displayed—including, specifically, "common men of the land."[52]

Whatever the sources of Moser's convictions may have been—and his political background was probably as important as his Pietism in this[53]—his conclusions on the necessity for general recognition of the importance of all classes of society for one another and for the common work of all in securing the welfare of the entire community were quite similar in many ways to those of Justus Möser, and in fact to those of numerous political and social commentators of the *"städtisch-ständischer"* stripe in pre-revolutionary Germany. Their notion of equality, while very specifically restricted to the context of a hierarchical society, was none the less of great importance to the evolution of a new evaluation of the peasant. Without attacking in any of its fundamentals the system of social stratification which placed the peasant on the bottom rung of the ladder, these men successfully raised the peasant to a level of equal social responsibility and function with burghers, nobles, and princes. The consequences they drew from this kind of equality were chiefly moral rather than legal; but this was not unusual for a time in which social problems were quite generally held to originate in moral deficiencies, and in which the study of social data was still a very haphazard and unsystematic affair.

In making this limited but significant contribution to the

---

[52] F. C. von Moser, *Gesammelte moralische und politische Schriften*, I, 476.

[53] Friedrich Carl von Moser grew up in Württemberg, where the importance of the Diet of the Estates in the government was much greater than in most German principalities. His father, Johann Jakob, was a Councillor of the Estates, and taught his son a reverence for this brand of representative government which stayed with him for the rest of his life. Friedrich Carl had unpleasant experiences with despotic government while an official in Hesse, as had his father with the cantankerous Duke Karl Eugen in Württemberg, and these practical insights into the evils of absolute rule confirmed Moser in his belief in a "liberty" defined by the representation and influence of the estates in government.

foundations of a new peasant image, these *"städtisch-ständische Patrioten"*[54] and Pietists were joined, for quite different reasons, by another group of individuals. These were the officials, servants, and apologists of the German princes, who formed a homogeneous group insofar as their social polity was determined by statist considerations within the specific framework of late eighteenth-century absolutism. In all fundamentals, this group accepted the hierarchical division of society into estates, as did the princes whom they served. But while all paid lipservice to an idea of the state as a kind of pyramid, with gradations from the mass of peasants and laborers at the bottom through the burghers and nobles to the prince at the top, the whole development of absolutism had tended, in fact as well as in the nightmares of the noble estates, towards an elevation of the prince above the various estates of his territory in such a way that his sovereign control of persons tended to become equally complete for all estates. Theorists of absolutism in virtually all European countries almost uniformly characterized the central authority as implying the common subjection of all subjects to the sovereign prince, even though they admitted the possibility of ranked subcategories within the major division of "subject." In Germany, the practical difficulties of implementing the control suggested by this purely political theory in states where powerful organizations of nobles or burghers existed had resulted in anomalous political structures whose shape was eclectically determined by the varying results of the continuing struggles of princes and estates.

But one of the tactics involved in this struggle of princes to become truly sovereign (in the sense which theory proposed) was that of appealing to the country at large against the "selfish" or "egotistical" machinations of whatever group happened to be in the absolutist shooting-gallery at the moment. From this was developed the picture of the prince as a force standing outside the social hierarchy, or above it entirely; he was no longer merely the *primus inter pares*, the first nobleman of the realm, but rather

---

[54] The words *Patriot* and *Patriotismus* at this time carried very few of the nationalist connotations they acquired somewhat later. They were roughly synonymous with "humanitarian" and "humanitarianism," in the sense that a man who loved his country (*patria*) strove for the welfare of its inhabitants. They were just beginning to take on the narrower, nationalistic meaning in these years.

an objective arbiter of interests whose goal was the welfare of all persons within his sovereign jurisdiction. In the tasks which he set for himself and for the state, he established a standard of judgment which weighed men and actions, institutions and ideas, in terms not of an intrinsic superiority or inferiority, but in terms of the contribution they could make to the fulfillment of the state's task as defined by the prince. Of special importance, too, was the later adoption by some princes of much of the cant and some of the practice suggested by enlightened *philosophes,* for their doctrines legitimized absolute authority by making of the enlightened prince in theory the executive (or, in Frederick II's words, the "first servant") of an abstract state, whose goals of humanitarian welfare, independent of the person of the reigning prince, opened up vast areas of potential executive intervention which under older definitions of welfare were closed to state action.[55]

Once the state had become conceived as an abstract mechanism for the achievement of a welfare vaguely defined as "the general good," then the stage was set for the reduction of political virtue to a single and, for that society, universal definition. In Prussia, a young professor at the University in Frankfurt an der Oder, Thomas Abbt, provided an excellent example of such an idea in a writing intended to serve as propaganda for Frederick the Great's recruiting officers in their desperate attempts to find men for the Prussian army after the disastrous defeat at Kunersdorf in 1759. "Some divisions of estates, necessary in monarchies, have perhaps been the reason that the connection of efforts towards the general good has been too much dissolved," he wrote. "Each of these estates soon began to believe that it could contribute its share thereto only in one particular way." But if there is in fact a "general good" (as there is in every society), he continued, then there must be but one political virtue. Regarded from this standpoint, "the difference between peasant, burgher,

---

[55] For the relationship between these ideas of enlightened absolutism and the development of the concept of the *Rechtsstaat,* the idea of the state as the instrument of law, and the connection of both to democratic-republican principles, see especially Fritz Hartung, "Der aufgeklärte Absolutismus," *Historische Zeitschrift,* CLXXX, Heft 1 (August 1955), 15-42. See also John G. Gagliardo, *Enlightened Despotism* (New York, 1967), 86-102.

soldier and nobleman disappears." Everyone is merely a *citizen*.[56]
For the political theorist Christian Wolff, also, every individual
within a civil society was equally bound to contribute to the
advancement of the common good as much as lay within his
power.[57] What emerges here, and very explicitly so in Wolff's
works, is the notion of a civil equality of duties, and therefore
also of rights. Here again, as may be seen from Abbt's approval
of the existence of social classes or estates, there is little or no
attempt to translate this particular definition of civil equality
into a social equality; but every individual and every class in its
duty to work for the common good of society and its instrument,
the state, has thereby also claims on society and the state, the
right to participate equally, if admittedly differently, in the benefits of the common good.

The special kinds of "equality" spoken of by all these various
groups posited no exalted place for the peasantry relative to other
social groups, of course. But as the emphases of all these groups
in their writings suggests, it was the peasantry more than any
other social class which benefited from any mention of social
equality, however restricted its meaning may have been. Where

56 Thomas Abbt, "Vom Tode für das Vaterland" (1761), in *Deutsche Literatur,*
Reihe Aufklärung, IX (Leipzig, 1935), 52-53. In Prussia, especially, the canton
system of universal military enrollment or registration and the subsequent service
in the armed forces of large numbers of peasants may well have provided an
important channel of contact between the peasant and the state in this larger,
abstract sense. The peasant's view of and sense of participation in the state was,
under normal circumstances, largely blocked by the high degree of social control
exercised over him by his lord and by the extreme parochialism of his life. Once
he was in the army, however, he became subject to a number of influences which
tended to broaden his mental horizons, and to establish a sense of loyalty to a
social unit larger than the village and the lord's estate. The organs of military
administration—military courts, for example—usually retained their jurisdiction over
peasants even when they were on temporary furlough at home, and provided the
peasant with a suggestive contrast to the local authority of his lord. Military
service, then, served the "enlightened" Prussian monarchy, and that of other states
as well, as a method of establishing a direct link between king and peasant in much
the same way that it had served the earlier monarchy as a method of bringing the
nobility of the scattered Prussian provinces to some semblance of a uniform state
allegiance. These points have been discussed in detail by Otto Büsch, *Militärsystem
und Sozialleben im alten Preussen, 1713-1807: die Anfänge der sozialen Militarisierung der preussisch-deutschen Gesellschaft* (Berlin, 1962), especially 51-74.
57 See Krieger, *The German Idea of Freedom,* 66-71.

the talk was of social inequalities, it was nearly always the peasantry which came most quickly and clearly to mind. That this was so indicates not only that the peasantry had in fact sunk to a social level far below that of any other class, but also that the condition of the peasantry was itself a prime reason for the raising of the social problem in these years, even before the French Revolution brought more immediate and obvious reasons for doing so.

It is not surprising, however, in view of the general failure to propose any really concrete social legislation as a consequence of these kinds of desired equality for the peasantry, that political consequences would be almost entirely lacking also. Political representation of the peasantry by peasants themselves, for example, could normally only be seen as a consequence of an actual existing equality of their estate with others, a thing which had clearly not yet been achieved; or at least of ownership of land, which was as much in abeyance as political representation. It is quite true that peasant participation in the diets of territorial estates was not unknown: Johann Jakob Moser indicated that there were about twenty German principalities in which peasants were represented in the estates,[58] but he was mistaken on some of them, and the principalities were for the most part small in any case. It was decidedly unusual for peasants to sit in diets, and where they did, the nobility often did not attend at all. In some instances—Württemberg and the Palatinate being the best examples—peasants were often said to be represented by the fact that the urban deputies technically sat in for the rural districts surrounding the towns as well as for the towns themselves; and there were a number of principalities in which peasants sat in local assemblies, and were thus said to have representation.[59] In general, however, it was more commonly through the "virtual representation" of the landed interest by the nobility that the peasantry was assumed to exercise a sufficient influence on political affairs.

[58] Frederick Hertz, *The Development of the German Public Mind: A Social History of German Political Sentiments, Aspirations, and Ideas,* Vol. II (London, 1962), 24, note.

[59] Francis L. Carsten, *Princes and Parliaments in Germany from the Fifteenth to the Eighteenth Century* (Oxford, 1959), 424-25.

In spite of his strong Physiocratic beliefs, it therefore appears somewhat unusual that Johann Georg Schlosser recommended a stronger participation of the peasant in legislation and especially in the imposition of taxes; he alone was chained to the land, said Schlosser, and he alone made up the nation.[60] In few other writings was this sentiment so directly expressed, although a number of publicists spoke of the desirability of a peasant "estate," and thereby presumably indicated their approval of its participation in diets in common with other estates. In Austria, Joseph II's tax reforms called forth a declaration from Minister Count Zinzendorf (not the famous Pietist) in 1787 that only an assembly of all landowners could decide about the reform of direct taxation, thus including otherwise disenfranchised peasants; and in Prussia, Frederick II's Minister Count Hertzberg proposed in a lecture to the Berlin Academy in 1784 that estates in the future should include peasant representatives—though it is likely that he had rather consultative than deliberative estates in mind.[61]

The political question seemed to present more difficulties than the social one, partly, no doubt, because it touched the center, the ruler, more obviously (if, in the long run, no more directly) than did criticism of the social order, and was therefore rather dangerous as a subject of too much earnest discussion. But there were other problems associated with the patent political immaturity of the peasants themselves. Even the radical publicist August Ludwig Schlözer showed a certain rather unusual reserve about the political readiness of the peasant; while thoroughly convinced that the peasantry ought to be represented in the *Reichstag* by virtue both of its numbers and its importance, he printed extracts from the proceedings of the Swedish *Ryksdag* of 1786 in order to point up the complexities involved in such representation. The extracts proved conclusively that the peasant deputies themselves frequently misbehaved, spoke out of turn, cursed, appeared late (or drunk), and in some cases could not understand Swedish. Schlözer tentatively wondered, on the basis of this evidence, whether it was a very good idea for "peasants, *qua* peasants, *in naturalibus*," to sit in a legislative group, and

[60] Schlosser, *Kleine Schriften*, II, 239.
[61] Hertz, *The Development of the German Public Mind*, II, 423, note 1.

appeared to lean towards the somewhat more traditional approach that peasants ought perhaps to elect their deputies from other classes.[62]

"Moralist literature," finally, appears to have laid much of the groundwork of an increased regard for the peasant as a human being and as a citizen capable of individual and social moral decisions. It was not merely the importance of his occupation to society which was hereafter to influence thinking about the possibilities of a more active role for the peasant in society, but also the kind of man his occupation made of him. Briefly stated, he had come to be conceived as a kind of "natural man," whose instincts, left to themselves, were entirely good. There was perhaps less agreement on his innate ability to channel those instincts towards beneficial social goals. There were many commentators, it is true, who believed that one implied the other; but there were just as many, or more, who saw a special need to educate the peasant in the application of his faculties to his own and society's requirements. "Pedagogical reformism," as it may be called, was thus (in the period of the old regime, especially) important to all the reformist directions so far discussed; the next chapter is therefore devoted to the contributions of pedagogical thought to the further growth of the social respectability of the peasant.

[62] "Auszüge aus den Protocollen des BauerStandes beim Reichstag in Stockholm 1786," *Staats-Anzeigen,* XII (1788), 458-61, 458, note, 459, note.

4 Pedagogical Reformism

Apart from the almost innumerable proposals for the technical improvement of agriculture and the improvement of material living conditions, no facet of the peasant's life appears to have awakened more interest in this period than his education. A surprisingly large proportion of the book and periodical literature in which peasant problems were discussed before 1800 was devoted to the question of rural education. As will subsequently emerge, it was to some considerable extent the practical limitations under which agrarian reformers worked—the apparent impossibility of basic social change—which created the astounding quantity of writings on peasant education in this time. As a substitute for alterations in the relationship between the peasantry and other classes, these tracts proposed to accomplish reform within the peasant class itself. This literature deserves special attention not only because of its sheer bulk, but also because of the unique way in which it catches up the various motives and directions of the new and heightened interest in the peasant, and because, in the end, it not only strengthened some other arguments for the social importance and individual dignity of the peasant, but added important new ones of its own. In it can be seen a reflection of the image of the peasant as it was conceived by different individuals and groups, and illustrated and extended by them in more or less concrete pedagogical proposals and theories.

It should come as no surprise, in view of foregoing chapters, that it was the vocational education of peasants which was of greatest importance to most of those who wrote on the problem. The discussion of agrarian reform proposals in earlier chapters has sufficiently attested to the fact that in this as in other areas, almost all problems of public life before the revolution were looked at from an economic point of view, and were regarded as soluble from that standpoint. The education of the peasant, seen largely in terms of his vocation, was to make of him a better farmer, a more efficient producer. There were numerous precedents for the vastly increased interest in peasant education characteristic of this time. Such venerable Cameralist thinkers as Veit Ludwig von Seckendorff and Johann Joachim Becher, both in the seventeenth century, had demonstrated the interest of the absolute state in securing efficient performance from citizens through purposeful instruction when they placed concern for education high on the list of obligations for princes who wished to cultivate the resources of their countries. The schools they had in mind were not the Latin grammar schools of the traditional classical education, but were instead highly vocational in the sense that they were to train citizens for an active role in the modern state— which meant providing them with knowledge of the eminently practical sort which a *"Hausvater, Bürger, und Inwohner des Landes"* could use with benefit to his prince and his country. The kind of education here projected became standard statist policy in Germany in the eighteenth century—insofar as the state really developed an educational policy—and well illustrates Andreas Flitner's generalization that "education for the state was in its primary form education for the economic policy of the state."[1]

Most justifications for the proposition that the peasant should be educated started from the economic point of view, and emphasized the benefits the state would derive from the superior talents which education would develop in him. "The lower classes of the people are still almost entirely disregarded and their education, as that of the most important part of the nation, should nevertheless be the first concern of the ruler," wrote a nobleman in Moser's *Patriotisches Archiv;*[2] and he left no doubt that what he meant by "the most important part of the nation" was the economically most productive part. What was wrong with the peasant's current level of productivity, insofar as that was a function of his own activity,[3] was the fact that his ignorance prevented him from

---

[1] Andreas Flitner, *Die politische Erziehung in Deutschland: Geschichte und Probleme, 1750-1880* (Tübingen, 1957), 16-17.

[2] "Volks-Schulen besser, nüzlicher, nöthiger, als Universitäten," *Patriotisches Archiv* (Moser), X (1789), 555-56.

[3] Very few people were so naive as to suppose that it was merely the peasant's ignorance which kept agricultural production down. The objective conditions of the agrarian constitution under which he lived were just as important. Isaak Iselin pointed to this rather obvious fact when he stated that if a government were wise enough to recognize peasant education as a desirable goal, then it ought also to be

making beneficial improvements; after all, it was said, "No peasant knows any more about agriculture than he has learned from his father."[4] The peasant's own income suffered from his ignorance, but so did that of the state, of course. Writing in the mid-1780s, one official made this connection quite clear as he argued that the current deflation of land values, and therefore also a major part of the entire agricultural depression which so adversely affected the economy of the state, were merely a result of the peasant's unfortunate ignorance. It was a commonplace, he noted, that the earth produced more in proportion as the cultivator was enlightened; all consumers should therefore remember the importance of educated cultivators, since their own existence and well-being depended on them.[5]

What the economic argument implied, left to itself, was that a technical training in agricultural methods and practices was about the only education a peasant needed; it regarded the peasant as an outdated machine producing a certain type of goods, and suggested that readjustments in its mechanism were all that were required to make it run faster and better. In fact, however, this argument was swallowed whole by almost no one, not even the most ironhearted statists. In the first place, while there was a good deal of argumentation about just how much the peasant really did need to know, it was commonly admitted that he had to have more than a mere catechism of agricultural principles. Even Frederick II, who was a noted skeptic on such questions, realized that some reading and writing were essential tools of understanding; and his chief of the Department of Ecclesiastical Affairs and Public Instruction, Karl Abraham Freiherr von Zedlitz, proposed a curriculum for peasant schools which would include religion, writing, exercises in reading and arithmetic, some mechanics, a bit of natural science, diet and medical care, some knowledge of the constitution of the country, and vocational

---

wise enough to see that both *raison d'état* and considerations of humanity demanded the release of the peasant from humiliation and actual oppression. Iselin, *Vermischte Schriften*, II, 113-14.

[4] F. C. von Moser, "Bauren-Politik und Bauren-Weisheit," *Patriotische Archiv* (Moser), VII (1787), 413.

[5] Braun, "Ursachen und Beweise, woher und warum der Grund und Boden bey dem Bauernvolke noch immer einen so geringen Werth gehabt," *Neues Archiv für den Menschen und Bürger in allen Verhältnissen*, II (1785), 5-20.

training in occupations outside the school itself.[6] While a few shortsighted souls might regard even this meager curriculum as too extensive,[7] it can generally be taken to represent a minimum acceptable standard. Even from the state's standpoint, therefore, there was reason to suppose that no peasant could produce what was asked of him without the rudiments of a general education.

It was quickly perceived also that moral education could contribute to increase the peasant's productivity. With all the specialized information in the world, no peasant who did not have the desire to get ahead would make use of new tools at his command. Moral training was thus advocated as the method of infusing him with an aroused spirit and an eagerness to advance himself.[8] In a narrower sense, it was valuable to prevent the peasant from wasting his substance in drinking, gambling, and other unproductive amusements. The mutually supporting relationship between moral and vocational training was seen clearly enough, but there was little agreement on which should precede the other. Friedrich Carl von Moser's journal published an article strongly condemning any attempt to imbue the people with any political, economic, or moral truths without first having established a firm foundation in vocational education;[9] but many others, including especially religious figures, were convinced that only harm could come to the man who increased his wealth without knowing how to make proper use of it. Only a moral education which taught the relative value of different ways of spending time and money could satisfy the hopes of such a person as Lorenz Westenrieder, who hoped that properly enlightened peasants would spend their leisure time with good books rather than in riotous living.[10]

[6] Karl Abraham Freiherr von Zedlitz, "Vorschläge zur Verbesserung des Schulwesens in den Königlichen Landen," *Berlinische Monatsschrift*, X (July-December 1787), 103-105.

[7] One writer, for example, attacked von Zedlitz' plan, avowing that domestic arts would be learned by peasant children through experience, and that natural science was of no use whatever to peasants. "Ueber einen Plan zur Verbesserung der Schulen in den preussischen Ländern; ein Schreiben," *Deutsches Museum* (July-December 1788), 249.

[8] "Gedanken und Vorschläge von der besten Erziehung des Landvolkes, in Absicht auf die Landwirthschaft," *Archiv für den Menschen und Bürger*, IV (1782), 64.

[9] "Romanen-Bauren," *Patriotisches Archiv* (Moser), VIII (1788), 570-71.

[10] [L. Westenrieder], "Ob man Bürger und Bauern aufklären soll?" *Beyträge zur vaterländischen Historie*, III (1790), 348-49.

An essentially unpolitical social morality, too, was part of the program of many pedagogical thinkers, especially the so-called Philanthropists, a number of individuals who put their educational ideas to work in "model" institutions set up for the purpose. J. B. Basedow, P. E. Fellenberg, F. E. von Rochow, and many others belong to this group, which saw its chief function in the general dissemination among the lower classes of the idea of humanity and the development of the powers of the individual for the benefit of himself and his society. Through various procedures, the schoolchildren were to be introduced to the concept of the love of one's fellow man and to "exercises in patriotism," meaning the process of denying one's own selfish desires in favor of the common good. In one such school, it was reported, the pupils created a little republic on the model of the Roman state, administered it, gave justice impartially, and in general ruled themselves as an ideal community. Festivals were held during the school year, in which virtuous men were praised and examples of sacrifice for the fatherland were celebrated. "Fatherland" of course meant the existing state—whatever it was—as the social institution to which one owed security and welfare. And in this sense the "social morality" preached by the Philanthropists was thoroughly congenial with the existing relationships of the old regime.[11]

The concept and practice of enlightened despotism itself broadened considerably the field of subject matter which should be covered in peasant education, and enlightened rulers certainly found their own reasons for supporting the teaching of social morality. Among other things, it opened up still more fully the area of "citizen education," which implied many more facets of instruction than did mere vocational training. When von Zedlitz proposed that some knowledge of the constitution of the country be included as a part of peasant education, he was expressing the pedagogical implication of the emphasis upon government by laws which the theory of enlightened absolutism had created. If government was to operate according to known laws, then the citizen of the state must be educated to know and understand those laws, in order that government would no longer be based upon the mechanical obedience of ignorant subjects, but upon an

[11] Flitner, *Die politische Erziehung*, 18-20.

active cooperation of citizens, stemming from a rational understanding of rights and duties.[12] As one writer very aptly put it, the best intentions and most vigorous undertakings of any ruler would necessarily remain without the desired effect if the people to whom he addressed himself lacked the understanding to perceive the goal and the method, and were therefore unable to cooperate to the extent necessary to carry out the recommendations.[13] The Physiocrats, who were for the most part devoted partisans of the theory of enlightened despotism in any case, reinforced this expanded view of the knowledge necessary to the proper fulfillment of one's role in society. For them, government and all economic activity were also subject to the rule of law—natural law—whose recognition was essential to the proper ordering of both private and public affairs. "When the schoolmaster and the priest have taught [the peasants] to read the calendar and to recite the catechism, their education is completed; thus one believes to have done everything which is necessary to educate the most precious, the most venerable part of this class," wrote the Physiocrat Isaak Iselin disgustedly. Against this, he proposed a real education which would enable the peasant to become as capable as any man of balancing the cost and efforts of his labor against the advantages and profits and which would inculcate a love of work and order.[14] These goals presupposed the introduction of the peasant to both natural and positive law to some extent, since the ultimate insight which the peasant was to derive from this education was the necessary connection between work and order (seen also in the broader sense as "natural order"), on the one hand, and prosperity or happiness on the other.

Frederick II, like many other German rulers of his time, was never quite sure where all these educational efforts on behalf of the peasant were going to end. If instruction in religion and morality were sufficient to keep the rural folk away from the pernicious influences of Catholicism and to prevent them from robbing and murdering, that was fine; but one could carry this

[12] *Ibid.*, 22-23.

[13] [L. Westenrieder], "Ob man Bürger und Bauern aufklären soll?" *Beyträge zur vaterländischen Historie,* III (1790), 351.

[14] Iselin, *Vermischte Schriften,* II, 109-14.

business too far, said Frederick, and while it was commendable to give peasants all the education they could really use to become more valuable as farmers, too much might simply induce them to leave the land and find work in the cities as "secretaries and such things." This he certainly wished to avoid.[15] It was in fact one of the most common criticisms of persons who opposed education of the peasant that the countryside would be depopulated when peasants became educated and considered themselves too exalted for the vulgar pursuits of agriculture. This attitude had changed but little by 1803, when Frederick William III, replying to a request of his Minister-of-State Voss that a Prussian teacher be sent at state expense to learn the newest pedagogical techniques from Pestalozzi at Burgdorf, admitted that reading, writing, arithmetic, and religion were valuable tools for the common people, but said that anything more was hardly necessary for their "temporal progress and true happiness." Whoever wished to teach them more, said the monarch, involved himself in a vain and thankless task, for "if the great mass acquires a taste for reading, then their hands would be diverted from mechanical work and their attention from the most essential necessities, [and] they would be robbed of their contentment with the simplest, most laborious, and lowest occupations."[16]

But for proponents of rural education, many of these arguments could now be turned around: only those peasants who *were* educated in the knowledge of the dignity, value, and acceptability of their class and their occupation would have really firm reasons to stay on the land, because only they could feel happy and worthwhile.[17] In this way, the notion became current that the best and most enlightened rulers necessarily had to be concerned for peasant education; there was nothing degrading about being a peasant, and in contrast to the early days of absolutism, it was said, one no longer had to believe that sheer force was necessary to keep peasants on the land. Enlightenment was the surest way

---

[15] Arthur Eichler, *Die Landbewegung des 18. Jahrhunderts und ihre Pädagogik* (Langensalza, 1933), 37.

[16] Mathys Jolles, *Das deutsche Nationalbewusstsein im Zeitalter Napoleons* (Frankfurt am Main, 1936), 75-76.

[17] Iselin, *Vermischte Schriften*, II, 112. See also "Gedanken und Vorschläge," *Archiv für den Menschen und Bürger*, IV (1782), 80-81.

to bring a peasant to a true understanding and love of his work, and that ruler who refused him an education became thereby, as it were, a self-confessed tyrant, one who in the mistaken belief that the peasant necessarily disliked his work because it was in itself hateful, was therefore prepared to hold him to it by main force if necessary.[18]

All these different elements, in any case, were more or less successfully combined into integrated curricula in the writings of the advocates of peasant education. An idea of what such a curriculum might look like can be derived from the proposals of Rudolph Z. Becker (1759-1822). Becker, educated at Jena, became interested in educational reform from his contact with Basedow's famous philanthropic school at Dessau; a prolific writer, he at one time published a young people's newspaper, in which he put his own ideas to work, and later, in Gotha, established a publishing house to facilitate the publication of his own writings. Becker proposed the following order and substance for the education of peasant children: first, they were to be instructed in the areas essential to their existence,—clothing, food, basic agricultural practices. Superstitions and outmoded or inefficient agricultural methods should not be forbidden, but abolished by example of the opposite. Secondly, the moral truths connected with family, friends, love, and society should be set before them, again by the use of example in true stories of outstanding behavior. Next, the children should be instructed in the principle that agriculture was for them the means of procuring all the civilized qualities brought out in the earlier stages, and that order, diligence, and a capacity to think and make decisions were important in agricultural progress. Fourthly, they should be taught that they owed the undisturbed enjoyment of all necessities and pleasures to civilized society, that every social class contributed in its own way to their utility and enjoyment, and that laws, rulers, and taxes were necessary for the existence of society. Finally, their eyes must be directed to the heavens and the

[18] Views such as these may be found in a citation from C. F. D. Schubart in Erich Schairer, *Christian Friedrich Daniel Schubart als politischer Journalist* (Tübingen, 1914), 77. See also Johann Georg Büsch, "Vortheile der niedern Stände aus der Verbesserung der Volks- und Landschulen," *Sämmtliche vermischte Schriften*, 2d ed. (Hamburg and Altona, 1801), I, 142.

eternal powers, so that religion and the worship of God would become important for them.[19]

Becker here sketched out a nearly ideal and very typical picture of the educational process as it was conceived by the majority of pedagogical thinkers in the last two decades of the eighteenth century. Starting the children out in the things most familiar to them and most easily understood by them, he wished to progress with them from the concrete and familiar to the abstract and unfamiliar. Every step was to be the necessary precondition for the next, until finally a stage was reached at which it would be possible for the children to realize the complexity and value of the world in which they lived, and saw their own work and their general social role in that world in some perspective. This was emphatically not a "philosophical" education in the sense of an education for a life to be lived among abstractions; quite the contrary, it was designed to bring generalities home to the students always by the use of concrete and specific examples and illustrations, corresponding to the concreteness of the very real world in which the peasant worked. But it set out quite unmistakably the idea that knowledge brings understanding, that understanding brings consent, and that the peasant who made a voluntary commitment to his work would do that work better than the one to whom it was merely the chief part of his misery.[20]

[19] R. Z. Becker, "Versuch über die Aufklärung des Landmannes," *Der teutsche Merkur* (August 1785), 120-25.

[20] In some quarters, however, there was strong skepticism of the principle that peasants in whom sensitivity and understanding had been awakened would actually be happier and work harder. Isaak Iselin, for example, felt that under prevailing conditions of tenure and servitude, education would merely make the peasant's misery more perceptible to him, and could therefore constitute a real cruelty. Iselin, *Vermischte Schriften*, II, 113. This rather strange argument appeared with some frequency, and was often received with feelings approaching horror; as one writer said, it suggested a conviction that the peasant's condition could not be ameliorated, and that the greatest good deed lay in perpetuating his lack of feeling. Martin Engelmann, "Der preussische Bauer," *Das Rothe Blatt, eine Monatsschrift*, I (2d Trimester, Heft 3, 1798), in Joseph Görres, *Gesammelte Schriften* (Cologne, 1926-1939), I, 244-45. An argument such as that of Iselin was actually employed to prove opposite points, however. It was used to point out the necessity of social reform in conjunction with attempts to improve education (this was Iselin's intent); but it was also used to oppose any educational reform, on the unstated assumption that the social constitution should not be touched, and in the explicit belief that no enlightenment was necessary for the peasant in his occupation. Most educational reformers fought both uses of the argument: the latter for obvious reasons, and the former because it tied education too closely to reforms which, however

Most of the progressive theories put forth in this time could be implemented only on a small scale, and usually only in private institutions. The state was normally unwilling to invest much money in experimental education, and in fact had a generally sorry record in any kind of public education below the university level. The private "model" schools established in various places in Germany had occasionally conspicuous successes with their students and their programs of instruction. One of these schools and its founder and patron, Friedrich Eberhard von Rochow (1734-1805) have generally been considered extremely important in the development of the system of village schools in Germany. Rochow, the son of a Prussian minister of state, began a career in the Prussian army, but was forced to retire because of wounds suffered in the Seven Years' War. He withdrew to his estate at Reckan, near Brandenburg, where he soon developed an interest in the education of his peasants. His first major writing for them, the *Versuch eines Schulbuches für Kinder der Landleute oder zum Gebrauch in Dorfschulen,* was the result of his sympathy at the plight of the confused and ignorant rural folk who, during two successive years of crop failure and an accompanying epidemic, turned rather to quacks and superstitions than to the trained physician whom he had hired to care for them. "I live among peasants," Rochow wrote: "I pitied the folk. In addition to the hardships of their class, they are oppressed by the heavy burden of their prejudices. Their ignorance of the most necessary skills robs them of the advantages and compensations which the gracious providence of God for all classes has also granted theirs."[21] Rochow's book was noticed by Freiherr von Zedlitz, and later by Frederick II himself, who as a result commissioned von Zedlitz to reorganize the Prussian village schools on Rochow's plan—a reform which had many beneficial effects, in spite of its highly spotty and incomplete application.

Rochow was best known not for his writings, however—at least in his own time—but for the model school he set up on his

---

desirable, were to them not essential to the efficacy of education in improving the peasant's lot, and which appeared to lie far in the future.

[21] Friedrich Eberhard von Rochow, "Versuch eines Schulbuches für Kinder der Landleute oder zum Gebrauch in Dorfschulen" (1772), *Sämtliche pädagogische Schriften* (Berlin, 1907-1910), I, 3.

estate at Reckan. Here he put his theories of practical and vocational education to work; curious educational reformers visited the place in some numbers, and a few wrote glowing descriptions of it. A visitor of 1775 praised the emphasis on religious and moral training at the institution, and called for a universal imitation of the school in Prussia.[22] The Royal (Prussian) Orphanage at Potsdam sent an observer who later published a book containing detailed and thorough descriptions of the content and method of instruction and praising Rochow for his excellent attempts to make of the children in his care good, sensible men and useful peasants.[23] An article from a still later time, with the apparent intent of answering some of Rochow's critics, recalled attention to the school, and its author, a professor at Braunschweig, stated his hope that the school and its methods would not be forgotten.[24] According to the figures of Frederick Hertz, there were by 1790 about sixty-four model schools of one kind or another in Germany;[25] not all of them were established primarily for peasant education, of course, but these appear to have received the most publicity—perhaps because of the enormity of the task they undertook. Rochow's school was probably the best known of its type in this period, and made a permanent impression on attempts to improve peasant education, even though its influence was not to bear fruit on a large scale until much later.

No matter how good the education offered by these model schools was, however, it affected a pitifully small part of the total peasant population. If anything of significance were to be accomplished in this area, it would have to come through a reform of the *Landschulen* or *Dorfschulen,* schools maintained with varying degrees of frequency and regularity in the villages, and taught either by the village priest, some artisan in the village or, less often, a schoolmaster hired for the purpose. The quality of the schools, while different from area to area, was generally deplorable, due chiefly to lack of respectable facilities and the money

[22] Anton Friedrich Büsching, *Beschreibung seiner Reise von Berlin über Potsdam nach Rekahn unweit Brandenburg* . . . (Leipzig, 1775), 233-34, 295.

[23] Carl Friedrich Riemann, *Versuch einer Beschreibung der Reckanschen Schuleinrichtung* (Berlin and Stettin, 1781), xxii.

[24] Johann Stuve, "Über die Rochowsche Schule zu Rekkahn," *Berlinische Monatsschrift*, X (Jully-December 1787), 325-41.

[25] Hertz, *The Development of the German Public Mind*, II, 385.

necessary to procure them. The feeling among those who concerned themselves with the school problem was almost unanimous that the state must intervene if these were ever to be brought up to a decent level. Allocation of tax moneys and other means were suggested, and one writer, reflecting the contempt in which the jejune activities of most eighteenth-century German universities were held, even recommended that state funds be diverted from universities and applied to rural and other schools at the elementary level, where they would do some good.[26]

The educational reformers could at least operate from the knowledge that every village had a school—this was virtually guaranteed by the state authority in all German territories, and had been for some time. Whether they were any good or not was another question. Besides facilities, the greatest problem appears to have been the quality of teachers. A Prussian official traveling in Brandenburg in 1780 remarked indignantly that the education of peasant children was valued as little as religion itself, and found that the largely recommendatory decrees concerning education and the schools were ignored. He noted especially the lack of respect shown for teachers, but was forced to confess that this attitude was not altogether unjustifiable, inasmuch as teaching positions were occupied mostly by tailors. As long as this situation continued, "the rural school system cannot be other than very imperfect: for the handicraft spirit is absolutely not fitted to [it], it admits of only mechanical, only statistical teachers, and the best schoolmasters from the crafts-class are seldom anything more than enthusiasts without understanding and irrational babblers."[27] Teaching positions were frequently offered to nearly anyone who was willing to take them —unemployed ex-soldiers, students who had flunked out of the universities, and to other equally unqualified persons; in some instances, jobs were virtually put up at auction and conferred upon the man who would accept the least money as salary. The

---

[26] "Volks-Schulen besser," *Patriotisches Archiv* (Moser), X (1789), 555-56.

[27] Anton Friedrich Büsching, *Beschreibung seiner Reise von Berlin nach Kyritz in der Prignitz* . . . (Leipzig, 1780), 148. The prevalence of tailors in village teaching was confirmed by Johann Georg Büsch, who would have disputed Büsching's characterization of them as "enthusiasts." All too often, they took on teaching as an "extra," and sometimes carried their sewing to class with them. Büsch, "Vortheile," *Sämmtliche vermischte Schriften*, I, 143.

most obvious and most commonly proposed solution to this problem lay in special teacher training—in the establishment of teachers' seminars such as that for which Prince Alexander of Ansbach had earmarked part of the funds derived from his state lottery.[28] More visionary, in view of peasant indifference, was the proposal that ten or fifteen peasant families as a group might pool their funds to hire a teacher for their children and thus enjoy the advantages offered by smaller classes and better-trained teachers than those provided by the usual village schools. A further feature of this system was that the teacher, responsible only to the peasants, could be cashiered immediately if his charges were not learning anything.[29]

Judging from the frequent complaints of educational reformers, a scarcely less formidable obstacle to the amelioration of peasant education than the quality of teaching was the attitude of the peasantry itself towards education. The peasant was often hard to convince that education had something to offer him and his children; even where schools were readily available, peasants sometimes kept their children home to work, and when they were chastised for this, they replied that the children spent too much time in school already. A system of compulsory education was one possibility suggested as a means of keeping children in school; but one writer illustrated the difficulties of such a scheme in a detailed narrative of a system of compulsory education introduced on a certain nobleman's lands. According to the plan, the parents of schoolchildren were to be fined if their children were absent from school for any reason other than illness. This high-minded plan ended in miserable failure as the landlord was driven to the very brink of madness by the constant stream of complaints from the peasants.[30] Getting funds from peasants to maintain schools was like squeezing blood from a stone: the peasants were sure they had better uses for their money.[31] They also grumbled about the cost of books their children used, a complaint which

28 Schairer, *Christian Friedrich Daniel Schubart*, 82.
29 "Unterthäniges Gutachten, die Aufhebung der Gemeinheiten der Felder in den Markungen der Dörfer . . . betreffend," *Archiv für den Menschen und Bürger*, IV (1782), 418-19.
30 "Über einen Plan zur Verbesserung der Schulen," *Deutsches Museum* (July-December 1788), 251-56.
31 Büsching, *Beschreibung seiner Reise . . . nach Kyritz*, 51.

caused some despair among reformers, who feared that unless the peasants could assume some of the burden of expense of books, teachers' salaries, and school buildings, the total expense would be too great for the state to assume, and it might refuse to give any help at all.[32] These sorts of considerations made a kind of propagandization of the peasantry itself necessary, and a substantial amount of pedagogical literature was devoted to convincing the peasant of the benefits of education to himself and his entire family.

Material of this sort was frequently included in the growing body of *Volksliteratur,* which experienced a tremendous expansion in the last quarter of the eighteenth century. Fritz Valjavec has called attention to a noticeable increase in the reading of books and periodicals among peasants in this period,[33] and certainly a part of this increase must be ascribed to the greater availability of reading material intended for the common folk, itself called forth by the efforts of educational reformers in no small measure. The enthusiasm for putting educational materials in the hands of peasants had a number of sources. It was partly the result of a realistic appraisal of the difficulties to be overcome in reforming and bolstering the school system in such a way as to secure formal classroom education for peasants: this problem could be sidestepped to some extent if private reading in the home could be encouraged—a prospect which presupposed the existence of appropriate printed materials. This proposal would also provide a solution of sorts to the problem of what to do about the education of adult peasants, who had no access to schools in any case. Finally, it was generally recognized that a permanent and continuing body of literature for the common man was desirable so that he might benefit from education morally and vocationally for the rest of his life instead of for the short period of his formal schooling only.

There was already a literature of sorts available to the common man, but its quality and value left much to be desired. A writer of the 1780s surveyed with great disgust the sorts of books actually

---

[32] "Ueber einen Plan zur Verbesserung der Schulen," *Deutsches Museum* (July-December 1788), 256-58.

[33] Fritz Valjavec, *Die Entstehung der politischen Strömungen in Deutschland, 1770-1815* (Munich, 1951), 95.

being read by the people, and listed about fifty titles of popular works, among which lurid novels of adventure predominated. After commenting on a number of other works intended for the real education of the folk, and concluding that these were either too expensive or not sufficiently simple to fulfill their purpose, he called for a "patriot" who might write for the people without thought of compensation, and for private funds to support the printing of his works, which should be sold for a very small price.[34] Realizing that peasants would not necessarily jump at the chance to possess such works even if they could afford them, further proposals were made by reformers to clothe didacticism in the raiment of the adventure story, with arresting tales (albeit always instructional ones) and plentiful woodcuts.[35]

There were several categories of literature for which a need existed. Some periodicals were founded expressly for the consumption of the common man, with the aim of providing general and timely information. In his study of peasant newspapers, Ernst Grathoff distinguishes three categories of such periodicals, according to the nature of their primary content: the "didactic-discursive," the political, and the "scientific-agricultural." The first of these was in essence a lower-class equivalent to the moral weeklies of the middle class, containing warnings against immorality of all kinds and its evil effects, and devoting itself largely to issues such as the raising of children, health and hygiene, diligence and good working habits. The second, for the most part reportorial rather than editorial, contained more or less current information on the activities of members of ruling houses and news of international and local military and political affairs. The third was given over to specifically pragmatic news and information relating to a wide variety of farming needs. It is difficult to know how large the combined circulation of these periodicals may have been, but the number of separate papers was very impressive: at least 104 different titles of periodicals of the "scientific-agricultural" sort alone had appeared by 1790. The publishers of these news-

---

[34] "Über die Mittel, bessere Bücher in die Hände der niedrigern lesenden Menschen-Klasse zu bringen," *Berlinische Monatsschrift,* VI (July-December 1785), 295-311.

[35] R. Z. Becker, "Versuch über die Aufklärung des Landmannes," *Der teutsche Merkur* (August 1785), 129-30.

papers suffered from cost problems occasioned by their failure to look into the market realities for their product, with the result that demand was usually much smaller than production. Bad postal communications in spite of high postal rates meant stale news, and advertising income was low, since advertisements, when not actually prohibited, were in any case unfamiliar to and unpopular with readers. The relatively high cost of periodicals to the reader was a major factor in reducing circulation, even though deliberate attempts were made to keep prices down.[36]

Occasionally, a government would establish a peasant newspaper as a method of spreading agricultural information. Following the Seven Years' War, for example, Frederick II's concern to see that practical vocational information was passed around from one enlightened agriculturist to another led directly to the founding of the *"Ökonomisch-patriotische Sozietät,"* under the aegis of Grand Chancellor von Carmer; out of this society, somewhat later, grew the *Schlesische Volkszeitung*, superintended by Minister of State Hoym. By official order, this periodical was to be distributed in every Silesian village community. Originally, it was sold at a low price, but later came to be distributed free, and reached a yearly edition of 33,000 German and 10,000 Polish copies. Founded in 1789, the *Volkszeitung* collapsed in 1803.[37]

The quality of these peasant papers was anything but uniform, and as is perhaps usual with totally new media, they often showed little awareness of the real tastes of the audience at which they were aimed. And if a given periodical managed to attract a readership outside a local area, it often lost its character as a publication for the peasant, and became one about the peasant. Occasionally, such a publication achieved an almost national circulation: the *Magazin für den Landmann* (Oldisleben, 1784-1785), for example, contained subscriber lists which indicated a geographically widespread circulation throughout Prussia, and a socially diverse readership, including professional men, preachers, and officials of the magistracy. As its circulation outside of the Oldisleben area increased, it dropped both its peasant idiom and its more or less exclusive attention to local affairs.[38] Christian

[36] Grathoff, *Deutsche Bauern- und Dorfzeitungen*, 43-46, 62.
[37] *Ibid.*, 50-52.
[38] *Ibid.*, 46.

August Wichmann complained that two of the best known of the peasant periodicals, the *Wochenblatt für den gemeinen Mann* (Leipzig, 1775 and 1777) and the *Volkslehrer* (Leipzig, 1781-1783; Nürnberg, 1785 and after) seldom found their way into peasant hands, that both were too expensive, and that the *Volkslehrer,* which affected the actual language of the peasant, disgusted rural inhabitants so much that they refused to read it.[39]

Wichmann's own preference ran to another type of publication: peasant calendars and almanacs, which could be distributed very cheaply, and which the peasant was already familiar with in some degree. This type of literature was probably more common than any other intended for the peasant, and was broadened in this time to include a much wider variety of information than the traditional almanacs. A good example of this general category of the *Hausfreund* was R. Z. Becker's *Noth- und Hülfs-Büchlein für Bauersleute,* published in several editions in the last quarter of the eighteenth century, and quite well known in northern Germany, especially. The book was divided into three sections: 1) how the peasant might live happily, 2) how he might bring honor to himself, and 3) how he might help himself in emergencies. Individual chapters, fifty-six in all, covered such diverse topics as poisonous plants, spoiled meat, the dangers of uncleanliness, various uses of the potato, ways of saving money, medical care, fires, and storms. Information on social and legal relationships, with much gratuitous advice, was thrown in for good measure.

The almanac was a mine of practical information presented in straightforward topical form. Less direct but more elegant, and intentionally more persuasive, were the many books which painted agrarian scenes more or less corresponding to reality, and in those scenes dealt with real agricultural problems through central fictional characters around whom episodic stories were organized. One of the first of these was H. C. Hirzel's *Die Wirthschaft eines philosophischen Bauers* (Zürich, 1761). Hirzel introduced to the public the "philosophical" and enlightened peasant Kleinjogg, whose character was an ideally perfect representation of informed practicality, and whose farm was a model of modern agricultural methods. In a discursive manner, Kleinjogg was made to explain

---

[39] C. A. Wichmann, "Ueber die natürlichsten Mittel," *Leipziger Magazin,* Zweites Stük (1784), 183-88.

the various facets of his farm economy, and to invite general imitation of his own success. Hirzel's method was widely copied, and in a number of books based on fictional "success stories," various authors in later years attempted to present peasants with current agricultural information. Johann Evangelist Fürst's *Der verständige Bauer Simon Strüf, eine Familiengeschichte,* published in the second and third decades of the nineteenth century, demonstrated the progress and happiness which could come to the peasant through the understanding and application of new ideas, and still later there was a great demand for A. von Rothe's *Der Landmann, wie er sein sollte, oder Franz Nowak, der wohlberathene Bauer,* which carried the same motif through several editions from 1838 until well past the mid-century. The use of fictional characters lent a personal tone to these instructional works which made them vastly popular among peasants, who believed everything said in them as a personal experience of the invented characters.

Finally, there were the actual schoolbooks or primers prepared for the use of peasant children, of which Rochow's efforts were fairly typical. In addition to his *Versuch eines Schulbuches* of 1772, which was widely circulated, praised, and emulated, he published in 1802 a still more famous work, *Der Kinderfreund,* in two parts; this was a collection of little stories pertaining to various situations of public and private life, and was almost painfully didactic: every story, of course, had its moral. But it was cheap, with its price (two Groschen) printed on the cover; and Rochow's intention that its low cost might enable every school child to possess one came closer to fulfillment than he himself might have guessed, for it achieved a total circulation of about a hundred thousand copies through the last edition of 1834.[40] The exact content of books in this category varied with the predilections of their authors and the age of the children for whom they were intended, but moral instruction was almost always of major importance.

The concern for peasant education which was such a large part of the agitation for agrarian reform in the prerevolutionary period in Germany was of considerable importance in providing the theoretical basis for the actual improvement of the level of knowledge and education of rural inhabitants. It did this through the development of experimental curricula, which were tested in private philanthropic schools; through the publication of hundreds of books, pamphlets, and periodicals intended to be read by the peasant or to him by village priests, schoolmasters, benevolent landlords, or other interested persons; and, most important of all, perhaps, through emphasis upon the value of educated peasants to the state and to society in general in the most practical terms. It is perfectly clear that for the most part pedagogical theory did not stray very far from the limits imposed by the social and political constitution of the old regime; in this sense, the most common and most acceptable justification for the education of the peasantry lay in the greater efficiency of its performance as an economic group, a justification which corresponds quite closely to the pragmatic interest in the reform of agrarian economic relationships on the part of Cameralists, Physiocrats, and others. The interest in peasant education was, after all, to a certain extent shaped and developed from the essentially economic interests of Cameralism and Physiocracy, as a legitimate extension of the means necessary to achieve their goals.

It speaks for the importance of these economic considerations in the minds of educational theorists that the social basis of their thought was almost entirely consonant with the class structure and theory of the established order. Not all of them, certainly, would have agreed with the famous Austrian Cameralist Joseph von Sonnenfels (1732-1817), who disputed the possibility of public education in any state "as long as the diversity of Estates and property lasts"; but they would have found little to quarrel with, for the most part, in his opinion that the modern state, based as it was on a diversity of classes, required different kinds of education for different classes, and that the lower classes must not be spoiled for their work by an education suitable only for the upper classes.[41] Freiherr von Zedlitz expressed much the same idea when he emphasized that through education the peasant "should

---

[41] Kann, *A Study in Austrian Intellectual History*, 190.

become a good and, *in his class,* a sensible, useful, and active man"
(italics mine);[42] and Rochow was typical of many educators in his
deliberate effort to explain to his pupils that a class *(Stand)* which
one did not choose for oneself was a vocation *(Beruf),* and that
there was little they could do to change this; they had, none the
less, reason to be happy, for "If any one class of society is useful,
indeed inexpendable, it is the class of plowmen or peasants, and it
is extraordinarily important for you, my friends, who are born to
agriculture as well as to the home economy bound up with it,
that you learn and know what is actually required of you."[43]
Behind the concern manifested by Frederick the Great and others
that educated peasants might develop a desire to leave the land
was not only a fear of losing workers from an essential part of the
national economy, but also, and perhaps more fundamentally, a
suspicion that education would change class patterns; the vehement denials that this was so on the part of educators were
implemented with special care in their concern to impress the
necessity of the old social order upon students—usually as a part
of their "moral education."

On the other hand, the development of the theory of enlightened
despotism had so broadened the conception of what constituted
good citizenship that it was no longer thought sufficient that a
man make his contribution through the performance of economic
tasks alone. Those tasks were important, of course, and education
should enable him to perform them efficiently; but if government
and the positive laws on which it rested were indeed a reflection
of natural law, and therefore in the highest sense rational, as
theorists of enlightened absolutism said they ought to be, then, to
achieve the highest operational efficiency, it was necessary to
make the citizen aware of the scheme of government and laws.
An ignorant citizen was not capable of the rational cooperation,
even in his economic work, which functional excellence in government demanded. This meant a broadening of what was considered the minimum necessary curriculum to include a certain
kind of instruction in political and social morality, for the peas-

---

[42] K. A. Freiherr von Zedlitz, "Vorschläge zur Verbesserung des Schulwesens,"
Berlinische Monatsschrift, X (July-December 1787), 103.

[43] von Rochow, "Versuch eines Schulbuches," *Sämtliche pädagogische Schriften,*
I, 72-73.

antry as for other classes. It also meant that it was now virtually impossible to establish a curriculum which was entirely class-bound, for the type of insight necessary to good citizenship was the same for all classes. This is as much as to say, then, that educational theory both reflected and reinforced a peculiar idea of political equality which stemmed from the politically leveling tendencies of absolutism combined with the enlightened belief in the possibilities of a truly rational foundation for law and government. The peasantry benefited from these conceptions, for although this was hardly democratic government in the modern sense, it was a government which professed a need for consent through understanding: this consent was not that of the class, but of the citizen; and the understanding upon which it was to be based, awakened through education, was the same for all citizens —thus placing the peasant in this restricted respect on a footing of equality with all other persons in the state.

Finally, it must not be forgotten that the entire pedagogical movement for the education of the peasant was based upon the assumption of his educability; more than that, it was based upon the assumption of his equality with other men with respect to the innate quality of his mind. That the peasant was ignorant was almost everywhere admitted; but that he was constitutionally stupid was disputed most vehemently in all pedagogical literature. Such an allegation was indeed raised by some who, for whatever reason, opposed any real attempts to educate the lower classes; but it was answered by the rather obvious retort that intelligence was not a function of class, and that the amount and rapidity with which a peasant learned depended entirely upon the teacher and the method and quality of instruction.[44] F. E. von Rochow quite explicitly embraced the principle of the equality of the human soul, and his educational philosophy revolved around the corollary that all classes had an equal right to the relative perfection of humanity through enlightenment concerning the morality of their goals and their methods in attaining them.[45] The equality spoken of here did not mean that every individual was equal to

---

[44] "Gedanken und Vorschläge," *Archiv für den Menschen und Bürger,* IV (1782), 81.

[45] Friedrich Eberhard von Rochow, "Vorrede," in Riemann, *Versuch einer Beschreibung,* vi-vii.

every other in his ability to learn: as the economist Johann Georg Büsch pointed out, children are not born equal, but with different abilities and capacities. Still, these do not depend on class or rank, and peasant children possess in their souls powers of understanding equal to those of the prince's son. Acquired knowledge may depend upon the accident of birth, and commonly does to a large extent; but no class distinction could be made relative to ability to learn.[46] While deliberate caution was exercised to prevent any social consequences being drawn from this kind of recognized equality, it was of great importance that the peasant in this pedagogical literature of the later eighteenth century was given the full measure of common humanity with respect to the single criterion which all agreed separated man from animal—reason; it had not been too many years, after all, since the peasant's very humanity had been a subject of serious dispute in some quarters.

In view of what has been said above, however, it is interesting to note that one of the first major rifts in the otherwise substantial agreement of reform-minded writers before 1790 came on the question of peasant education. Justus Möser, in spite of a certain equivocation, illustrates this disagreement perhaps better than any other single figure. In an essay directed against the exclusion of certain classes of society from educational opportunities, Möser appeared to place himself on the side of the advocates of peasant education; the denial of the possibility of education, he said, would hit the lower class first, whereas it was precisely in this class that the people with the most stamina, diligence, and willingness to work would be found. From the ranks of so-called children of good family, by contrast, came almost nothing but "tender fops and hypochondriacs."[47] Yet the majority of Möser's comments on education were anything but favorable, and indeed he seems to have spent much of his energy on this question in attempts to demonstrate how little the peasant could gain from education. He brought out in several ways, first of all, that it was a luxury the peasant could ill afford. The sciences, he remarked in one

---

[46] J. G. Büsch, "Vortheile," *Sämmtliche vermischte Schriften*, I, 137-38; also, "Ueber die Erziehung der Kinder auf dem Lande," I, 304-305.

[47] Möser, "Also soll man das Studieren nicht verbieten," *Sämtliche Werke*, VI, 114.

essay, belonged very much to the luxuries of the soul, and in households or estates where essential things were still a matter of concern, the forces of the soul had to be used in a better way.[48] He even suggested, at another point, that vocational education was not especially desirable, since it normally tended to institute new agricultural tools and methods among peasants who had no economic margin for experimentation: "Experiments and trials are for the nobleman, who can [afford to] lose something; not for the peasant, who must be economical with every hand's-width of land."[49]

More than this, Möser seems to have felt that education was necessary for the peasant in neither a vocational nor a moral sense: where his cultivation of the earth was concerned, "The peasant follows a long experience, or a venerable prejudice, and it is dangerous to disturb him."[50] It was, in Möser's opinion, a fashionable and attractive but thoroughly groundless notion of his own time that "reason" according to the narrow concept of the enlightened philosophers must be made the foundation for all action and all morality. He sneered at the concept of genius, saying that "incomparably more is accomplished by durability, diligence, and work than by so-called genius,"[51] and announced that no right-thinking man could maintain that the praiseworthy steadfastness so characteristic of the peasant in time of social or natural catastrophe had anything to do with formal education.[52] The ideas of the philosophers were worth nothing in a pragmatic context, Möser thought, and illustrated his opinion in a little story in which a traveler, marveling at the marked improvement in agriculture in a certain region, asked an inhabitant whether this had come about through the appearance of a "philosopher" who had taught the peasants a better method of cultivation. Answered firmly in the negative, he was told that "the philosophers do enough if they keep the publishing houses in business, [but] they

---

[48] Möser, "Die Spinnstube," *ibid.*, V, 43.

[49] Möser, "Vom Hüten der Schweine," *ibid.*, IV, 185.

[50] Möser, *Osnabrückische Geschichte*, I, 96.

[51] Möser, "Also soll man das Studieren nicht verbieten," *Sämtliche Werke*, VI, 114.

[52] Möser, "Also soll der handelnde Teil der Menschen nicht wie der spekulierende erzogen werden," *ibid.*, VII, 26-27.

will never awaken diligence as long as they themselves do not put a hand to it and persuade by means of successful results."[53] By contrast with the philosopher, the peasant derived his knowledge not from reading the *Encyclopédie* but from experience alone—and was better off for doing so.[54] Furthermore, in opposition to enlightened or rational morality, Möser set up "Passion, this noble gift of God," which "leads [man] more surely than the most enlightened reason."[55] If one were led to right action by the dictates of passion, an intuitive guide, then one had little use for reason and for the information and education which instructed one in its application.

One source of Möser's singular position on the question of peasant education has already been discussed in another context: it need not again be insisted that his concept of society as a cooperation of functionally different estates or corporations which needed to be kept apart if each was to do its own social work best led him to keep a sharp eye cocked for any blurring or overlapping of corporative prerogatives or functions. Education, for Möser, and as understood by him, was essentially an attribute of the "speculative" estate, not of the "active"; one of his essays was entitled "Thus the Active Part of Mankind ought not be educated as the Speculative," and it seems quite clear that the socially valuable qualities which he saw in the peasantry really could not be improved upon by education. Steadfastness, solidity, religious faith, and the innate ability to do the right thing in practical situations were the very definition of the distinctive social role of the peasant. Education, which emphasized thought rather than action, reason rather than passion, could only introduce into the peasantry methods of thought and action which were at best useless to it in its proper work, and at worst actually harmful. Education, philosophy, and luxury formed a kind of continuum in Möser's mind, which he associated with city life, with artificiality, in short with amorality or immorality which was the

[53] Möser, "Beantwortung der Frage: Was muss die erste Sorge zur Bereicherung eines Landes sein?" *ibid.,* V, 116.

[54] Möser, "Die Spinnstube," *ibid.,* V, 50. Möser went so far as to question the utility of a peasant's being able to read at all.

[55] Möser, "Schreiben einer Mutter an einen philosophischen Kinderlehrer," *ibid.,* V, 262.

furthest possible thing from the proper life and contribution of the peasant.

Möser's emphasis on passion or intuition, his tendency to praise the value of experience, and to call attention constantly to the efficacy of tradition as a guide to present action were all part of what Andreas Flitner has referred to as a sharp reaction against the common tendency of both the Enlightenment and the disciples of Rousseau to place the judgment of living man, whether based in the mind or in the heart, in the center of social reality.[56] For Möser, it was not possible to regard society merely as the creation of the men who at any one time composed it; it was the result of the thought and action of countless generations, an edifice which any one generation received as an inheritance from previous generations, to which it made its contribution, and which it then passed on to the future. The *philosophes* and Rousseauists had all forgotten that society was a historical reality, and had arrogantly placed the judgment of the present generation above the judgments of many past generations. Möser's fear of "philosophical" education was a fear that this evil prejudice of the social and moral self-sufficiency of contemporary man would be disseminated to ever-wider circles of the population. The greatest tragedy of all would be its dissemination among the peasantry, for it was precisely in this class that Möser saw the living and unself-conscious embodiment of the historical elements which had shaped contemporary society; it had the incomparably important role as the bridge between the tasks of the present and the insights of the past. Given Möser's frame of reference, therefore, it was an almost imperious necessity that the philosopher be kept away from the peasant—even if it was necessary to protect the peasant's illiteracy to do so!

There are two interesting things about the disagreement which separated Möser from his contemporaries on the issue of peasant education. First, it illustrates that the growth of favorable elements in the public image of the peasant could result from philosophical convictions which were in most respects almost diametrically opposed. The enlightened and rational approach to educa-

[56] Flitner, *Die politische Erziehung*, 76-77.

tion and social problems contributed its part to the growth of such favorable elements through the assumption that rational understanding as a human ability was not restricted to any social class, and that the individual peasant, all other things being equal, had as much of it as anyone else. From this standpoint, it was precisely his individuality which made him equal to other men. Möser's argument, on the other hand, lent a special respectability to the peasant because he was *not* in the first instance an individual, but a member of a class which performed the most valuable sort of corporate function, that of carrying within itself the *Volksgeist,* the summation of the historical experience of the people and of the moral values, above all, to which that historical experience had given rise. The peasant could do this because he was not conscious of himself as an individual who possessed an existence in any sense apart from his group, or, as his dependence upon tradition indicated, apart from his group past. But: different as were the ways in which Möser and the rationalists helped to rehabilitate the peasant in society, each appealed to a different group of contemporaries, and thus in their very difference both together reached more people than could either alone.

At the same time, one can see in Möser's arguments against the *philosophes* on the education question the beginnings of what was later to be an even more explicit divergence of views on the peasant and his role in society. For Möser, the peasant deserved respect and honor because of his unique position as the guarantor of the morality upon which society was or ought to be based. In this sense, it was the peasant as the representative of a way of life which preserved a set of absolute moral values which formed the justification for Möser's advocacy of his interests. By contrast, the *philosophes* found no special merit in the peasant as peasant; interest displayed by them in ameliorating agrarian conditions had little or nothing to do with an admiration for his way of life, but only with the principle that, as an individual, the peasant must have the same freedom and opportunity to exercise his reason for his own and society's benefit which other men possessed. As long as the peasant was a social pariah, as long as he was oppressed and held in bondage, there could be a large amount of substantive agreement between Möser's moralism and the utilitarianism of the *philosophes*: both demanded the release of the peasant from an inferior status. But whereas the achievement of a formal "equality of opportunity" could satisfy the demands of the *philosophes*, it could not provide the added guarantee demanded by the moralists that the absolute and unchanging ethical considerations which they prized would continue to prevail. After the actual attainment of legal equality for the peasant, it was therefore to be expected that the freely competitive or "open" society foreseen by many rationalists would awaken opposition from those whose idea of morality was spiritual and absolute rather than empirical and relative, and who, in the absence of other guarantees, thus had to continue to demand a special social honor for the peasant as a means of preserving the social morality which only he represented. As will subsequently be shown, this conflict between two fundamentally different approaches to the foundations of society, insofar as it touched on the peasant question, became really severe only after 1815 or 1820, when a serious threat to the existence of a large and newly independent peasantry arose. But its beginnings can be seen quite clearly in the protests of Justus Möser against an educational theory which in his mind sought to convert the peasant into the tool of an abstract and therefore false social theory.

After 1800 or more especially, after the reform period in Prussia, the amount of literature devoted to discussion of the education of the peasant declined markedly. This was in part the result of the increasing prominence of certain more pressing issues related to political affairs of immediate importance, which simply shoved educational problems to one side. But it was in part also due to the introduction of a new theory of the self-education of the peasant through property ownership. This theory, associated not only with the names of individuals who can properly lay a claim to the title of pedagogues, but also with officials and statesmen such as Freiherr vom Stein of Prussia, was largely rooted in the teachings and philosophical assumptions of Adam Smith, whose doctrines had been penetrating the German intellectual world for some years prior to 1800. The specific nature of this theory will be discussed below; what is important here is to indicate that the unusually great pedagogical interest treated in this chapter was as widespread as it was precisely because it was predicated upon the existence of serfdom and the lack of proprietary rights among the peasantry. The creation of vocational interest and technical skill among the peasants and the infusion of moral attitudes towards which much of this educational theorizing aimed were quite obviously based upon the assumption that few peasants, left to themselves under prevailing conditions, would develop these attributes and therefore would have to be stimulated from the outside. The theory was also based to some extent upon the assumption or, rather, the hope, that agrarian problems could adequately be solved by a change in the attitudes of the lower classes, to be effected through deliberate propagandization. This hope proved illusory in the course of the two decades following 1789, but especially after 1806. With the enlightened precept of *amour propre*, interpreted and carried into Germany most successfully by Adam Smith in the principles of personal freedom and proprietorship, and with the increasingly obvious bankruptcy of noninstitutional approaches to agrarian problems, this outside "pump-priming" became at once unnecessary and insufficient: the enlightenment of the peasant thus to a great extent became subsumed under the even older reform goals of freedom and proprietorship, and as a separate concern tended for some decades to take a back seat to more concrete and material reforms.

Part Three

The Call to Duty

By the 1780s, there had begun to occur in much German public literature a slow transformation of attitude towards the peasant and the nature of the role he played in society. As previous chapters have suggested, part of this transformation consisted of an enlargement of the picture of the peasant from that of a purely economic unit to that of a certain moral type which preserved universally praiseworthy ethical norms. And it was from some combination of these two fundamental views of the nature of the peasant as a social being that contemporary attitudes towards the social role of the peasant and towards agrarian reform were to continue to take their direction. But the great problems of social theory relative to the peasant before 1780 revolved around the questions of how the economic services of the peasant could be increased and how his peculiarly valuable morality could be placed in the active service of his society. Cameralists, Physiocrats, and agricultural writers of all kinds had spilled much ink to recommend certain kinds of reforms which they believed would increase the efficiency of the peasant as producer; moralists of various stripes had ground out tracts to demonstrate the moral superiority of peasant life; and pedagogical writers had devoted their best efforts to combine schemes for vocational and moral education in such a way as to evoke from the peasant the best possible contribution to the economic and ethical life of his society.

But among all these writers, the peasant was in all essentials still regarded as "subject"; and indeed, he was just that. He was subject to the social, economic, and political constitution of a regime whose very essence was patriarchal, and which assumed the dependence of the subject peasant on the state. As his economic and social life was assumed to be regulated only by command from higher authority, so even the social application of his morality was normally thought to be subject to the precept of the pulpit and the chancellery; changes or improvements in both cases were of course assumed to come from above. Aside from scattered hints in economic and pedagogical writings to the effect that individual voluntarism was a prerequisite for the maximum contribution on the part of the individual members of a society, the prevalent political assumption into the 1780s was that society was held together only by the most strenuous efforts of rulers who, assisted by a highly organized and artificial governmental structure, prevented the otherwise ineluctable conflict of individual interests from converting social harmony into complete chaos. The notion that the stability and duration of states might be enhanced by, or even dependent on, the *active* consent of the governed had not penetrated very far into the governing classes, and was maintained chiefly by philosophers, a few officials, and still fewer rulers, who paid lipservice to it under the rubric of enlightened despotism. Still less was the idea entertained that subjects, acting on their own initiative, might actually produce social results more beneficial than those ordained by sovereign decree.

Events of the 1780s and after, however, were to bring about an increasingly rapid transformation of "subject" into "citizen." This means, above all, that the dependence of the subject on the state is converted into, or at least reduced to an equal level with, the dependence of the state on the voluntary cooperation and even the initiative of all the individuals who composed it. The peasant had a singularly large role in the literature and the public discussions which accompanied this transformation. Again, his economic function and the supposedly unique character of his morality—both of which were developed in their essentials, at least, in the literature before 1780—remained the central points of discussion; but the manner in which both were to be made maximally useful to society, and the definition of their usefulness itself, changed with the new ideas and events of the 1780s and after. Novel concepts of the worth of the peasant, coupled with the newly perceived necessity for him to make his contributions willingly, overcame the previously only rather mild and abstract interest in the peasant and in agrarian conditions, and led eventually to the first real call to duty for the peasant—a call which was no longer to the subject, but to the citizen. This section, then, deals with the development of the conception of the peasant as an active citizen-patriot—a man, that is, whose qualities made him no longer merely the "feet" of society, to use a favorite metaphor of medieval political thinkers, but its very backbone as well. Of primary importance in the growth of the idea of voluntarism and individual freedom as preconditions for a strong and healthy society, affecting not only the peasant but all members of society as well, were the economic doctrines of Adam Smith.

5 Adam Smith in Germany

Much of the importance of the introduction and spread of the works of the great Scottish economist Adam Smith (d. 1790) into Germany lay not in the economic principles of the "wealth of nations," but in the philosophical framework within which those works were conceived and written. Free trade, the concept of the market, the "invisible hand"—all of these were in one sense but specific economic (and therefore, from a contemporary point of view, practical) applications of a more general world-view which also contained certain assumptions about the nature of man, the role and purpose of the state, and the proper relationship to be observed between individuals themselves and between individuals and collective authority. These assumptions, partly obscured though they may have been by the specific uses to which they were put by Smith in his best known work, *The Wealth of Nations*, could nevertheless scarcely have been missed by even the least discerning student. For this reason, and because of the nature of the connection between these assumptions and his economic recommendations, those classes of society which tended to benefit materially from Smith's corrections of earlier economic theory also tended to benefit in other less tangible ways from the philosophical premises necessary to the acceptance of the Smithian economic world. This was especially true of the peasantry, whose position in society was greatly elevated, relative to its previous one, in the minds of many hardheaded German economists, officials, and others, who might well never have accepted such an idea had it come in any form other than that of an economic treatise. A brief survey of the influence of Smithian ideas in Germany for this period should clarify these points.[1]

Smith's great work, *An Inquiry into the Nature and Causes of the Wealth of Nations*, published in English in 1776, was quickly translated into many European languages, including German, and enjoyed virtually undisputed preeminence in the field of theoretical economics for well over half a century. In this work, Smith challenged the system of governmental paternalism characteristic of mercantilist economics, and set in its place the principle of natural economic law, based upon the operation of individual self-interest in a freely competitive society. Identifying the interests of the individual and of society, Smith maintained that in pursuing his own economic interest, the individual would naturally seek out an employment for his capital (or labor) which would bring him the greatest profit, and that society's need would determine where the capital could most profitably be employed. In thus seeking to enrich himself, the individual would infallibly benefit society. Such a happy relationship could only exist, however, where the individual was allowed freely to determine the use of his capital; all governmental restrictions on production, trade, commerce, and property relationships would have to be abolished, together with artificial encouragement of industries or other acquisitive activities through monopolies, subsidies, and tariff protection.

The first German translation of Smith appeared in 1776-1778, and his work was known and discussed in Germany as early as 1777, when Isaak Iselin reviewed it in his periodical, *Ephemeriden der Menschheit*. The first really influential group of Smithians, however, developed at the University of Göttingen, among it such important figures as Georg Sartorius, Johann Stephan Pütter, and Ludwig Timotheus Spittler. There is good evidence that these professors and others like them were putting Smith's doctrines before their students in lectures as early as the 1780s; the later writings of Göttingen students of this time, such as Michael Alexander Lips, Albrecht Thaer, Friedrich Karl Fulda, and Chris-

---

1 The theoretical impact of Adam Smith in Germany has been treated in the following works: Carl William Hasek, *The Introduction of Adam Smith's Doctrines into Germany*, Columbia University Studies in History, Economics, and Public Law, vol. CXVII, No. 2 (New York, 1925); Hugo Graul, *Das Eindringen der Smithschen Nationalökonomie in Deutschland und ihre Weiterbildung bis zu Hermann*, Inaugural-Diss., Halle-Wittenberg (Halle, 1928); and Alfred Nahrgang, *Die Aufnahme der wirtschaftspolitischen Ideen von Adam Smith in Deutschland zu Beginn des XIX. Jahrhunderts*, Inaugural-Diss., Frankfurt (Gelnhausen, 1933-1934). The development of a more specifically national German economic theory beyond Smith has been examined by Judith Grünfeld, *Die leitenden sozial- und wirtschaftsphilosophischen Ideen in der Nationalökonomie und die Überwindung des Smithianismus bis auf Mohl und Hermann*, Inaugural-Diss., Tübingen (Vienna, 1913).

tian Jakob Kraus sufficiently attest to the influence Smith had on them by way of their professors. Nor was the Smithian influence restricted to those who were to make their careers in academics: Göttingen, like most German universities of the time, produced many officials who staffed important administrative and other governmental posts all over Germany, and among these were many who had learned their political economy from Smithian professors. Prince Hardenberg and Freiherr vom Stein were among the most important officials who had read and expressed approval of Smithian economics.[2]

It was not until the 1790s, however, that Smith's ideas began to appear consistently in the works of German political economists. In 1794, the second and improved German translation of Smith, by Christian Garve, appeared, and was received with greater attention than the first; by 1810 this translation had gone through another printing and two more editions. The greater interest awakened by the new translation was reflected in Georg Sartorius' *Handbuch der Staatswirthschaft zum Gebrauche bei akademischen Vorlesungen, nach Adam Smith's Grundsätzen ausgearbeitet* (1796), which was a pure abstract of Smith's work and showed a complete acceptance of his principles. A tendency to swallow Smith whole was not untypical of the writings of early German Smithians, although many of them later modified his writings in accordance with their own ideas and experience.

With respect to reform ideas for the German agricultural situation, it is sometimes hard to identify specifically Smithian ideas in the writings of the German economists, for little that Smith wrote with regard to the ideal agricultural condition was absent from earlier economic writings, especially those of the Physiocrats. Freedom of the grain trade, the abolition of serfdom and the establishment of free proprietorship for peasants, the abolition of forced labor services and of laws of primogeniture and entail, all of which were advocated in *The Wealth of Nations,* were integral parts of the Physiocratic program before Smith. Indeed, Smith's reasoning for these recommendations was not

---

[2] The influence of Smith on German academicians is the subject of an essay by Wilhelm Treue, "Adam Smith in Deutschland; zum Problem des 'Politischen Professors' zwischen 1776 und 1810," *Deutschland und Europa: historische Studien zur Völker- und Staatenordnung des Abendlandes* (Düsseldorf, 1951).

substantially different from that of the Physiocrats: both were interested in increasing production from the land, and both felt that the abolition of all these essentially feudal restrictions was necessary to obtain maximum efficiency in agriculture. Smith himself called the Physiocrats' doctrines "the nearest approximation to the truth that has yet been published upon the subject of political economy," and went on to say that "though in representing the labour which is employed upon land as the only productive labour, the notions which it [Physiocracy] inculcates are perhaps too narrow and confined; yet in representing the wealth of nations as consisting, not in the unconsumable riches of money, but in the consumable goods annually reproduced by the labour of the society; and in representing perfect liberty as the only effectual expedient for rendering this annual reproduction the greatest possible, its doctrine seems to be in every respect as just as it is generous and liberal."[3]

On the question of the relative importance of agriculture to the economy as a whole, Smith was of course much less narrow in his views than the Physiocrats. He saw much more clearly than they that the increase of wealth was not a one-way circular movement beginning and ending in the agricultural sector, and he was actually much more eclectic than they, in that the amounts of labor and capital invested properly in agriculture as opposed to other sectors of the economy was for him always a matter of circumstance and varying natural balance rather than of immutable principle. Inevitably, therefore, there arose disputes between Smithian and Physiocratic economists. Smith's concept of the free market tended to clash at some points with Physiocratic doctrine, which would have resolved at least certain kinds of competitive situations by government action, if necessary, in favor of the agricultural interest. The single land tax, the much-cherished *impôt unique* of the Physiocrats, was regarded by Smithians as a clear restraint on one category of producers, which would merely have to be made up somewhere else, and saw it therefore as useless or actually damaging. Another favorite Physiocratic goal, large population, did not square with Smith's

[3] Adam Smith, *An Inquiry into the Nature and Causes of the Wealth of Nations* (New York, 1937), Book IV, Chapter 9, 642.

emphasis on wealth as a function of the ratio between population and the production of goods for consumption, and was often specifically repudiated by his followers.[4]

As suggested above, however, there were many bases for an alliance between Smithians and Physiocrats as far as their attitudes towards the means necessary to improve production within the agricultural sector were concerned. And their agreement on the conditions most conducive to the actual progress of profitable cultivation was probably more important to the realization of reform than their disagreement on systematic economics. Each could support the other on the most pressing questions of reform, and this mutual support was generally recognized: Gottlieb Hufeland, sometime professor at Landshut and finally at Halle, pointed out in 1807, for example, that the principle of free labor as better, cheaper, and more efficient than slave or forced labor had already been virtually universally recognized, even by those whose principles differed considerably in other respects—and he cited both Smith and the Physiocrat Turgot as proof.[5]

In many instances, Smith's influence on German economists' views of agriculture can be seen rather readily. One case among many is that of August Ferdinand Lueder, professor at Braunschweig, Göttingen, and Jena. His work *Ueber Nationalindustrie und Staatswirthschaft* also carried the subscript *"nach Adam Smith bearbeitet,"* and is a virtual paraphrasing of *The Wealth of Nations.* Lueder did, however, see in Smith's survey of the discouragement of agriculture after the fall of Rome not only the history of a past catastrophe, but also a commentary on

---

[4] An author writing on the question of whether agriculture was really the foundation of the wealth of nations, for example, vigorously maintained that a large population as a goal in itself was, in fact, evil, and that the goal of the state should rather be the greatest happiness for the existing citizenry, regardless of numbers. V(on) K(öpken?), "Ob der Ackerbau wirklich den Grund des Reichthums der Staaten ausmacht?" *Der teutsche Merkur* (August 1789), 148.

[5] Gottlieb Hufeland, *Neue Grundlegung der Staatswirthschaftskunst,* erster Theil (Biesen and Wetzlar, 1807), 209. In the two or three decades following 1790, it appears that most Physiocrats in Germany were more or less completely converted to Smith's teachings by the force and profundity of his great work, as well as by the development of objective economic relationships in Germany. Of the still rather considerable number of persons who continued to maintain the absolute primacy of the agricultural sector of the economy after 1820 or so, very few were trained economists.

contemporary agricultural relationships in Germany; and while he repeated Smith's statement of the reasons for men's natural preference for agriculture over other occupations (the attractions of outdoor life, the security of the landowner by reason of his proprietorship in soil, and the independence of the rural capitalist), he was also careful to point out that this preference would exist only where circumstances did not oppress the peasant or farmer, and he really went beyond Smith in saying that the free peasant "does not know that despotism which the manufacturer never escapes; he is not, like the craftsman, a servant of his clients."[6] From this and similar statements, one might fairly assume that Smith's doctrines in this case had fallen upon ears which were already receptive to a rationale for the improvement of agriculture and the condition of the peasant.

Smith's principle of absolute economic freedom had a profound influence on the formulation of complaints against the prevailing agrarian order and of solutions offered for agrarian problems by German economists. One well-known economist of this period, Ludwig Heinrich Jakob of the University at Halle, for example, again used Smith's argument of the manifold advantages of the agricultural occupation to prove that if artificial hindrances were abolished, more capital would be invested in agriculture and more products would be forthcoming from it.[7] Jakob classified the obstacles to agriculture under the following categories: 1) artificial property relationships, such as entail, communal lands, hunting, pasturing, and stock-driving rights on other people's lands, and restrictions on traffic in landed property; 2) restrictions on the actual use of the soil; 3) restrictions on free traffic in the produce of the soil; 4) the miserable personal relationships of many peasants, including slavery, personal servitude, and all sorts of dependence on noble landlords; and 5) an improper tax system, which frightened many people away from agriculture, especially because of personal services and payments in kind.[8] He further listed the following restrictions on property as not

[6] August Ferdinand Lueder, *Über Nationalindustrie und Staatswirthschaft*, 3 vols. (Berlin, 1800-1804), I, 328-29.
[7] Ludwig Heinrich Jakob, *Grundsätze der National-Oekonomie oder National-Wirthschaftslehre* (Halle, 1805), 193.
[8] *Ibid.*, 191-93.

resulting from the "natural law," and therefore damaging: 1) all restrictions with respect to the ownership of property which prohibited the selling of property at will, and which thereby decreased the value of property and prevented it from coming into the hands of the most willing and able cultivators; 2) all restrictions with respect to the partition of fields, communal lands, and all other collective aspects of land tenure; 3) all restrictions with respect to the use and cultivation of the soil.

Jakob introduced his section dealing with restrictions on the freedom of the worker with the following statement, which might have been taken word for word from Smith: "All restrictions . . . which confine the freedom of the worker lessen, in general, the product of labor, and are therefore disadvantageous to the increase of national wealth, even if they are of use to him who derives advantage from these restrictions. But his advantage is indeed never as great as the disadvantage which the country has from it, and it is therefore better that he be recompensed for his advantage, but [that] the freedom of the worker be brought about." The restrictions discussed by Jakob included all forms of direct or indirect coercion which held people to agricultural work for which they had no desire. "Complete freedom of landed property, of all proprietors, and all labor is the first and necessary condition, if the perfection of agriculture is to attain its highest peak," he concluded in this section.[9]

His statement of the right of property was similarly Smithian. No one, he wrote, would have the desire to invest labor or capital in a farm if he were not convinced that he alone would own and control the product of his industry; if, therefore, wealth in a nation were to be increased, the right of property had to be recognized—and not only for society as a whole, but for every individual as well.[10] Bound up with the right of property, wrote Jakob, was the freedom to sell or exchange property at will, for behind the creation of surplus was always the intention of exchange to the profit of the producer.[11] If it were left entirely to the farmers themselves to decide how they wished to divide

[9] *Ibid.*, 269-72.
[10] *Ibid.*, 21.
[11] *Ibid.*, 22-23.

or cultivate their lands, said Jakob, the self-interest of every proprietor would shortly dictate the most advantageous method of cultivation.[12] Jakob manifested a typically Smithian disapproval of state ownership of domains (crown lands), and advocated that such lands be sold to private owners or at least rented out hereditarily. The state, he wrote, could not get as much produce from the land as could private owners, since in general it looked at domains as sources of income rather than as opportunities for investment, and therefore seldom put any money into them.[13]

Fundamentally Smithian in his attitudes, too, and quite influential in his time, was the agriculturist and economist Albrecht Thaer (1752-1828), whose attempts to apply scientific advances to agriculture were only one part of the real service he performed for German agriculture in his lifetime. Thaer was educated in medicine at Göttingen, and returned to his home in Celle to practice. During this time he developed an interest in agriculture and became a member of the Royal Agricultural Society in Celle and a close follower of agricultural theory and practice. From humanitarian motives, largely, Thaer decided to create a model farm as an example of scientific agriculture for farmers in that area. He bought up some lands around his home and directed their cultivation, an enterprise which, owing to his lack of experience, at first caused him a certain amount of financial loss. Within a few years, however, the farm showed a substantial profit.

Once his estate had begun to attract national attention among agriculturists, Thaer came to the notice of the Prussian government, which arranged his entry into the Academy of Sciences in Berlin. He was authorized by the government in 1804 to establish an agricultural school on land provided for that purpose, and the school was ultimately as successful as his model farm. Thaer was active in the formation of agrarian reform policy in Prussia in 1807 and after, and he was appointed professor of Cameral Sciences at Berlin in 1810. After his retirement from this post in 1819, he devoted virtually all his time to the model farm and school at Möglin. Thaer may be regarded as the first authority

---

[12] *Ibid.*, 181-82.
[13] *Ibid.*, 306-12.

who sought to give agriculture a really scientific basis; and much of his effort was directed towards the achievement of rational agricultural procedure by competent farmers.[14]

As part of his general concern for agriculture, Thaer spent a great deal of time in the study of agricultural economics. In his *Leitfaden zur allgemeinen landwirthschaftlichen Gewerbslehre*, he acknowledged his debt to Adam Smith, the "immortal" founder of national economic theory *(National-Wirthschaftslehre)*, who had proposed the correct concept of capital and its application.[15] He followed Smith in stating that the natural attractions of outdoor life as well as the security of capital invested in land would attract more capital to rural occupations, if only the restrictions on land and labor were removed.[16] In this connection, he argued for the introduction of consolidation of fields *(Zusammenlegung)*, the abolition of labor services as advantageous to both parties, and the modification or abolition of such institutions as the tenth, pasturing and stock-driving rights, communal ownership of land, and hunting laws.[17] His very close relationship to Smith may further be observed in his statement that once freedom to buy, sell, and exchange had been established, the good farmers would soon be successful, and the bad ones would go out of business—but others would appear on the scene with money, industry, and knowledge sufficient to make up for those lost.[18]

Even the most convinced of Smith's followers among the German economists could not, however, accept the full implications of Smithian doctrines in the German situation as it then existed. If, for example, Christian Garve, the translator of the most widely known German editions of Smith in this period, wished to leave basic peasant reforms to the good will of the

---

[14] *Allgemeine deutsche Biographie*, XXXVII, 636-41. Thaer's most important technical work on agriculture was his four-volume *Grundsätze der rationellen Landwirthschaft* (Berlin, 1809-1812). For a good account of Thaer's life, see Walter Simons, *Albrecht Thaer, nach amtlichen und privaten Dokumenten aus einer grossen Zeit* (Berlin, 1929).

[15] Albrecht Thaer, *Leitfaden zur allgemeinen landwirthschaftlichen Gewerbslehre* (Berlin, 1815), 16.

[16] *Ibid.*, 29-30.

[17] *Ibid.*, 81-112, *passim*.

[18] Albrecht Thaer, *Einleitung zur Kenntniss der englischen Landwirthschaft* (Hannover, 1798), 700.

landlords, thus following completely in this particular the Smithian formula of denying the government any active role in the interplay of natural economic forces, then in this he stood virtually alone among German economic thinkers.[19] For every voice which spoke out in favor of "self-regulation" of the old feudal agrarian order, there were many whose proposals for reform clearly depended on government intervention. "The peasant is the first rung in the ladder of the state," wrote one economist; "but the peasant, and the state with him, can arrive at his true greatness and happiness only through support, encouragement, only under an economic scepter."[20] It was still very much open to question whether this "arrival" would be expedited by piecemeal reform or by vast changes such as that suggested by a Physiocratic writer, who envisioned the establishment of a special State Agricultural Ministry (*Staats-Ackerbau-Kollegium*) with central and provincial branches, which would eventually produce and implement a general agricultural statute based on "the unchangeable laws of nature."[21] But it was commonly agreed that the aegis of the state was essential to almost any really beneficial reform.[22]

Many German thinkers were thus faced with an insurmountable dilemma in attempting to reconcile laissez faire principles with an agricultural system which labored under great artificial restrictions, and they solved the problem only by junking, provisionally, this part of Smith's system. Thus Georg Sartorius (d. 1828), professor of history and political economy at Göttingen, who had originally supported Smith's theories point by point,

---

[19] Roscher, *Geschichte der National-Oekonomik*, 607-608.

[20] Stumpf, "Stumpf's (Oekonomie Rath) über die vollkommenste Dorfwirthschaft," *Leipziger Magazin*, Viertes Stük (1787), 463.

[21] "Vorschlag zu einem besondern hohen Staatskollegio für den Ackerbau," *Neues Archiv für den Menschen und Bürger*, IV (1787), 348-60.

[22] The hopeful but perhaps rather naïve individuals who thought that the peasants themselves might be able to bring about helpful reforms were given little comfort by Johann Christian Schubart, who disputed the notion that the peasants even had the freedom to do so: "Whoever may think freely, thinks well, says Haller. But candid thought is unfortunately absolutely not permitted the peasant in many areas; and if he wished to proceed completely according to his insights, hatred and persecution would in a few years deprive him of his few belongings. In order barely to preserve [what he has], he has nothing else to do but what he . . . can do without much thought; namely, to follow tradition blindly and not to deviate from it in the slightest." Quoted in von Moser, "Ob der Bauer frey denken und handeln dürfe?" *Patriotisches Archiv* (Moser), V (1786), 528-29.

was led to accept and elaborate upon Lauderdale's criticism of Smith—that the sum total of interests and wealth of individuals was not necessarily identical with the interest and wealth of the nation as a whole. He sought to show that in many cases government must indeed take a hand to help the economy along, sometimes even by restrictions and prohibitions. He felt that this was particularly true with regard to German agriculture, where servitude, labor services, and other such institutions required a reform which could only be imposed by the state, as well as in the grain trade, which ultimately could not operate for the welfare of all under complete free trade.[23]

Other writers modified Smith's doctrine to the point of approving laissez faire only after freedom of person and property had everywhere been established in the state. L. H. Jakob reached this conclusion, and agreed with Smith in regarding government fundamentally only as a watchdog with police functions.[24] On the other hand, the watchdog would have to be a strong one, wrote Jakob, for "the security of property rests on the establishment of a state which alone is strong enough to repel any force which wishes to invade a right."[25] Albrecht Thaer, too, writing in 1798, recognized that laissez faire under then-obtaining agrarian relationships would not serve to increase agricultural production substantially, and in an examination of the English agricultural system he stated that "one can assume that a state can approximate its agriculture to [that of] the English only to the degree in which it is in a position to make the relationships of its agricultural class comparable to those in England." But if cultivation of the land were left largely to peasants, and if these were oppressed by servitude, labor services, the tenth, and other dues and fees, then certainly little improvement could be expected. The situation, then, called not for "decrees, admonitions, instructions, and premiums," but for a reform of the whole agrarian constitution.[26]

But if in these respects Smith's work was not found universally

---

[23] Georg Sartorius, *Abhandlungen, die Elemente des National-Reichthums und die Staatswirthschaft betreffend,* erster Theil (Göttingen, 1806), Abhandlung IV, 199-519, *passim.*
[24] Jakob, *Grundsätze,* 274.
[25] *Ibid.,* 22-23.
[26] Thaer, *Einleitung,* 698-700.

applicable in Germany, its importance in its effect on German economic theory and, more specifically, on German agrarian reform literature cannot be denied. Smith, perhaps, contributed few if any original thoughts to specific reform proposals—a review of pre-Smithian literature certainly tends towards this conclusion —but he at least contributed a systematic rationale for reform which gave added impetus to reform literature. And although the effect of orthodox Smithian economics was such as to deemphasize the importance of agriculture as a sector in the economy as a whole, at least by comparison with Physiocracy, the more realistic and balanced appraisal of the new system by no means neglected agriculture, and may indeed have helped to evoke a more favorable attitude towards agricultural reform on the part of the growing German commercial and industrial middle classes. These groups, seeing the intimate relationship which Smith showed to exist between increased productivity in all fields of economic endeavor, and feeling now no longer ignored as producers of real wealth, as they had been in Physiocratic doctrine, could support agricultural reform as a matter of putting money into their own pockets while at the same time aiding the peasant, instead of giving aid and comfort to an economic group which, according to many previous theorists, already far outweighed them in importance.

Nor is it without significance that Smith, to an extent previously unknown in economic thought, assumed as the basic human agent in his system a man who with respect to his judgment on his own interest and on the things which conduced to it was the equal of every other man. This economic world, that is, depended not just on the principle of self-interest, but also upon the ability of men to perceive where their self-interest lay. When Smith therefore posited at the center of the economic world a man with this ability, he established rationality as a universal human characteristic. To accept Smith's great analysis was to accept this axiom; and above all others, on the German scene, the peasant acquired stature from Smith's scheme, for the basic principles of agrarian reform—personal freedom and ownership of land—presupposed something by no means yet generally accepted in Germany, namely, the ability of the peasant to make rational use of his instruments of production to benefit himself and, through himself, the rest of society.[27]

In this way, an important new argument to reinforce the idea of the peasant as a man equal to other men was introduced. What was of such great significance here was that a scheme which purported infallibly to point the way to maximum material progress depended for its success upon an assumption of at least one kind of equality of man. From any such formula, but especially from one as widely accepted as that of Smith came to be (not all enlightened and utilitarian doctrines were as readily taken as Smith's, after all), the peasant could not fail to benefit. The peasant, it must be remembered, began his ascent to social respectability from a position which at the outset was commonly assumed to be *below* humanity; to achieve equality, to achieve humanity itself, was a major part of his social rehabilitation.

[27] Smith made this point quite clearly in his discussion of the differences between the lower classes of town and country. The following illustrative quotations, though lengthy, are of some importance: "No apprenticeship has ever been thought necessary to qualify for husbandry, the great trade of the country. After what are called the fine arts, and the liberal professions, however, there is perhaps no trade which requires so great a variety of knowledge and experience. The innumerable volumes which have been written upon it in all languages, may satisfy us, that among the wisest and most learned nations, it has never been regarded as a matter very easily understood. And from all those volumes we shall in vain attempt to collect that knowledge of its various and complicated operations, which is commonly possessed even by the common farmer; how contemptuously soever the very contemptible authors of some of them may sometimes affect to speak of him." "The common ploughman, though generally regarded as the pattern of stupidity and ignorance, is seldom defective in this judgment and discretion [i.e., relative to the instruments and objects of his work]. He is less accustomed, indeed, to social intercourse than the mechanic who lives in a town. His voice and language are more uncouth and more difficult to be understood by those who are not used to them. His understanding, however, being accustomed to consider a greater variety of objects, is generally much superior to that of the other, whose whole attention from morning till night is commonly occupied in performing one or two very simple operations. How much the lower ranks of people in the country are really superior to those of the town, is well known to every man whom either business or curiosity has led to converse much with both." Smith, *The Wealth of Nations*, Book I, Chapter 10, Part 2, 126-27. This argument was frequently used in future years in Germany both by those who wished to emphasize the intelligence and versatility of the peasant, as for example by Carl von Clausewitz (see below, p. 179), and by individuals such as Adam Müller and Ludwig Börne, who for different reasons opposed the prevalent tendency towards the division of labor and thus used Smith's own examples of the peasant as a "whole man" as a club to cudgel the growth of an "economic man," i.e., a man who, in virtue of the extreme specialization of his work, would become stupified and dehumanized. (See below, pp. 230-32.)

6 The Awakening of National Consciousness

The influence of Smithian economic doctrine in Germany power-
fully reinforced earlier economic arguments for the liberation
and proprietorship of the German peasant. It laid down in a
systematic fashion the apparently undeniable principles of a
natural economic order in which virtually unrestricted freedom
of competition occupied a central position. The implications of
the Smithian system were revolutionary insofar as they pointed
to freedom as an absolutely necessary part of the natural economic
world, without which other wealth increasing mechanisms would
not function with maximum efficiency. But in spite of the
rationality ascribed to the peasant, the role and picture of him
which emerged directly from the Smithian schema were actually
little different from those posited by earlier economic thinkers.
However necessary the peasant may have been to the economy,
and however necessary his freedom, a strictly economic view
could do no more than raise him to a level of equality of economic
function with his fellow subjects; it had nothing whatever, in
principle, to say about the relative position of the peasantry to
other classes with respect to anything but purely economic
standards. If it was an economic argument which most firmly
established the pragmatic efficacy of freedom and proprietorship
for the peasant, his legal equality with the members of other
classes as concerned market competition, it could scarcely be
an economic argument which established his social equality—his
right to claim a special social honor which would entitle him to a
status in society entailing attitudes of respect on the part of other
classes. The economic point of view, in other words, implied
changes in the legal status of persons and property, but nothing
more.

The realization of these legal changes was clearly felt to depend
upon changes in the attitudes of those classes whose influence
was necessary to the introduction of social reforms. Even the
economists, who were not in the first instance moralist humani-

tarians, therefore buttressed their pleas for agrarian reforms with noneconomic, moral arguments designed to show the justice of reform in terms of the peasant's character and wider social role; they had to create the picture of a man deserving of the reform of his material circumstances and capable of taking advantage of that reform in the interest of himself and society as a whole. The discovery of a particular set of virtues common to the peasants as a group, and only to them, was then given further impetus by an essentially intellectual reaction to the philosophical morality and social implications of leading currents of enlightened thought, as well as to the actual progress of certain social changes felt to be undesirable. The beginnings of a movement which created for the peasant not merely a common equality with the members of other social classes but also an especially honorable and even exalted status in public opinion in Germany came with this coupling of moral virtue and the peasant life—a development discussed above in chapter III. When to this mixture was added the peculiarly virulent impulse of nationalism, the foundation was laid for the transformation of the virtuous peasant into the standard definition of a distinct German national character.

The general historical problem of the origins of national sentiment in Germany is a topic much too broad to be treated systematically in this study. It has been explored in a number of important works since the end of the First World War, especially, and is as complicated a development as any with which the German historian must deal. For present purposes, it will be possible only to touch upon those aspects of awakening nationalism which are of most direct importance to the development of the peasant image.

The opposition to the Enlightenment pointed out above was more than an opposition to certain ideas or concepts; it was also part of a rising tide of sentiment against foreign influence in Germany in general, and it is difficult to separate the two. In view of the virtual tyranny exercised by France over Germany with respect to style, fashion, literary expression, manners, mores, and the development of philosophical thought, it was not unnatural that reactions against foreign influence should direct themselves chiefly against France. Examples of a rapidly growing

Gallophobia in the last decades of the eighteenth century are too numerous to mention in detail. Justus Möser expressed himself against the French influence in Germany in very direct and caustic ways as well as indirectly through his numerous attacks on fashions, ideas, and habits whose source, though not mentioned by him, was clearly understood to be France. Friedrich Carl von Moser was so disturbed by the pernicious effects of French influence on the government and society of Germany that he at one time thought of writing a book, to be called *Von der französischen Influenza,* which would be "a pragmatic presentation of all the results brought about by the influence of French principles, literature, morals, and customs on German princes, princesses, and ministers, on the education and development of the youth and on the government of land and people."[1]

It would be difficult, however, to find a major publicist in Germany in this time who was more hostile to France and the French influence than Christian Friedrich Daniel Schubart, the editor of the southern German periodical *Deutsche Chronik.* He scolded Germans for their habit of sending German money out of the country, chiefly to France, for various kinds of goods to flatter their vanity ("Frazen der Mode und der Eitelkeit"), especially when they had their own goods and manufactures, and he announced that such practices were neither German nor upright—qualities which belonged together.[2] He damned the French for their overrefinement and for its transplantation to Germany, and called for "a little of the old coarseness of our character. A refined nation does not rise, but falls; and my heart bleeds if I should think this of my fatherland."[3] Consciously turning inwards, Schubart sought to locate the positive properties of a German national character which he could oppose to the superficiality of the French and to the strange half-Germans who aped French manners in Germany and thereby denied their own character. At various times he mentioned valor, loyalty, simplicity, solidity, purity, sincerity, and honesty as fundamental and distinguishing characteristics of Germans.[4] At the same time,

---

[1] Quoted from von Moser in Pinson, *Pietism,* 185.
[2] Schairer, *Christian Friedrich Daniel Schubart,* 65.
[3] Quoted from Schubart in *ibid.,* 77.
[4] *Ibid.,* 113.

he really despaired over what he saw as an ingrained "subject-mentality" *(Unterthansgeist)* among Germans, a tendency to suffer everything without showing initiative to improve themselves. He made some rather halfhearted attempts to justify this characteristic by glimpsing in it a philosophical calmness, an ability to observe the course of affairs with a certain admirable stoicism; or even to relate it, as a virtue, to a fundamental love of order and harmony.[5]

Schubart was certainly at base a pessimist about the possibility of creating a German national self-consciousness; but the strength of this self-consciousness in him did not allow him to be utterly without hope. Towards the end of his life, he published an interesting poem which in a sense summed up his national aspirations and recommendations:

> Wenn Deutschland seine Würde fühlt,
> Nicht mehr mit Auslands Puppen spielt,
> Die alte deutsche Sitt' und Art
> In Wort und Wandel treu bewahrt
> Den Christenglauben nie verletzt,
> Und Wahrheit über alles schätzt,
> Nicht Irrwischlicht Aufklärung nennt,
> Weil es die Leuchte Gottes kennt,
> Wenn Mannkraft, wie zu Hermanns Zeit,
> Den Enkel stärkt und Tapferkeit,
> Wenn Deutschland all diss thut und hält,
> So wirds das erste Land der Welt.[6]

> If Germany its worth can feel,
> No more 'fore foreign playthings kneel,
> Preserve the ancient German ways
> In word and action all its days
> Ne'er let the Christian faith to fall,
> And value truth well over all,
> And does not call Enlightenment
> What not from God's own light is sent,
> If courage, as in Hermann's age,
> In his descendants' hearts can rage,
> Should Germany do all this, and stand,
> The world will know no better land.

He calls here on the German past as the guide to Germanness,

[5] *Ibid.,* 105-107.
[6] Quoted in *ibid.,* 112.

and demands the preservation of the "ancient German ways" to steady the German eye against what he called the false "*Irrwischlicht*" of a decadent and supercilious age calling itself the "Enlightenment." It is no accident that the masculinity or courage of the age of Hermann, or Arminius, appears in this poem; German antiquity was a favorite theme for Schubart's reference, and on one occasion he expressed the view that if Tacitus should return to Germany, he would still find among the Germans many people with the same firm character traits which he had once used to put his own decadent Rome to shame.[7]

The connection between Schubart's national feeling and the peasant is direct and palpable: the coarseness which he demanded as a counterweight to overrefinement, the traditional German customs he praised, and indeed the very image of the primitive German which he conjured up from the time of Arminius could be found nowhere as distinctly and purely as in the German peasant. What Schubart had done was to construct a composite of characteristics which to him constituted all the traits necessary to a German national character—and the result looked astoundingly like the descriptions of the peasant which Schubart himself and a number of other writers and publicists had begun to put forth.

Schubart, like Möser and other more or less politically oriented writers in Germany, reacted quickly and with some violence to the criticisms of the crudity of German life which were very much a part of European public opinion in the eighteenth century. The lower standards of living, the inferiority of most German manufacturing and especially luxury industries, and the general lack of elegance in the conduct of life—all hangovers from the Thirty Years' War—were an object of mockery to travelers and members of upper classes in France, England, and even Italy and Spain. For those Germans who had personal contact with the fiscal contortions of German rulers who horribly overtaxed their lands in vain attempts to achieve for their courts the standards of luxury and elegance of a Versailles, these criticisms of German crudity were stupid and pernicious (in that they produced

[7] *Ibid.*

redoubled efforts on the part of petty princes to make themselves and their courts respectable), and their retorts were essentially countercriticisms of wasteful and effeminate societies.[8] Some criticisms were less easily answered, however. In literary circles, it was extremely difficult to counter the gibes that Germany was plainly backwards with regard to the development of a literary language. French culture, in particular, was nowhere as self-assured as in the realm of belles-lettres, and it was impossible for Germans to compare their meager literary efforts with those of the great seventeenth- and eighteenth-century French essayists, dramatists, and poets. Here, as elsewhere in German cultural life, a sterile imitation had become the rule of the day.

It was Friedrich Gottlieb Klopstock (1724-1803) who, in deliberate reaction to this slavish imitation, first sought to create a new and self-conscious German national literature. His efforts were one part of a somewhat vague but fervent desire to revive a pan-German cultural national spirit. In strophes resplendent with scarcely remembered mythologic names, Klopstock addressed his fellow Germans, telling them of ancient Germanic bards inhabiting the primeval forests, who with no resources other than their own folk-past, their feelings, and the raw nature which surrounded them, were yet able to create songs of intense emotional beauty. Klopstock mixed Celtic, Anglo-Saxon, and Scandinavian folklore and primitive religion together with Tacitus' relations of ancient Germania to produce an utterly unrecognizable and thoroughly fantastic picture of old Teutonic life and beliefs.[9] By shortly after the midcentury, he had attained a remarkable reputation in Germany, which however diminished

---

[8] One can get some idea of the violence and bitterness with which the petty German courts were denounced for their spendthrift ways from an article of 1781 by J. C. Schmohl, a little-known publicist, who referred to the standing armies of the ruler as a "consuming cancer," and to the type of the petty ruler himself as a "little prince who wants to be emperor and Lord God and strains his little country, like the frog who wanted to become an ox [strained] his stomach, in unholy torture, until everything must burst." J. C. Schmohl, "Vermischte land- und staatswirthschaftliche Ideen," *Deutsches Museum* (January-June 1781), 46. A lively and often humorous survey of the petty German courts in this period has been written by Adrien Fauchier-Magnan, *The Small German Courts in the Eighteenth Century* (London, 1958).

[9] Hertz, *The Development of the German Public Mind*, II, 390-91.

slowly thereafter in spite of later spurts of favorable attention he evoked from the literary public with such dramas as the *Hermanns Schlacht* (1769) and *Hermanns Tod* (1787).

In the long run, it was not Klopstock's own artistic contributions which made him the idol of much of the younger German literary world; these were perhaps only somewhat better than mediocre. But the significance of his literary patriotism was not lost on his contemporaries, who saw in it the beginnings of a liberation from a shallow and frivolous subservience to foreign influence. Klopstock was made the patron saint of the Göttingen *Hainbund,* whose members drank toasts to Luther, Arminius, Goethe, Herder, and other German figures whose work appeared to them to represent native German genius in high degree. It need scarcely be pointed out that the simple morality preached or suggested in their poems and ballads by the members of the *Hainbund,* as described in Chapter III, was very closely related to the intoxication of these early feelings of literary emancipation from a foreign yoke: their rediscovery of the peasant and his simple, uncorrupted life and the refuge they found in his hut were to them the closest possible approximation to a visit with the tribesmen of the *Urgermane,* Arminius, in the sylvan purity of their folk-life.

The reaction to foreign influence in Germany was often enough transformed into a dislike of the very idea of cosmopolitanism; some Germans, that is, reacting to criticism that Germany was in effect making no significant contribution to "world culture" as defined by Europeans in that time, simply denied the validity or utility of a truly international cultural community. But perhaps a more important, if also a more tortuous path to nationalism was laid down by a group of German intellectuals who were, initially at least, firmly committed to the ideal of *Weltbürgertum* (cosmopolitanism). They, too, reacted against foreign criticism that Germany was culturally sterile; but they did so not merely in returning tit-for-tat criticism to their critics, but by opening and broadening the whole question of what culture was, and how cultural contribution was made. When they were done, they had not only proven a positive contribution of Germany to cultural life, but had changed the entire meaning of the word "culture."

The central figure in this movement was Johann Gottfried Herder (1744-1803), whose major contribution lay in the exposition of the idea that poetry must be regarded as the evolutionary product of particular peoples and could not be judged by abstract and universal canons. With this principle, a historical as well as a literary insight of absolutely first-rate importance, Herder at once denied the typical enlightened view that literary endeavors could be subjected to any single set of standards, and also suggested that the peculiar genius of any people's literature lay in the peculiar genius of its language. Herder's German contemporaries pounced on his ideas and shook them in the faces of the foreign mockers of Germany's "coarse and crude" language; here was a basis for self-respect which had hitherto been lacking, for how could a respectable German literature arise if the medium of its expression, the German language, were inferior by its nature to French, Italian, or other languages? The sense of Herder's argument was that no language is intrinsically inferior or superior to any other: all languages are but the result of the peculiar needs and experiences of the people who speak them. For any particular people to make its contribution to a "world culture," it was therefore necessary not that it imitate other peoples' modes of expression, but that it become fully conscious of itself and out of this consciousness strive to bring to literary expression the most characteristic of its own peculiarities. The true cosmopolitanism would therefore consist not in some artificially contrived and universally imitated world literature (or world language), but in the sum total of the individual, natural, and therefore true insights of particular peoples.

In a fascinating study of the origins of national consciousness in northwestern Germany for the period 1790-1830, Wolfgang von Groote has illustrated the path taken by German cosmopolitanism to German nationalism in the concrete example of Gerhard Anton von Halem, a leading literary figure and founder of the *Oldenburgische Literarische Gesellschaft*—a society established in 1780 on the model of Klopstock's famous literary club in Hamburg. Von Halem was one of a number of essentially middle-class Germans who sought the erection of a new German "elite," one of writers and thinkers, primarily, which would securely anchor and give direction to a renewed feeling of German honor and dignity. Although his goals were clearly cosmopolitan, von Halem early attached himself to Herder's language mystique and began to see the goals for which the nation should strive as somehow inherent in the German language itself. Rousseau, perhaps, had provided the key notion that what is good is what the folk has produced naturally, in the course of its unselfconscious activity. How the good is to be found appears in this formulation of von Halem: "Knowest thou the touchstone of the True?—The language of the Germans! What it proclaims to thee in its own words is true." The great Lessing had once announced that the Germans were not yet a nation, "since they lack not only the political constitution, but also the moral character."[10] This was now interpreted, in von Halem's circle, to mean not that the Germans had much to learn from others about morality, but rather that they had much to learn from themselves: the bases of morality were not to be found in the denial of Germanness and in the imitation of foreign ideas, which were *ipso facto* unnatural for Germany,[11] but in the rediscovery of Germanness through the infallible tool of the German language— that is, through a process of coming to self-consciousness.

What arose from this new emphasis on language was a new definition of "nation." Earlier usage had in effect included in that term only the intellectual leaders of this or that country; but now, if language was indeed to be the criterion, "nation" included all who spoke a certain language. For the first time, therefore, the "folk," the broad masses of the people, became a part of the

[10] Wolfgang von Groote, *Die Entstehung des Nationalbewusstseins in Nordwest-deutschland, 1790-1830* (Göttingen, 1955), 10-13; the citations from von Halem and Lessing are on p. 13.

[11] Herder, for example, had numerous bitter comments for those Germans who maligned their own language because of their belief in the real superiority of other languages, especially French. He once wrote: "Whoever despises the language of his nation dishonors its most noble public; he becomes the most dangerous murderer of its spirit, of its domestic and foreign renown, of its inventions, its finer morality and industriousness." Johann Gottfried Herder, "Haben wir noch das Publicum und Vaterland der Alten?" *Sämtliche Werke*, ed. Bernhard Suphan, 33 vols. (Berlin, 1877-1913), XVII, 287.

nation. The significance of this development has been summarized by von Groote: "Beyond the language, there are soon
found in the folk itself, which speaks this language, praiseworthy
characteristics. Be it in blame or in praise—one began to feel an
identity with the folk. With the leadership responsibility which
the new elite had taken over, it now self-consciously defended not
only its own group, but also the dignity of the entire folk."[12] Von
Halem himself certainly never came to a complete identification
with the people, and he did not even see very clearly the possibility that a people united by a language might carry, as a
national community, certain common traits which might add up
to a national character;[13] he was even further from suggesting
that the peasantry or the common people were really identical
with "the nation." But this was not a hard step to take. It was
prepared by the desire to find the German language in its most
natural and purest state—which suggested that one had best go
to those among whom foreign and unnatural influences had made
least progress, i.e., to the peasantry.

And so it indeed happened that the most immediate and
obvious expression of the interest in the origins and character
of the German language took shape as a fascination with the
Volkslied, the folksong. In the early years of awakening interest
in the folksong, Herder was again a figure of major importance.
His sympathy for the masses was deep and strong, and in it and
its customs and language he glimpsed the living embodiment of
the nation's history and the dynamo of its progress. Already in
his early twenties, he was impressed with the ability of the
common man to express himself clearly and to the point about
things with which he was familiar, and he praised the practical
common sense of the lower classes.[14] His interest in the *Volkslied*
was to a large extent sparked by his conviction that it provided
a sure path to the essence of the folk, a knowledge of it in its
completeness: "With mild forbearance," he wrote, "one thus sets
oneself back into the old times, down into the way of thinking of
the folk, lies, listens, perhaps smiles, rejoices with [them] or pon-

---

[12] von Groote, *Die Entstehung des Nationalbewusstseins*, 12.
[13] *Ibid.*, 13.
[14] Herder, "Über die neuere deutsche Litteratur: Dritte Sammlung, 1767.
1768," *Sämtliche Werke*, I, 387.

ders and learns."[15] The folksong, the peasants' own poetry, provided a most direct glimpse into the peasant mentality for, as Herder put it, the peasant's soul and his language were two sisters, raised together in society, used to one another, and absolutely inseparable.[16]

Herder had a definite idea of what constituted a real folksong: in 1772, he wrote that only those songs which were conceived and born in the midst of the folk itself possessed that great vitality and boldness which were the earmark of the true folksong.[17] And at the end of his life, nearly thirty years later, he still cautioned that it was wrong to attempt to improve on *Volkslieder,* for in so doing the heart was removed from the poetic method, "which actually should be all heart."[18] The further the mass of the people was from an artistic, scientific way of thinking, and from its language, the less its songs must be thought of as formal or "dead letter-verses," Herder wrote,[19] and in this indicated his sincere belief in the reality of popular life and thought as expressed in the simple folksong.

Herder himself published a collection of folksongs from various lands, the *Stimmen der Völker,* in 1778 and 1779; but even before this, other interested persons had begun to fill literary journals, of which there were a considerable number in Germany in the later eighteenth century, with individual folksongs, whether originally German or translations from other languages. The pages of such important journals as the *Göttinger Musenalmanach,* the *Hamburger Musenalmanach, Der teutsche Merkur,* and many others, began to reflect the heightened interest in the *Volkslied.* Some poets took it upon themselves to imitate both the forms and content of the folksong, with an almost uniform lack of success; but their attempts were indicative of the beginnings of a major reversal of interests among German literati. It was a long step from Gottsched's contempt for the common folk as the object

---

[15] Herder, "Von Ähnlichkeit der mittlern englischen und deutschen Dichtkunst," *ibid.,* IX, 530.

[16] Herder, "Über die neuere deutsche Litteratur: Dritte Sammlung, 1767. 1768," *ibid.,* I, 387.

[17] Herder, "Auszug aus einem Briefwechsel über Ossian und die Lieder alter Völker," *ibid.,* V, 186.

[18] Herder, "Adrastea," *ibid.,* XXIV, 264-65.

[19] Herder, "Auszug aus einem Briefwechsel über Ossian," *ibid.,* V, 164.

of literary attention[20] to Gottfried August Bürger's plea, a quarter-century later, that the poets and writers of his day begin writing for the whole people, and that "Apollo and his Muses" might come to earth and wander among all men, whether in palaces or in huts, in order to become acquainted with the entire folk.[21]

The years 1805-1808 saw the height of the folksong fever, for in these years the three volumes of *Des Knaben Wunderhorn*, edited by Achim von Arnim and Clemens Brentano, appeared and were received enthusiastically by the public. Von Arnim and Brentano were interested not only in the collection of songs taken from the mouth of the folk, but also in producing a useful book of songs for the whole German people; and more than any other work, this one was accepted as the most popular collection of *Volkslieder*. The materials included here were entirely German in origin, and later collections, such as *Die teutschen Volksbücher* (1807) and *Altteutsche Volks- und Meisterlieder* (1817) of Johann Joseph Görres, took their cue from this particularistic national interest rather than from the more cosmopolitan bent of Herder's compendium. Interest in the *Volkslied* in Germany abated but little in the years following the publication of *Des Knaben Wunderhorn*, and it was soon broadened into a more general interest in the folk as a storehouse of national history and legend. In addition to the famous fairy tales collected and published by Jakob and Wilhelm Grimm, the philological and ethnological researches of numerous German scholars focused a sympathetic attention on the masses of the common people; and an imposing body of literature grew out of this attention.[22]

In sum, the revivification of the idea of a German fatherland, still at this point seen largely in cultural terms, but with a firm principle of inclusion based on language, was of inestimable importance in the growth of a public opinion favorable to the peasant, and in the development of his public image. The search for a

---

[20] See above, pp. 29-30.
[21] G. A. Bürger, "Aus Daniel Wunderlichs Buche," *Sämmtliche Werke*, III, 170-71.
[22] See below, Chapter XII, for a more complete discussion of the appearance of the peasant in imaginative literature for the period 1770-1840.

distinctive German national character had been attended by the discovery of language as the key to the singularity of peoples. The common man, the peasant, benefited from this insight not only because he, speaking his national language, thus automatically became a part of the German nation as thus newly defined; but also—and perhaps more important—because it was he most of all who in his very existence guarded the purity of the language which separated the German from the non-German. It was not the peasant, after all, who in an attempt to be modish corrupted his speech, his natural language, with an admixture of foreign words and phrases, or who tried to adulterate his native language by Germanizing foreign words. And it was also not the peasant who corrupted his native customs, morals, habits, and beliefs—all of which were of course merely the behavioral side of his language —by the adoption of foreign practices out of a feeling of the inferiority of his own. Herder expressed the vital role which the common folk was now felt to play: "Indeed," he wrote, "it remains eternally and always, that if we have no folk, we have no public, no language and poetry which is ours, which lives and works in us."[23]

"Germanness" and "folkness" *(Deutschtum* and *Volkstum)* have begun to merge into one. In 1798, the famous young romantic poet Novalis expressed a confidence in the cultural progress of the Germans which he couched in these terms: "The German has long been the 'Little Hans.' But he might well soon become the Hans of all Hanses. It is with him as it is said to be with many dumb children: he will live and be wise when his precocious siblings have long mouldered, and he now alone is master in the household."[24] The most fascinating aspect of this quotation is that Novalis has spoken of the foreign contempt for the *German* in precisely the same terms commonly used by Germans to refer to the *peasant*. What has taken place in his mind is a conscious or unconscious identification of the German with the common man. This is not to say that Novalis or others like him had yet become admirers of all that the peasant was, but rather that a

[23] Herder, "Von Ähnlichkeit der mittlern englischen und deutschen Dichtkunst," *Sämtliche Werke,* IX, 529.
[24] Novalis [Friedrich von Hardenberg], "Blüthenstaub," *Athenaeum,* I (1798), 87.

feeling had been developed for an intimate connection, however ill-defined still, between the qualities of the "typical" peasant and those of the "typical" German just now coming into existence. This sentiment was still further reinforced by Novalis when he wrote that "The folk is an idea. We should become a folk. A complete man is a small folk. Genuine popularity [*Popularität*] is the highest goal of man."[25] The ideal German, as the ideal man, should be one who catches up within himself all that which his folk is—which is another way of saying that the ideal for the German lies nowhere but in the folk, and must be sought there.

It was this cultural nationalism, too, which provided the greatest impetus for the conquest of one of the biggest obstacles to the development of a really sympathetic public attitude towards the peasant. That obstacle was the all too obvious unfavorable side of the peasant—his general boorishness, lack of initiative, suspicion of things new, and so forth. Under the aegis of a rising national awareness, these qualities were simply converted from vices to virtues—with different names, of course. What made them virtues was not primarily any quality they possessed of beneficial effect, but rather their mere Germanness. Later, of course, it could be shown that they were intimately connected with observable evidences of German genius, but for the time being it sufficed to point out that, being German, they were good. It is thus in one sense meaningless to ask whether the picture of the peasant as it was here evolved was an accurate one or not; it was certainly a recognizable one, judging from descriptions of external actions and characteristics—but the meaning of these and the judgments passed on them were not inherent in the externals; they received their specific value from the broader picture into which the peasant and his qualities were fitted.

Vastly more important than the moral role suggested by the particular virtues spotted in the peasant by critics of one or another social evil as discussed above in chapter III was the new moral role of the peasant as *Volk* in the cultural-national awakening. He was far more than a passive example of right conduct to whom the degenerate elements of society might look for hints to improve their own living; he had become the great guarantor not

25 *Ibid.*, 83-84.

only of moral integrity but also of national identity: without him, there was no nation. Yet, typical of the period before the French Revolution or even the time of the Napoleonic conquest of Germany, the leading figures of this literary nationalism did not translate their feelings for the folk into any concrete reform proposals which went much beyond headshaking about the harsh realities of servitude. Herder, for example, while convinced that the real evaluation of human ability was greatly hindered by the concept of land as indivisible and servitude-ridden, also believed that society required men to exist in a number of vocations and professions.[26] He seemed to feel that social problems would not exist if people regarded their class as an "office," again suggesting the by-now familiar formula that all classes had equal public responsibilities, and that the knowledge of this equality should make class distinctions only functional ones.[27] However unimportant formal class distinctions may have been to him, however, he did not suggest their abolition. This common view, that the importance of the peasant or the folk, heightened though it now was, did not require any basically new social forms, was acceptable as long as the nation was not threatened by anything more serious than moral decay: this internal disease could presumably be cured by means of sermons and moral tracts using the new insights of nationality as a text. Whether these remedies would suffice when the nation was endangered by the conquest of a foreign enemy remained to be seen, however. In fact, the social and political implications of the new doctrines of nationality for the peasant, and the full meaning of those doctrines themselves, became obvious only through the confrontation of Germany with the French Revolution and its stepson, Napoleon.

[26] Herder, "Ideen zur Philosophie der Geschichte der Menschheit," *Sämtliche Werke*, XIV, 394-95; also, an undated, unaddressed letter, *ibid.*, XVIII, 331.
[27] Herder, "Gespräche" (No. 3 in *Aurora* [1799]), *ibid.*, XXIII, 15.

7 The Revolutionary Period to 1806

"If the folk feels itself really unhappy under a ruler and a state administration; if it has hope with an altered governmental constitution, and with another course of state affairs, to be happier or even less unhappy; if it even knows with conviction, that the subjects of other states live in a greater well-being under a state administration quite different from its own; then it will naturally lose confidence and love for its ruler, detest the previous leadership of state affairs, and await with longing opportunities to be able to bring about a revolution in the constitution of the state."[1]

With these words, Johann August Schlettwein in 1791 expressed the principle which was to dominate the German mind in its practical thinking about the peasant question for nearly two decades following the French Revolution of 1789. The world-shaking transformation which occurred in France was greeted with mixed emotions in Germany, running the scale from ecstatic joy in those who saw it as the inauguration of a new and higher stage of human existence, through the vaguer hopes and fears of those who could but dimly perceive its direction and significance, to the abject horror of those who saw in its revolutionary leadership the four horsemen of destruction of a time-honored constitution. But however different their judgments on the revolution may have been, literate and thoughtful Germans were agreed that it had introduced into political and social affairs in Germany an important series of factors of potentially explosive significance. It was not just that revolution was somehow by its very nature feared to be infectious, nor even that French ideas might by themselves incite Germans of the lower classes to attempt a revolution similar to that in France; it was also that Germans perceived, in many instances for the first time under the eye-opening influence of a major political catastrophe, that the conditions which contributed to the outbreak of revolution in France had their counterpart in Germany as well. And for all those who were opposed to revolution, whether because of a hatred of violence and a love of order, or because they were attached by strong ties of self-interest to the old order of things —and these categories embraced all but a real fringe element of the most radical thinkers—it came as a hair raising insight that the force of internal dissatisfactions did not always have to be dissipated in mere grumbling. Friedrich Carl von Moser might complain that the common man in Germany too often looked upon himself as a creature created to suffer and keep silent, comforting himself with the hope that when the present ruler died, his successor would be better, or being comforted by the priest with images of a pleasant afterlife;[2] but most members of the upper classes would more likely have agreed with Schlettwein, who pointed out that when people lived in misery, the contrast between their lot and their sweat, produced in toil, and the easy carelessness with which their taxes and dues were spent by the grandees of the country on luxuries and amusements resulted in an "indignation against this condition of things." Such a people, Schlettwein warned, "easily ventures to destroy with force and impetuosity those relationships which it regards as the causes of its miserable life."[3]

Such insights as these were not entirely speculative; they were also based upon actual observation of a heightened degree of agrarian unrest in some parts of Germany following the revolution in France. As early as 1790, a number of local uprisings in Saxony culminated in a particularly severe revolt in August of that year, and various evidences have been cited to indicate that in some instances the peasants involved in these disturbances were fairly well informed about revolutionary events in France through peasant newspapers and pamphlets.[4] Radical and violent peasant complaints appeared with some frequency throughout the 1790s, especially after the entrance of the German states into war with revolutionary France.[5] In 1793 and 1794, certain areas

---

[1] Johann August Schlettwein, *Die in den teutschen Reichsgesetzen bestimmte weise Ordnung der Gerechtigkeit wider Aufruhr und Empörung der Untertanen gegen ihre Obrigkeiten* (Leipzig, 1791), 72.

[2] Friedrich Carl von Moser, *Politische Wahrheiten*, 2 vols. (Zürich, 1796), I, 85.

[3] Schlettwein, *Die in den teutschen Reichsgesetzen bestimmte weise Ordnung*, 82-83.

[4] Percy Stulz and Alfred Opitz, *Volksbewegungen in Kursachsen zur Zeit der Französischen Revolution* (Berlin, 1956), *passim*.

of Prussia, especially Silesia, experienced agrarian unrest, some of which was suppressed only with military force and the application of severe penalties. The General Directory of the monarchy was in fact for a time terrorized by the prospect of a general peasant revolt.[6] Peasant uprisings were neither as numerous nor as severe as they were often imagined to be by terrified members of the upper classes; but under the tense and fearful conditions of the revolutionary epoch, only a little new unrest was required to give substance to some suspicions that general revolution was just around the corner.

It was from considerations and realities such as these that the example of the revolution came to be a powerful stimulus for the support of at least certain kinds of agrarian reform, even among landlords and others who had previously opposed reform schemes with vehemence. They recognized the truth of statements such as that of the Hanoverian and later Thuringian official Freiherr von Münchhausen, who warned in 1793 that there was in his time more than ever before reason to believe that a lack of regard for the peasant was not only dishonorable and contrary to self-interest, but also dangerously damaging to the constitution of the state.[7] Still more pointed, for those who remained unconvinced, was the analysis of Christian August Wichmann, whose lengthy book on the abolition of forced labor services was published in 1795, after the French had already occupied and annexed some sections of Germany west of the Rhine. The times called unequivocally for the removal of every cause of dissatisfaction among the common classes of the people, wrote Wichmann, since the French Revolution had everywhere awakened a great love of freedom. At all costs, the obstacles preventing the rapprochement of the almost totally alienated classes of powerful and humble, rich and poor, had to be removed. Violent revolutions, when undertaken by the common folk, were invariably the result of long, repeated, and incessant

[5] Heinrich Scheel, *Süddeutsche Jakobiner: Klassenkämpfe und republikanische Bestrebungen im deutschen Süden Ende des 18. Jahrhunderts* (Berlin, 1962), *passim.*

[6] Max Lehmann, "Das alte Preussen," *Historische Zeitschrift,* XC (1903), 414.

[7] Phillip Adolf Freiherr von Münchhausen, *Über Lehnherrn und Dienstmann* (Leipzig, 1793), 29.

oppression, and of a stubborn disregard for every request for reform. A state in which the different classes lived in discord, Wichmann warned, was particularly susceptible to social difficulties, especially when the government was not concerned to eliminate discord and rather wished to maintain discord for its own sake, i.e., for the government's own ends; in such a case, "the smallest spark . . . is sufficient to excite a rebellion and to kindle a fiery conflagration, which thereafter will not otherwise be extinguished than with the blood of thousands." Wichmann specifically admonished landlords that far-reaching agrarian reform was in their own interest, if only to prevent the occurrence of events such as those which had taken place in France.[8]

While the idea of agrarian reform itself thus received support from the immediate necessity of staving off a potential and much-feared revolution, not every kind of reform was approved by the majority of publicists. The theoretical economists, marching under Adam Smith's banner, tended to go their own way, advocating total peasant emancipation and proprietorship; but the more politically oriented publicists in general stopped far short of this ideal solution. This does not mean that no radical proposals were made by political publicists: one can find evidences of a desire to confiscate monastic lands, to force the partition of landlords' own domains, and, as with the fiery Johann Gottlieb Fichte, much talk of nature and reason, by which servitude or the ownership of one man by another of any kind was absolutely impossible.[9] But more important than any other particular reform in the emphasis it received in the writings of the period 1789-1806 was the abolition of peasant labor services. A vast amount of attention was paid to this question, and some very sophisticated and complex proposals were made for doing away with forced labor while at the same time granting compensation to landlords so that their domainal economy would not go to ruin.[10]

[8] Christian August Wichmann, *Über die natürlichsten Mittel, die Frohn-Dienste bey Kammer- und Ritter-Güthern ohne Nachtheil der Grundherren aufzuheben* (Leipzig, 1795), 3-4, 276, 280-81.

[9] Johann Gottlieb Fichte, "Zurückforderung der Denkfreiheit von den Fürsten Europens, die sie bisher unterdrückten" (1793), *Sämmtliche Werke* (Berlin, 1834-1846), VI, 11.

It is not difficult to establish the reasons for the preoccupation with this reform, sometimes to the virtual exclusion of all others. In the first place, there was a quite general feeling among those persons who were deeply concerned about the possibility of revolution in Germany that the necessity to perform labor services was a greater irritant to the peasantry than any other facet of the agrarian constitution which oppressed them. Wichmann, for example, was convinced that feudal services, of which forced labor was the most onerous, were directly responsible for the smoldering hatred of the oppressed for their oppressors; the peasant was no longer unaware that they were unjust and, receiving nothing for labors which he thought should be remunerated, often showed his indignation by stealing from the lord's garden or woods as "compensation."[11] Fichte, too, expressed the opinion that the slavishness which was so pernicious to the peasant arose from his being at the beck and call of the lord to perform services, and asserted that the elimination of services would cause complaints between lords and peasants to disappear and the dissatisfaction of the peasant with his class to lessen.[12]

Nor was it especially difficult to illustrate these opinions, to show the very real basis for the hatred of forced labor among peasants. What sorts of things did it entail? Freiherr von Münchhausen listed a series of services containing vicious contradictions of which the most stupid peasant could not have been unaware: 1) transportation of the fruits of an earlier harvest across the countryside while a present harvest rotted on the fields for lack of labor to gather it in; 2) the erection of elegant buildings for the lord while the peasant's own hut was falling to pieces; 3) the carrying of unimportant messages while the peasant's dying mother might be calling for him; 4) the necessity of traveling several miles with a team of horses to carry something for which

[10] Two of the most exhaustive treatments of this problem were Wichmann, *Über die natürlichsten Mittel,* already cited, and Karl Dietrich Hüllmann, *Historische und staatswissenschaftliche Untersuchungen über die Natural-Dienste der Gutsunterthanen, nach Fränkisch-Deutscher Verfassung; und die Verwandlung derselben in Geld-Dienste* (Berlin and Stettin, 1803). Also, of course, nearly every Smithian economist devoted lengthy passages in their works to the same question.

[11] Wichmann, *Über die natürlichsten Mittel,* 1-2, 159.

[12] Fichte, "Beitrag zur Berichtigung der Urtheile des Publicums über die französische Revolution" (1793), *Sämmtliche Werke,* VI, 232.

a single horse would suffice; 5) the necessity of traveling great distances to pay a few pennies in dues; 6) all-night guard duty at the lord's farm after a hard day's work; 7) the necessity of driving a team eight miles in order to take a few bushels of the lord's grain four miles further to the warehouse; and 8) the necessity of staying at the appointed place to perform services while the peasant's own house burned to the ground before his eyes. If these examples (exaggerated though they may have been as everyday occurrences) were not enough to bring tears of anger and disgust to the eyes of his readers, then surely no one could fail to be impressed with the stories of the physical mistreatment of peasants by lords or overseers during the time reserved for the lord's service, or by the terrifying picture Münchhausen painted of the psychological effects possible under a system in which a creditor might have to perform services for one of his debtors, or even—the final horror—a father for the seducer of his own daughter![13]

The abolition of labor services, even when its implementation called for generous compensation for the lords, could not be called a minor reform; from the peasant's standpoint, in any case, it would have made him a free man with respect at least to the allocation of his own time on his own farm. But it could not be called a really major reform either, because its realization would not have entailed any fundamental readjustments of the agrarian social constitution. If indeed this reform could satisfy a disgruntled and perhaps restless peasantry, then even some conservative elements would be willing to go along with it—at least for purposes of discussion—in the hope that such a timely measure would both prevent revolution and also make further and more basic reforms unnecessary.[14] Even among those who were convinced that more reforms should ultimately be instituted, there was enough pragmatism to welcome any step forward, and perhaps also enough uncertainty about the wisdom of radical reform

[13] von Münchhausen, *Über Lehnherrn und Dienstmann*, 23-24, 43, 45.

[14] This rationale is well illustrated by the Hessian Diet of 1797-1798, in which the Estates, at the prodding of the towns, petitioned the Landgrave for commutation of labor services on the grounds that "the subjects' dizzy ideas have grown everywhere and make them rebel against their masters." Carsten, *Princes and Parliaments*, 188.

in a revolutionary age to make them hesitate to wish any more change than this at this time.

But in general, the reaction to the agrarian problem among German conservative elements in the years following 1789 was a myopic one, which often did not even penetrate into reformism as far as the abolition of labor services. It was not untypical of the obtuse resistance to change of some of these groups that they should give support to proposals which called for the entirely voluntary renunciation of certain essentially unimportant privileges whose exercise tended to exacerbate peasant feelings. Thus an anonymous author wrote that peasants would not begrudge hunting privileges to any who did not misuse them, but that, on the other hand, anyone who possessed such privileges would wish to forgo all abuses if the welfare of the peasants was more important to him than a transitory pleasure—not because of the "voice of the people," but because his own feelings of justice and humanitarian benevolence required it.[15] Similarly, another individual developed the point of view that any right or privilege, whether originally usurped or not, must be regarded as sacred if it had been approved through tacit consent, treaty, or long tradition; as one of these, the hunting privilege could not be destroyed arbitrarily, but one might hope for a voluntary renunciation of it by the nobility or princes.[16]

In these views, there was a hidden assumption about the nature and causes of the agrarian problem. In effect, so this assumption had it, there had been a misunderstanding between peasants and lords, slight but none the less regrettable. Poor and ignorant peasants had been hoodwinked by revolutionary rabble-rousers into believing that the misdeeds of a few wicked landowners were typical of all, and thus had come to cherish hatred in their hearts against all noble lords. Still, it was not too late to make the essentially minor readjustments necessary to put things aright again. It was, first of all, possible to work on the peasant's understanding—to educate him as a counterweight to the pernicious doctrines of revolution, and to make

---

[15] "So machen unpatriotische Staatsdiener gute Fürsten verhasst," *Patriotisches Archiv für Deutschland: der Gottheit, den Fürsten, dem Vaterlande gewidmet,* II (Part 1) (1799), 13.   Hereafter cited as *Patriotisches Archiv* (Wagener).

[16] "Jagdgerechtigkeit," *ibid.,* I (Part 1) (1799), 240.

manifest to him the advantages of the society in which he lived. As Fritz Valjavec has pointed out, the late 1780s and 1790s witnessed the growth of several conservative groups in Germany, consisting mostly of officials, nobles, and intellectuals, who made a deliberate attempt to emphasize a kind of affinity between nobility and peasants; often strongly Pietistic, antiabsolutist, and antirevolutionary, their goal was that of winning over the peasant population to "the conscious preservation of religion and tradition." Valjavec further indicates that in some such circles, educational activity was a common expression of this concern, as may be seen especially in the development of a kind of "village pedagogics," which involved a propagandization of peasants against the Enlightenment and later also the revolution.[17]

Typically, it was sound moral and religious training for the peasant which was emphasized in these groups—all of which was supposed to inculcate brotherly love and an abhorrence of violence, together with strongly antimaterialist sentiments. As long as these things formed the subject matter of education, and not intellectual frivolities such as "natural rights" and "the spirit of the laws," popular instruction was to be recommended; for, as one writer put it, "A dumb middle-creature between man and beast brings the fatherland, for which it has no feeling, no magnanimous sacrifice, and by no means does, endures, and suffers what an educated man tolerates." This author then went on to admonish his contemporaries that no one should see in the revolution a reason to cease working for popular education; history, after all, was full of such events, where luxury, need, bad economy, and oppression had always dragged such bad results in their train.[18]

These educational proposals were to be implemented in a

---

[17] Valjavec, *Die Entstehung der politischen Strömungen*, 262-64. One of the most important such groups was the so-called "Emkendorf Circle" of Schleswig-Holstein, led by the nobleman Count Fritz Reventlow and his wife, Juliane Friederike. The poet Matthias Claudius was associated with this group, and brought to it not only his innate literary talents, but also his valuable experience as editor of the *Wandsbecker Bothe,* from 1771 to 1775, and later as one of the founders and contributors of a peasant newspaper, the *Hessendarmstädtische Landzeitung,* which for a time after its establishment in 1777 was widely read in its locality. Some of the specific directions taken by this conservative propaganda can be seen in various educational proposals such as those dealt with in Chapter IV.

[18] [Westenrieder, L.], "Ob man Bürger and Bauern aufklären soll?" *Beyträge zur vaterländischen Historie,* III (1790), 343-46, 346, note.

number of ways. One proposal for *Volksbücher* to be distributed to the people envisioned a work in two volumes, the first of which would comprise a series of catechisms for religion, health, patriotism, and sound reason, while the second would contain passages from the Bible, a hymnal, and a collection of prayers.[19] Other writings were much more pointedly directed towards the suppression of revolutionary sentiment. Such was the proposal for the writing of a frankly counterrevolutionary German history for the burgher and peasant, with stress to be laid on the horrors of anarchy of the Thirty Years' War and of the feudal wars, as well as upon the noble deeds of princes for the moral and economic well-being of their subjects.[20] Similarly, in 1793, the *Erfurter Gesellschaft oder Akademie gemeinnütziger Wissenschaften,* whose patron was the Elector of Mainz, set up a prize question for the best popular writing intended for the common folk, "whereby it may be taught of the goodness of its constitution and warned of the evils of immoderate freedom and equality."[21]

Any readjustment of lord-peasant relationships which might indeed be called for could, according to these views, he brought about without any of the evils attendant to revolutionary agitation. The Pietistic author Johann Heinrich Jung-Stilling, for example, gently reminded the peasant that the tenth and various other lord's dues were a part of his inheritance, and that he should not seek to avoid paying them in the name of the "rights of man." Every forcible measure which the peasants might use to ameliorate their governmental constitution would be much more horrible and more dangerous to the rights of man than the worst tyranny; "There is truly only one mild, peaceable, and beneficent way in which all abuses . . . can be abolished," Jung-Stilling concluded, "and this is very certainly general striving for moral perfection, refinement of oneself and avoidance of luxury; in a word: general and practical cultivation of the pure and true Christian religion."[22]

[19] "Zur Abhelfung eines dringenden Volksbedürfnisses," *Patriotisches Archiv* (Wagener), I (Part 1) (1799), 111-12.

[20] "Sehnsucht nach einem Geschichtsbuche für das Volk," *ibid.,* II (Part 2) (1799), 382-83.

[21] Flitner, *Die politische Erziehung,* 51-52.

[22] Heinrich Jung-Stilling, "Über den Revolutionsgeist unserer Zeit zur Belehrung der bürgerlichen Stände" (1793), *Sämmtliche Werke,* 12 vols. (Stuttgart, 1841-1842), XI, 582-84, 618-19.

This injunction to the true practice of Christianity was applicable to nobles as well as to peasants. And it speaks for the sincerity of conviction of at least some members of the conservative groups that they did not hesitate to chastise conscienceless nobles for their part in creating dissatisfactions among the peasantry. The poet Matthias Claudius turned out a number of poems on the theme of proper observance of religious social morality, and directed them equally to nobles and peasants; if nobles would take care to be "pious men and Christians," he suggested in one of them, then their peasants would be obedient and would not chatter so much about the rights of man.[23] It was entirely characteristic of the kindly but rather obtuse sentiments of these groups that they should believe that a greater attention to land and peasants on the part of the landowning nobility should be sufficient to abolish all agrarian problems; for surely once they became aware of the abuses which had arisen through their own lack of attention to their estates, they would take immediate steps to correct them. It was even suggested by one zealous defender of the nobility that the landlord more often deserved pity than censure, because his wicked officials and overseers robbed him of the devotion and love of the peasants who otherwise would gladly fulfill the obligations which traditionally had rested on their land.[24] This attempt to shift blame from the nobles to their subordinate officials may or may not have stemmed from sincere conviction (this clearly varied from one individual to another), but it was an important part of the campaign to convince the peasant that whoever might be the cause of his misfortune, it was certainly not the noble, who in the vast majority of cases was his friend and benefactor.

A classic example of the mixture of these themes was the drama *Der deutsche Hausvater,* written in 1790 by the Freiherr von Gemmingen. The chief character in the play was a count, a man who, as the name *Hausvater* suggests, was a model of kindness to his peasants, and who manifested a constant interest in their affairs. In one typical scene, an honest peasant complained

---

[23] Claudius, "Lied der Bauern zu—an ihre Gutsherrschaft," *Matthias Claudius Werke,* II, 65-66.

[24] Samuel Christian Wagener, "Wer sind die Beförderer gewaltsamer Staatsrevolutionen in Deutschland?" *Patriotisches Archiv* (Wagener), I (Part 1) (1799), 39-40.

to the count about mistreatment at the hands of the overseer. The count called in the accused official and, upon hearing from him that the peasant in question was simply a stubborn trouble-maker, commented that his experience taught him that when a peasant was obstinate, the fault usually lay with his superiors. He then informed the overseer that he would personally examine the peasant's complaints, and was assured by the official that it would be a great favor for him to do so. No, said the count, "Say duty. Is it not enough that the nobleman is nourished by the poor peasant's sweat? We must apply great effort in order to rectify even in slight measure what the nobility does in harm to the food-producing class, [and] consequently to the general condition."[25] Here were all the elements of an ideal agrarian relationship: honest peasants and thoughtful lords, working to-gether for each other's welfare in a mutually satisfactory arrange-ment, marred only by the singular wickedness of self-seeking subordinates—different creatures indeed from the model lord!

The implications of these attitudes and opinions was, of course, that agrarian Germany would be peaceful again under a return to conditions of the past, before revolutionary ideas had spread their poison, and before materialism and perhaps even atheism had closed men's minds to injunctions of Christian love and charity and had provided lords with the temptation to leave their lands in the hands of overseers while they spent their substance in riotous amusements. Yet for all this, the proposals of this and earlier decades for the abolition of servitude were seldom attacked directly by conservatives; they dwelt rather upon the manifold advantages which the peasant derived from the nexus between himself and the lord, or else tended merely to emphasize the dangers of a too-rapid emancipation—which usually boiled down to various sorts of excess and debauchery, stemming from the heady feelings of freedom which long-servile peasants would surely feel if freed too prematurely.[26] It is

[25] Otto Heinrich Freiherr von Gemmingen, *Der deutsche Hausvater: ein Schau-spiel* (Mannheim, 1790), 55.
[26] For example, Christoph Meiners, *Geschichte der Ungleichheit der Stände unter den vornehmsten Europäischen Völkern*, 2 vols. (Hannover, 1792), II, 625-29; also, Parhysius, "Über die mancherley Missgriffe derer, welche aus Reformationssucht überall stürmend zu Werke gehen," *Patriotisches Archiv* (Wagener), I (Part 2) (1799), 329-30.

interesting, however, and not without significance, that in addition to much talk about landlords' rights and the traditional order of agrarian relationships, the peasant and his welfare had here thrust themselves into the center of at least the public discussion of reform issues even among the most fainthearted of those who saw minimal reforms as necessary to prevent possible revolution in Germany. Johann Stephan Pütter, professor at Göttingen and the eighteenth century's most renowned expert on the German imperial constitution, was a marked conservative on the issue of agrarian reform, who regarded the dispute over servitude as something of a tempest in a teapot; he was convinced that misdeeds of landlords would inevitably produce their own evil results for them, and thus required no external correction. He even made the statement, which would be incredible from anyone who knew the reality rather than merely the theory of the imperial structure, that peasants *in extremis* could go before an imperial court to obtain judgment against a cruel landlord. But even the stuffy and archconservative Pütter felt perfectly comfortable in saying that "servant and serving-girl by nature and in relation to a higher being are not cattle but humans just as much as lord and lady," and in admonishing all landlords not to forget it.[27] It was, in other words, a major step forward that even for the conservatives the efficacy of this or that reform, and indeed the whole question of whether reform ought to take place, and how much, were now discussed not merely in terms of the advantage of the state, or in terms of the advantage of the landlord, or in terms of the more or less spurious legality of reform—but in terms of the concrete benefits to the peasant, seen as a human being.

The revolutionary period had the further remarkable effect of forcing the German nobility, which itself was almost nowhere under direct and active popular attack, into a defensive position —all of which had a certain favorable result for the peasantry. As late as the 1770s, reform writers were pleading on behalf of the peasant that every class, including the peasantry, had a useful social function, and were complaining about the prejudice

<hr>

[27] Johann Stephan Pütter, *Über den Unterschied der Stände, besonders des hohen und niedern Adels in Teutschland* (Göttingen, 1795), 27.

against the peasant everywhere in society. Now, as early as 1789, could be found an article in a leading journal entitled "Concerning the Noble Estate and its Present Oppression," in which the aristocratic author complained about the prejudice shown towards the nobility on every hand. "No class in the world," he pleaded, "is in itself despicable, or useless, if well-ordered states, through centuries, have had advantages from it."[28] And just as this writer justified the nobility by what he called its function as the shield of the people against the ruler, so another found it expedient to defend the integrity of the noble estates of one territory, Detmold-Lippe, in terms of a record of fifty years of uninterrupted concern for the welfare of the peasantry.[29] Here, then, was an attempt of the privileged classes to embrace the peasant, to identify with him and to claim a special concern for him: this attempt to identify was indicative of the enlistment of a new group of persons in the building of a new image of the peasant.

One of the new ways in which the peasant benefited from the search of conservative groups for allies among the peasantry was in the praise given him as a public-spirited defender of the fatherland. For the first time, because of the direct military threat of revolutionary France, stories began to appear in which the peasant, the common man, figured as a thoughtful individual whose public spirit was second to none. The necessity for proof of this point lay in the frequent avowal by nobles and other traditional public servants from the privileged classes that the peasant, by virtue of his parochial heritage and situation, could not conceive the notion of duty to anything higher than his own selfish interest. Quite typical of this view were the statements of Friedrich August Ludwig von der Marwitz, member of an ancient and honorable Prussian noble house, who as late as 1812 was stoutly maintaining that as long as the peasantry remained peasantry, it could not be possessed of insights and considered judgments, and that "if there are peasants anywhere who, beyond their work, can see the state, then they must be reckoned equal

---

28 "Über den Adelstand, und dessen jetzige Bedrückung," *Politisches Journal nebst Anzeige von gelehrten und andern Sachen* (December 1789), 1373.
29 "Detmold, 21 Jun. 1793," *Staats-Anzeigen*, XVIII (1793), 351.

to the nobility."[30] For Marwitz, this was merely another way of saying that peasants were, in fact, unable to see the state, or, for that matter, any abstract public concern at all. To counter such ideas as these, a story related in a leading conservative journal told of the adoption by poor peasants of children from a neghboring village whose parents, in consequence of a terrible fire, could no longer assume financial responsibility for them; the narrator specifically admonished his readers that this act of benevolence should serve as a lesson to those who attached the title of "crude rabble" to the peasantry.[31] In the same vein, a poem in a Berlin periodical praised the actions of a peasant serving-girl who gave her life to capture a rabid dog which threatened an entire community. The poet closed with a reminder that greatness of soul is not dependent on class, and that whereas the sight of heroic monuments might prepare the warrior for a hero's death, this peasant girl died solely to further human happiness, and her monument was but a pauper's grave.[32]

The significance of these proofs of the peasant's ability to think in terms wider than his own selfish interest appears rather clearly in a series of articles published in Samuel Christian Wagener's *Patriotisches Archiv* in 1799. In these, the peasant suddenly emerges as the most patriotic of Germans in his devotion and fidelity to prince, law, and fatherland. Here is a peasant in the duchy of Gotha who on his own initiative proposed to the duke that peasants be armed to keep the marauding French out of the country, and who combated radical French propaganda in speeches before his fellow peasants, denouncing a "seducer of the people" in the area, and declaring that it was un-Christian and a disturbance of the peace to suggest, even in jest, the deposition of the reigning prince.[33] The story was told of a peasant in Westphalia who struck down a publican after the

<hr>

[30] Friedrich August Ludwig von der Marwitz, "Von den Ursachen des Verfalls des preussischen Staates" (1812), *Friedrich August Ludwig von der Marwitz: ein märkischer Edelmann im Zeitalter der Befreiungskriege*, ed. Friedrich Meusel, 2 vols. in 3 (Berlin, 1908-1913), II (Part 2), 61, note 2.

[31] Wagener, "Lüderlin der Edle und seine Bauern," *Patriotisches Archiv* (Wagener), I (Part 2) (1799), 413-15.

[32] von Köpken, "Seelengrösse einer Bauermagd," *Berlinische Monatsschrift*, XXV (January-June 1795), 52-53.

[33] Wagener, "J. E. Lange zu Bienstädt," *Patriotisches Archiv* (Wagener), I (Part 2) (1799), 417-20.

latter had jokingly declared that, since the French were coming, the peasant might no longer have to deliver his grain quota to the royal warehouse. The peasant, it was said, proudly announced that the blow had been struck for his prince.[34] These incidents provided proof to the editor of the periodical that peasants were by no means as inclined to support rebellion as they were sometimes thought to be; rather, they tended to give full credit to their vague sense of law and duty and of the high value of peace and order. Where peasant communities did occasionally act contrary to law, one might normally assume that gross injustice on the part of judges and superiors was responsible. The editor realized that a few stories of this nature were hardly sufficient to illustrate the loyalty of the peasant, but he requested his coworkers and also village preachers to submit to the journal further evidence of the peasants' "pure love of fatherland."

There was some basis in fact, furthermore, for the repeated assertion that the peasant was prepared to defend his country in time of crisis. French invasions of southern and southwestern Germany after 1795 had in some instances been met by spontaneous and stubborn local resistance of varying strength. Usually this occurred as protest against French marauders who, in the absence of supplies from military bases in France, seized crops and livestock as they moved through Germany. Whatever their motives, however, the peasants who resisted the French—often in guerrilla-type actions—were given credit for aiding the cause of the German states. A particularly interesting perspective on the association of the peasantry with defense of the fatherland is provided by a letter of Archduke Karl of Austria to the French General Jourdan, written in 1796; the French commander was informed that his strong measures against captured German peasant guerrillas, including summary executions and the punitive burning of entire villages, must forthwith cease, or else French National Guardsmen captured by the Austrians would be similarly dealt with. The peasants, asserted the Archduke, constituted the German National Guard, and had every right to defend their persons and property.[35]

[34] Wagener, "Der Westphälische Bauer Spönemann," *ibid.*, I (Part 1) (1799), 152-54.
[35] Scheel, *Süddeutsche Jakobiner,* 276.

(It must be admitted, however, that the spectacle of armed peasants was not a cause of universal rejoicing in Germany. There existed a general uneasiness in many circles that peasant uprisings against the French were at best a mixed blessing. An article in R. Z. Becker's *Nationalzeitung der Teutschen* of September 22, 1796, called peasant resistance to the French an "unhappy result" of the war, warned of French revenge, and concluded that the worst effect on the state lay in the feeling of power and arbitrariness awakened in the peasant, who could kill and despoil the French without fear of punishment.[36] Similarly, C. U. D. von Eggers, editor of the Hamburg *Deutsches Magazin,* expressed the fear that the "uneducated mob" under these conditions might not only develop a permanent taste for war, and become lazy, but also begin to acquire a sense of its own strength against traditional authority. Eggers called on the princes and leaders of the nation to obtain peace as soon as possible, "in order that every German peasant may peacefully return home to his plow, [and] the sooner the better."[37])

But it was under these critical circumstances, in any case, that the peasant was for the first time admitted to the role of an active member of his society. The importance of the peasant to society had already been established in a number of ways before this time: he produced the nourishment for all classes, he was the primary producer on whose efforts the entire economy depended, and, according to the more recent nationalistic insights, he was the cultural core or nucleus of the nation itself. But all of these were essentially passive attributes: they had little to do with conscious and deliberate participation in the active affairs of the country. There was a basis in these for the peasant as a defender of the fatherland—the natural attachment to the earth and soil of the place where a man was born, found his first nourishment, and developed his abilities, as one writer put it[38]—but the actual manifestation of the peasant as the unyielding backbone of the nation could not be perceived clearly until the nation was threat-

[36] *Ibid.,* 277.

[37] C. U. D. von Eggers, "Ist es gut, dass sich die Bauern in Deutschland bewafnen?" *Deutsches Magazin,* XII (July-December 1796), 717-20.

[38] Parisius, "Wie wird wahre Vaterlandsliebe in dem Menschen geweckt und erhalten?" *Patriotisches Archiv* (Wagener), I (Part I) (1799), 44.

ened from without. Here was at least part of a foundation for real citizenship: the assumption of common interests and common efforts in defense of those interests suggested the beginnings of a kind of equality which could no longer adequately be contained within traditional social categories establishing distinctions in the right of persons to take part in the public business of the nation.

Certainly the full force of this conclusion was not perceived by the conservatives, who sought merely to bridge an immediately dangerous situation by emphasizing the close connections of peasant to fatherland, in order to propagandize the common man into an antirevolutionary stance. Insofar as they drew any practical injunctions to action from the assumption that the noble and the peasant were bound together by common interests, it was that the nobility should shore up its lagging attention to the interests of its peasants—that it should, in other words, increase its benevolent patronization of the peasant. And there was little doubt in these circles that nobles could and would reform themselves in this sense to the extent necessary to lay at rest all serious problems relating to the agrarian social constitution.

This attitude was not reflected among all German publicists, however. With the revolutionary epoch came the beginnings of a really serious critique of the German nobility, which no longer restricted itself to essentially moral criticisms of aristocratic debauchery and irresponsibility, but which began to dig at the very roots of the special social position occupied by the nobility. With regard to the relationship of noble to peasant, this critique first cropped up as a questioning of the assumption that the nobility, left to itself, either could or would institute reforms sufficient to alleviate the supposedly inflamed conscience of the oppressed peasantry. Freiherr von Münchhausen spoke for a number of thoughtful critics on this point. He admitted that nobles were occasionally successful in winning the confidence of their peasants through reforms, but pointed out that voluntary reform of this kind always lay in the hands of men whose opinions were, after all, changeable; that good intentions were easily and all too often forgotten; and, most important, that the goal of reform left entirely in the hands of the noble proprietor could at most be only the amelioration of the old, worthless constitution, never its abolition.[39]

Involved in the attempted identification of noble and peasant interests was the tacit assumption that the nobility would continue to represent the peasants' interest as its own in all political questions. Johann Stephan Pütter was merely making explicit the almost unquestioned tradition of "virtual representation" of the peasant by the noble when he showed himself very cool to proposals for peasant representation in legislative assemblies, and declared that the welfare of both country and peasantry was better looked after when peasants were represented by princes and lords, as long as the latter remembered that their interest was inseparable from that of the peasants.[40] But this point of view came under increasing attack, in which the facts of history were used to demonstrate, among other things, that where in the past the nobility had been strong, and able to assert its influence politically, the peasantry was always weak and oppressed. Also given historical sanction was the fact that a lack of peasant representation in the estates had resulted in laws and actions prejudicial to the peasant, passed into force by a nobility which in fact, if not in theory, apparently had no difficulty in locating and adjusting to its advantage questions in which the interests of peasants and aristocrats differed, and in fundamental ways.[41] August Ludwig Schlözer was rabid on the subject of the patronization of peasants by nobles, and in one particularly wrathful article declared that the nobility looked after its peasants in general exactly as it would for its horses, cows, and other farm animals—and no more.[42]

What Schlözer was pointing out, with considerable justification, was the fact that all the pragmatic reforms in the world would not change the actual and apparently deeply inculcated contempt with which the nobleman looked at the peasant and treated his affairs. In one instance, Schlözer printed the comments

---

[39] von Münchhausen, *Über Lehnherrn und Dienstmann*, 20.

[40] Pütter, *Über den Unterschied*, 25.

[41] These views are contained in Michael Ignaz Schmidt, *Geschichte der Deutschen*, 22 vols. (Ulm, 1785-1808), III, 193, and IV, 596-97.

[42] "Detmold, 3 Sept. 1793," *Staats-Anzeigen*, XVIII (1793), 466, note 1.

of one of his readers on the statement of a certain Hungarian nobleman who had written that peasants were determined by nature to be peasants just as he himself was determined by nature to be a nobleman; Schlözer's reader warned that in this absurd belief the nobleman was just as simple-minded and in as much danger as the stupid child who teased and mistreated a dog until he was torn to pieces by it.[43] On still another occasion, Schlözer himself warned the "lords-landowners" that in their references to the peasant they had best stop using traditional and obviously inhuman expressions which emphasized his servitude, and would find it more proper now to speak of peasants as "fellow citizens" or "fellow subjects."[44] All these comments were in effect wedges pounded into the crack separating nobles from peasants which the conservatives were doing their best to plaster over, if only by verbal argument: for when, as an example, the notion of peasants representing their own political interests in Diets ever got as far as serious legislative discussion, it was usually voted down with little ado.[45]

Gradually, therefore, the right of the nobility to make itself the mouthpiece for the peasantry was broached. It was in this period still raised in a somewhat indirect fashion, for the most part, except for a few radical publicists, and was in many ways a rather academic argument.[46] But it was characteristic of the slowly growing utilitarianism of political thought that the nobility should be asked to defend its privileged position in terms of function. It was brought out by more than one author of this time that the original distinction which gave the nobleman his feudal rights of tenure was based on his performance of military services as a public responsibility. Since he no longer devoted his life to the personal fulfillment of this responsibility, but rather discharged it by grants of money to the sovereign, voted through the Diet of the estates, and since it was the peasant who paid

[43] "Anzeige von einer in Ungern handschriftlich umlaufenden AufrursSchrift," *ibid.*, XVI (1791), 371-72.

[44] "Detmold, 21 Jun. 1793," *ibid.*, XVIII (1793), 351 and note (a).

[45] As in the Hessian Diet of 1797-1798, for example, where the delegates from the towns actually proposed peasant representation. The proposal was voted down by the nobles and did not even come before the Landgrave. Carsten, *Princes and Parliaments*, 188.

[46] On the question of peasant representation, see also above, pp. 88-90.

the nobleman the money he voted and who also did the actual fighting, why should the nobleman continue to enjoy feudal rights over the peasant? This argument, along with many similarly historical ones, cropped up with increasing frequency in the decade following the events of 1789;[47] but it was not common for them to be used as part of a scheme for the abolition of the aristocracy. Much more usual was the use to which they were put by an advocate of reform such as Karl Dietrich Hüllmann, who mentioned them as a reason for lords to approve the abolition of labor services against compensation, before the public authority (the sovereign), tiring of their resistance, abolished them without remuneration.[48]

The actual course of military and political events in Germany before the great Napoleonic campaigns of 1806-1807 was not, in fact, sufficiently alarming to create a really serious questioning of the fact of noble privilege and its utility in the state and society. Not until the collapse of an old and venerable regime in Prussia before the onslaught of French armies could fundamental criticisms of the old society win numerous and influential supporters. Still, there was a kind of prophetic suggestiveness in the tendency of a number of writers in the 1790s to toy with new definitions of "nobility." Christian August Wichmann, for example, declared himself opposed to a nobility of birth, and advocated the introduction of a nobility of service open to all citizens of the state;[49] and even a conservative journal printed an article by a man who wished for a new meaning for the word "nobility" whose application would be restricted to those who were "wiser and better, more understanding and nobler" than others, and who "stand out in true wisdom and morality above ordinary men."[50] As much as any other statements of this period, these references to a "new nobility" represent the application of outdated but not yet outlived language of an old social order to express a concept belonging to a new order: a civic recognition, not a social distinction, based on merit only, one which was open to all who performed

47 See below, Chapter X.
48 Hüllmann, *Historische und Staatswissenschaftliche Untersuchungen*, 142-45.
49 Wichmann, *Über die natürlichsten Mittel*, 291-366.
50 G. A. L. Hanstein, "Über die Gewalt patriotischer Beispiele," *Patriotisches Archiv* (Wagener), I (Part 1) (1799), 69.

signal services for the fatherland or for humanity; and this was an important basis for a political redefinition of citizenship. Johann Heinrich Jung-Stilling in his rambling novel *The Gray Man* showed something of the direction which this discussion of a "new nobility" could take when he singled out the peasant class as containing many noble members, indicated that the greatest part of the nobility in God's realm consisted of middle class and peasants, and then went on to emphasize that the nation was actually made up of its burghers and peasants, who were the best Christians and remained firm and solid while the upper classes sopped in luxury and comfort.[51] For Jung-Stilling, the "noble" man was quite obviously the ideal citizen who constituted the nation—and it was for him precisely the commoner, especially the peasant, who possessed in fullest measure the characteristics of this nobility.

The revolutionary period, in sum, intensified the attention focused on the peasant by the German upper classes. Not only did it lend renewed hope for basic agrarian reforms to radical publicists who had damned the oppressiveness of the agrarian constitution for some time already, but it also provided a clear reason for reform to some conservative groups which had previously been loath to admit their necessity. But among both moderates and conservatives, it had the perhaps even more significant effect of raising up an image of the peasant as the defender of the fatherland. Now, "fatherland" was grasped somewhat differently by each group: sometimes it was the new and as yet ill-defined nationalist impulse which came to the fore, and at other times—especially with the conservatives—it was the old regime of territorial constitutions and a feudal social order which was meant. But however it was conceived, the proportions of the presumed internal threat of revolution and the quite well recognized external menace of foreign invasion caused a new concern to win the allegiance of the peasant to this variously understood fatherland. In the course of the attempt to do this, a picture of the peasantry as the great line of defense against foreign domination was

51 J. H. Jung-Stilling, "Der graue Mann," *Sämmtliche Werke*, VII, 65-66, 112.

created by those who hoped it was true and accurate. In so doing, they merged their ideas with other streams of thought, already discussed in earlier chapters, which were finding a new importance in the peasant; suffice it to recall that it was the 1790s which witnessed the hitherto most direct associations of the peasant with the German national character. Certainly these associations themselves gained much from the fact that the threats to Germany during the revolutionary period were after all also French threats. There can be little question but that the growth of sentiment favorable to the peasant was reinforced among the conservatives by their attempt to embrace the peasant for their cause; it helped not only to create a certain willingness to reform on the part of landlords, but also to provide virtually the first occasion for a really new look at the peasant (if for the most part only a fearful one) by his noble lord.

At the same time, however, liberal and moderate groups had taken a long step towards the realization of the social implications of the increasing identification of peasant with "nation." Their slaps at the nobility, cautious and academic though many of them may have been, and for the most part certainly not revolutionary in intent, were extremely important in casting doubt on the traditional claims of the aristocracy to represent the peasant in all public business. The sharpest kind of difference was sketched out between the respective roles of noble and peasant in society. It was the peasant, not the noble, who possessed the morality and performed the social functions which were truly "noble" according to the new definitions now put forward; it was the peasant, not the noble, who was the nation. It was not far from here to the suggestion that the peasant who fed the fatherland, who guaranteed its national identity, who kept its moral fiber strong, and who was now also said to be its surest hope against internal revolution and foreign invasion, should be allowed to receive the common benefits of the society to which he contributed so much, and more important, that he be given the freedom or the opportunity to utilize to the fullest possible extent for himself and for society all of those insights and personal characteristics for which he was praised. This meant nothing more or less than that he should be freed from the political and social tutelage of the state and of the nobility to which he had so long been subject. It meant, ultimately, conferral of the status of citizen.

The growing realization of this fundamental fact in publicistic circles in Germany found some echo in the ranks of responsible and influential governmental figures in various states even before the end of the century. But the occasion for the implementation of reforms embodying the conferral of a citizenship upon the peasant did not come with the still uncertain conditions imposed by the ferment and change of the revolutionary period. It required the shock and finality of a national collapse to thrust it to the fore; this came to Prussia and, through Prussia, to much of Germany with the catastrophes of Jena and Auerstädt.

8 Prussian Collapse and National Regeneration

The defeat of Prussian armies at Jena and Auerstädt and the subsequent occupation and partition of the kingdom by Napoleon's armies were events much too serious and shocking to be explained away as mere military failures on the part of an army which had lamentably deteriorated since the great days of Frederick II. Not that there would have been no truth in such a charge: the military organization was certainly not the high-spirited and well-disciplined creature it had once been. But a torpor, a strange lassitude, had settled over all of Prussia in the twenty years since the death of the great Frederick, and this was manifest in the almost mechanical way in which the defeat was received and announced by the bureaucracy, and in the fatalistic and virtually paralytic reaction of much of the Prussian upper classes to the catastrophe.

Yet among a certain section of the bureaucracy and the governing classes of Prussia, the victory of Napoleon called forth a deep and serious self-examination, which in some cases was in fact merely a sudden intensification or refocusing of doubts and questions about the nature of Prussian society and government which had existed among a few largely younger officials and administrators in the Prussian government since the accession of Frederick William III in 1797. Whatever its origins, however, the criticism of state and society which appeared in the years immediately following the Prussian defeat was responsible for bringing together for the first time in a practical context all of the various strands of thought which had developed in previous decades concerning the role and importance of the peasant in society, and for creating out of them the very picture of the citizen which was to activate the reforms of Stein and Hardenberg and which was to find its vindication in the Wars of Liberation beginning in 1813.

When Johann Gottlieb Fichte in his famous *Reden an die deutsche Nation* in 1808 thundered to the upper or educated classes of Germany that now, for the first time in history, they were given the opportunity and the responsibility for pushing the German nation forward,[1] it was as yet by no means certain that they would in fact be adequate to this challenge. Indeed, to judge from the publicistics of the time, one of the most commonly offered answers to the question of why Prussia had failed to measure up to the demands of this epoch was precisely that her upper classes had failed her at a decisive moment—or, rather, in a decisive age. This was formulated in a number of ways, some less harsh than others, but it was nowhere more flatly stated than by Paul Ferdinand Friedrich Buchholz, an early herald of the French Revolution in Germany and a liberal writer throughout the first two decades of the new century. Almost before the last shot of the Franco-Prussian battles of 1806 had been fired, Buchholz went to press with an analysis of Prussian society and an indictment of its shortcomings, the tone of which was set early in the work by his statement that a continuation of the pre-1806 social order after the return of the government from Königsberg was impossible.[2] Buchholz' point of view was that the court was in effect a captive of the nobility, and that the nobility in its turn was not concerned about the welfare of the country as a whole, but only about its own. This became clear in a later work, when he carefully distinguished between "nobility" and "feudal nobility" in a sense already made familiar by other writers.[3] The former was different from the latter chiefly in that it consisted of persons whose own interest was the same as that of society as a whole, or who were not hindered by some special interest from developing the highest degree of variety in their ideas. The "feudal nobility," on the other hand, had at one time had a very real and useful function in a society totally restricted to agricultural pursuits; but the principles which guided its action—and also oppressed the peasantry—in that society could no longer be considered valid.[4]

Buchholz' arguments on the nobility received a great deal of

---

[1] J. G. Fichte, "Reden an die deutsche Nation" (1808), *Sämmtliche Werke*, VII, 278.

[2] Paul Ferdinand Friedrich Buchholz, *Gemählde des gesellschaftlichen Zustandes im Königreiche Preussen, bis zum 14ten Oktober des Jahres 1806*, 2 vols. (Berlin and Leipzig, 1808), I, v.

[3] See above, pp. 163-64.

[4] Paul Ferdinand Friedrich Buchholz, *Hermes oder über die Natur der Gesellschaft mit Blicken in die Zukunft* (Tübingen, 1810), 110-11.

support from the Prussian official Friedrich von Coelln, who in his anonymously published periodical *Neue Feuerbrände* took an extremely critical stance towards the unreformed Prussia of 1806. Von Coelln pointed out that the nobility no longer went to war nor yet paid any taxes as a substitute for doing so, but left both to the poor peasant. "Long enough," he warned, "have the small farms had to pay for the large, long enough has the nobility enjoyed the advantages of its class, without fulfilling its noble responsibilities like its brave ancestors. The world is now enlightened, and the third estate educated enough to work with force towards an equal distribution of taxes."[5] Similarly, with an ill-concealed contempt which laid the causes of Prussia's disaster right on the doorstep of the aristocracy, von Coelln declared that the contemporary spirit and soul of the nobility consisted in contributing nothing and enjoying everything; and while the small peasant worked his fingers to the bone, "not a thing stirred" on the great estates. Could one call this situation "state, order, and righteousness," he asked, and still be in doubt as to the source of the public misfortune?[6]

The key to the problem Prussia faced was not in its innermost kernel only a political one, much less a military one; it was also a moral problem, and it required also a moral solution. This, at least, was the perception of the most thoughtful reformers, who found the contrast between French enthusiasm and Prussian indifference profoundly disturbing. What was lacking in Prussia, in particular, was *Gemeingeist,* or public spirit, in the true sense of the term: a losing of oneself (or perhaps rather a finding or identification of oneself) in the whole of society, implying self-denial, a spirit of sacrifice for one's fellows and nation. The characteristic of nobility (and even, to a much lesser extent, of the middle class) which was condemned again and again in the writings of the early reform period in Prussia was the inability to see beyond immediate class interest. The nobility was lost in the petty toils of a struggle to protect its privilege and a now-

[5] "Ist es wahr, dass in dem Lande, in welchem vorzüglich das landwirthschaftliche Gewerbe getrieben wird, jede Art von Abgaben die Grundeigenthümer treffe?" *Neue Feuerbrände,* I (Erstes Heft), 31, 33.

[6] "Über Gerechtigkeit, Freiheit, Feudale etc. nach S.—Eine Apologie unsrer Tage," *ibid.,* VI (Sechszehntes Heft), 87.

meaningless honor, while the middle classes were, as usual, too preoccupied with the rattle of the cashbox to hear the rumblings of the destruction of their country.

In this context of disillusionment with the traditional leadership classes, it was the *Volk*, the masses of the people, to whom worried reformers turned for the hope of a patriotic German regeneration. With the memory of defeat still strong in his mind, one German wrote to Friedrich Gentz as follows: "From the depths I await our salvation; from the heights, unfortunately! no longer. I still count on Germany, [but] on no single state of the common fatherland. What has been dissolved and separated through raw force or faithless cunning will be bound together again and united in the depths of the folk character according to the laws of a higher elective relationship *(Wahlverwandtschaft)*."[7] The upper classes of Prussian society possessed only egoism, wrote another observer, and egoism was the very opposite of that self-sacrifice which was the most necessary ingredient of patriotism; true national spirit would be found most readily in the lower classes.[8]

In view of the military reorganization which in 1813 was to give a semipopular character to the Prussian army through the twin devices of the *Landwehr* and the *Landsturm*, it is interesting to note the rapidity with which some of the later members and associates of the Military Reorganization Committee grasped the idea of the *Volk* as a revitalizing force in military and other public concerns. It was not the Prussian collapse which first brought attention to the necessity for the expansion of the size of the army: such ideas had been in the air since the first revolutionary *levée en masse* in France had presented European military commanders with the prospect of the huge "citizen army" which would somehow have to be met out of the manpower resources of their own states.[9] But the rout of Prussia's "professional army" in 1806-1807 became the occasion for much more purposeful

[7] Letter of Gustav von Brinkmann to Friedrich Gentz, dated in Memel, November 12, 1807, in *Die Franzosenzeit in deutschen Landen, 1806-1815: in Wort und Bild der Mitlebenden,* ed. Friedrich Schulze, 2 vols. (Leipzig, 1908), I, 158.

[8] "Unser Adel," *Neue Feuerbrände,* III (Achtes Heft), 31.

[9] A brief discussion of proposals for military reform in Prussia before 1806 is contained in William O. Shanahan, *Prussian Military Reforms, 1786-1813* (New York, 1945), Chapter 3.

reflection among Prussian liberal military reformers as they pondered the causes of French success.

August Neithardt von Gneisenau, a member of the Reorganization Committee and an early advocate of popular insurrection against French occupation armies, indicated in an essay of 1807 that France's greatness under Napoleon stemmed essentially from the awakening of all national and popular forces in the revolution, and through the opportunity given these forces to develop themselves fully. "What infinite forces sleep in the lap of a nation, undeveloped and unused!" he wrote; "in the breasts of thousands and thousands of men there lives a great genius, whose aspiring wings are crippled by its abased relationships. While an empire perishes in its weakness and disgrace, perhaps a Caesar is following his plow in his most wretched village, and an Epaminondas is living scantily off the income of the work of his hands." Why, asked Genisenau, did the German courts not make use of this genius—wherever and in whatever class or estate of the people they might find it? "Why did they not choose this means to multiply their forces a thousandfold, and open to the ordinary citizen the portals of triumph through which only the nobility is now supposed to go?"[10] Gneisenau, for his part, would have facilitated not only the participation of the common man in public affairs through the creation of a citizen army, as opposed to the purely professional standing army, but also the willingness of the peasant to participate by freeing those peasants who fought to the end for independence of all services which might attach to their lands and tenures.[11]

The interest in the common man which appears so strongly in Gneisenau's statements was echoed by many others, including Carl von Clausewitz, pupil and adjutant of the great General Scharnhorst and a participant in the drafting of the military

[10] Cited from an unnamed essay of August Neithardt von Gneisenau of 1807, in *Die Franzosenzeit in deutschen Landen*, I, 158-59. The rather complex development of Gneisenau's views is well summed up for the English reader in Eugene N. Anderson, *Nationalism and the Cultural Crisis in Prussia, 1806-1815* (New York, 1939), Chapter 3.

[11] A. W. A. Neithardt von Gneisenau, "Denkschrift" (1808), *Denkschriften zum Volksaufstand von 1808 und 1811* (Berlin, 1936), 15; also, "Auszug aus der Konstitution für die allgemeine Waffenerhebung des nördlichen Deutschlands gegen Frankreich" (1808), *ibid.*, 18.

reform work. After the Prussian defeat, Clausewitz became quite interested in comparisons between the French and German national spirit or national character; this interest was evoked largely in consequence of the Franco-German confrontations of recent years and the final subjection of Germany by Napoleon. What is particularly striking about Clausewitz' thoughts in this matter is not so much his conclusion that the German was superior to the Frenchman, but the fact that it was the common man, and specifically the peasant, who emerged as the basis of the comparison of the two peoples. Clausewitz explained this partly by the fact that the criterion of *haute culture*, by which the French had once asserted their superiority to the Germans, was no longer applicable, since the remarkable growth of German literary culture in the later eighteenth century had placed the two peoples on an equal footing in that respect. But it was at the level of the common man that comparisons should be undertaken in the first place—for it is there, said Clausewitz, that the "raw original material" *(der rohe Urstoff)* of a nation is most clearly manifested, and at this level it could be seen that the German common man was superior to his French counterpart.[12]

The chief characteristics of the French spirit were closely tied to a kind of national urban orientation, in Clausewitz' mind, and these contrasted sharply with the elements of the German national spirit, which were closer to the land, to agriculture. And in explaining the superiority of the German to the Frenchman, Clausewitz cited Adam Smith to the effect that if it were indeed true that the occupation of the lower classes was actually also its education, then the peasant would have to be placed on a higher level of intelligence than the city dweller. "His business is a great whole of diverse changes; a continual activity of his power of judgment is necessary, [and] a certain freedom of procedure is possible," wrote Clausewitz of the peasant; "it is otherwise with the city man, whose whole life and business often consists in the eternal repetition of a skilled movement of his hand."[13] Again in the moment of crisis and defeat, then, there

---

[12] Carl von Clausewitz, "Aus dem Reisejournal von 1807," *Politische Schriften und Briefe* (Munich, 1922), 25-28.

[13] von Clausewitz, "Bekenntnisdenkschrift" (1812), *ibid.*, 111.

was a search for the original essence of a national power which could assert itself against a foreign foe and reestablish the integrity of the German nation. Gneisenau and Clausewitz demonstrate for this period and for an important group of military theorists how the common man was evoked in an active role as the potential saviour of the fatherland, how he was placed in a role as the symbol of Germanness, and, just as important, how "common man" was specifically interpreted as "peasant."

This German peasant as the hope of a national reawakening of course required the noble qualities commensurate with his function. A variety of such qualities were quick to be developed. Close connections were drawn between the ability to love one's country and the ability to love and honor God; between patriotism and piety. Both were outward-looking and unselfish, and depended upon the steady cultivation of virtue. When an article in *Neue Feuerbrände* compared the life of city folk with that of peasants, it was pointed out that "whoever lives most naturally is the most pious, [and] that the peasant does, and after him the smalltown dweller"; the city man had more needs, real or imagined, than the rural inhabitant, and the satisfaction of these led him from the path of righteousness; only he who had few needs could be virtuous, the author of this piece concluded, and the city man could always find an opportunity to sin if he were so inclined.[14] The same could no doubt be said of the nobles, who again possessed in plenty the material temptations to sin.

If patriotism presupposed virtue, of which the peasant had more than anyone else, it was also a completely natural outgrowth of his life on the land. Buchholz made this point by comparing field husbandry to the pastoral life: the former, he said, brings man for the first time to a recognition of himself as a moral being, because it could prosper only through the making of agreements and contracts which had to be observed. Agriculture was therefore the foundation, the original *raison d'être* of legislation, and automatically instilled a sense of patriotism for the state which guaranteed that legislation. The longer a man had a fixed place of dwelling, the dearer it must become to him—not

[14] "Relationen aus Berlin, vom 16ten Juny 1807," *Neue Feuerbrände*, III (Achtes Heft), 33-34.

because of sheer force of habit, but because the man, as an active being possessing freedom, becomes a creator through agriculture and through his creations for the first time sees himself in perspective as a man.[15] In the course of his analysis of the causes of the Prussian collapse, Buchholz had thus gone back to the beginnings of society itself. He found the origin of all institutions of state in agriculture and in the necessity for fostering and preserving its contributions.

In this opinion, Buchholz was far from alone. Speculation about the origins and nature of government and of society was one aspect of the political thought called into being by the events of the reform period, and it is not at all uncommon to find agriculture occupying a major position in the minds of those who were seeking the first principles of social organization. For Karl Dietrich Hüllmann, writing on the history of the origins of classes in Germany, agriculture was "the cornerstone of civilized culture, of the independence and strength of a people when [it] deserts the impermanent hunting and pastoral life, accustoms itself to fixed habitations, and begins to cultivate fields";[16] while for Heinrich Luden, professor of history at Jena and himself the son of a Hanoverian peasant, field husbandry always remained "the basis for culture and humanity in the life of the citizen."[17] What gives real meaning to these references to agriculture in this time was their connection with citizenship, where ideally a uniformity of occupation in agrarian pursuits among all members of the state, together with the virtue acquired from those pursuits and the life they entailed, would come together to confer a single-mindedness of common purpose which was so visibly lacking in Prussia in 1806. Indicative of this relationship between agriculture and citizenship was the preoccupation with the great "citizen-states" of ancient times among many writers which now began to be apparent. Michael Alexander Lips, professor of political economy at Erlangen and Marburg, was typical of many another writer in his conclusion that the greatness of Rome,

---

[15] [Buchholz], *Gemählde*, I, 56-58.

[16] Karl Dietrich Hüllmann, *Geschichte des Ursprungs der Stände in Deutschland,* 3 vols. (Frankfurt an der Oder, 1806-1808), I, 18.

[17] Heinrich Luden, *Handbuch der Staatsweisheit oder der Politik: erste Abtheilung* (Jena, 1811), 238.

Greece, Carthage, and Corinth was firmly based on agriculture, and not on economic pursuits which predicated the existence of cities.[18] To a steadily increasing extent, it was perceived that a common national effort was needed to shore up a shattered Prussia: and agriculture as the occupation and the way of life still common to an overwhelming majority of the population—including, in this sense, most of the nobility—was therefore almost necessarily taken to be the primary social fact from which the new public spirit would be derived. In sum, agriculture and with it the peasant came to be regarded as the chief integral elements in the establishment of citizenship, which itself at this moment had a quite specific moral meaning: it meant simply the virtue of common dedication to a national purpose, often seen in rather vague terms merely as "regeneration," and it received this meaning from the actual situation of a politically and militarily bankrupt Prussia after Jena and Auerstädt.

With these factors in mind, it is easy to understand why the reform issues of personal emancipation and peasant proprietorship suddenly took on a vastly increased urgency in the minds of those reformers who saw Prussia's trouble as a political failure rooted in a moral problem. The connection can be illustrated directly by Hüllmann's history of class origins in Germany. In the early middle ages, he wrote, property was the sole measure of civic worth, and the noble class at that time was constituted of those who owned large amounts of land. The disdain with which these nobles regarded the common people underwent no change until the revival of trade in Europe, when the true value of agriculture was seen in some sort of perspective, and the peasant began to make some progress as an outgrowth of increased respect for agriculture.[19] But in the later middle ages, the growing propensity of violent temporal and spiritual lords to increase the size of their landed property, together with the growing pressure of the princes to erect powerful military establishments and a certain "misconceived religiosity" (the peasants' misunderstanding of Luther's "Christian liberty") combined to produce a

---

[18] Michael Alexander Lips, *Principien der Ackergesetzgebung als Grundlage eines künftigen Ackercodex für Gesezgeber und rationelle Landwirthe* (Nürnberg, 1811), 231.

[19] Hüllmann, *Geschichte des Ursprungs*, I, 7.

catastrophe (the Peasants' War of 1525) in which free peasant landowners were reduced to propertyless serfs.[20] "Thus has it occurred," wrote Hüllmann, "that in most areas of Germany the common man on the land possesses so little property, [and] is so heavily burdened with services and duties to landlords. Thus did the curse come over the folk, under which it has groaned for centuries."[21]

The contemporary relationships under which most oppressed peasants were living could in no way be compared with those of the original German colonists, Hüllmann emphasized: only the hereditary lessees who received their lands for moderate real (not personal) considerations had ever made a free contract with a lord; the rest had been illegally subjected in "that remarkable catastrophe of German constitutional history" during the middle ages.[22] Hüllmann's emphasis here on constitutional history is important: the subjection of the peasant was for him a constitutional catastrophe precisely and expressly because it meant the expulsion of the peasant from the ranks of the citizen. And Hüllmann declared that his own century had its work cut out for it in correcting the work of the past if it was to earn the title of a just and humane century.[23] At this critical point in Prussia's history, the peasant had to be freed from his condition of abject humiliation; when this had finally occurred, then a new order would have been created—an assuredly blessed order—for the fatherland would have been enriched with *men*.[24]

For its regeneration, then, Prussia needed *men*, defined as free moral agents whose strength and virtue would reinvigorate all of society through the medium of citizenship, the channel through which virtue expressed itself politically. Peasant servitude was absolutely incompatible with this need: it represented not only a denial of citizenship, but more basically still a strongly repressive force against the development and expression of those moral virtues which, left to himself, the peasant possessed in greater measure than anyone. Thus the "natural condition" of the peasant

[20] *Ibid.*, 195.
[21] *Ibid.*, 205.
[22] *Ibid.*, 205-206.
[23] *Ibid.*, 208-209.
[24] *Ibid.*, II, 326-27.

in an occupation which awakened in him only benevolent affections and attitudes, strengthened his health, lent him candor and vigor, and conduced to happiness, was contrasted sharply with the "unnatural" perversion of these qualities under servitude into laziness, sulkiness, mistrustfulness, maliciousness, and greed. Simply being a peasant was hardly sufficient to account for all these evil character traits; "in fact, how could the man who spends the greatest part of his time in the lap of nature become brutish?" asked Buchholz. The reasons for the peasant's oft-cited antisocial nature must therefore lie in the peculiar relationship to state and lord in which he was forced to stand. It required only a change in this relationship, in the sense described above, to allow the most noble qualities to develop themselves and to be placed at the service of the community.[25]

The existence of personal servitude and unfavorable rights of tenure on the land was detrimental in a double sense to the realization of a national reawakening as this had come to be conceived, in general terms, by Prussian and German publicists in 1806-1807 and after. It first of all restricted the contribution the peasant could make to the state by severely limiting the sphere of his independent decision and action. According to the new theory, the state, if it was to raise itself out of its present difficulties, might no longer regard itself as the tutor of its people, but must become the pupil of the people in the sense of allowing them, indeed encouraging them, to bring forth their own insights on public affairs, as well as on their private occupations. But the conditions for the development of initiative on the part of the citizen lay in freedom; as M. A. Lips expressed it, in a somewhat narrower context, the greatest production from agriculture could come only with the realization of the principle that "desire should cultivate the land." "Joy is the inner sun in which the deed ripens," he wrote, "and this joy, this desire to cultivate the land, is only a product of the feeling of freedom."[26] Servitude was not compatible with this kind of freedom, nor was the political and social system which permitted servitude to exist:

[25] [Paul Ferdinand Friedrich Buchholz], *Untersuchungen über den Geburtsadel und die Möglichkeit seiner Fortdauer im neunzehnten Jahrhundert* (Berlin and Leipzig, 1807), 119-20.
[26] Lips, *Principien*, 97.

it was again because of its limitations on the development of independent thought and judgment that Buchholz attacked the paternalism of "enlightened" educational theory under the old regime, accusing it of merely enjoining the peasant to humility, patience, and subordination to the will of God as pronounced from the pulpit.[27]

In another and equally important way, servitude worked against the national reinvigoration: it blocked and distorted the peasant's view of the state. The necessity for giving the individual citizen a feeling of his participation in the state as a way of bringing him into a close emotional association with the state and public affairs was regarded as an established fact by the reforming writers of this period. The problem of how to do so was most severe where the peasant was concerned. No one doubted the special importance of bringing the peasant into the state: Heinrich Luden emphasized the imperative necessity for making the peasant feel as if he were not merely tolerated in the state as a necessary evil, not the mat on which others might arbitrarily wipe their feet, but rather the very basis of civil society, whose occupation conditioned the preservation of the state and of life for all citizens.[28] Servitude, because it represented an unequal relationship between rights and duties, interfered with any attempt to make the peasant feel wanted and necessary in the state; what was really wrong, as Buchholz pointed out, was that no one could efficiently serve two masters,[29] and the peasant, who produced for both his lord and the state, could not even see the state as such beyond the onerous condition of his subjection to his lord. The only aspect of the state which had penetrated to the level of the servile peasant was the administration of justice in certain types of cases—but the peasant could scarcely have a very favorable picture of the state because its administrators sought their own advantage before justice.[30]

The abolition of servitude thus became a method of making immediate the relationship of state to peasant, the final fulfillment of a process begun long since under absolutism. This meant

27 [Buchholz], *Gemählde*, I, 14-15.
28 Luden, *Handbuch*, 245-46.
29 [Buchholz], *Gemählde*, I, 7, 12.
30 *Ibid.*, 7-8.

not only that all justice ought to be an affair of the state, and that court cases involving peasants—or anyone else, for that matter—ought all to come before regularly constituted state courts,[31] but also that all public functions ought ideally to be in the hands of officials who represented only the public interest, not a private one also. The elimination of the mediative role of the noble in the peasant's relationship to public authority in this way became the key to the problem of converting the serf into a citizen whose vigor, initiative, and affections could be tapped by the state for its renewal. It was precisely these two ideas—that the individual could best develop his own potential and must be given the freedom to do so, and that all artificial barriers to the utilization of that potential by the state must be removed—which motivated the actions of the high Prussian officials who actually instituted the remarkable changes which formed the basis of the Prussian revival. In the reform period of the first decade of the nineteenth century, the most important of these officials was Karl Freiherr vom Stein.

The fundamental necessity of a Prussian reform, as Stein saw it, was the creation of a civic spirit in the broad masses of the people—that is, a desire to participate in the affairs of the state and of the nation. Stein saw in the people a vast potential source of moral energy which heretofore had not been utilized by the state for its national purposes, and his problem reduced therefore in one sense to the double question of how this energy could be created and how it could then be placed at the service of the state. According to Stein's insight, which was comparable to that of many officials and publicists in less responsible positions than his, popular participation in the state was not essentially a political problem, but a moral one; it related primarily to the spirit which activated political life, and only secondarily to its forms and structure. What was most important was precisely the creation of "public spirit," which was characterized at one point by Stein as the feeling among the people "of so loving King and Fatherland that they will gladly sacrifice

---

[31] At the level of the county *(Kreis)*, for example, as proposed in "Welche Veränderungen sind in der Preussischen Staats-Verfassung und Verwaltung nothwendig?" *Neue Feuerbrände*, II (Sechstes Heft), 18.

property and life for them."[32] The emphasis here is on the people's immediate connection with sovereign and fatherland, and of such a sort that love, freely given, will call forth sacrifice. What is desired is that sacrifice or, in the broader sense, all civic duty, become a voluntary, self-imposed obligation, not a false front evoked and maintained by artificial sophistries or outright force. Stein thus really aimed at the creation of the good citizen at the base of society—a man who would possess a real desire to contribute to his fatherland, who would be vigorous in his pursuit of that desire, and who would possess the resources to pursue it purposefully. In short, voluntarism, activism, and responsibility in its individual citizens were for Stein the keys to the strength of the state.

The thought-processes and personal experiences which went into the making of this briefly summarized conception of state and citizen cannot be dealt with in any great detail here. The synthesis which Stein made of the various ideas which came to him at one time or another in his career and the use to which he put that synthesis, above all, were quite original and unique; yet it is possible to trace the most important elements of this new political concept to influences which exercised some sway over Stein in the years prior to his reform ministry in 1807-1808. It is in fact necessary to track these influences down in order to understand just how the emancipation of the peasant from personal servitude and the first steps towards the grant of proprietorship of his land, two of the most important of the Stein reforms, were related to the idea of political strengthening through moral regeneration.

One of the most powerful influences on Stein's political thought came from the philosophy of Adam Smith. As a student in Göttingen, Stein heard lectures in political economy from various professors upon whom Smith's work had made a deep impression, and many evidences indicate that Stein himself was to a large extent a convert to the economic doctrines of Smith. As an official

[32] Karl Freiherr vom Stein, "Rundschreiben Steins an die Mitglieder des Generaldepartements, sogenanntes 'Politisches Testament' Steins, Königsberg, 24. Nov., 1808," *Freiherr vom Stein: Briefwechsel, Denkschriften, und Aufzeichnungen,* ed. Erich Botzenhart, 7 vols. (Berlin, 1931-1937), II, 583. Hereafter cited as *Freiherr vom Stein.*

in the western provinces of Prussia after 1780, with special competence in economic affairs, particularly in mining, Stein showed his hand in his tendency to reverse the policy of his predecessors and his colleagues in other areas of Prussia by encouraging wherever possible the exploitation of coal and iron deposits by private undertakings. Earlier and basically mercantilistic policy had operated under the assumption that only the state could provide the capital, technical equipment, and skilled labor necessary to an efficient mining enterprise. Stein, by providing a skilled general supervision of mining regulations and by putting government money into the development of transport facilities, was able to keep mining in private hands while at the same time vastly increasing its total output. It is significant also, that in spite of certain financial difficulties, Stein refused to use forced labor from peasants in the construction of highways in this area —thus indicating at this time already (late 1780s) his disapproval of servile obligations.[33]

Stein's position on personal servitude and unfavorable property relationships among the peasantry was perhaps the strongest and most consistent of all his attitudes on public affairs; and certainly this had its Smithian side. His own copy of *The Wealth of Nations* was underlined at the following passage: "It appears accordingly, from the experiences of all ages and nations, I believe, that the work done by freemen comes cheaper in the end than that performed by slaves."[34] And it was probably not only Smith but a host of German Smithians to whom Stein was referring when he noted, in 1797, that experience "and the opinion of all writers" tended to the conclusion that freedom and property were most conducive to the peasant's individual happiness and to the greatest possible advancement of his acquisitive activity.[35] He felt quite strongly that in order for agriculture to achieve a permanent prosperity, the peasant had to know his business, possess the capital necessary for the improvement of his property, and be given and assured of freedom in the use of his abilities and of his property. If he possessed any of these in an only

[33] W. O. Henderson, *The State and the Industrial Revolution in Prussia, 1740-1870* (Liverpool, 1958), 32-38.

[34] *Ibid.*, 38, note 1.

[35] vom Stein, "Denkschrift" (June 1, 1797), *Freiherr vom Stein*, I, 274.

incomplete degree, nothing but a relatively weak and scanty cultivation could ever be expected.[36]

Personal servitude was for Stein the expression of the most oppressive relationship of the peasant to his lord, and was disadvantageous in equal measure to happiness, morality, and prosperity.[37] Legislation was fully entitled to abolish personal servitude and the practice of arbitrary removal of peasants from their farms: the former contradicted "the original and inalienable rights of man," while the latter, giving little advantage to the lord, kept the peasant in a continual state of minority *(Unmündigkeit)*, which resulted in a miserable condition of land, buildings, and inventory.[38] Stein's personal observation more than confirmed statistical and theoretical objections to servitude: after a trip through Mecklenburg, noted for the prevalence of harsh conditions of peasant servitude, he wrote: "The dwelling of the Mecklenburg nobleman, who [takes the peasants' land] instead of bettering their condition, seems to me like the den of a beast of prey, which lays waste all round it and surrounds itself with the stillness of the grave. Certainly the advantage is only apparent, and a high energy of culture, [and] complete cultivation [are] only possible where there is no lack of men and of human abilities." The price of land, its produce, and the assurance of sale of produce, together with the possibility of executing great public undertakings, he went on, must surely be greater in lands where a large population and industriousness existed than in those where men were degraded "to an integral part of the cattle-inventory of an estate."[39]

For Stein the economist, there was no question but that freedom and proprietorship were essential ingredients of increased production and material prosperity for the peasant and for the state in which he worked; and in this judgment Stein was no more original than any of the economists who had adopted this principle from Adam Smith or from the Physiocrats. But Stein

[36] vom Stein, "Verwaltungsbericht des Oberkammerpräsidenten vom Stein" (March 10, 1801), cited in Georg Heinrich Pertz, *Das Leben des Ministers Freiherrn vom Stein*, 2d ed., 6 vols. in 7 (Berlin, 1850-1855), I, 199.

[37] *Ibid.*, 202-203.

[38] Cited from an untitled document of vom Stein in *ibid.*, II, 29.

[39] vom Stein, (Letter to Frau von Berg, April 22, 1802), *ibid.*, I, 192.

was more than an economist; he was also a governmental official and a man of intelligence and initiative, whose administrative (and therefore public) concerns were broader than those of the academic economist, and whose insights were at once more incisive and more thoughtful than those of the average post-Friderician bureaucrat. Stein saw more in the philosophy of Smith than its economic principles, and applied what he took from it to more than the economic sector of public life. More important to Stein, ultimately, than the idea of a freely competitive economy as such was the idea that human ability was able to develop itself only in situations of challenge, and that freedom was necessary to the existence of such challenge. This may be expressed in a different way: no individual who was prohibited from enjoying the fruits of his own assiduity could feel the challenge of seeing what his labors could accomplish, and he therefore would not develop those abilities latent within him on which his assiduity depended. In order, then, to develop in the individual the quality of self-reliance, it would be necessary to give him an arena in which he could feel challenged, and at the same time the freedom to develop his own response to the challenge. For the Prussian peasant, the abolition of servitude was the necessary answer to the latter requirement, and private property was the answer to the former. What Stein really took from Smith, then, was the idea that an individual works best and with most vigor when he works most voluntarily, and that he works most voluntarily when his own interest is most closely involved.

This important idea was reinforced by certain developments in pedagogical thought in the last two decades or so of the eighteenth century. Most educational theory of the eighteenth century which concerned itself with popular education got little further than the insight that meaningful instruction had not only to present students with principles of right action, whether vocational or moral, but also to connect these principles to concrete examples. This was of course a major step forward over the older and still widely held notion that education consisted of the presentation and memorization of "catechisms" of principles; but it still held fast to the idea that education dealt solely with a body of knowledge, whether facts or principles, and merely sought to facilitate the understanding or memorization of such information by connecting it with objects of everyday familiarity to the student. Gradually, out of the experiences of educators in model schools and other institutions which actually taught children of the lower classes, came a new and pedagogically revolutionary insight: education had to do not just with the inculcation of information, but with the development of the power of the individual *to think for himself*. The conclusion to which this led was that the presentation of information was of less importance than the confrontation of the student with real problem situations in which the individual could develop his own capacities not just to solve this problem, but to solve problems in general. It was, in other words, self-developed independence of thought in the student which was to be striven for, not an externally developed dependence on general precepts which might or might not fit particular situations.

A number of individuals were important in the dissemination of this new idea. Christian Salzmann, the founder of a model school at Schnepfenthal, was certainly one of the first to implement a conception of the educational importance of purposeful activity, or labor, itself: at his institution, every pupil—these were peasant children—was assigned a particular piece of land to cultivate, and was put in charge of caring for a number of animals—rabbits, fish, bees, and the like. The value of this work, said Salzmann, lay not only in health and physical vigor, but in teaching the worth of property, the value of one's own labor, in the growth of the love of one's fellow man, and in the joy of being able to do something important by oneself.[40] Here appears quite clearly the notion that labor—in agriculture, in this case—is not only a goal to be attained, but a means to the achievement of other goals, of which economic and moral self-reliance were perhaps the most important. The point was still more sharply made by Wehrli, a longtime collaborator of Philipp Emanuel von Fellenberg, the Swiss philanthropist who established an agricultural school on his estate near the turn of the century. Speaking of the educational value of agricultural labor, Wehrli had this to say: "No other calling [*Beruf*] offers such a variety and richness of useful

[40] Eichler, *Die Landbewegung*, 108-11.

occupations, conducive to health, for every age and condition. It stands in [a] manifold reciprocal relationship with many other kinds of callings and easily makes possible for the skilled peasant the transition to other occupations. No other calling provides as much material and opportunity for comparison and distinction, for many-sided views, sharp observations, connections, differentiations, conclusions, so much opportunity for thanks, for love and adoration of the All-Father and for edification of the mind."[41] In Wehrli's formulation, agriculture had ceased to be primarily an object of education, and had become a means for educating an individual for the widest possible variety of social tasks and for the development of a mind capable of independent thought and moral judgment.

The most comprehensive and influential statements of this new conception of education were not made by any of the foregoing figures, however, but by the Swiss educator Johann Heinrich Pestalozzi (1746-1827), whose name became almost a household word in European pedagogical circles from 1790 until his death. It was Pestalozzi's service to have formulated the idea of education through *Selbstkraft* and *Selbstbetätigung* in a systematic fashion in a number of books and articles, to have popularized it for general understanding, and to have implemented it in what were generally agreed to have been the most successful and in any case the most famous model schools in all of central Europe. Pestalozzi's most famous and popular work was *Lienhard und Gertrud,* a rather loose three-volume compendium of didactic stories and dialogues centering around the "rational" peasant parents Lienhard and Gertrud, who with their children as pupils in numerous different situations brought out the virtues of education conceived as the development of the powers of observation and reasoning of the individual. The setting of *Lienhard und Gertrud*—the home, the farm, and the village—was not a random choice. It was one of Pestalozzi's most cherished convictions that an education which based itself on known or familiar (also from the root word "family") situations and objects—which is what he meant by the term "concrete"—was of infinitely more

[41] Quoted in *ibid.,* 111.

value in awakening interest in the student than one in which abstractions without connection to the pupil's own world were preached. Pestalozzi's own major interest was in peasant children, and he was convinced that for them the best school was the natural one of fields, meadows, stalls, and barn. He insisted that books and schoolroom exercises should not interrupt the process of experience, which was the real basis of the children's education. The school's proper function should accordingly be limited to introducing consideration, consciousness of purpose, order, and perspective into the children's way of looking at things, in order that they might make full use of their "natural school."[42]

While Pestalozzi was of course forced to recognize and deal with the harsh fact of servitude in most German-speaking lands, and while he considered it beneficial for servile peasants to be educated, he also attacked serfdom itself in numerous writings and quite obviously felt that freedom was absolutely necessary to the full realization of the educational goal of self-fulfillment or self-development. He illustrated this very cleverly in a story of a benevolent Junker and his serfs. The Junker asked his peasants whether they felt that he was doing all he could for their benefit. All dutifully replied in the affirmative but one; he in turn asked the Junker which of two fields would produce more: one which was heavily manured, but badly plowed and full of weeds, or one which was sparingly fertilized but well plowed and free of weeds. The Junker answered that the latter would of course produce more, for full justice had been done to it. The peasant thereupon replied that peasants, too, would thrive better if the Junker would do full justice to them instead of "over-manuring" them with good deeds. Discussing this bit of rustic wisdom later in the presence of an old priest and a young vicar, the Junker was told by the inexperienced vicar that the opinion expressed by the peasant in question was a typical manifestation of a characteristic ingratitude among peasants. But the wise old priest would have none of this, and broke in: "Dear Junker! thankfulness is not a weed, which thrives in any soil; it is a tender

[42] Johann Heinrich Pestalozzi, *Lienhard und Gertrud* (Zürich and Leipzig, 1790-1792), 226-27.

fine plant which . . . grows as little in hard, dried-up earth as in wet, flooded soil; and it has been an evil prejudice of my age, that in general it has been considered easy to cover up injustice with good deeds."[43] This was of course not intended as a slap at benevolence, but as a typically gentle Pestalozzian criticism of a system in which the peasant was not free to bring about by himself the improvements in his cultivation and in his own abilities which now depended on the uncertainties of someone else's kindness.

Pestalozzi's ideas were quite well known in many official circles in the German states, and especially in Prussia. It is highly probable that Freiherr vom Stein himself had read some of the famous pedagogue's writings; his circle of friends, in any case, included a number of men who were quite familiar with Pestalozzi's educational philosophy. Among them, in fact, was a very close personal friend of Pestalozzi, Ludwig Nicolovius, whom the Swiss had designated the "heir" of his work. While it is perhaps not possible to draw any direct connections between Pestalozzi and Stein, it is certainly possible to see striking similarities in their thought.[44] Both directed their interest—in different contexts, of course—to the common man rather than to the intellectually or politically "mature" upper classes; both attempted to work changes by concentrating on abilities which they assumed to be latent within the individual, rather than by reworking human nature; and both saw the labor and the continual necessity for facing and solving problems in the situations of a man's everyday life as the essential condition of the self-development of every individual's abilities. For Stein, the first two of the above could perhaps be explained from the exigencies of the situation of Prussia in 1806-1807. Certainly it required no Pestalozzian influence to perceive that mass support for the government was highly desirable in the present circumstances; furthermore, given Stein's fundamentally unrevolutionary attitudes, it was completely consistent that he should wish to implement the development of a civic spirit through the cultivation and direction of already-existing inclina-

---

[43][Johann Heinrich Pestalozzi], *Figuren zu meinem A B C Buch oder zu den Anfangsgründen meines Denkens* (Basel, 1797), 52-58.

[44] Flitner, *Die politische Erziehung*, 80-81.

tions and through connection with already-existing institutions of social life.[45] But the third point, the value of concrete experience as education for informed self-reliance, appears to be much more closely related than the others to the specific contributions of Pestalozzian thought, or at least to the philosophical current of which Pestalozzi's ideas were a part.

It was, in any case, largely the combination of the pedagogical idea of the educational value of agricultural work in building the personality with the Smithian principle that willingness to work was a function of the individual's perceived self-interest which led Stein to the conclusion that personal freedom and proprietorship were necessary to the preparation of the peasantry for an active role in political life. The abolition of servitude would mean that a man had the legal freedom to act in his self-interest, and the possession of property meant that he had the economic freedom to follow through his own ideas. But just as important in Stein's mind as the opportunities for economic self-development provided the individual by property were the doors it opened to the growth and exercise of social consciousness. Here is a fundamental difference between Stein's concept of the position of property in the social order and that of eighteenth-century "liberal" or Smithian thought; whereas the latter pointed to property as the arena for the essentially amoral aggrandizement of the individual, and was chiefly economically oriented, Stein's idea was that property was a means towards a social end, and was therefore largely morally oriented. As one historian puts it: "Property is for [Stein] . . . the means whereby the econom-

---

[45] Flitner quite correctly points to a major difference on this question between vom Stein and a national reformer such as J. G. Fichte. It was vom Stein's view, to quote Flitner, that "neither politics nor education can create a new man or in general ignore reality, the personal and social forces which determine life," and that any improvements in public life had therefore to utilize and work with these forces. For Fichte, on the other hand, who in his *Reden an die deutsche Nation* preached an education for the entire German people without any reference to class or circumstance, a "peculiarly German national education" (*Sämmtliche Werke*, VII, 276-77), it was necessary to change the individual's whole frame of reference, making use of state force to do so, in order to create a new man. In other words, whereas vom Stein would use Pestalozzi's pragmatic or "concrete" method in the actually existing social milieu in all its variety as Pestalozzi conceived it, Fichte would apply only the method, and would attempt to implement it in a uniform milieu yet to be created by state power. Flitner, *Die politische Erziehung*, 81.

ically independent and morally autonomous personality can develop itself. Property concerned him essentially as the area in which the virtues of the future citizen, activity, personal responsibility and public-mindedness are contained."[46] As a statesman, Stein was less interested in the free play of economic factors leading to the most efficient utilization of property judged in terms of production than he was in the opportunity for every man to be a proprietor, the results of which were judged in terms of the morality and self-reliance of as many individuals as possible.[47]

With this insight, Stein's most basic conception of the state as "a great national educational institution" becomes clear; he did not conceive of the reform measures which were made law in 1807-1808 as conferring political responsibility in the largest sense upon individuals who had absolutely no maturity, no experience, in political affairs. He thought of them instead as an "enabling act," or, as he and many others were fond of putting it, as the "Habeas Corpus Act" of the Prussian state, which provided an opportunity for individuals to develop themselves into responsible and politically mature citizens. Municipal self-government was to be for the middle class exactly what freedom and property were to be for the peasantry: a real-life school of practical instruction in citizenship. This is the meaning of the state, seen as the totality of its social relationships, as a "national educational institution." Thus, Stein's plans for political representation for the peasantry in a national Diet were clearly for the future, not the immediate present, and were therefore fully in harmony with his conviction that the peasant would for a time still be in the process of social (self-) education. And just as different groups of the peasantry would achieve political maturity at different times, in accordance with the different social conditions which obtained in the various groups at the time of the reform edicts, so Stein foresaw the provisional necessity of a differential scale for electoral franchise and candidacy. But he

[46] Eichler, *Die Landbewegung,* 69-70.

[47] Property was also important as a bridge between the individual and his larger social world, for it was through property that the individual might come to see the logic and necessity of laws, to develop his feelings of responsibility for the defense of law and the authority which guaranteed them, and so forth.

was firm in his conviction that peasants should elect their representatives from their own midst, for this would bind them more firmly to the constitution and educate them in the actual tasks of government. Criticisms that peasants might prove to be too untutored or too unsophisticated to represent their class were answered by Stein with the statement that men of sufficient power and plain understanding would indeed be found in the peasantry.[48]

The independence which Stein demanded as an absolute necessity for self-development towards citizenship was for the peasantry not only a right, but a duty; and Stein was remarkably stubborn in his insistence that the peasant be left alone—even when that was not the peasant's own desire. He must not only be given the *opportunity* to develop his own resources, said Stein, but the *necessity* of doing so, in the sense of being deprived of the ultimately pernicious, if well-intentioned, guiding hand from the outside, which could only have the final effect of undermining the peasant's own initiative. Thus Stein's opposition to labor services, expressed on numerous occasions, stemmed not from a feeling that there was anything intrinsically wrong with one man performing services for another, as long as both were free, but from the conviction that "these services carry with themselves a sort of dependence and arbitrary treatment of the servant, which is disadvantageous to the national spirit."[49] He rejected a proposal that the new lessees of royal domains should exercise a general administrative control over the peasants on the land and collect their taxes because to him this represented simply one way of bringing back the old disadvantageous dependence of the peasant on the lord which, making advice and assistance too close at hand, would prohibit the peasant from developing independence of thought and action.[50] On the very morning of his departure from Königsberg, and from his ministerial post, he expressed his concern about the number of provincial and local peasant codes (*Gesindeordnungen*) still in existence, and warned that in some cases new codes were even then being

---

[48] vom Stein, "Denkschrift" (November 7, 1808), *Freiherr vom Stein*, II, 566.
[49] vom Stein, "Rundschreiben" (November 24, 1808), in Pertz, *Das Leben des Ministers*, II, 312-13.
[50] vom Stein (Letter to Schroetter, May 10, 1808), *Freiherr vom Stein*, II, 424.

established which, restricting the freedom of the people, would restore the substance if not the form of hereditary servitude.[51]

The Prussian reform period, and especially Stein's participation in it, occupies a position of major importance in the social rehabilitation of the German peasant. It provided a direct and immediate impetus for a concern with the foundations of national power in a specific crisis, a situation which was soon enough perceived to be merely an indication of the extent to which Prussian and other German political constitutions had become antiquated in a new Europe which dated from 1789. What resulted from the introspection occasioned by the defeat of Prussia and the subsequent hegemony over Germany exercised by Napoleon was a general recognition of the necessity for genuine popular support of the regime. The necessity mothered the possibility, and it was not long before the peasant was invested with all the requisite intrinsic qualities of good citizenship as that was defined under the determining influence of the external situation: these qualities were altruism, loyalty, perseverance, and a willingness to sacrifice. In the discussion which centered around these points, it is impossible to overlook the powerful influence exercised by earlier writers, who provided for these reformers an almost ready-made picture of the kind of man they wanted as their "citizen."

It was Freiherr vom Stein's great contribution to unite the moral dignity which was an essential part of this definition of "citizen" with the practical reforms which would give the peasant the opportunity to actualize that dignity in his social and political life. He gave to the peasantry its first real opportunity to participate in a common task on a level of equality with other Germans; and this was no longer a merely passive equality based on an economic function, but an active one, assuming a conscious and deliberate cooperation of individuals. The lessons which Stein taught Prussia were received elsewhere in Germany as well; and their effect was permanent.

For Freiherr vom Stein, citizenship was a concept which in

[51] vom Stein, "Rundschreiben" (November 24, 1808), in Pertz, *Das Leben des Ministers*, II, 310.

neither theory nor practice was class-bound; in this, indeed, lay his great contribution to the progress of the peasant. No single individual was incapable of developing the attitudes and the moral foundation which it entailed, and it was therefore an integrative social idea with absolutely no divisive connotations. In principle, therefore, Stein was interested in no one class more than another except insofar as class circumstances tended to create for groups of individuals similar obstacles to the development of a *milieu* favorable to the psychological growth necessary to citizenship. Stein was, for example, especially concerned about the peasantry precisely because its material position required the most reform to create such a *milieu*. But aside from the numerical importance of the peasantry vis-à-vis other estates or classes in Prussian society, Stein had no special concern for it. What his reforms accomplished for it were of inestimable importance, of course; and his assumption of the equality of the individual with respect to citizenship was of major significance for the rise of the peasant to social equality.

But there was another stream of thought connected with Prussian regeneration and with the national German liberation that followed which posited a much more singular association of the peasant with the moral, military, and political demands of the crisis than did Stein and the group of bureaucratic liberals which surrounded him. In this other conception, it was the peasant *more* than any other person who could give to his fatherland the vigor and moral fiber which were necessary to endure or prevent national catastrophe. In consequence, there were reasons for the preservation of the peasantry *qua* peasantry which did not stem from a conception of a universally applicable citizenship, but from an idea of a special civic worth inherent only in the peasantry and incapable of being transmitted. These ideas and their implications can best be explained by reference to the works of Ernst Moritz Arndt (1769-1860), the northern German poet and writer who was at once their most ardent and most famous exponent.

Arndt was born the son of a freed peasant in Swedish Pomerania, and his first memories were those of the hard, pious, and frugal life of the small peasant. He attended school at Stralsund with the help of an unknown benefactor, and later studied theology at Greifswald and Jena. He became a minister at the completion of his studies, in 1796, but found the religious life little to his liking, and gave it up in order to travel for about a year and a half in various European countries. It is thought that his sense of German patriotism may have been fired for the first time during this trip as a defensive reaction to the scorn of many Europeans, especially French and Italians, for Germany and German life.

In 1800, he became professor of history at Greifswald, and as early as 1805 he began to warn Germans about French contempt and enmity for things German, and to attack the German tendency to overestimate and overvalue foreign culture. The vigor of his literary attacks on the French prompted him to flee to Sweden after Jena and Auerstädt, and he remained there in an official post until 1808. He returned to Germany in that year and settled in Berlin, gathering around him a number of Prussian patriots, while he himself developed an ardent feeling for Prussia. When peace was made between France and Sweden in 1810, Arndt was reappointed to his professorship at Greifswald, but left it in 1811 in order to travel—first to Prague, where he met such figures as Blücher, Scharnhorst, and Gneisenau, and then to St. Petersburg, where he was one member of the circle of exiles grouped around Freiherr vom Stein. With the Wars of Liberation, Arndt followed the Prussian troops through Germany, turning out prodigious quantities of nationalistic songs, poems, and pamphlets all the while. He again traveled between 1815 and 1818, but finally settled down to a professorship in history at the newly founded Prussian university in Bonn. His outspoken criticism of reactionary German government eventually led to an order forbidding him to teach, and he was put under investigation by the Prussian government. No taint of guilt was proved, but it was not until 1840 that Frederick William IV returned him to his position. With the revolution of 1848, he was elected to the Frankfurt Parliament, and was a member of the delegation which offered the imperial crown to Frederick William in 1849. He died in retirement in 1860.[52]

Arndt's own peasant background was probably chiefly respon-

---

[52] *Allgemeine deutsche Biographie,* I, 541-48,

sible for the impulse behind his first major writing on the peasantry, a history of personal servitude in Pomerania and in Rügen,
the island on which he had grown up. As was the case with
many such works in this time, his "history" was perhaps less
instructional than polemical in intent, for he used it as a vehicle
to attack the foes of emancipation. His chief stated objection to
servitude lay in the fact that it was an unnecessary restriction of
activity, and he declared that no state might permit any restrictions on human energies which did not result directly from the
necessity of its own preservation and security.[53] He buttressed
this objection with his own feelings of the injustice and unright-
eousness of servitude, with the old arguments of the efficacy of
freedom in the increase of agricultural production, and with his
convictions of what protestant Christianity meant in terms of
brotherly love and Christian liberty.

It was not until after the Napoleonic incursion into Germany
had forced his heretofore vague feelings of German cultural
nationalism into some sort of focus, and after Arndt had actually
become associated with the Prussian patriotic movement, however, that he became the fiery nationalist of the Liberation who
placed the free peasant proprietor at the head of the forces which
defended the fatherland. In other words, the basis of Arndt's
publicistic defense of the peasant underwent a considerable
change between 1803 and 1810; whereas servitude in 1803 was
merely unjust and un-Christian, for example, it had by 1810
become also the means to German national disaster. Conversely,
the maintenance of a free peasantry was a sure guarantee of
national freedom. One way to explain this change, keeping in
mind the great events which occurred in the period 1803-1810,
is to examine Arndt's own proofs for his conviction that the
peasantry stood as the great wall against tyranny and subjection.
More common than any other of these proofs was a historical
one, which was heavily dependent on examples from antiquity.
Fritz Valjavec has pointed to the importance assumed by antiquity
in the vocabulary of politics in Europe after 1789, and has sug-

---

[53] Ernst Moritz Arndt, "Versuch einer Geschichte der Leibeigenschaft in
Pommern und in Rügen" (1803), *Agrarpolitische Schriften*, ed. W. O. W. Terstegen 2d. ed. (Goslar, 1942), 173.

gested that the American and French Revolutions with their popular aspect evoked not only imitations of the political forms and symbols of the great republics of antiquity, but also a vast amount of analogizing between the events of contemporary Europe and those of the ancient republics, especially with regard to the idea of the participation of the totality of citizens in affairs of the state, opposition to tyranny, and so forth. The influence of antiquity on the German political vocabulary was perhaps most apparent in the period of the Napoleonic hegemony. Valjavec refers to the translation and publication in 1805 of Demosthenes' "First Philippic Oration" by Barthold Georg Niebuhr as a rather obvious use of the antityrannical tradition of the ancient democracies, and notes that the violently anti-imperial Tacitus enjoyed a considerable revival in Germany during Napoleon's sway.[54] The temptations to analogize or at least to draw examples from antiquity were scarcely less powerful for Arndt, the professor of history, than for anyone else: the resistance to French tyranny and the atmosphere of revivification in Prussia after 1807, based on Stein's reforms and the idea of popular participation in civic affairs, appear to have combined with Arndt's nascent nationalism and his already strong views on the moral strength of the peasant to effect in his somewhat romantic mind a conversion of Stein's "citizen" into a kind of amalgam of the Roman Cincinnatus and the Teuton Arminius—the picture of a man which, by simple extension and association, came to look suspiciously like the contemporary German peasant.

Arndt provides sufficient evidence of this connection. Over and over he repeated his conviction that the ancients, when not ruled despotically, based their freedom and the stability of their states on agrarian laws, which indicated to him that free peasants meant even then a brave people and a free land.[55] It was no accident that the wisest founders of states and legislators of the nations of antiquity based their states on agricultural laws, for they recognized that a measure of equality in the ownership of agriculturally productive lands had to be introduced if a reason-

---

[54] Valjavec, *Die Entstehung der politischen Strömungen*, 35-36.

[55] Ernst Moritz Arndt, "Der Bauernstand, politisch betrachtet" (1810), *Arndts Werke: Auswahl in zwölf Teilen*, ed. August Leffson and Wilhelm Steffens, 12 parts in 4 vols. (Berlin, 1912), IV (Part 10), 41, 43.

able balance of fortunes between the citizens were to be achieved and maintained.[56] The great victories and achievements of Rome and Sparta, he declared, were based on a peasant culture, and when Arminius defeated the Roman legions, he did so with an army of free peasants. Rome's glory and virtue had by that time long since disappeared, of course—coincidentally with the gradual replacement of free peasants by slave laborers. In more recent times, Arndt asserted, the Swiss had attained their freedom and maintain it still through the vigor of the free peasant; further, to bring the story right up to the present, the brave attempts of Catalonians and Tyroleans to wrest their freedoms back from the conqueror Napoleon were peasant efforts; and, finally, the well-known freedom-loving character of the Scandinavians was based on the existence of a free peasant class. The conclusion which Arndt drew from all this was that "as old as history is, it pronounces in the clearest and most variegated manner: that a people was always courageous, free, and happy in measure as it had free and vigorous peasants."[57]

It is quite clear from everything Arndt wrote that it was for him largely the direct and active role of the peasant as warrior which raised him above the level of his fellow countrymen. The ability and the readiness of the peasant to take up arms against foreign enemies was always the prize jewel in Arndt's collection of services which the peasant performed for the fatherland. The force of this argument could be clearly understood in the Germany of the Wars of Liberation, when the primary task was a military one; and Arndt, whose greatest patriotic contribution came in precisely this period and in relation to that military task, developed from this specific crisis a Gallophobia and a general super-sensitivity to foreign threats which continued to play a very important part in the shaping of his thought on the role of the peasantry in the decades following 1815. Their overall effect

[56] Arndt, "Erinnerungen aus dem äusseren Leben" (1839-1840), *Werke*, I (Part 2), 198. Much of this material first appeared in Arndt, "Ein Wort über die Pflegung und Erhaltung der Forsten und Bauern im Sinne einer höheren, d.h. menschlichen Gesetzgebung," *Der Wächter: eine Zeitschrift in zwanglosen Heften* (Cologne, 1815-1816). The article was also printed, with a few omissions, as a small book in Schleswig in 1820.

[57] Ernst Moritz Arndt, *Über den Bauernstand und über seine Stellvertretung im Staate* (Berlin, 1815), 16-17.

was that of confirming his belief in the constantly pressing need for the maintenance of a people from which a willing and able soldiery could instantaneously be drawn. On the other hand, the military virtues of the peasant were only one facet or expression (if indeed the most important) of a praiseworthy morality peculiar to the peasantry. It was this morality which was basic to Arndt's views on the social value of the peasant, who through his moral strength acted as a necessary counterweight to the most degenerate and "accursed" elements in society and supplanted or revivified those weakened or scorched by what Arndt called the "fiery elements" of the spirit.[58] The peasantry constituted a "forest," as he picturesquely described it, from which the masts and beams of power must be hewn.[59]

Agriculture was responsible for the content of this morality: it was the first occupation to ennoble and educate man, it had always been associated with freedom, and the free peasant in turn had always preserved more than anyone else all the virtues of body and spirit.[60] The peasant was indeed the very picture of the original active and loyal man, for it was in his hut that the primary virtues of the human race were most truly preserved and nurtured: strength, simplicity, honesty, piety, and courage.[61] His connection with the land had everything to do with his readiness to fight for the preservation of his country. In the first place, his source of income and the location of his work were fixed in the land; unlike those whose wealth consisted in money or other movable treasure, therefore, the peasant could not carry his livelihood with him, and was not inclined to run away in time of national danger.[62] His modest economic circumstances also made him less selfish and materialistic than others; with less to lose than the noble or the rich man, and with the means for his support in his own two hands, he was more easily convinced than they to leave his land and go to battle.[63] Furthermore, the peasant's own feelings of self-identification were most closely bound

[58] Arndt, "Der Bauernstand, politisch betrachtet," *Werke*, IV (Part 10), 47.
[59] Arndt, "Erinnerungen," *ibid.*, I (Part 2), 193.
[60] Arndt, "Der Bauernstand, politisch betrachtet," *ibid.*, IV (Part 10), 44.
[61] Arndt, *Über den Bauernstand*, 16.
[62] Arndt, "Erinnerungen," *Werke*, I (Part 2), 199.
[63] Arndt, "Der Bauernstand, politisch betrachtet," *ibid.*, IV (Part 10), 55.

to his land and to the morality it nurtured: "In the firm and secure ownership of the soil down through long generations from the furthest ancestor to the last grandson, morality, law, honor, loyalty, [and] love [are] fortified: the peasant is the first son of the fatherland; when he becomes a slave, when his heart becomes cold and his arm lax for the fatherland, then it has truly perished."[64] The peasant's land was his history and his identity; and the emotional feeling he had for these were a sure warranty against indifference in times of national danger. As Arndt more than once put it, the peasant thinks more with his heart than with his head, and would therefore rather die in a noble, if hopeless, cause than to lead a safe but cowardly life which betrayed his own deepest sense of what was right.[65]

Arndt was not a thoroughly consistent political thinker; but the successful participation of the people in the mass armies which swept Napoleon out of Germany appeared to him to have proved to others what he professed to know already—the readiness of the people to participate in the public affairs of the nation. He therefore worked hard in the years following 1815 for the acceptance and implementation of a representative constitution on a territorial basis for all of Germany. It was, in fact, his criticism of Prussia's feet-dragging on this and similar issues and of the reactionary elements which tended to gain the upper hand in official circles in the postwar period which led to his suspension from teaching at Bonn. His own version of a national assembly inevitably included recognition of the peasant, and he felt that the peasantry should be represented by deputies from its own midst. His partiality for a continuation of the traditional system of representation by estates is explained to a certain extent by his conviction that more democratic schemes whereby all classes would vote together for general representatives would have the effect of excluding peasants from actually sitting in the legislative body. The only way to be positively sure that peasants themselves sat as representatives was to constitute the peasantry as an estate, and give it representation as such. Certainly Arndt recognized

---

[64] Ernst Moritz Arndt, *Schriften für und an seine lieben Deutschen*, 4 vols. (Leipzig, 1845-1855), II, 113.

[65] Arndt, "Der Bauernstand, politisch betrachtet," *Werke*, IV (Part 10), 54-55.

objections that the peasant was ignorant of political affairs, and that he was one-sided in his views; but he declared the latter to be desirable in a truly representative assembly, and dismissed the former by saying that a start had to be made somewhere in the political participation of the peasant, and that he would be quick to learn once given the opportunity to participate.[66] The electorate of the peasant class would consist of free peasants, whom Arndt defined as those who occupied indivisible peasant farms and who lived or appeared to live entirely from agriculture or directly associated industries. No person already represented in another class would be allowed to vote with the peasantry.[67]

Arndt's devotion to the idea of political representation for the peasantry in a real legislative—as opposed to a merely consultative —assembly was not so much an end in itself, however, as it was a means to an end. Nothing in Arndt's conception of society was as important as the maintenance of a free and independent peasantry; and to give the peasant a voice in legislation was the political guarantee for the preservation of the freedom and independence of his class. Arndt saw, specifically, two methods by which the peasantry might be destroyed: 1) through the accumulation of wealth in particular families, which in various ways could restrict the independence of smaller peasants; and 2) through actual suppression or enslavement of smaller landowners by outright usurpations in times of great need and disorder, when powerful men could arbitrarily dictate conditions of tenure to the small, impotent peasants.[68] He felt that in most instances a man had to be free in the disposition of his property, and in any case absolutely free in his person: but he opposed any provisions which might make it too easy for the peasant to sell, partition, or otherwise alienate his land, for when the peasant lost his sense of responsibility to the land, he also lost his endurance and all moral attitude.[69] Arndt's wish was therefore for a large, widespread class of independent peasants with moderate holdings: "the more free peasants with small or middle-sized property in

[66] *Ibid.*, 74-78.
[67] *Ibid.*, 78-79.
[68] Arndt, *Schriften*, II, 109.
[69] Arndt, "Erinnerungen," *Werke*, I (Part 2), 223.

land a country has, the stronger, more secure, and more valiant such a country is."[70]

How was such a class to be preserved, with respect to both numbers and quality? Arndt proposed that legislation might seek to ensure that at least half or two-thirds, and perhaps even as much as three-quarters of the total arable land of the country be and remain in the hands of peasants with only small or medium-sized holdings. The remainder could be occupied by the nobility and larger peasant or bourgeois owners.[71] In areas where the number of peasants without full ownership of a certain minimum area of land was disproportionately large, the domain lands of the ruling prince should be sold to the highest bidders in lots of from one to three hides. Primogeniture and entail should be introduced on all peasant lands, and no peasant might possess a farm larger than three hides; if a peasant should somehow come into the ownership of a larger amount of land, he would be required to get rid of it: the intent of these measures was after all that the number of free and independent landowners as the food-providers and preservers of the industry and bravery of the folk be maintained, and if two or more farms, each of which would be sufficient for the livelihood of a peasant family, were amalgamated, then their owner ceased to be a peasant and became a lord.[72] Where sale of royal domains was in question, furthermore, Arndt would have permitted only peasants, that is, those who would actually live on the land, to buy, and would have allowed only outright ownership, no lease relationship, to exist.[73]

There is a striking similarity between Arndt's views and those of Freiherr vom Stein as far as the necessity for peasant freedom and proprietorship was concerned. The two were close associates from the time Arndt arrived in St. Petersburg through the period of the military campaigns against Napoleon, and there is no question but that the ideas of each were influenced by those of the other. Certainly both were in full agreement on the value of property for the development (Stein) or the manifestation

---

[70] Arndt, *Über den Bauernstand*, 16-17.
[71] *Ibid.*, 36-37.
[72] Arndt, *Schriften*, II, 110-12.
[73] Arndt, "Erinnerungen," *Werke*, I (Part 2), 226-28.

(Arndt) of the abilities and social-political consciousness of the peasant, and both were absolutely convinced of the desirability of the greatest possible distribution of property among the masses, which in effect meant the maintenance of a numerically large peasantry with small but adequate holdings in land. On the other hand, there was from another viewpoint a substantial difference between Arndt and Stein, one which is indicative of a quite different set of assumptions about the nature and value of the peasantry. Whereas Stein wanted to confer freedom and property on the peasant as a way of developing moral qualities in the peasant of a socially useful sort, Arndt was concerned to grant the same things as a way of releasing moral qualities already possessed by the peasant but momentarily hostage to his legal, social, and economic circumstances. Stein, in other words, did not see the peasantry as the porter of any exclusive moral qualities inherent in its nature. Arndt certainly did, and made no secret of his belief that the close connection of man with land produced invaluable characteristics in men which could not be duplicated elsewhere.

It was of course true that Arndt was intensely concerned with national unity, both in the period of the Wars of Liberation and afterwards, and that he made strenuous efforts to keep his concept of the moral superiority of the peasant from operating as a socially divisive influence on the minds of his readers. He was careful to note that the burgher and the peasant stood in a certain "natural contrast" to one another: the restlessness and inequality of the city and the composite and artificial character of the life and creations of the burgher were sharply different from the tranquillity and equality of the country and the simple and natural life and creative activities of the peasant.[74] But he modified the real harshness of this judgment by saying that although conflicts would arise from this contrast, there was no freedom without lively contention,[75] and by declaring that burghers belonged together with peasants as the "greatest and most honorable part of every people," whose representation in a constitution made

[74] Arndt, *Schriften*, II, 114.
[75] *Ibid.*, 120.

that constitution a democratic one.[76] Similarly, he attempted (with some reluctance, one feels) to broaden his definition of the peasantry to include all men who possessed any landed property of their own: to the peasantry (with its name taken from the root word *bauen*) thus belonged not only the high nobility, which represented a class in itself, but also all noble and bourgeois landowners and "the peasant in the proper sense," who actually guided the plow in the furrow and personally threshed his grain.[77] Arndt vigorously disclaimed any dislike of the nobility, and said that he wrote for the peasant only because he could not speak for himself; but then belied his own impartiality by noting that the nobility needed no spokesmen, for it had enough of a mouth of its own, which indeed it never kept still.[78]

In spite of his attempts to be fair, Arndt possessed an ultimately inescapable feeling that it was the peasantry alone which formed the deepest and most solid foundation for the state and the nation; and his belief that Germany could not afford social division and conflict, strong though it was, was balanced by an equally strong conviction that a readjustment of social relationships was necessary to provide the requisite guarantees of national strength. This dualism led him to conscientious (if tortuous) attempts to develop a formula of social unity, on the one hand, but also to an extreme suspiciousness of the reactionary members of the upper classes whose immediate interests would be adversely affected by such a readjustment, on the other hand, which induced him as early as 1810 to issue a warning against a spirit of reaction to the reform decrees of the Stein ministry.[79] For the times in which he lived and for the foreseeable future, he thought, no virtues were more necessary or more important for the nation than those possessed by the peasant; and this fact tended to determine his scale of social priorities. As has been suggested above, Arndt's viewpoint was shaped to a very large extent by what he conceived to be the most elemental tasks of a national movement; and these

[76] *Ibid.*, 100.
[77] *Ibid.*, 108.
[78] Arndt, "Erinnerungen," *Werke*, I (Part 2), 193-94.
[79] Arndt, "Der Bauernstand, politisch betrachtet: Beilage" (1810), *Werke*, IV (Part 10), 89.

were in turn strongly influenced by armed conflict and foreign invasion, the specific historical conditions under which his nationalism attained its greatest fervency. The primary national task was therefore conceived by Arndt as the preservation of national integrity seen in military terms, or ultimately reducible to such terms: and in an age which had introduced and already made extensive use of the mass army, national defense was unthinkable without reliance on the peasant.[80]

Arndt, finally, was the major figure among those participants in the great national crisis of 1806-1815 who derived the possibility and ultimately also the success of popular participation in the Wars of Liberation from the intrinsic moral worth of the peasant. In many respects, Arndt stood closer to the Justus Mösers and the Friedrich Carl von Mosers of the old regime in his evaluation of the peasant than to the liberal bureaucrats of the Stein era, who indeed foresaw the reinvigoration of the state through the participation of the burgher and peasant, but who conceived this in largely quantitative terms and by a more or less universal standard of civic morality to which the peasant would be educated. Arndt's position that the peasant represented the most essential foundation of the German nation really turned the Stein formula around and advocated the education of the nation to the peasant's morality rather than the raising of the peasant to an upper-class "maturity." Stein felt that the peasant must acquire moral maturity as a basis for political judgment; Arndt, by contrast, saw in the peasantry perhaps the only class whose morality was unimpeachable, and which required only a little experience to convert this into political wisdom. Judged from the standpoint of the practical reforms advocated by each, the two men were quite similar. But it was Arndt far more than Stein who propagated and contributed to the further formation of a special image of the peasant whose content was such as to exalt him above other men.

[80] Arndt's preoccupation with military virtues should not obscure his deeply religious nature, which led him to an identification of Germany's cause with that of God in the period of the Wars of Liberation. Piety (the protestant variety) was a characteristic of Germans, Arndt believed, and he, like many others before him, tended to locate piety in its purest and best form in the peasantry.

9 Restoration Constitutionalism and Liberalism

The experience of the Wars of Liberation proved to the triumphant Prussian reformers that the emancipation of the peasant was a political success. With Arndt, most of them rightly or wrongly believed the surge of popular support for the expulsion of French armies from Prussian soil to have arisen in large measure from the connections established between peasant and fatherland through the machinery of freedom and proprietorship, and in this sense fully to have justified the principles which underlay the reforms.[1] But the insights which led the Prussians to make associations between the moral freedom of the individual, guaranteed by his legal and economic freedom; his participation in public affairs; and the strength of his devotion to his country—these insights were not the sole property of the Prussians. If it was indeed true that Prussia's conspicuous success in 1813-1814 had focused attention on freedom and property for the peasant as efficacious means of politicizing him and thus of enlisting his active cooperation in state business, it was also true that economic and social pressures inherited from before the revolution and from the period of Napoleonic supremacy in Germany had brought many other Germans to the conclusion that the problems of the lower classes demanded a new attention if the instability of the revolutionary period were to be ended and if governments were to develop the human resources of their states for an age in which the masses would perforce play a more important role than had heretofore been the case.[2]

In the years following 1815, the characteristic expression of the desire to integrate the popular element into the political structure of states took shape as a movement towards constitutionalism, a movement to secure a formal and legally guaranteed framework within which was recognized the right of some kind of popular participation in public affairs. The initial successes of this movement in achieving the granting of constitutions in a number of important German states within a few years after the Congress of Vienna were due to several factors. More important than the pressures from political liberals upon conservative governments, probably, was the voluntary acceptance—even imposition—of constitutions by governments or rulers who had become convinced that it was possible to accommodate economic and social changes and the increasing political self-consciousness of the German middle class within the structure of a monarchical state without disturbing its most fundamental values. These governments glimpsed in the constitutional movement an opportunity to create among the people a "state-consciousness," as Fritz Hartung has called it, which would operate as a strong support for prince, state, and law. While the liberals had something quite different in mind, and wished to establish a real political liberty for the people through their influence on legislation and administration, it was yet possible for them, in these early years at least, to cooperate with the more conservative view, since both had in common the intention to establish a *Grundgesetz*, a constitutional law, which in principle would end the legal arbitrariness of absolutism.

As far as agrarian reform was concerned, both liberal and

[1] It is extremely difficult, however, to know with any degree of precision just how much real popular enthusiasm went into the military phase of the German liberation from Napoleon. W. O. Shanahan indicates that desertions from the Prussian *Landwehr* in the first stages of the autumn campaign of 1813 reached 29,000—or about one-quarter of the *Landwehr* strength of 120,000. On the other hand, Shanahan notes that the *Landwehr* formations acquitted themselves honorably in the famous Battle of the Nations at Leipzig from October 16-19, 1813, and that the Silesian *Landwehr,* comprising about 50,000 of the total *Landwehr* strength, was conscripted from a most unwilling population which had been exempt from Prussian military service since the acquisition of the province by Frederick II and which had suffered not at all from the French. Shanahan, *Prussian Military Reforms,* 210, 222-24. Furthermore, a 25 percent desertion rate, extremely high though it may be according to present standards, was certainly no higher than in the time of Frederick II. In any case, contemporaries did not appear to think the rate abnormally high, and were on the whole more than pleased with the popular participation represented by the *Landwehr* system.

[2] For those western and southwestern German areas whose governments had been modified or totally changed under French occupation, the influence of socially progressive French legislation proved to be ineradicable in certain respects; certainly the peasantry benefited a great deal from this period of French hegemony in many of these areas, for even though much of the most revolutionary legislation was voided after the expulsion of the French, a complete return to pre-war conditions was regarded by the restored German governments as neither possible nor even desirable, and the peasantry in almost all cases carried away some material benefits from the Napoleonic period.

conservative constitutionalists in this period accepted the idea that personal freedom was a virtually inescapable necessity for any constitutional state, and the liberals were almost uniformly favorable to the notion that property was a necessary corollary to freedom. On the more conservative side, governments were perhaps generally more favorable to proprietorship as a necessary ingredient of citizenship than were the aristocratic landowners, and many difficulties arose in the implementation of reform laws embodying property rights for the peasantry. In many instances, even in the relatively more progressive states, these difficulties were not resolved until the second half of the nineteenth century. For present purposes, however, it is of much greater importance to note that the principle of citizenship for the peasant had survived the patriotic frenzy of the Napoleonic period which had given it substance for the first time, and that it continued even through the reaction of the 1820s and 1830s to enjoy the support of quite diverse political groups. The establishment of political representation for the peasantry, however modified or vitiated in its actual effect on legislation by constitutional restrictions on the prerogatives and functions of representative assemblies generally or on the position of the peasantry within such assemblies, was a common feature of constitutions adopted in the various German states between 1815 and the late 1830s.[3]

With the realization of a kind of political representation for the peasantry, as provided for in the new constitutions, a final major step in the legal recognition of peasant civic equality was taken. As yet, of course, this did not mean a democratic society with even universal manhood suffrage, or even a society in which individuals rather than estates received political representation. In almost every instance in the new constitutions, franchise was severely restricted, usually by a property qualification, and just as universal was the qualification that different classes were to be represented by deputies sitting in separate houses, chambers, or curiae. In the first few years after 1815, there was a very substantial agreement on the principle of class representation

[3] A brief but cogent survey of such constitutions in the small and medium-sized states of Germany is given in Fritz Hartung, *Deutsche Verfassungsgeschichte vom 15. Jahrhundert bis zur Gegenwart,* 7th ed. (Stuttgart, 1950), 199-212.

among political thinkers and publicists, from the conservative Adam Müller through Freiherr vom Stein and the "official liberals" within governments to republicans such as Joseph Görres. The constitutions were intended by no one to be revolutionary in character, and even the most liberal of them were deliberately calculated to provide recognition of traditional social distinctions. Freiherr vom Stein, for example, emphasized the necessity for reliance on historical law in the drawing-up of constitutions, as opposed to the theories of "political metaphysicians," and advocated that nobility and burghers, each with honor and respect for the other, should be set side-by-side with a strong and prosperous peasantry, and not mixed.[4] In the *Landtag*, the peasantry should no longer be represented by nobles, but by peasants themselves, and the representative assembly would be divided between one group elected by nobles and clergy and another chosen by the towns and the peasantry.[5] Görres was somewhat more democratic than Stein, in that he proposed a single chamber as the representative body for a future German national constitution, and suggested that the number of delegates from the peasantry and middle class should exceed that of the upper classes; but even he stipulated that the nobility and the clergy should each sit in curiae separate from that of the burghers and peasants.[6]

Regardless of the class distinctions which were established in representative bodies, however, the fact of peasant representation remained. It was of course attacked by some. The influential Brandenburg nobleman Friedrich August Ludwig von der Marwitz, for example, disputed all attempts to constitute the peasantry as a separate estate which could claim a right to representation as such. As little as apprentices and shop-servants could claim to be a proper estate in society, so little also could the peasants, said he. Never had peasants been constituted a separate estate without great damage to the state in which this occurred, Marwitz declared, for as long as the peasantry remained peasantry, it could have no real political judgment. Small, free land-

---

[4] K. Freiherr vom Stein (Letter to Nesselrode, December 17, 1817), *Freiherr vom Stein*, V, 426-27.

[5] vom Stein, "Denkschrift" (May 3, 1817), *ibid.*, V, 388-89.

[6] Joseph Görres, "Teutschland und die Revolution" (1819), *Gesammelte Schriften*, XIII, 130.

owners as they existed in some places in Germany were actually not peasants at all, and "if there are peasants anywhere who, beyond their work, can see the state, then they must be reckoned equal to the nobility." If the "producing" class were therefore to be represented, it was the nobles as owners of the land who came under consideration, not the peasants who were their servants.[7] For Marwitz, then, there was no reason to discontinue the traditional representation of the peasantry through the nobility; and in this opinion he was seconded by many other rural nobles.

On the other hand, abolition of servitude and the growth of proprietorship among the peasantry after 1815 had really made at least part of Marwitz' argument inapplicable: the peasant was no longer the servant of the nobility, and as a property owner in his own right it could no longer be maintained that his interests were always the same as those of the nobleman. Furthermore, if it was true that the peasant was politically immature, it was also thought possible that he could be raised to maturity by his participation in representative assemblies. Thus the Freiherr von Wedekind, who by his own admission was convinced that the rural nobility by virtue of its education and experience was best suited to represent the entire rural population, none the less proposed that only half the representatives of the rural areas be nobles, and the other half non-noble landowners. While he would have established a property qualification for the latter, in order to ensure that only the better-educated would be eligible for election, he also thoroughly approved the principle that roturiers from the land should take part in legislative bodies as deputies, "because nothing can contribute more to removing the peasant from his filthy egoism and to infusing him with patriotic opinions than if he might take part in public affairs through people who are of his [own] kind."[8] The kind of support which Wedekind thus lent to the inclusion of peasant interests and peasant repre-

[7] F. A. L. von der Marwitz, "Von den Ursachen des Verfalls des preussischen Staates" (1812), *Friedrich August Ludwig von der Marwitz*, II (Part 2), 60-61, note 2.

[8] Georg Christian Freiherr von Wedekind, *Über den Werth des Adels und über die Ansprüche des Zeitgeistes auf Verbesserung des Adelsinstitutes*, new ed., 2 vols., (Darmstadt, 1817), I, 241-42.

sentatives in legislative assemblies was echoed years later by Ernst von Bülow-Cummerow, an influential member of the Pomeranian estates, a leading agricultural entrepreneur, and a political publicist of some reputation in Prussia. Bülow-Cummerow expressed himself strongly in favor of a class representation precisely because the property qualifications normally attached to the eligibility of candidates in schemes for popular representation had the effect of excluding the less well-to-do from appearing in assemblies. He declared that men of some education would not necessarily speak better for the peasantry than would peasants themselves; the latter knew their true interests quite well, said he, and "their voice makes a much greater impression on every assembly than that of a legal expert not belonging to their class, who, as experience in many countries only too often proves, regards his position more as a bridge to attain influence and high offices than to be useful to his fellow-delegates."[9] In the course of the two decades or so following 1815, then, even the landowning nobility had in some numbers been brought to accept the principle of political representation for the peasant—a principle which guaranteed an active role for the citizenship he had won.

Finally, in the late 1820s and the 1830s, the idea of class representation began to come under heavy attack as the principle gained ground among the liberal intellectuals, especially in the favorable political and parliamentary climate of the German southwest, that the time had come for general popular representation in which traditional class distinctions no longer played an important role. For these liberals, the sense of the reforms which had created a more open society economically by abolishing servitude and granting a more or less universal freedom to acquire and dispose of property was that of doing away generally with the tutelage of individuals by corporate groups of any kind. When Carl Theodor Welcker, the well-known liberal politician from Baden, wrote that the more highly developed and liberal political relationships of his time (the 1830s) meant that all castelike, feudalistic, in short *forced* distinctions had to give way

9 Ernst Gottfried Georg von Bülow-Cummerow, *Preussen, seine Verfassung, seine Verwaltung, sein Verhältniss zu Deutschland*, 2 vols. (Berlin, 1842-1843), I, 49-50,

to natural relationships and differences, he was merely giving expression to an increasingly common conviction among the essentially middle-class liberals that the liberation of the energies of the individual had reduced and simplified social interactions to transactions between individuals of such a sort that group identifications or privileges were not only unnecessary but even harmful. The new and better relationships which Welcker praised were, as he himself said, formed freely through the give-and-take of life itself, through "free practice and autonomic agreements," which permeated one another in a truly organic manner.[10] This was, in other words, a "natural" social world of free individuals acting in their own interest (through "autonomic agreements") quite similar in conception and very closely related to Adam Smith's "natural" economic world. And just as Smith condemned artificial combinations as injurious to the increase of wealth, so did these German liberals, in politicizing Smith's economic man, condemn social corporatism as detrimental to the increase of real freedom. With this general conceptual scheme in mind, it was thus possible for Welcker to proclaim that the word "peasant" had already lost all legal or class meaning, and had come to be used merely to designate those "who live in the country and practice agriculture themselves as their life's work."[11] What emerged from these considerations, in any case, was the idea that *individuals*, not *classes*, were to be represented in legislative assemblies; and it was the growing strength of this idea which was ultimately to confer complete political equality on the peasant, for it was completely to efface all formal political consequences of the individual's occupation. But this was to occur long after the time with which this study is concerned.

For a certain time after 1815, it appeared that the implications of liberal political ideas in the formulations of Welcker and other middle-class theorists would actually tend to destroy the peculiar moral foundation which had heretofore so often formed the basis

---

[10] Carl Welcker, "Bauern," *Staats-Lexikon oder Encyclopädie der Staatswissenschaften*, 15 vols. (Altona, 1834-1843), II, 256.
[11] *Ibid.*, 254.

of attempts to secure equal social treatment for the peasant. If in the scheme of Ernst Moritz Arndt the peasant deserved an increased consideration because of the singular value of his morality or moral qualities to the preservation of the general social morality which Arndt believed necessary to the cohesion of any social group, the universalistic standards of liberal thought implied merely that the peasant, like any other individual, must have his freedom if the natural mechanisms of self-interest (the new basis of moral thought) were to operate as they ought. For the liberal, that is, in theory, the word "peasant" was to have no special moral connotations any more than it had legal ones; the society he wished to create, and which he saw taking shape around him, was one in which individuals, not groups, were the units of social action, and in which "social morality" was a term descriptive of natural processes rather than of a group of particular attitudes which had to be learned or cultivated. And so, it seemed, the picture which had been developed of the peasant as an irreplaceable moral agent from whom society derived continuing strength might well go by the boards in a highly individualistic and freely competitive society such as that which the new liberal thought envisioned.

But, as it happened, before even the liberals could draw this consequence from their own reasoning, a crisis in German agriculture occurred which seemed to pose a threat to the very foundations of the existence of a newly freed peasantry. This was a major agrarian depression in the decade following 1820, a minor catastrophe for large portions of rural Germany, which witnessed the first large-scale migrations of peasants to cities in Germany, which caused widespread rural bankruptcy, and which resulted in the formation of many large land holdings or estates through the purchase of the smaller farms of ruined peasants by entrepreneurs who had sufficient farming capital to make of agriculture a profitable enterprise even in these times of huge crop surpluses and consequent low prices. This crisis raised for the first time the real possibility of a mass expropriation of the peasantry and its consequent proletarianization, a prospect which was alarming enough to put the agrarian problem back among the most central public issues until the middle of the century.

And certainly insofar as discussion of and attitudes towards the peasant were concerned, these matters were of fundamental importance, for they brought German thinkers face-to-face with the disturbing picture of a nation devoid of a strong proprietary class, and consequently gave rise to a reconsideration of the social value and the character of the free peasant proprietor. The end effect of this reconsideration was such as to strengthen the old moral image of the peasant, as well as to add new reasons for his social utility.

The influence exercised on writers by the agrarian crisis of the 1820s and the legacy of problems it bequeathed to later decades may be seen in a number of emphases in the literature of the time. One rather frequent theme is typified by a writing of Friedrich Bülau, economist and professor at the University of Leipzig. His *Der Staat und der Landbau* (Leipzig, 1834) was a lengthy plea for governments to take up once again an initiative in the encouragement of agriculture and the reform of agrarian relationships. Bülau believed that an excessive concern for the commercial and manufacturing sectors of the economy on the part of economic experts and governments had contributed to produce a potentially dangerous lack of interest in the problems of agriculture and its social importance; and he attempted to point out in detail just why agriculture ought to remain the most essential concern of statesmen.

Bülau's arguments, for the most part, were not new. He emphasized that an assured food supply was essential to the independence of a nation in its foreign relations, as well as to its internal social stability; the success of ancient Sparta against Athens and of Rome against Carthage provided historical evidence for the former, while the tumultuous behavior of the lower classes of ancient Rome and of early revolutionary France, stemming from fear of starvation, adequately demonstrated the truth of the latter assertion.[12] In other respects, a healthy and stable agricultural sector tended to give stability to all other aspects of economic activity, because the steadiness of peasant consumer power worked against the occurrence of economic fluctuations

---

[12] Friedrich Bülau, *Der Staat und der Landbau: Beiträge zur Agricu̇ltṳ*· (Leipzig, 1834), 9-11, 18.

which were already becoming endemic in commercial societies. The primary characteristic of the agricultural society, in economic terms, is the preservation of a standard of well-being for all which is midway between the extremes of wealth and misery.[13]

Finally, and perhaps most important, the very character of a people itself will degenerate in a state in which trade and manufacturing are allowed by default to efface agriculture and its allied pursuits: "Who can fail to recognize that the class of lower workers which stands in the service of trade and industry is a frivolous and undisciplined folk, that it easily squanders the easily acquired, that it has no stomach for hard work (or) for harsh privations, that it panders to the moment, is changeable, easily moved, ready for any foolish scheme. Its work is unhealthy, debilitating, preparing the germs of chronic ill health for the days of old age." Bülau hinted darkly at what such a class of people would do when its momentary and frivolous satisfactions were taken away by temporary bad times, and concluded that the very considerable "shadow side" of the commercial state consisted of depravity in the best of times, and in the worst in misdeeds, pestilence, and revolution.[14]

An agricultural state, on the other hand, contains a large peasant population which, Bülau freely admitted, was often sulky, obstinate, prejudiced, and wedded to old customs, but whose vices were entirely in the nature of inconveniences for social accessibility rather than matters of concern for state and society. As for the peasants themselves, "The hard work to which they are obliged, the simple life which they lead, have made diligence and moderation their hereditary virtues. Just as the profit of agriculture is only moderate, comes but gradually and is only possible through frugality, so also is the character of the peasant moderate, peaceful, and hostile to every extreme. His life style, his habitation, his activities are the healthiest for the nature of man. The health of the body also reacts on the health of the spirit. To be sure, even the peasant is subject to sensual desire, and no one can believe in the idyllic dreams of a rural world of innocence. But therein he only embraces the drive of a power-

[13] *Ibid.*, 13.
[14] *Ibid.*, 15-16.

ful nature, which is not overexcited by artificial stimuli. The simple life in the lap of nature continually preserves a sound kernel which also breaks through the crude shell. Loose the fetters of agriculture, see to it that the peasant finds an adequate return for his diligence and insight, encourage education and instruction around him, make it possible for him to acquire a consciousness of his human dignity and citizenship, and you will be able to look with pride upon the class *(Stand)* you have created."[15]

The appeal to stop the decay of agriculture which Bülau made in this writing was thus based as much on the value of the peasant's character to society and the state as it was on the purely economic advantages of a strong and healthy agriculture. He suggested that the stability of the social order itself was at stake in the solution of the problems of agriculture, and that the peasant himself was in many respects the most important social product of agriculture. Among other things, Bülau's work demonstrates that it had become almost impossible for social commentators by the 1830s to separate the economics from the social and political implications of agricultural and agrarian conditions.

The reform proposals which appeared as a consequence of the depression of the 1820s continued to reflect a wide variety of concerns, among which was the immediate desire to reestablish stability in the agricultural sector of the economy by helping the smaller peasant to weather the depression. The political economist Michael Alexander Lips, surveying the agrarian scene in the year 1830, cited the heavy burdens of taxes and fees borne by the peasantry as particular causes of the depression, and asserted that while no other class paid as much in taxes as the peasantry, none enjoyed less advantage from the state. In spite of the progress made in other areas of human life and endeavor, agriculture still remained society's beast of burden; while indeed the Physiocratic injunction to tax only the land had been followed assiduously, none of the benefits which should flow back to the land had been conferred.[16] Quoting a satirist of his day

---

[15] *Ibid.*, 16-17.

[16] Michael Alexander Lips, *Deutschlands National-Oekonomie* (Giessen, 1830), 57,

—and perhaps intending it as a slap at doctrinaire economic liberals—Lips noted that the well-known phrase "live and let live" must, with regard to the peasant, be a typographical error, for from all of scripture the only phrase which properly applied to him was that "it is more blessed to give than to receive."[17] While the ultimate solution to Germany's agrarian problems lay in the permanent severance of the connection between landlord and peasant, Lips believed, the immediate crisis demanded remission of state taxes on peasants, since the failure to do so might well result in the destruction of the taxable object.[18] His own pet project for the future was a single, uniform, and equal income tax with enough built-in elasticity to spare particular individuals in time of great need.[19] Lips' concern with the excessive tax load carried by the peasantry was echoed by numerous others in this time, among them Carl Welcker, who emphasized his plea for a lessening of financial requirements by quoting one source to the effect that in a certain area in Germany the yearly taxes per *Morgen* of land amounted to two Thaler, two Groschen, two Pfennig, whereas the total income per *Morgen* was only two Thaler, three Groschen—leaving a net yearly profit to the peasant of only six Pfennig![20]

A renewal of interest in agricultural credit institutions was related to the preservation of the small cultivator. An article of the early 1840s praised a number of institutions which provided lending capital for rural landowners, but deplored the fact that only nobles had access to them and that the peasantry was so far totally deprived of dependable sources of credit. The author recommended establishment of credit collectives similar to the *Landschaften* of Frederick II,[21] in which the resources of numerous peasants would be merged in such a way that all would bear liability for those who had to borrow.[22] The agriculturist

[17] *Ibid.*, 63 note.
[18] *Ibid.*, 137.
[19] *Ibid.*, 210-12, 218-19.
[20] C. Welcker, "Bauern," *Staats-Lexikon*, II, 254. A *Morgen* was a unit of field-measure which in this time varied, according to locality, from about six-tenths to about nine-tenths of an acre.
[21] See above, p. 5, for the *Landschaften.*
[22] Alexander Schneer, "Über die Errichtung von Credit-Instituten für Rustical-Grundstücke," *Archiv der politischen Oekonomie und Polizeiwissenschaft*, V (1843), 315-36.

Georg von Forstner proposed a quite different plan: royal domains, where they existed, should be sold outright to private persons, and the money thus taken in by the government administered as a credit fund for peasants. What was sought by von Forstner, as by most of his contemporaries, was not merely an increase in possibilities for credit in rural areas, but, more specifically, sources of credit which did not charge ruinously high rates of interest. Von Forstner went so far as to say that the maintenance of the peasantry, and thus of the agricultural industry itself, depended on the freedom of the peasant from the "haggling Jew." "Agricultural credit institutions," he wrote, contrasting these with private moneylenders, "are, *rebus sic stantibus,* an indispensable requirement for the German peasant. In them lies the only means to protect him against usury."[23]

Since the immediate economic symptom of the depression lay in the inability of the peasant to sell his crops at reasonable prices, a number of suggestions designed to solve this particular problem also appeared. These ranged from recommendations for a diversification of crops to cut down the amounts of basic grains glutting the market, to cooperative or governmental grain storage and control of distribution, to the suggestion of M. A. Lips for the more widespread cultivation of potatoes and their conversion get better with every passing day![24] Perhaps the most commonly proposed solution to this and other economic problems, however, was free trade. This doctrine had been hawked about in Germany at least since the 1760s (it was a major part of the Physiocratic program) and had been given great support by German Smithians since the 1780s. The French had gone ahead in the abolition of some internal customs duties and various other imposts even before the revolution, and agitation for the same policy in Germany had achieved results in Prussia in the formation of the Tariff Union in 1818, which was later expanded into the German Customs Union *(Zollverein)* in 1834. The atmosphere for a gradual introduction of free trade was looked on by many writers after 1815 as a favorable one, and there was no lack of free-trade

---

[23] Georg von Forstner, *Gegenwärtiger Zustand der deutschen Landwirthschaft bey ihren dringenden Bedürfnissen* (Tübingen, 1829), 81-82.
[24] Lips, *Deutschlands National-Oekonomie,* 83.

literature in the period. Carl Welcker and his contemporary and coworker Carl Rotteck were convinced free traders, and Rotteck, who saw the maintenance of agricultural prices at a level which would result in a steady real profit for the peasant as the most obvious means of furthering agriculture, theorized that a "middle price" was always the best, imposing hardship on neither producer nor consumer, and that free trade, domestic and foreign, was the best way to assure this middle price.[25] Free movement of grain was therefore quite generally supported as a method of balancing out the shortages of one area with the surplus of another, and of preserving a reasonable price level.

If the decade of agrarian depression gave new impetus to the liberal economists in their advocacy of free trade, it also infused reformers with a new vigor to push towards the completion of specific agrarian legislation which would make proprietors of all peasants in Germany. Prussia was not the only state in Germany whose agrarian lawmaking had begun to experience a conservative reaction almost immediately after 1815; and in 1830 it was possible for Carl Stüve, a Hanoverian statesman and moderate liberal, to write that in such major states as Saxony, Hanover, and Kurhessen virtually nothing had been done for the betterment of the peasantry.[26] Yet, as Stüve pointed out, it was at precisely this time that the greatest necessity existed for the independence of the peasant from his landlord: for just when the peasants desperately needed a relaxation of the obligations required by their landlords, the financial embarrassment of the lords was resulting in a greater pressure on the peasants; the mighty landlord, remarked Stüve drily, was not always benevolent, for his own indebtedness sometimes inclined him to transfer his burdens to others.[27] Thus for Stüve, as for many of his contemporaries, full proprietorship was the only permanent answer to the peasant's problems, as indeed to the problems of German agriculture in general. But it should be noted that a myriad of continuing suggestions from various quarters for less fundamental

[25] Carl von Rotteck, *Lehrbuch des Vernunftrechts und der Staatswissenschaften,* 4 vols. (Stuttgart, 1829-1835), IV, 187.

[26] Carl Stüve, *Über die Lasten des Grundeigenthums und Verminderung derselben in Rücksicht auf das Königreich Hannover* (Hannover, 1830), 67-69.

[27] *Ibid.,* 32-34.

reforms—abolition of labor services, reductions of dues and fees, and so forth—indicate that full proprietorship was not everywhere thought of as a reform likely to be enacted immediately. As late as 1844, indeed, the industrialist, entrepreneur, and prominent liberal Friedrich Harkort still despaired over the realization of widespread full proprietorship for the peasantry when he wrote: "The peasant as he should be is a king on his farm, but as things now stand it will be a long time before we see a people of kings!"[28]

Even more indicative of the concern for the peasant awakened by the depression than the heightened interest in his proprietorship, perhaps, was a marked tendency among reform writers to drop the traditionally conciliatory tone of earlier writers towards the established order, with respect both to extent and method of reform. Not many people, certainly, would have gone quite as far as Carl Rotteck, who impatiently demanded the abolition not only of those peasant obligations which were the results of usurpation and misuse of prerogative, but also of those which in their content or conception appeared to be unjust "in themselves";[29] but a growing dissatisfaction with the slow and cautious progress of reform legislation which had to consider vested interests is obvious in a number of statements. Lips, for example, denied the necessity of considering the rights of the lords in agrarian legislation; the whole problem, he said, had no relation to "rights," but only to the question of whether servitude and its associated evils were in harmony with the long term existence of mankind. In all cases, the public welfare and the "law of humanity" took precedence over historical right, which meant, in this instance, that the lord-peasant nexus had to be destroyed.[30] Carl Stüve expressed much the same sentiment when he wrote that, after all, no rights were invaded when relationships were gently dissolved which, upon close examination, and in the presence of immediate danger to society, could and might have to be totally destroyed for society's protection; reference to the untouchable sanctity of the *status quo* could have no validity where the *status quo* could be demonstrated to be injurious and the

[28] Friedrich Harkort, *Bemerkungen über die Hindernisse der Civilisation und Emancipation der untern Klassen* (Elberfeld, 1844), 33.
[29] von Rotteck, *Lehrbuch*, IV, 145.
[30] Lips, *Deutschlands National-Oekonomie*, 220-21.

result of an injustice which arose from the usurpations of the strong.[31]

The general sentiment expressed in such statements as these found concrete application in proposals which would in effect have reversed the heretofore usual policy of requiring the peasant to bear the burden of proof against his lord in most legal questions relating to servitude or to the obligations arising from either real or personal dependence. It was a common attitude among reformers that most of the services, fees, and dues of the peasant did not arise from free contract, and therefore had no actual legal basis; therefore, as one writer argued, in the establishment of the principles and conditions governing the redemption of feudal obligations their extra-legal origins should be kept in mind, and where no free contract could be proven as their origin, then the presumption of the courts must be more on the side of the peasant than had heretofore been the case.[32]   Similarly, in 1837, Ludwig Duncker, professor at Göttingen and later at Marburg, noted approvingly that it was in his time generally recognized that the burden of proof in the requirement of services and dues was on the person who wished to require them, not on him from whom required.[33] These arguments were of course in one sense merely a specific application of the general principle, characteristic of much nineteenth-century liberal legal and political thought, that contract rather than status was the only admissible basis for valid legal relationships—a view which was extended to the principles of social organization itself, insofar as constitutionalism and the *Rechtsstaat,* with their utilitarian roots, were also the *Vertragsstaat,* or contract-state. But, practically speaking, they also represented a method of relieving the new peasant proprietor from the necessity of remunerating his one time landlord for real dues and services he had once paid in those many instances where no freely contracted agreement could be shown to have provided what was now regarded as a valid legal basis for the obligations; and in this respect they were designed to

[31] Stüve, *Über die Lasten,* 29-30.

[32] Johann Christian Fleischhauer, *Die deutsche privilegirte Lehn und Erbaristokratie, vernunftmässig und geschichtlich gewürdigt, für gebildete Deutsche aller Classen* (Neustadt an der Oder, 1831), 182-83.

[33] Ludwig Duncker, *Die Lehre von den Reallasten, in ihren Grundzügen* (Marburg, 1837), 220.

provide a financial freedom for the peasant which might be sufficient to enable him to develop and maintain an independent farm economy.

Finally, of course, it became impossible to avoid facing a basic question which had become more and more obvious since the principles of peasant proprietorship and the opening of land purchase to all classes had actually been translated into law: were the economic freedoms demanded and achieved for the peasant to be conceived merely as an end in themselves, or were they also the means to another end, an essentially political one? In more specific terms, was "the agrarian problem" to be regarded as an economic one, in which the desired goal was the greatest possible production of commodities from the land, or was it also a political problem, in which the desired goal was a certain kind of political man? Before the 1820s or so, the question had not often arisen in this form, because it was not generally perceived that there could be any real conflict between these as alternatives: if most commentators were agreed that individual ownership made the peasant a politically more responsible person, they were also nearly unanimous in believing that agricultural production would be increased by free proprietorship.

Too few individuals, however, had seen what Freiherr vom Stein saw as early as 1807: that individual ownership of property and complete freedom to acquire and dispose of property were neither the same thing nor even necessarily compatible as principles. It is significant that the major restriction Stein wished to place on the peasant proprietor with regard to property rights was one which would hinder very rich peasants with large amounts of land from buying out their less fortunate neighbors.[34] Stein's goal was a political freedom which depended on the moral responsibility of every individual within the state, and no one was more convinced than he that economic freedom, expressed as the right to be a proprietor, was necessary to build that moral responsibility; but he was also convinced that political freedom in his conception could only be maintained if limits were set to economic freedom. He illustrated this view through his opposition to the freedom of the peasant to sell or bequeath his original

[34] K. Freiherr vom Stein, "Denkschrift" (October 8, 1807), in Pertz, *Das Leben des Ministers*, II, 19-20.

holdings in pieces to different people. The constant decrease in the size of individual farms which would result from such a freedom, he wrote, would lead first to the degradation of the peasantry into a class of virtually landless paupers, but then also to the consolidation of lands into great holdings—for poverty would force peasants to sell out to rich men and "usurers," who would buy up as much land as possible in order to have it worked by agricultural day laborers. The final result would be a small number of great landowners and a great mass of proletarians, as in Italy and England.[35]

What Stein himself favored was a forced preservation, if necessary, of a range of individual farm sizes which would be small enough to insure a numerically large peasantry yet large enough to guarantee the economic viability of each farm. He recognized, certainly, that this "middle size" was fully satisfactory neither to advocates of sheer population increase nor to those who saw the huge estate as the best unit for the maximum production of foodstuffs. But the tiny farm size demanded by the former and the large size required by the latter both contained the danger which Stein most wanted to avoid: the increase of propertyless-ness among the masses. The state's purpose, as he saw it, should be its own perfection in a religio-moral, intellectual, and political sense, and this could never be accomplished if the population dissolved into day laborers, poor landed proprietors, and "Christian and Jewish usurers," officials, and other undesirables who were driven through life solely by greed and the search for pleasure.[36]

However much Stein may have wished to maintain certain social controls which, while conferring freedom and property on the peasant, would also have prevented him from ruining himself, neither he nor his successors actually put through or saw passed into law any of the legal qualifications which would have to have been attached to the original emancipation legislation if the latter objective were to be realized.[37] The most famous

[35] vom Stein (Letter to Spiegel, January 29, 1822), *Freiherr vom Stein*, VI, 62.

[36] vom Stein (Letter to Spiegel, March 28, 1820), *ibid.*, V, 620-21.

[37] It is of course true, however, that those provisions of the Prussian law which in effect stipulated a certain standard of well-being as the qualification for proprietorship were an attempt to guarantee a safe start for those peasants who could become proprietors.

of his successors in the "reform period," Prince Hardenberg, was in fact a Smithian of considerably more one-sided conviction than Stein, and at the same time a bureaucrat in the traditions of enlightened absolutism, who was not at all interested in the preservation of any of the corporate groups or corporate privileges of the traditional estates or occupational groups. The legislation he sponsored tended towards a much more homogeneous society, economically and politically, than did that of Stein, and, with specific regard to agrarian relationships, sought to establish the proprietorship or economic freedom of even marginal peasants without making provision for any sort of protection for their scarcely viable farms. The ruinous effects of such a policy did not become strikingly apparent until the 1820s; but they had been foreseen and feared as possibilities much earlier. The later eighteenth century was filled with warnings about the dangers of emancipation of peasants who, losing their lords' protection at the same time they gained their freedom from his dominion, might in a crisis find themselves bankrupt without any source of help, and thus completely ruined.

Despite the obvious tendentiousness of this argument as a tool of landlords who opposed peasant emancipation from selfish motives, there was more than a grain of truth in it, as was recognized by many reformers themselves, who spilled much ink in attempts to show how this objection might be overcome. Other fears appeared after the turn of the century. An interesting radical indictment of Stein's reform work which appeared shortly after the emancipation edict of October 9, 1807, for example, declared that this ostensibly liberal enactment was in fact a coup for the nobility, in that by making land purchase available to anyone it had in effect abolished the old legal prohibition against the incorporation of peasant farms by the nobility, and raised the specter of peasant expropriation through the various subtle and not-so-subtle pressures to sell which a nobleman could still bring to bear on neighboring peasants.[38] This critic's solution to the problem here raised was contained in a suggestion for an agrarian law which would fix the maximum and minimum legal sizes of landed property, for "a people whose landed property

[38] "Über die neuerlich geschehene Aufhebung des Adels im preussischen Staate," *Neue Feuerbrände*, II (Achtes Heft), 135-36.

is distributed in great portions among a few owners must consist of a few free citizens and many slaves."[39] This attack on Stein's reform thus stemmed from the same fears which Stein himself harbored, and recommended measures which, left to himself, Stein would quite possibly have added to the original reform decrees had his ministry lasted a few years longer.

Furthermore, some of the criticism of the economic "liberation" of society which proceeded apace in Germany in the first two decades of the nineteenth century originated from precisely the same kind of moral-political concerns which moved Stein deliberately to cut off his reforms far short of total economic freedom. When in 1800 the German philosopher and critic Friedrich Schlegel commented that "Where politics or economy is [concerned], there is no morality,"[40] he was stating as an accomplished fact a condition of public affairs which Stein was intensely concerned to correct or prevent. Morality was for Stein the basis of a strong and sound state, indeed of politics itself, and his use of Smithian economic ideas was to extend only as far as they bolstered a moral sense and responsibility among the citizenry. For Smith's world, conceived as an essentially amoral social order based on competition or mutual exploitation of citizens by one another, he had no use whatever. Clearly Schlegel's inclusion of "economy" in his aphorism had to do with this tendency of utilitarian thought among liberal rationalists. The philosopher and conservative Austrian official Adam Müller further illustrates the growing concern of political moralists with the potentially pernicious effects of rationalist (Smithian) economics on society. In a fascinating dispute which appeared in the pages of the *Berliner Abendblätter* late in 1810, a series of somewhat indirect disputations on Adam Smith's doctrines emerged in the framework of what at first began as a eulogy of the newly deceased Königsberg economics professor Christian Jakob Kraus. Müller's contribution came in the form of faint praise for Kraus, who was generally recognized as a figure of major importance in the spread of Smithian ideas in Prussia, especially among younger bureaucrats; while giving Kraus full credit for good intentions,

[39] "Welche Veränderungen," *ibid.*, II (Sechstes Heft), 53.
[40] Friedrich Schlegel, "Ideen," *Athenaeum*, III (1800), 22.

Müller yet took this occasion to wonder about the utility and validity of *The Wealth of Nations,* warned prospective economists against the "seductive certainty" of the book, and expressed great doubt that the science of economics could attain absolute principles and unconditional precision outside the science of law, from which, he said, economics was inseparable, and while the "theory of the state itself is still in dispute."[41] What worried Müller was the possibility that Smith's economic model would be allowed to determine social organization in such a way that the operation of alleged "natural laws" would remove all necessity for deliberate moral choice from the individual and, by forcing him into a narrow and confined occupation through the specialization of labor, make it impossible for him to face the variety of human situations which alone could make of him a political man in a moral sense, a man who could see his own life and work in perspective to that of other men and to society as a whole. This was the purpose of Müller's citation in another work of an English author who had written that the lower classes in England had dreadfully low moral standards, and that they had lost the simple, natural feeling of justice which characterized the uncorrupted peasant; in England, Müller's authority continued, the greatest crimes were committed by the lower classes, whereas in other countries, where the people preserved their rural and pastoral habits, the worst crimes were committed by the privileged classes. For Müller, who swallowed these generalizations whole, this constituted sure proof of a connection between crime and the division of labor, and he concluded that a moral man needed a wide range of different activities for his life —something which the versatility of the agrarian life, as Adam Smith himself admitted, afforded the peasant.[42]

It was precisely the same concern which moved the social critic Ludwig Börne to inveigh against the division of labor as a principle which restricted the human spirit, cut the individual off from his fellow man, and made him lonely and solitary as he had never been before. And, referring specifically to the peas-

---

[41] Ps. [Adam Müller], "Über Christian Jakob Kraus," *Berliner Abendblätter,* No. 11 (October 12, 1810), 44.

[42] Adam Müller, *Vermischte Schriften über Staat, Philosophie, und Kunst: erster Theil,* 2d ed. (Vienna, 1817), 233-35.

antry, Börne questioned whether the personal servitude *(Leibei-genschaft)* of peasants in antiquity was an any more unhappy condition than the spiritual servitude *(Geisteseigenschaft)* of the 1820s: the former, after all, at least had the fatherly care of their lords, while the latter are "orphaned and free of all bonds of relationship."[43] The pessimism awakened by this state of affairs and by the increase of propertylessness among the peasantry which was its most obvious economic earmark can be seen in the dire predictions of social disorder and moral degeneracy for the future made by such a person as Ernst Moritz Arndt throughout the 1820s and 1830s, but beginning as early as 1817, soon after it became apparent that the high hopes of the Liberation had a good chance of remaining merely hopes: "What is the mass of men as compared to the goodness and the fine and faithful sense and the pure kernel of power and the simplicity of morality and sense which alone can protect the peasant?" he wrote. "Who can save a land against the inundation which the overflow of factories, the riches of trade, and the exaggerated partition of land will bring; against the rabble of men, that nameless misery, which England now partly has, and which one sees in Germany here and there, where 500 to 1000 too many men live on one square mile?"[44]

Much the same sense of discouragement can be detected in the writings of Barthold Georg Niebuhr, the famous historian of Rome, whose views on the historical and contemporary importance of a free and independent peasantry were similar to those of Arndt. The very plenitude of freedom given the peasant proprietor contained the seeds of slavery, thought Niebuhr: with unimpeachable motives and in the sincere belief that they were doing the peasant a favor, liberal government circles were in fact destroying him through the unrestricted right granted him to sell, partition, and mortgage his lands. Quoting a contemporary, Niebuhr wrote that all German states which were not completely stationary were by their legislation creating within themselves the same situation which then obtained in Italy: bungling

[43] Ludwig Börne, "Vorrede," *Die Spende,* Offenbach, 1823, in *Ludwig Börnes gesammelte Schriften,* 8 vols in 3 (Leipzig, n.d.), I, 192-93.
[44] Ernst Moritz Arndt, "Briefe an Franz Hegewisch" (Letter of August 5, 1820), *Preussische Jahrbücher,* LVI (1885), 395.

artisans and small shopkeepers in the cities, and in the country a rabble of day-laborers and peasants without property.[45]

In the minds of almost all the writers who worried about the decline of the peasant, delivered over, as they thought, to exploitation in an economic world which he could neither comprehend nor cope with, existed actually a double concern: there was, first, a fear of the general economic dislocations which could result from the collapse of agricultural prices and land values; but there was also a perhaps even more fundamental anxiety about a political and moral decay in society, of which the worsening economic situation of the peasant appeared to be a symbol. The first of these worries, the economic crisis itself, was reflected not only in the proposals for further reforms within the agricultural sector described earlier in this chapter, but also in renewed attempts to define and emphasize the importance of the place of agriculture within the economy as a whole. These took the form of reminders that agriculture or the extractive industries in general formed the basis of economic life, and that no facet of the economy could long prosper if agriculture remained in a depressed condition. Ernst von Bülow-Cummerow, for example, ascribed the continuing lack of general attention to the agricultural sector to a stubborn refusal of nonagrarian interests to recognize that the interests of trade, manufacturing, and agriculture were not separate, but one and the same—a mistake whose origins he found in a deep-seated antinoble prejudice for which there was no longer any justification.[46] Other important figures such as Carl Rotteck, K. H. L. Pölitz, L. T. Spittler, and Karl Friedrich Schenck emphasized the interdependence of various sectors of the economy, pointing out, however, that there was scarcely an industry or manufacture which did not depend on agriculture.[47] Schenck, for example, assured advocates of German industrial expansion that the possibility of growth in that sector was greater in countries where a strong agriculture existed than

[45] Barthold Georg Niebuhr, *Lebensnachrichten über Barthold Georg Niebuhr*, ed. Dora Hensler, 3 vols. (Hamburg, 1838-1839), III, 65.

[46] von Bülow-Cummerow, *Preussen*, I, 48.

[47] von Rotteck, *Lehrbuch*, IV, 135; Ludwig Timotheus Spittler, *Vorlesungen über Politik*, ed. Karl Wächter (Stuttgart and Tübingen, 1828), 364-68, 385; Karl Heinrich Ludwig Pölitz, *Staatswissenschaftliche Vorlesungen für die gebildeten Stände in constitutionellen Staaten*, 2 vols. in 1 (Leipzig, 1831-1832), II, 177-79.

in those where it was poorly developed, both because the need for foreign raw materials in the former was less than in the latter, and because the former could be more sure of its food supply than the latter.[48] Behind these views one can find evidence not only of a greater sophistication in the understanding of economic interdependence, but also of a recognition of some of the requirements of a complex national economy in the midst of a vastly expanded international economic competition—an essentially nationalist reinforcement for the argument of national economic integration.[49]

While it is perhaps not difficult to understand why the crisis of agriculture as a productive industry would cause great concern and would evoke proposals to arrest any decrease in production, it is yet not entirely clear why this crisis would produce a universal sentiment for the maintenance of a large, independent peasantry. The preservation of agriculture and the preservation of the independent peasant were not the same thing, and could even be conceived as mutually exclusive: Adam Smith, after all, had clearly pointed out the advantages of large-scale cultivation over small farms as far as maximum output of marketable produce was concerned, and a number of his followers in Germany accepted his conclusions, among them the famous agriculturist Albrecht Thaer. It is true that there was some opposition to this principle almost from the very beginning, in that some economists valued the intensive cultivation which they claimed was the prime advantage of the small farm over the possibilities for division of labor and more efficient use of new tools in extensive cultivation advocated by Smithians as the chief advantage of the large estate. But it is striking that in the 1820s and 1830s there could only rarely be found a statement supporting the view that perhaps the growth of the large estate was, in the long run, a beneficial development. On the contrary, this eventuality was seen almost exclusively in terms of the expropriation and disappearance of the smallholder, and was loudly lamented by all—

[48] Karl Friedrich Schenck, *Das Bedürfniss der Volks-Wirthschaft*, 2 vols (Stuttgart, 1831), II, 2-3.

[49] The economist Friedrich Bülau in his *Handbuch der Staatswirthschaftslehre* (Leipzig, 1835), for example, emphasized that the economic independence of the state from foreign countries depended on the prosperity of agriculture.

economists, officials, agriculturists, politicians. It is very unusual to find in this period a treatment of the departure from the land of the ruined or bought-out peasant which appears to recognize even faintly the possibility that the migrations of peasants from the rural areas might be anything but an unmitigated disaster. Since these migrations were almost universally damned, there were, naturally enough, few attempts to propose measures to accommodate them. Instead, everyone's attention was turned to the question of how to stop the exodus, or, differently stated, how to create conditions of social stability in rural areas and, increasingly, in urban areas as well.

The characteristic solution to this question, by the 1830s, was expressed in terms of the correct distribution of land among the rural population. And, as suggested above, those who occupied themselves with this question almost without exception came down on the side of a society consisting of essentially small peasant proprietary holdings. The development of this argument is very revealing of the continuing vitality of the conception of the peasantry as the moral cement of society at large, as well as of the hopes and fears of social thinkers who in these years found a new application for that conception in the solution of the most pressing social and political problems of their own day. This can be illustrated in the thought of two professorial representatives of the social thought of the 1830s, both of them economists: Robert von Mohl and C. W. C. Schüz.[50]

Von Mohl, whose *Die Polizei-Wissenschaft nach den Grundsätzen des Rechtsstaates,* first published in 1832-1834, is one of the most important early works in the development of liberal political theory in Germany, regarded the correct distribution of land as an absolutely fundamental prerequisite for a free and healthy society. The most essential principles of correct distribution were the preservation of the possibility of land ownership

[50] Aside from the statements of Freiherr vom Stein and Ernst Moritz Arndt, as well as these men, other views favoring some sort of regulation of farm size may also be found in Theodor Hartleben, "Akerbau," *Geschäfts-Lexikon* (Leipzig, 1824), I, 22-26; C. Welcker, "Bauerngut," *Staats-Lexikon,* II, 263-67; Schenck, *Das Bedürfniss,* I, 104-105; Stüve, *Über die Lasten,* 168-71; and Georg von Forstner, *Landwirthschafts-Polizey, ein Ding, das da seyn sollte—und nicht ist und Domainen-Wirthschaft, ein Ding, welches nicht seyn sollte, und doch ist* (Tübingen, 1810), 42-43.

for all, as well as the establishment and maintenance of small and middle-sized estates. Where these principles were not observed, said von Mohl, the result would be an exodus of peasants from the land, who would then either have to leave the country entirely or else go to the cities to seek their livelihood. If they emigrated, the state would lose capital both in labor resources and in money; if they went to the cities, then the urban areas would grow in a manner potentially dangerous for the moral and physical strength of the country as well as for the security and order of the state.[51]

Even more important was the fact that when only a few men had rights of ownership of land, the great mass of citizens feel themselves robbed of a native right, the right to acquire, which produces a constant sense of social grievance. Furthermore, exclusion from land ownership deprives the majority of citizens of a major civilizing influence: "Not only for savages is the ownership of landed property and its cultivation the first step of civilization: favorable effects accompany this relationship through all stages of society. Order, industriousness and foresight are attached to it. The landowner, in the enjoyment of a home, participates in the preservation of lawfulness, peace and order in the state; while a propertyless mass of agricultural day laborers *(Kolonen)* is easily inclined to any kind of change."[52] Von Mohl was particularly concerned to keep alive the possibility of very small-scale ownership of land for artisans and factory workers, because he felt that this kind of ownership was important in creating a sense of satisfaction and material well-being among these working classes; cultivated by the worker and his family in their spare time, such small pieces of land provided a change of pace, relaxation in the open air, and some produce for men whose usual work was often debilitating.

Another direct result of concentration of ownership of land in the hands of a few was a lack of "inner political energy." This, said von Mohl, results from one or both of two things: 1) the suffocation of the feeling of freedom on the part of agricultural

[51] Robert von Mohl, *Die Polizei-Wissenschaft nach den Grundsätzen des Rechtsstaates,* 3d ed., 3 vols. (Tübingen, 1866), II, 19-23. The first edition was published 1832-1834.
[52] *Ibid.,* 16.

workers who recognize their abject dependence on the owners, who are unable to develop a free public opinion of any value, and who permit eventual misrule within the state resulting in a lack of active support from the people in case of foreign war; or 2) there is a "secret struggle" between the "soil-monopolists" and the workers, which then allows a foreign enemy to find willing allies within the body of the people itself. The growth of both rural and urban proletariats, bad in itself as far as the living conditions of the masses are concerned, is made even more terrible because of the political danger it represents to the state.

Finally, von Mohl attacked the concept of land monopolization by a few with the argument that the resulting poverty of the huge mass of the peasantry necessarily affected adversely the industrial sector of the economy, by reducing consumer power and substantially lessening the amount of goods which could be sold to domestic consumers by the various manufacturing industries. In this, he added a powerful economic argument to a point of view which in other respects was conditioned largely by his concern for the social and political prerequisites for a healthy and stable free society.[53]

To encourage general extension of landed proprietorship, von Mohl recommended the sale of state domains to private buyers, limitation of the mortmain of religious institutions, the general alienation or sale of village common lands to private individuals, restrictions on the use of primogeniture and entail, and general abolition of feudal ties of all kinds.[54] He was not in favor of any very massive intervention of legislative power to regulate property size, however; the dictates of economic freedom did not permit it, and like many of his liberal contemporaries, von Mohl escaped the apparent contradiction between economic freedom and social stability by almost deliberate evasions. For example, he saw nearly as much danger in excessively small holdings as in too large ones, but he wrote that it would be almost impossible to prevent fragmentation of land by state intervention while still preserving a necessary freedom; he concluded rather lamely that education and propagandization of landowners themselves

[53] *Ibid.*, 14-19.
[54] *Ibid.*, 40-70.

was perhaps the best way to prevent excessive division of land.[55]

Von Mohl was not so ambiguous on the questions of servitude and peasant proprietorship. He favored the abolition of all forms of servitude by state action, and was emphatic in his belief that nothing less than full ownership for the peasantry could approach the social desiderata of the *Rechtsstaat*.[56] Nor did he believe that peasant emancipation would automatically lead to peasant proprietorship: "a correct economic relationship of those who are freed must be solicited. Nothing would be less desirable for the general interest, as well as for that of the freedmen themselves, than if through the emancipation a widespread agricultural proletariat of the worst kind, namely of day laborers or small lessees, should arise. . . . Rather, a peasantry with free landed property is to be created."[57]

For von Mohl, quite clearly, the avoidance of the growth of a proletariat was a major problem; it was essential to the stability of a free society such as he envisioned that its citizens be free men not only in a formal or legal sense, but that they be free with respect also to a moral independence which could not exist (at least not optimally so) under the conditions of wage labor. The establishment of small landed properties was a means towards the goal of a society free in both respects. But the negative purpose of preventing the growth of a proletariat was but one side of a coin, the other side of which was a positive appreciation of the specific benefits brought to society by a strong, free peasantry; von Mohl put them this way: "The occupation of the peasant is healthier for body and spirit; he remains a man, and does not become merely a piece of a machine. The family life of the peasant is natural and essentially moral. Through these characteristics he forms the firmest foundation of a sound condition of people and state. Surely reasons enough for the state to extend to agriculture all the encouragement which it requires and which is compatible with correct principles."[58] Reasons enough, too, to be persuaded of von Mohl's convictions on the importance of the peasantry as the desired foundation of social and political stability

[55] *Ibid.*, 26-29.
[56] *Ibid.*, 17, n. 6.
[57] *Ibid.*, 12-13.
[58] *Ibid.*, 165.

in an age when property was to provide the moral nexus linking the individual to his state and society.

More explicit even than von Mohl's work in making the connection between the *Rechtsstaat*, the peasantry as one of its most essential guarantors, and the consequent necessity of widespread small landed holdings, was a book entitled *Über den Einfluss der Vertheilung des Grundeigenthums auf das Volks- und Staatsleben*, published in 1836 by a young economist at the University of Tübingen, Carl Wolfgang Christoph Schüz. After examining at length the entire question of whether large estates were better or worse for society than small estates, Schüz concluded that in every respect the small estate was more beneficial. Like von Mohl, by whom he was undoubtedly influenced, Schüz believed that the traditional legal protection afforded large estates to prevent their dissolution was an evil which tended to exclude the masses from the possibility of land ownership. "In this exclusion of a large, especially poor part of the population from landed property lies the germ of a later dissolution of the legal order, and the state, which ought to be a lasting realization of the idea of law, takes up into itself something which is in contradiction to itself; it nourishes a serpent in its breast. There arises, namely . . . a poor population in the state without landed property—the great working class. [Once] this population has grown to such a degree that a great part of it can almost never be sure of its existence, then it will make use of illegal and forcible means to secure it. These means, however, will consist of nothing other than that which lies before its eyes: namely, in robbery of the wealthier . . . through deceit or by the superior power of physical force. But this is the destruction of the legal order."[59]

For Schüz, the *Rechtsstaat* meant freedom for every individual to set and pursue his own life's goals. This implied the right of every individual to acquire landed property, and to dispose of it as he chose. He admitted that there was no sure way to guarantee that full freedom to buy and sell land would not result in a detrimental overfragmentation of land; but he worried much less about this possibility than about the known evils of large estates.

[59] Carl Wolfgang Christoph Schüz, *Über den Einfluss der Vertheilung des Grundeigenthums auf das Volks- und Staatsleben* (Stuttgart and Tübingen, 1836), 101-102.

Historically, he wrote, the development of a small, wealthy landed aristocracy, ruling over a class of dependents, had resulted in the growth of such evils as slavery, personal servitude, and feudal political and social privileges: "One can therefore say: that where landed property is piled up in the hands of a few, popular freedom will be very limited."[60] A system of large estates, furthermore, is politically damaging to the state in its foreign relations, for it develops a large class of day laborers: "how will that class of day laborers fight for the fatherland, [when] neither attachment to its masters, nor material interests, nor an idea binds it to the fatherland—slaves are also cowards."[61]

By contrast, the free divisibility of land, leading to widespread free proprietorship, "encourages the cultivation of the soil, and creates a large farming population, which through the ownership of a firm property forms a solid and broad foundation for the social pyramid."[62] Public stability in the state is greatly strengthened, "in that a great propertyless mass . . . is not formed, but rather the largest part of the citizens is bound to the existence of a firm legal order through the interest for peace and security that an immobile property, a family, and the possibility of providing for oneself honestly instill."[63] Finally, since the independent proprietor is challenged by the varieties of his work to a much greater extent than is the day laborer, said Schüz, a system of small land holdings produces more men with more developed understandings; and this, in turn, leads to the possibility of a free and democratic community life among sober and thoughtful citizens, something which is highly improbable in a society consisting of large, scattered estates, where aristocratic ideas tend to predominate and where the agricultural laborer is sunk in ignorance and apathy.[64]

The treatment accorded the question of land divisibility and the correct size of landed properties by both von Mohl and Schüz (as well as by many others of their contemporaries) reveals one very significant fact: the nature of this agrarian problem was

[60] *Ibid.*, 103.
[61] *Ibid.*, 107-108.
[62] *Ibid.*, 135.
[63] *Ibid.*, 133.
[64] *Ibid.*, 130-32.

seen largely as a political and social one, not as an essentially economic one. It is true that both authors justified a system of widespread small proprietorship on economic grounds, claiming that it not only resulted in a greater total of agricultural produce than a system of large estates, but that it also benefited the industrial sector by increasing the number of reasonably affluent consumers. But these economic justifications took a distinct back seat to a manifestly greater concern for simple social stability. Both men feared the proletarianization of the peasant, and this fear stemmed not just from the obvious possibilities of social disturbances arising from the rootlessness, jealousies, and economic misery of propertyless wage earners, but also from an awareness that the very essence of the liberal constitutionalism which both men so strongly favored for the German states rested on the voluntary acceptance and observance of the principles of law and order by intelligent citizens. If the precept that free citizens ought to participate in the making of law were to hope to win permanent acceptance, then it would have to be demonstrated that they were willing and able to observe the laws which they helped to make for themselves. The principles of constitutionalism and popular participation were still extremely fragile ones in the Germany of the 1830s; and for such thinkers as von Mohl and Schüz, only the moral independence which came from property ownership and the understanding which came from the social manipulation of property could provide the basis for proper citizenship in the *Rechtsstaat*. A proletariat, by contrast, tended by its very nature to be hostile to the legal orderliness which was the essential foundation of a popularized constitutional state.

Of course, much of the advocacy of the small proprietary estate was merely one aspect of a liberal program which demanded general freedom for all individuals to acquire property according to their means. But this itself was inextricably tied to a conception of politics which saw in property the basis of political life itself; as the industrialist Friedrich Harkort put it in 1844, "in order to guarantee the fundamental law of states, [which is] the sanctity of ownership, the path to acquire property in a lawful fashion must be opened to all, and the opposing limitations fall away." Harkort stated the essential problem in the clearest and most concise terms: "The poor man is prevented from acquiring property, [and] therefore thinks about division by physical force. We make laws against the fragmentation of estates, favor primogeniture—[but] look at Ireland and the results."[65]

The whole debate over the proper size of proprietary land holdings was therefore really, in the end, a political debate. It is not surprising that the peasantry was regarded as a key element in the success or failure of constitutional government, conceived in these terms, because its sheer numbers could provide either the positive alternative of a society firmly anchored in proprietorship or the negative one of millions of rural and urban proletarians. But for present purposes, it is perhaps most important to note not only that the personal qualities of the peasantry—its stability, conservatism, morality, and stubborn independence—were here again used as a major reason to work for its preservation as a large social class, but also that these arguments gave to the peasantry a more specific political and social significance than it had ever had: the guarantor of a political order based on the rule of law.

The writings of Carl Rotteck and Carl Welcker, two of the most important figures in the development of German political liberalism after 1815, provide another interesting commentary on the adoption of the peasant as the guardian of social integrity and morality by the representatives of the new and powerful strain of liberal political thought in Germany after 1830. Rotteck gave agriculture credit as the pioneer of civilization and its continuing tutor, which protected it from the evil results of excessive refinement and the overcrowded life of the cities. As for the peasant himself, Rotteck asserted that steady intercourse with nature opened the peasant's heart to all natural and good feelings, and that his constantly changing work, in the open air and always connected with the enjoyment of nature, kept him physically and spiritually strong and healthy. He was by nature happy and frugal, and, where oppressive force and injustice did not weigh upon him, normally contented, for his pleasures were simple and not accompanied by bad aftereffects. His importance for society was derived from these characteristics: "The peasant class is the

[65] Harkort, *Bemerkungen,* 9.

constantly fresh source of life from which the other classes of society, which all have the inclination to gradual languor or to corruption, draw their continual refreshment or renovation. Love for the fatherland and all virtue which flows from it is especially characteristic [of the peasant class]. Through the land and soil which it possesses and which yearly yields its gifts to it, which it loves as its nourisher, it is tied with the firmest bonds to the fatherland, of which this soil is a part." The peasant, who could not tear himself away from his fatherland, would fight much harder for it than merchants, manufacturers, and capitalists, who could easily move their fluid wealth from one land to another; and he would move from his land only under the most catastrophic conditions, so that if he were but treated with some semblance of justice, the state and the government could count on him in every emergency and danger. It was for these reasons (repetitious, for the most part, of those offered by various writers for the previous half century), said Rotteck, that all wise lawgivers and rulers of the past had honored and improved agriculture, and had received manifold blessings and advantages in return.[66]

Carl Welcker was even more rapturous than Rotteck in his praise of agriculture and the peasant. The best and most important example of progress in his time, wrote Welcker, was the gradual accession of the peasantry to an honorable position and a more nearly free and just relationship in society. It was more than a figure of speech, he said, to characterize agriculture as the most important, one of the healthiest, and, by virtue of its natural moral effect, also one of the noblest occupations. Earth and soil were, after all, the most important property of the nation which, together with the citizens, formed the very basis of the state and the most solid foundation for the independent personality of the citizens. Of particular importance was the fact that the peasant class, always the most numerous in a state, could, and if properly treated, would provide healthy stock, a morally and physically sound foundation for the rejuvenation of the state and its old virtues and freedoms. Welcker spoke of the beneficial influences of life in open nature and of the peasant in his "still, fresh valleys" and his "forested heights," leading an

[66] von Rotteck, *Lehrbuch*, IV, 134-36.

idyllic life, where no feudal destruction of his freedom, pressure of servile dues and services, and the arbitrariness of officials had dragged him down and made him suspicious, where "clerical obscurantism and fanaticism" had not stupified him, and where, finally, proximity to large cities or main highways had not corrupted him with metropolitan luxury and usury. A person who was privileged to observe peasants who lived without any of the pernicious influences described above, Welcker maintained, would wonder at their "physical health and vigor, as [at] their uncorrupted and forceful disposition and their sound, accurate judgment, the manly preservation of old loyalty and old principles and customs, of old freedom and rights." For these reasons, the simple and healthy peasant life, always opposed to the growth and transformations of corrupting modes and "modelasters," constituted a storehouse of virtue which could save the nation even if corruption threatened the rulers, the upper classes, city folk, and along with them the constitutional structure and administrative institutions of the state.[67]

The explanation of the wildly laudatory effusions of liberal-national thinkers such as Rotteck and Welcker on the character and utility of the peasant has several aspects. First, it is hardly necessary to insist on the importance the peasantry assumed in any framework of liberal political ideas which included the notion of constitutionalism based on widespread popular participation in legislation and government. For doctrinaire liberal political thinkers, especially, among whom Carl Rotteck must certainly be numbered, concepts of popular sovereignty could not be validated without the inclusion of the peasantry, which still formed an overwhelming majority of the population of Germany. Even apart from any personal convictions on the matter, it was good propaganda for their political ideas to raise the peasantry to the exalted level suggested in the above descriptions; for having thus demonstrated the essential contributions of the peasant to state and society, it was then possible to demand that formal provision be made to facilitate the exercise of the peasant's beneficial influence on state and society through government—that is, through some sort of constitutionally guaranteed participation in legisla-

[67] C. Welcker, "Bauern," *Staats-Lexikon*, II, 254-56.

tion. Furthermore, the heavy emphasis placed by both Rotteck and Welcker on the connection of peasant to fatherland, and their singular view of the *nature* of that connection, point up the gradual growth of an assumption on the part of liberal-national reformers that the numerous peasant class could perhaps give the fundamental cohesion to the structure of a national Germany yet to be realized. The national element, it is true, does not yet predominate; but it is quite clear that in these writings the peasantry is regarded as a socially integrative element, which could perhaps provide one answer to the rather serious problem of how a basic social unity was to be preserved beneath the free play of conflicting interests of a "free" society. The problem here may be stated as follows: it was commonly agreed by liberal political theorists in this time that a free society implied the conflict of differing ideas and interests, with full opportunity for differing groups to air their arguments and, ultimately, to reach compromises with one another in conclusions which expressed a common agreement on the public welfare. But underlying the whole structure of this view was the assumption that conflicting groups would reach agreements before their conflicts degenerated into social struggles whose intensity could destroy the very foundations of any community cooperation. In other words, some integrative principle had to bind these groups to one another so that the social effect of their disputes would ultimately be constructive rather than destructive.

In the search for a new integral principle, the "natural order" of politics and society as represented by stereotyped interpretations of the teachings of Adam Smith and the utilitarian disciples of the rationalistic political theory of the Enlightenment proved unsatisfactory almost as soon as the actual possibility of its implementation was foreseen. The great agrarian crisis beginning in 1820 was only one of a number of events which created among German thinkers a profound anxiety about the future of a society in which the economic liberation of some members of society had apparently fostered an economic libertinism for all—an unbridled greed and acquisitiveness which resulted in feelings of insecurity and personal and class antagonisms fully as destructive as those of the unreformed old regime. It was becoming all too obvious that, in the words of Carl Stüve, "the advantage of the [individual] is seldom that of the whole." Some way had to be found, he felt, to make particular endeavors serve the common welfare.[68] In the minds of many men, the mutual exploitation of all by all represented the disappearance of political and social morality, and meant the eventual conversion of society into a jungle, where the propertied and the propertyless would contend with one another in an eternal and mutually destructive struggle. The peasant as a social saviour fitted into this picture in several ways. His motivations, first of all, were supposed to have very little to do with materialistic considerations: he loved his land, not the money it gave him, and he loved it not merely because it nourished him, but also, and primarily, because it gave him full opportunity to express his individuality. It is no accident that one of the most recurrent themes in the eulogistic literature on agriculture concerns the beneficial effects of the variety of tasks and problems which necessarily faced the peasant, forcing him to develop strength and balance in judgment, perspective, versatility, and associated virtues. These various tasks fostered within the peasant a sense of his individuality, but also a concept of his responsibility to the society (fatherland) which made the enjoyment of property possible in this way, and which connected him with the past generations which had bequeathed this property to him. The peasant, through his land, was converted into an almost necessarily moral man; and this morality was put at the service of society not only in times of military danger, when the peasant was the first to take up arms, but at *all* times, by the constant passing-over of members of the peasant class into the other classes of society, carrying their superior moral standards and physical constitution with them. Most essentially, then, the peasant grew up and developed his standards of behavior in an atmosphere in which materialism and consequently also greed and the evil acts necessary to satisfy greed had no place; mutuality of cooperation, not of exploitation, was natural to the peasant's mentality. In a social sense, therefore, his most valuable contribution lay in his devotion to the general welfare, which was a necessary outgrowth of his devotion to his own particular interest.

[68] Stüve, *Über die Lasten,* xi.

This dedication to the common cause could be spread throughout society by the personal influence of former peasants in other occupations, or it could be applied more generally through the influence of the peasantry as participant in national institutions such as the army or in legislation for the state as a whole.

It was of course not merely rural life, but also rural *ownership* which developed in the peasant the set of attitudes and virtues described above. The peasant who was an agricultural day laborer, a paid wage earner, was nowhere mentioned as a porter of valuable social virtues: indeed, it was of course the growth of precisely this class of men that was regarded with such horror by writers in this time. No contrast could be sharper than that drawn by such people as Stein, Arndt, von Mohl, and Schüz between the free peasant proprietor and the rural proletarian; in their minds, these two types were virtually polar opposites, and all the virtues of the former had their counterparts as vices in the latter. As has been indicated above, the desire to preserve the independent peasant proprietor was at the same time, therefore, the desire to prevent the development of the proletariat, and in fact the concern over the peasant's plight may be regarded in one sense as but one aspect of a more general uneasiness about the growth of a class of men who possessed neither property nor traditional roots of any kind. If the peasant in the period before the reform decrees of the various German states had indeed not owned his land, he at least had enjoyed hereditary tenure, in most places, and in theory was a dependent of his lord, who was bound to look after him in critically bad times. He thus had no property, perhaps, but he did have two of the most essential benefits which property could confer: security and a sense of belonging.

The peasant of postliberation years, by contrast, exposed to the vague yet powerful and frightening operations of an impersonal market, had little of this sense of security at any time, and a sense of belonging only as long as he managed to remain on his land, which meant avoiding bankruptcy and foreclosure of his mortgage. Much the same thing could be said of the artisan in the city, whose progress through the ranks of his guild may have been intolerably slow in the earlier period, but who had a security of place unknown to his counterpart of the 1830s and 1840s, whose individual skills and production, no longer protected by the privileged position of the guild, were no match for the growing quantity output of factories with their machines, division of labor, and vastly greater marketing capabilities. The landless peasant and the displaced artisan, both deprived of property and of the niche in society which it conferred, represented a fundamentally new phenomenon, and a very disquieting one, to political and social thinkers in Germany after 1820. The most obvious manifestation of this phenomenon was the proletarianization of the peasant: his departure from the land, though sometimes quantitatively exaggerated, could be observed quite clearly in the increases in rural beggary and the number of unoccupied farms, in the growth of large estates, and in the concomitant increase in city populations and urban unemployment. To some, it looked like the demise of an entire class.

The explanation of the praise of the peasant and of rural life which was again so freely given in the period after 1820 has, then, to do with two closely related convictions. First, there was the conviction that political morality, embodied in the concept of "good citizenship," was the cement which bound men to cooperate in society in spite of their many differences, and that this morality was in large part a function of the ownership of property. Property had the positive effect of inculcating an ability to make the decisions and choices which inevitably accompanied its administration, and of forcing a man to consider the social implications and consequences of his actions by involving himself in society through the institution of private property—which was as much "social" or "public" as private in the number of connections it necessarily established between the individual owner and other owners, and between him and the state. Second, there was the conviction that the creation of a group of propertyless men, having no wealth yet desiring it, would eventuate in an easy propensity among such people towards agitation for the redistribution of property, perhaps even the expropriation of the existing proprietors, and would result in an eternal series of dissatisfactions. The dichotomy was both clear and simple: to have property was to be an active, moral, responsible citizen; not to have it was to be a man without connection to the fatherland or to one's fellow citizens—an asocial and, by virtue of his envy, also a hostile agent within the body politic. The decline in the number of persons possessing individual property and the closing-off of opportunities for still others to accede to private property was thus conceived as the degeneration of men from citizens whose stake in the country through landed property assured the continuation of integrative social principles to creatures whose lack of a stake in society through property introduced dangerous potentialities for social disintegration.

Given the overwhelming numbers of the peasantry in German society, it was perhaps only natural that the peasant proprietor, though by no means typical of the real situation of the peasantry as a whole, should be taken—by bourgeois writers, primarily—as the "ideal type" of the property owner, and that he should be contrasted with the most extreme example of the non-owner, the city proletarian. The former was then supposed to possess freedom of mind and spirit, balance, stamina, solidity, strength, simplicity, purity of morals, piety, loyalty, and so on. The latter was seen as corrupt, vicious, even criminal, and was thought to lead an immoral and irresponsible existence amidst the artificialities, false pleasures, and manifold vices of a city within a society which he saw only as an oppressor and to which he felt no sense of responsibility. The emphasis on the opposition of the natures of land and city, urban and rural, is certainly as strong in this period, and perhaps even stronger in certain respects, than in earlier periods. But it was no longer the noble or the bourgeois city fop who was held up for contemptuous comparison with the strong, simple peasant—as in Justus Möser's time, for example; now it was the proletarian who was held off against the peasant. And behind the praise of peasant virtues and the condemnation of proletarian vices—indeed, behind all the antimaterialism and political idealism which R. Hinton Thomas has found so characteristic of middle-class intellectuals of the second quarter of the nineteenth century,[69] was in fact the specter of social revolution, conjured up by the fear of the social effects of propertylessness.

The fact that the peasant proprietor, as opposed to other kinds

[69] Richard Hinton Thomas, *Liberalism, Nationalism, and the German Intellectuals, 1822-1847* (Cambridge, 1951), *passim*.

of proprietors, was so much praised in this time appears to stem from two considerations: first, the economic crisis seemed to threaten the independent peasant proprietor more palpably and directly than any other group of property owners, and there existed thus a greater necessity to make out a case for his preservation than for that of any other kind of proprietor; second, in terms of roots and the firm anchorage of a man in and to his society through property, land appeared to be at once a more tangible and more permanent foundation than money or other things of value, no matter whether expressed in cash, investments, buildings, or goods. In the adoption of the latter view, writers in this time were actually merely continuing to propound an opinion which had been current for some decades already, and which had originally grown out of situations described in earlier chapters of this book. All this is as much as to suggest, then, that no matter how much the moral virtues of the peasant proprietor may fervently have been talked about and believed in by the commentators of this period, his fundamental virtue seems to have consisted foremost in the bald fact that he possessed property.

The final explanation for the frequent proposals to establish a small or middle size for peasant holdings thus lies primarily in the concern to maintain a propertied class as nearly as possible coextensive with the entire population of the state. It had become quite clear by 1830, and had been suspected long before that, that total freedom of property relationships would in fact destroy any hope of achieving a society conceived as a totality of propertied individuals. Ultimately, therefore, it was the moral content of property, *not* of the peasant, and the social meaning of that moral content which led to the conclusion that the freedom to dispose of property must be restricted, and a numerous class of peasant proprietors preserved. This conclusion, in turn, by its tendency to project the peasant as the ideal and typical proprietor, led to the further strengthening of an image of the peasant as the backbone of society, and perpetuated him as the living model of the best individual and social virtues.

Part Four

The Image Fixed

10 The Contribution of Historians and Littérateurs

There is some justification for surveying historiography and belles-lettres as categories distinct from the more direct and purposeful publicistic literature of politics and economics because of the importance of both in giving some permanence to the image of the peasant as it was built up in other types of literature. After 1848, especially, the agrarian problem diminished fairly rapidly as a social issue of first-rate importance in Germany, and, while it continued to provoke discussion in many circles on particular occasions, the progress of social legislation, the growth of agricultural markets, and the emergence of national political problems of a new and different sort combined to attenuate the most critical problems which had caused so much concern in earlier decades and to divert the public consciousness to other issues. As a result, interest in agrarian affairs and in the peasant tended to lessen in contemporary polemical publicistics after the mid-century, and these works ceased to operate as porters of the peasant image which they had chiefly been responsible for creating in the previous three-quarters of a century.

By this time, however, the "new peasant" had won a footing in the works of historians and literary figures: and it was these works which were to propagate this more favorable image forward into new times whose basic social concerns, in themselves, could scarcely have produced or maintained such an image. If, in other words, the new and positive picture of the peasant owed its origins and its essential features to certain practical social problems of the last decades of the eighteenth century and the first decades of the nineteenth, and to the publicistic literature which accompanied those problems, it owed much of its survival beyond the issues which had created it to the permanent impress it was to achieve on historians and literary artists. There is no intention here of developing a complete or detailed examination of the treatment accorded the peasant in historical and literary works over the entire period covered by this study. A separate volume could be devoted to each. Rather, the following discussion attempts simply to point out some of the stages of the growth of interest in the peasant in these types of literature, and to focus on the specific contribution made by each to the propagation of that interest. The reader should be cautioned to remember, however, that most of the interest shown in the peasantry by historians *as such,* and therefore also most of the influence of that interest, came well after 1840, and thus cannot be fully explored within the limits set for this study. Much the same thing must be said of belles-lettres.

Among historians, it is a commonplace too well accepted to require any special pleading here that historical works almost inevitably mirror in one way or another the concerns and interests of the historians who write them. It should come as no surprise, therefore, that in the period 1770-1840, especially, when the concept of "historical objectivity" was somewhat less analytically viewed than it is today, historical writing on the peasantry was not devoid of publicistic and polemical character and purpose. The appearance of the peasant in historical works in the early period of this study was indeed due chiefly to historians' interest in the contemporary scene; and in this sense, interest in the peasantry in contemporary society was reflected both in the attention of historians to the history of the peasantry and in their readiness to apply the "lessons of the past" to the present agrarian situation. The early combination of historical and polemical writing on this issue is clearly illustrated in the work of Justus Möser, whose convictions on the importance of landed property and of the landed proprietor were expressed not only in publicistic articles and tracts, but in his important *Osnabrückische Geschichte* as well. Since many of Möser's views have been discussed in detail above,[1] let it suffice here to point out that he did not merely include the peasant in his *Geschichte* as a class in society whose welfare through the ages and in present times had been too much neglected, but in fact built the history itself around the peasant. His periodization and the nature of the topics to which he addressed himself were strongly affected by his belief that the common landowners were "the true constituents of the nation,"

---

[1] See discussion above, beginning on p. 75.

and that the history of Germany was properly the history of the changes which had affected these common landowners: they were to constitute the "body" *(Körper)*, and all the great kings, princes, nobles, warriors, bishops, abbots, and other major historical figures of German history were to be regarded only as "accidents" of the body, and judged according to their effect on it. If indeed there were such a thing as an aristocracy for Möser, it was an aristocracy consisting of all landowners who in their obligations to the soil bore the responsibility for the welfare and progress of the entire nation. Möser's concern for the maintenance of the contemporary peasant as an effectively independent proprietor lay quite close to the base of his history, which sought to make direct connections between the condition of peasant proprietorship and the degree and nature of civic liberty and freedom in Germany since before the time of Charlemagne. By following the vicissitudes of the peasant and his relationship to the soil he cultivated, one was provided with a lens which gave the most accurate focus to the major political, constitutional, and social developments of German history.

In his own time, Möser was a distinct rarity, for he not only recognized the peasantry as deserving of attention within a historical context, but actually proclaimed that the history of society was in large measure the history of the peasant, and that, in effect, the chronicles of the deeds of kings and princes which had set standards for historical writing before his own time were merely histories of the external limbs of society, whose actions were indeed important, but important because of their effect on and relationship to the body of society, the nation, the common landowners. What Möser did, in other words, was much more than to assert that the history of the peasantry was an important constituent part of the history of Germany as a whole; he asserted that the history of property relationships, seen through the peasantry, was the key to German history, and that German history was virtually meaningless or at the very least falsely conceived unless the peasant were placed in the very center of it.[2]

---

[2] It is of course clear that Möser did not believe the Germany of his own day to consist of peasant landowners; and for this reason, he refused to recognize Germany as a "nation." See Carlo Antoni, *Der Kampf wider die Vernunft: zur Entstehungsgeschichte des deutschen Freiheitsgedankens* (Stuttgart, 1951), 129-32.

It can scarcely be expected that Möser's view would have been universally acclaimed or imitated among many other historians; and it was not, at least in his own time. In spite of many eulogies of his work and the adoption of many of his particular points of view by others, no other historian in this period gave to a general history the framework which Möser imposed on his. The form taken by the interest of contemporaries in the peasantry in works of history was generally much less drastic, though its utilitarian purpose was no less obvious than in Möser. Thus Ludwig Spittler in a history of Württemberg dwelt at some length on the peasant revolts which led to the Treaty of Tübingen of 1514, and was careful to state his conclusion that the claims and grievances of the peasants were justified.[3] Spittler's sentiments were quite similar to those of Johann Georg August Galletti, whose multivolume history of Thuringia included sections on agrarian life and the peasant in every major period. Galletti, referring to the servitude which fell upon much of the German peasantry after the thirteenth century, noted that "in those still so little-enlightened times, princes, lords, and prelates failed for the most part to recognize the rights of mankind which are due the peasant, the most useful part of the citizenry, and they considered themselves as it were the despots of their poor subjects."[4] He was notably happier when speaking of the gradual emancipation of the peasantry in the twelfth and thirteenth centuries, a development which, he said, redounded to the honor of mankind.[5] He adjudged fully justified the demands made in the fifteenth and sixteenth centuries by peasants, whose misery made them desire to achieve a better life, and capped his arguments with the observation that the history of the most perceptive and wisest rulers of modern times proved beyond dispute just how much the majority of peasants' claims were justified by standards of both rights of man and the benefit of the state.[6]

It was generally not until after the French Revolution had begun, however, that the tendencies already apparent in the

---

[3] Ludwig Timotheus Spittler, *Geschichte Wirtembergs unter der Regierung der Grafen und Herzöge* (Göttingen, 1783), 100-103.

[4] Johann Georg August Galletti, *Geschichte Thüringens,* 6 vols. in 3 (Gotha and Dessau, 1782-1784), IV, 285.

[5] *Ibid.,* II, 347.

[6] *Ibid.,* IV, 286-87.

above works towards the judgment of contemporary agrarian relationships in terms of their historical conditionality became a quite self-conscious endeavor linked to hopes and programs for agrarian reform. When Christian August Wichmann in 1795 published his detailed examination of the ways and means by which peasant labor services might be abolished, he found it desirable to devote a lengthy section of the book to a historical demonstration of the fact that labor requirements and other obligations of the peasant were in his time greater than they had once been, and that the basis for the increase lay largely in usurpations in the Middle Ages and in early modern times.[7] Much the same kind of motivation lay behind E. M. Arndt's *Versuch einer Geschichte der Leibeigenschaft in Pommern und in Rügen* (1803) and K. D. Hüllmann's *Historische und Staatswissenschaftliche Untersuchungen* (1803) and his *Geschichte des Ursprungs der Stände in Deutschland* (1806-1808); in his writing, Arndt sought to make clear that the necessity of servitude had been outlived, and that state and society now suffered from this anachronistic institution, while Hüllmann, arguing for the transformation of services into cash payments, warned landlords that if they would but take time to make historical inquiries, they would discover that the prince or sovereign could legally demand the complete abolition of services without compensation, and that they had therefore best accommodate themselves to reform without delay.

In the considerations of German agrarian history which began to appear with increasing frequency, either as prologue and support for reform proposals or as sections of general histories of Germany and its various territories, it was above all the origins and development of servitude or personal dependence which attracted close attention. A few examples will suffice to indicate the major focal points of historical interest. The Carolingian period, first of all, was usually regarded as the critical period in the origins of peasant servitude. P. F. F. Buchholz traced the beginnings of servitude back to the eighth and ninth centuries, when small landowners gave up their free title to land in return for freedom from military service, which they could not afford to

---

[7] Wichmann, *Über die natürlichsten Mittel*, 68-119, *passim*.

perform. The imperial ministerials to whom they gave up their lands then created their own subministeriality, and gave out their newly acquired lands to its members, with the ultimate result that the originally free owners, the peasants, sank into a position of servitude.[8] Ernst Ludwig Posselt similarly emphasized the unholy choice which the less well-to-do freemen had to make between agriculture and war; when the former was chosen, irrevocable damnation to servitude resulted. Personally servile peasants were not in that time regarded as members of the *Volk* at all, and in Posselt's eyes this fact had a clear parallel with his own day, in which the useful peasant class was not yet a member of the estates in most German territories.[9] The author of another general history of Germany, Michael Ignaz Schmidt, pounced upon the lack of any mention of the peasant in the otherwise very detailed Capitularies of this period, and wondered at the failure of Charlemagne to provide for this class, from which all others derived their living; he saw to the welfare of his own, his personal peasants, but as monarch was silent on the treatment of the peasantry which lived and labored under his own subordinates. "Reason . . . had to teach [this concern] to every other person who possessed estates," mused Schmidt; "but how often does it not occur, that the despot thinks about everything else before this!"[10]

Schmidt went on to trace a gradual increase in the peasant's well-being in the thirteenth and fourteenth centuries, an increase which in most areas continued until shortly after the beginning of the sixteenth century. But in the midst of their new prosperity, the seeds of future evil were sown: many new taxes came into existence, and fell almost entirely on the peasant. He had no representation at the estates, for he stood either directly under the prince, in which case he had no representation whatever, or else under his "virtual" representative, the noble, who of course looked after his own interest rather than that of the peasant.[11] K. D. Hüllmann, like Schmidt and almost every other historian,

[8] [Buchholz], *Untersuchungen,* 120-23.
[9] Ernst Ludwig Posselt, *Geschichte der Deutschen für alle Stände,* 4 vols. (Hamburg and Leipzig, 1808-1819), I, 206-207.
[10] Schmidt, *Geschichte der Deutschen,* I, 597-98.
[11] *Ibid.,* III, 193; IV, 596-97.

happily noted the rise of the dignity of the peasantry in the high Middle Ages, which he ascribed to the revival of trade in Europe: the true value of agriculture was finally seen in some sort of perspective, and the peasant began to make progress as an outgrowth of increased respect for agriculture. The usurpations of spiritual and temporal lords, the erection of standing armies, and, finally, the mistaken religious notions of peasants following the Lutheran reform suddenly reversed this development, however, producing a "catastrophe" in which free peasants were reduced to serfdom.[12]

The catastrophe to which Hüllmann referred was, of course, the great Peasants' War of 1525-1526, seen by all historians alike as a major event in the development of the German agrarian constitution, and a point of agreement for all in its lamentable consequences for the peasant. Discussions of the Peasants' War commonly centered around the inflictions suffered by the peasants from their lords. In nearly all cases the grievances of the peasants, if not their revolt, were held to be just. Christian August Wichmann, for example, discussing one of the preliminary revolts in Württemberg, suggested that rebellion might well have been expected under a ruler (Duke Ulrich) to whom a fine hunting dog was more important than a village full of good peasants. As far as Wichmann was concerned, the worst result of the Peasants' War lay in the worsening of the peasants' condition, wherein "the power of the little tyrants, whose yoke these poor people had sought to shake off, was still more fortified with barbaric vengefulness."[13] This was a decisive event in the humiliation of the peasant, for, as Schmidt put it elsewhere, "since he got it in his head all at once to wish to be master, [he] was so discouraged through his defeat that he learned from now on to bear everything, and sank back not only to his old, but to a yet much worse serfdom."[14]

The conclusions to which these historical insights led were varied. Schmidt made a strong case for the interconnection between the oppression of the peasant class and the failure of

---

12 Hüllmann, *Geschichte des Ursprungs*, I, 7, 195, 205.
13 Wichmann, *Über die natürlichsten Mittel*, 119.
14 Schmidt, *Geschichte der Deutschen*, VI, 322.

agriculture under Charlemagne to progress past the level it had attained in most ancient Germanic times—and in doing so, he made quite clear his opinion that such an interconnection was fortuitous neither in the time of Charlemagne nor in any other, including his own.[15] Perhaps even more important was the argument presented by Hüllmann, who maintained that the contract by which those who tilled the soil but performed no military service possessed their land was not a private one between them and the lord who held their lands as part of a benefice, but rather a public one, in which they stood in direct relationship to the overlord of the country. Services, dues, and other payments thus actually belonged to the sovereign, who had given them as appurtenances of the fief to his feudal vassals. That noble fief-estates had long since become hereditary rather than precarious made no difference, said Hüllmann: they were still fiscal lands, and whatever fees or services appertained to them still belonged theoretically to the sovereign. The threat here was clear: the sovereign could, if he wished, abolish whatever appurtenances to his fiefs he wished, and without consulting the nobility. Furthermore, Hüllmann argued relentlessly, since the nobility no longer performed the military service which constituted the original condition of its feudal rights of tenure, and instead paid a sum of money, voted through the *Landtag*, then the peasant ought to be able to do the same, especially since it was the peasant upon whom the chief burden for the defense of the country fell, while they *also* paid taxes to the government and performed services for their landlords.[16] The chief impact of all these writings came, however, not through the particular arguments from history which were raised in support of one or another reform proposal, but from the historically demonstrable fact that contemporary German agrarian social relationships had been shaped by imperative necessity on the one hand, and the usurpations of the mighty on the other, neither of which could lay any claim to permanent legal validity. It is hardly necessary to point out the connection between this historical research together with the conclusions drawn from it, and the beginnings of the French Revolution, the

[15] *Ibid.*, I, 568.
[16] Hüllmann, *Historische und staatswissenschaftliche Untersuchungen*, 151-52.

first serious agrarian reform attempts of many German princes affecting private peasants, and the rise of vehement protests from the nobility, whose theoretical arguments against reforms were quite commonly based on the assumption of the immutability of the prevailing set of legal relationships.

The introduction of basic agrarian reforms in many German states after the Prussian collapse and after the Wars of Liberation did nothing to change the desire to use history to illuminate and, if possible, to help solve the problems of peasant reform. The famous historian of the Roman Empire, Barthold Georg Niebuhr, might well have been speaking for numbers of his colleagues when, in commenting on a treatise he was writing on property laws and agrarian legislation in ancient Rome, he wrote that his work would be damned by many, and that no nobleman or landlord would much care to look through it.[17] Niebuhr's scarcely concealed conviction that the results of his work, when applied to the present, would tend to be unfriendly to the interest of great landowners and nobles was nearly as applicable to the work of other historians as to his own; but although the perhaps inevitable tendency of historical discussion concerning lord-peasant relationships was such as to favor the peasant interest in contemporary issues, the desire to serve the present at the same time in most cases prevented historians from proposing any measures which would literally disinherit the nobility by way of compensating the peasantry for past injustices and centuries of neglect. Thus in a history of servitude, for example, Wilhelm Gessner, while demonstrating the worsening of the peasant's condition in Germany from Frankish times to the French Revolution and while proposing the conviction that freedom and unrestricted proprietorship were absolutely essential ingredients of any state which wished to assure its continued existence, was primarily interested in enabling landlords and peasants to reach amicable agreements concerning their respective rights and obligations—a concern which presupposed compromise on both sides.[18]

The essentially moderate viewpoint represented by Gessner

---

[17] Niebuhr, *Lebensnachrichten*, II, 44.
[18] Wilhelm Gessner, *Geschichtliche Entwicklung der gutsherrlichen und bäuerlichen Verhältnisse Teutschlands* (Berlin, 1820), vi-vii, 1-20, especially.

was even more clearly apparent in a history of labor services by Heinrich Theophil Ebel. Ebel concluded in this work that peasant services could not be traced to an original property right of landlords; they were, rather, a product of conquest and enforced subjection, which had become a part of the positive law by mere sanction of time. But the positive law is not eternal, and because the origins and coercive sanction of this part of the law were now recognized as extra-legal, the law could and ought to be changed. The great goal for which the peasants originally gave up their freedom was liberation from military service; but now that the common man was subject to conscription, he ought also to be freed of the labor services which he had assumed as part of his servitude. But: while the landlords theoretically had no right whatever to any compensation for the services to be abolished, Ebel carefully pointed out, it would none the less be proper for them to be remunerated in order to avoid the social disorder which would otherwise surely result.[19] In spite of the very politic attitudes expressed by Gessner and Ebel, however, it is likely that they and many of their fellow historians would have agreed with the liberal Carl Welcker, for whom the historico-legal research of recent years had proved that the presumption of courts in litigation involving peasants and lords ought always to be with the former unless the latter produced complete and legally valid evidence for their case. "A consistent fulfillment of this demand of justice will be most highly beneficent," Welcker concluded, "although it cannot make good even a tenth of all the injustices which chiefly also by means of the opposite legal presumptions were inflicted upon the peasants."[20]

The implementation of important agrarian reforms after 1800 in many German states also stimulated many historians to attempt to place the reforms in some sort of historical perspective. Karl Heinrich Ludwig Pölitz believed it unnecessary to go back any further than the mid-eighteenth century to seek the causes of the amelioration of the peasant's condition. About that time, he declared, the principles of the Physiocratic system began to be

---

[19] Heinrich Theophil Ebel, *Über den Ursprung der Frohnen und die Ausführbarkeit ihrer Aufhebung* (Giessen, 1823), 84-90.
[20] Welcker, "Bauerngut," *Staats-Lexikon*, II, 257-58.

circulated widely, and many rulers and officials began to recognize the extreme importance of the peasantry and the necessity of freeing agriculture from the oppressive relationships which the middle ages had bequeathed to them. At the same time, the peasants themselves became better informed and, with the spread of more efficient techniques, began to work more diligently to obtain a profit beyond their immediate needs. As the peasants, by dint of hard work, came into the ownership of larger holdings which they successfully cultivated, governments were taken with the desire to improve agricultural activity still more, and made it possible for the peasant to achieve personal freedom and full property rights. The peasant thereupon began to be called to the meetings of the estates as delegates. This was both just and wise: just, because all who contributed to the support of the state through taxes had a right to be represented politically; and wise, because representation awakened and nourished within the peasantry the feeling of self-reliance and political responsibility. General education of the peasantry was now the next logical step for government to undertake in elevating the peasantry to the level of full and informed citizenship, a historical movement which had begun barely a century before.[21]

Other historians, however, tended increasingly to locate the origins of the modern emancipation of the peasantry in earlier centuries. Carl Welcker, writing in the 1830s, saw the main reason for the new recognition of the peasantry in the principles-of-state, historical, philosophical, political, and economic, which were first awakened in the sixteenth century, and which achieved general expression in the eighteenth century, especially through the French Revolution.[22] Occasionally there was even an attempt to make direct parallels between events of the sixteenth century and contemporary history, as when Wilhelm Zimmermann, author of a detailed and well-known history of the Peasants' War of 1525, emphasized the similarity in spirit between that revolt (which Zimmermann unequivocally termed "a struggle of . . . light against darkness") and the French Revolution: "The inherent spirit of the Peasants' War is the same spirit which two hundred

---

21 Pölitz, *Staatswissenschaftliche Vorlesungen*, I, 196-201.
22 Welcker, "Bauern," *Staats-Lexikon*, II, 255.

and fifty years later shook and transformed the entire state-edifice of Europe. [In] 1525, the people bled, [in] 1790 the aristocracy bled. [On] every guilt follows its revenge, every sacrifice its expiation, every sowing on the earth of life its fruit."[23] Parallels drawn between the grievances of the French people before 1789 and those of the German peasants before 1525 in a number of histories also tend to give substance to the suggestion that for some intellectuals in the period of the German Restoration the Peasants' War represented, in retrospect, a kind of premature, and therefore unsuccessful, French Revolution, in which the inhuman oppression of the masses of the people by feudal lords had missed by a hair being overturned in a truly popular revolt. The cleric Johann Gottfried Pahl, praising the peasants' movement, hardly concealed a note of wistfulness when he remarked that the revolt would undoubtedly have stood as a great, epoch-making event in the history of the German fatherland, had only one of the great heroes of the time stepped to the head of the movement and, uniting the separate forces, directed the energies of the people with a bold and noble spirit.[24]

It appeared, by 1840, that giant strides had been taken towards the achievement of the new direction in historiography for which Justus Möser had so fervently hoped nearly three generations earlier. Möser himself was of great importance in the origins of the systematic research into the genesis and development of the German peasantry which was to be taken up, for various reasons, by increasing numbers of historians after his time, until no history which might wish to lay a claim to comprehensiveness for any period of time or any territory could afford to neglect the conditions and development of the agrarian population. The insistence with which Möser put forth his conviction of the intimate connection between the history of the German peasantry and that of the German nation as a whole began to be echoed in the writings of later historians who pondered the historical and contemporary position of the peasant in Germany—as indeed the

[23] Wilhelm Zimmermann, *Allgemeine Geschichte des grossen Bauernkrieges*, 3 vols. in 2 (Stuttgart, 1841-1843), III, 907.
[24] J. G. Pahl, "Vorwort," in Ferdinand Friedrich Oechsle, *Beiträge zur Geschichte des Bauernkrieges in den schwäbisch-fränkischen Grenzlanden* (Heilbronn, 1830), xiii.

position of the tiller of the soil in the history of Europe as a whole. It need hardly be recalled that the works of Ernst Moritz Arndt, for example, manifest not only a firm persuasion that the elements of a Prussian-German regeneration lay close at hand in the peasantry, but also that in all times and in all places, the strongest and most solid foundations for a vigorous national life rested squarely on the shoulders of a strong, free peasantry.

These principles were accepted and used in different ways and with varying degrees of conviction by a host of political publicists and professional historians after 1800. Lotz, Lips, Hüllmann, Luden, Rotteck, and Welcker were but a very few of those who in some fashion reflected the tendency to relate the stages and progress of civilization itself to the level of welfare of the lower classes, as represented by the peasantry. Hüllmann expressed one of the tenets of the new historiography very well in an attack he launched upon a group of literary romantics whose praise of the Middle Ages had demonstrated to him that their understanding had been seduced by the legendary splendor of knighthood, the poetic and heroic life, and the moving ritual of the medieval church. "The friend of humanity and its history, who wishes to measure national happiness and welfare in a land, in an age," he admonished them, "should not start with the upper classes; then he is too easily corrupted. He should start from the opposite standpoint, from the lower classes, the majority. Then the German Middle Ages will appear less lovable to him. The upper and middle classes were united in castes; only the peasants [were] without a guild system, [and] therefore oppressed by the spiritual and temporal landlords, not deigned to be regarded by the learned, despised by the burghers, the pariahs of Germany. No warming spring was to be sensed . . . for the members of the highly important peasant class, benumbed in the abyss."[25] Even more important than the outraged sympathy for the peasant which this statement indicates is Hüllmann's adoption of the actual circumstances of the lower classes, the peasantry, as the standard of historical judgment of national welfare, regardless of time or place—further evidence that the peasant had not only won a place in German historiography, but also that he

[25] Hüllmann, *Geschichte des Ursprungs*, I, 314-15.

and his class were being shifted into the very center of the stage of German historical development by more than a few historians.

This new understanding of the role of the peasant in history, and particularly in German history, was also involved in the increasing reliance of political writers on historical arguments in their pleas for agrarian reform. History, for these publicists, provided the concrete evidence of the centrally important role of agriculture and the peasantry for national development, and they were not slow to make use of this evidence as support for agrarian reform, especially after 1789 and 1806. The arguments they used have been discussed in some detail in previous pages; let it only be emphasized here that while it is impossible to know with certainty just how much influence these arguments might have had on responsible governmental officials and major political thinkers, it is at least possible to find citations of historical arguments by such figures. Freiherr vom Stein, to give but one example, referred to Ludwig von Baczko's *Geschichte Preussens* (Königsberg, 1792-1800) as proof that the Prussian peasant had an original historical right to his land, and that he became personally servile and lost his rights only as the result of extraordinary and quite illegal distortions, disturbances, and usurpations.[26] Still more suggestive of his reliance on history was a statement he made in 1808 before the Komité of the East Prussian estates: "I have become convinced . . . from Prussian history and constitution, that the peasant farms, whether they belong to domains or to private holdings, were originally bestowed hereditarily on the peasants and that only in later times a reprehensible abuse, for which no inveteracy can procure legal sanction, suppressed the rights of the peasants and transformed their hereditary right into a temporary ownership, abandoned to the arbitrariness of the landlord."[27]

For a political theorist such as Carl Welcker, on the other hand, the investigations of historical scholars not only provided ammunition for the proponents of reform, but also gave a firm basis in historical perspective to the political theories upon which

---

[26] vom Stein, "Denkschrift" (June 14, 1808), *Freiherr vom Stein*, II, 441.

[27] vom Stein, (To the Komité of the East Prussian Estates, July 1, 1808), *ibid.*, II, 453-54.

he and other liberal intellectuals hoped to construct a new Germany. In consequence of "the constantly more thorough and comprehensive historicolegal research of our German social relationships in all parts of the German fatherland," he was able to dismiss the putative absolute validity of the "historical or positive legal relationship" under which the contemporary German peasant suffered. The results of recent research, he explained, presented a particularly happy conclusion: that aristocratic privilege and peasant servitude did not constitute the basic conditions from which German history necessarily took its course, but rather that complete freedom of person and property stood as an unassailable fact at the dawn of the history of the various German peoples.[28] To return to *these* roots, Welcker appeared to say, was not to deny native German historical development, but only to affirm the existence of another and better German tradition; the task of the present was to harness contemporary German development to the dynamo represented by the free, popular forces of the independent peasantry belonging to this "other" tradition.[29]

Historical literature, then, or at least the utilization of the historical perspective, made its own contribution to the shaping

[28] Welcker, "Bauerngut," *Staats-Lexikon*, II, 257-58.

[29] On the other hand, the work of the so-called "historical school of law" (*Historische Rechtsschule*) which Welcker seems here so closely to approach, while very important in stimulating research into the history of the legal relationships of all classes in German society, actually did not provide uniformly strong positive condemnation of the peasant's relatively inferior position in German society. Both of the men who are normally taken to be the "founders" of this school—Friedrich Carl von Savigny (1779-1861) and Karl Friedrich Eichhorn (1781-1854)—looked with favor on the improvement of the peasant's situation in recent legislation, for example, but did so because that improvement was itself the result of a certain kind of evolution which gave it reason and justification. Neither would have approved of Welcker's attempt to "stop" legal evolution at some convenient point in the past and to pick up the present from there, regarding what had transpired in the meantime as either illegitimate or irrelevant. Broadly speaking, the *Historische Rechtsschule* contributed to the growth of greater attention to the peasant less through its specific historical conclusions than through its general philosophy that law ought to be regarded as the embodiment of the cumulative experience of the entire people, as a product of the *Volksgeist*, and that the *Volk* of course included the peasantry. In this sense, the *Historische Rechtsschule* did for the peasantry in legal history what Herder and his successors did for him in the history of language and literature with their *Volkslieder*; nor should it be forgotten that the *Volksgeist* was the animating principle behind the collections of fairy tales of Jakob and Wilhelm Grimm—both of whom, it must be remembered, were serious students and devoted friends of Friedrich Carl von Savigny.

of a public opinion favorable to the peasant, and to the specific features of the peasant image with which this book has been concerned. It is of course necessary to emphasize the pragmatic concerns which led to the initial interest in peasant history, and which sustained it into the nineteenth century; for it is largely true that it was the impulse towards agrarian reform rather than any disinterested intellectual curiosity which stimulated the historical research described in this chapter. The direct dependence of this research on contemporary concerns can be seen in the uses to which its conclusions were put (in the sense of applications to the present) and in the kinds of events or periods on which interest was concentrated—those in which not merely the peasantry itself, but the peasantry in its relationship to the public life of the nation as a whole was affected (the breakup of the Carolingian Empire, the Peasants' War of 1525, the growth of territorial sovereignties, the Thirty Years' War). It was precisely the problems of contemporary national economy and politics which led historians to search the past for evidences of connections between the development of the peasantry and the main features of German social, political, and economic history as a whole. In discovering such connections—however mistaken their interpretations or even their information may have been in particular instances—these historians tended to discover also a new peasant, one whose original character was rather like that of the free peasant warrior whom Welcker believed to have stood at the dawn of German history. His subsequent misfortunes had done nothing to diminish his vigor and his capacity to perform the tasks of responsible citizenship which he had (supposedly) once discharged with honor (in the time of Charlemagne, for example). The practical conclusion to be drawn from this was that the truly national and popular character of a dynamic public life might be recaptured through the full reinstatement of the peasantry to its original civic status.

It can be asserted, on the other hand, that the historical literature of this period did more than merely support the arguments of agrarian reformers, and that it did more than provide evidence that the peasantry was a historically significant part of the German nation. It also contributed in a special way to the creation and the perpetuation of a "peasant type," a model man, whose significance lay not only in the essential economic functions he performed, but also in the moral and physical strength which he and he alone could give to a nation, and whose importance was universally demonstrable in the histories of Germany and all other countries as well. This "type" corresponded very closely to the new image of the peasant produced in the political polemics, agricultural tracts, economic arguments, and the poems and stories of the littérateurs of the same period; but it was the historical view, above all, which gave to the more or less gratuitous theories of these political and social writings the long-range perspective which constituted their test and—as contemporaries saw it—their positive justification. Important, too, is the fact that the "model peasant" of the historians soon enough gave rise to heroic, even romantic images, far beyond the wildest imaginings of the historians themselves, and in this form quickly passed over into popular literature and thence into the public mind; there it has survived to the present day in Germany the destruction by more recent historical research of the notion of the free and equal warrior-peasant community of ancient Germania upon which at least part of the original historical "model peasant" was built.

But a note of caution must be introduced here. It would certainly be an error to regard historians' greater interest in the peasantry as a phenomenon separable from their generally increased interest in the history of the nonprivileged orders of society as a whole. What is increasingly apparent from the 1770s onwards, in fact, in historical just as in political literature, is the growth of a distinct antiaristocratic bias, which as often as not was expressed by historians as a greater concentration on the contributions made to the history of Germany and its constituent parts not only by the peasantry, but also by the urban middle classes. Indeed, in the case of general histories of Germany or of its particular states, the amount of attention paid to the growth and development of cities and their bourgeoisies, and to their historical importance, often far outweighed that given to the peasantry. Thus, the peasantry benefitted in many instances only as a peripheral concern of what was essentially a bourgeois polemical historiography.

Furthermore, the polemical tone itself began to become progressively milder, especially after the mid-century. This was a consequence not only of the gradual quieting of many of the burning agrarian issues of the first decades of the century, but also of the growing strength of the "objectivist" school of historiography, symbolized by the name of Leopold von Ranke (1795-1886), which deliberately sought to take the study of history back to the sources and to write history "as it actually was." The influence of this school worked against exaggerated notions of the peasant's importance in history in a double way: first, its critical method tended to cut away at unfounded assumptions about the warrior-peasants of old Germany which some protagonists of the peasantry persisted in seeing as the historical origin of their "model peasant," and second, that same critical method required a thorough training and professional expertise which tended to exclude mere polemicists from the ranks of historians who were to be taken seriously. Consequently, the role of the peasant in history began to be regarded in a more objective and realistic perspective in historical works. But if this indeed tended to dissolve the more wild-eyed assessments of the peasant's historical importance, it also guaranteed the peasant a permanent place in historical works, because the emphasis on objectivity and comprehensiveness of this school of historians made it certain that the historical role of the lower classes would never again be ignored as it had so often been in the "aristocratic" historiography of the eighteenth and earlier centuries. While it is therefore true that moral and political subjectivity first put the peasant into historical works, it was historical objectivity that was ultimately to keep him there.

Finally, one must not mistake the gradualness and the tentative character of a really methodical inclusion of the peasantry as an integral part of historical works. It was perhaps not a completely common thing even by the end of this period. The liberal entrepreneur Friedrich Harkort as late as the mid-1840s bemoaned the still all-too-common tendency of historians to write of battles, the great leaders of mankind, the affairs of courts and kings, and so on, while ignoring the development of mankind in general. "Another spirit will have to guide historians in future," he wrote, "if the past is to act on the present of peoples in an instructive way and penetrate deeply into their life." To this goal, the "dry history of rulers and states" made little contribution.[30] Still, the beginnings of such a spirit had become apparent by 1840, and it was to grow stronger in succeeding decades.

If indeed the peasant had won at least an increasingly significant place in German historiography during the period 1770-1840, the rise of his class to the level of a legitimate subject of literary attention in the narrower sense, in belles-lettres, was perhaps of even greater importance. The appearance of the peasant and of village situations against a rural background in works of literature, though perhaps owing its beginnings to the timeliness of the agrarian problem in the contemporary social context, indicates a realization within literary circles of a new variety of thematic possibilities whose potential popularity did not necessarily depend on the continuation of the specific social issues which had first drawn literary attention to them. As literacy increased among the lower classes, including the peasantry, and as their literary tastes, along with those of the middle class, began to assert themselves as a demand for popular fictional works centering around the family, work, and credible or familiar situations and characters, the peasant village was discovered by writers virtually as a new world, replete with its heroes, villains, joys, sorrows, and suspenseful and exciting episodes—all set in the entirely believable context of the ordinary rural community.

The actual appearance of peasant life as a literary motif in itself came only at the very end of the period covered by this study, and for that reason will not be treated here in its fully developed form. The purpose here is that of tracing only very briefly the main outlines of the growth of this specific motif through literature to the point at which, in the late 1830s, the first real *Dorfgeschichte* (village story) made its debut. What is important here is not the mere mention or utilization of peasants in literary works, of which a fairly considerable catalog could be made, but rather the development of an entire genre surrounding the peasant and his life. Many of the greatest literary figures in Germany during this period actually did not much assist in this development—at least not directly so. Certainly this is not to say

<hr>

[30] Harkort, *Bemerkungen*, 5.

that the Goethes and the Schillers, for example, had no interest in the peasant or the lower classes and their social situation.[31] It is to say, however, that as they outgrew their youthful enthusiasms and passions they more or less consciously evolved away from narrowly social motifs and specific social criticism, and found society most congenial to their art as a foil and a condition for exploring the inner depths of the individual spirit. Again, one assuredly cannot ignore the contributions to a heightened respect for the *Volk* in literature by Klopstock, Herder, Achim von Arnim, Brentano and others discussed in earlier chapters, or by many more who were not separately discussed. But at the risk of appearing to ignore some of the great geniuses of German literature, this chapter concentrates on only one illustrative theme: the appearance of the village genre as an indication of the cultural permanence that the new awareness of the German peasant was to achieve by and after 1840.

From what has been said in earlier chapters, it might be expected that a concentration on a realistic though fictional portrayal of peasant life would develop only out of an original interest in peasant life which stemmed from essentially pragmatic concerns. As was the case with historiography, so also did belles-lettres develop a peasant-centered genre largely in consequence of the attention focused on agrarian problems from other, chiefly economic and political, sources. This can be demonstrated by an examination of the two broad categories of fictional literature which dealt with situations of peasant life prior to the actual *Dorfgeschichte*. The first of these was a literature of social criticism which, though based on real situations, included poems or short stories describing particular fictional episodes of rural life in order to awaken sympathy for the peasant suffering from one or another intolerable abuse and thereby to work for the abolition of the abuse in question. The poems of G. A. Bürger, J. A. Leisewitz, G. A. von Halem, as well as the prose works of F. C. von Moser, Justus Möser, and C. F. D. Schubart are good examples

---

[31] Goethe, after all, was an official at Weimar for a long period, and on one early occasion, in 1776, appeared before the young duke, his master, dressed in peasant garb, and read to him a poem asking the duke's gracious understanding and attention to the problems of the peasant. W. H. Bruford, *Culture and Society in Classical Weimar, 1776-1806* (Cambridge, 1962), 92.

of works of this sort. It cannot be said that these men established any kind of genre, in spite of the quantity of their works: their interest was not really in peasant life as such (if such a distinction can be made), but only in those aspects of it which were in need of reform. They merely used a literary form to present specific grievances which had been presented elsewhere in less imaginative ways.

On the other hand, it is of some significance that this artistic method was used, for in contrast to the dry and often very formal arguments of economists, statesmen, and agriculturists, which emphasized the evils resulting for the state from oppression of the peasantry, the emphasis in these poems and stories was much more directly connected to the personal sufferings of the peasant as an individual. If facts and figures on agricultural production and the tax-paying capacities of the peasantry could be used to good effect in convincing some segments of public opinion that agrarian reform was desirable, it was just as true that still other segments of public opinion could be swayed to the side of reform by appeal to the sympathy of the heart, which could best be aroused by reference to specific individuals in concrete situations, whether real or fictional, whose anguish and sorrows could be directly imagined by the reader. It should be noted, too, that in contrast to earlier writings whose authors advocated the growth of lovingkindness among the various classes of society on the basis of mutual and individual Christian sympathy, but for whom class and material distinctions were of little importance—one thinks here particularly of Pietist tracts—it was for these later writers the peasant in his natural setting of agrarian life and work which had to be brought out if his feelings were to be made comprehensible to other men whose life-situations differed widely from his. It was true that all souls were equal before God, their Maker; but the modifications of those equal souls by their differing material situations created obstacles to common feeling, or to mutual sympathy. It was therefore not enough to talk about the peasant's grief, or joy, or any other emotion; one had to create the situation which gave rise to that emotion, so that the reader might be subject to the same forces, vicariously, which worked to produce this feeling in the peasant in the story. However unintended by its originators, therefore, the creation of a kind of agrarian "naturalism" is already foreshadowed in certain little stories and poems of the last decades of the eighteenth century, whose conscious purpose was thoroughly pragmatic and decidedly limited by the well-defined objectives of their authors, but whose effect was that of facilitating the marriage of literary art and social criticism which most "correct" literary critics of the time would still have regarded as decidedly morganatic.[32]

Just as closely related to practical concerns and the need for reform as the works described above was a series of books built entirely around agrarian life at the peasant level, but with the avowed pedagogical intent of providing the peasant with information and insights necessary to improve his own cultivation and his entire farm economy. The standard for this sort of effort was set by Hirzel's *Die Wirthschaft eines philosophischen Bauers* of 1761, which has already been discussed in chapter IV. Hirzel, it will be recalled, created a fictional peasant, Kleinjogg, to illustrate the procedures and techniques of modern ("philosophical") farming. In so doing, he dwelt on the daily as well as the seasonal activities of this fictional character, and, incidentally to his purpose, created also a picture of peasant life which, though necessarily idealized in terms of his purpose, had much of reality in it. It was not necessary for Hirzel to choose this particular method of conveying agricultural information: there were, after all, a variety of other expository works dealing with farm improvements which merely catalogued and discoursed on ameliorative recommendations, leaving it to the reader to imagine the pleasures of their implementation, and of their results. But it was Hirzel's insight that a story, however fictional, which depicted the concrete circumstances of a particular peasant on a particular farm and which showed the step-by-step progress of improvements leading to increased production and increased happiness, rounded out with the necessary credible detail of a peasant's daily existence, might well win the attention of readers who otherwise would look with great skepticism on such proposals and regard them as the well-meant but utopian dreams of a philosophical

---

[32] See above, pp. 29-30, for example, for Gottsched's comments on the relationship of the contemporary peasantry to the poetic art.

innovator. Judging from the numbers of similar works which appeared in subsequent years, other writers—or at least many of those whose chief readership was intended to consist of peasants —apparently became convinced of the efficacy of Hirzel's method.

In spite of his attention to the problems of peasant farming in the context of a specific peasant's life, however, Hirzel's work did not approach the level of an interest in peasant life for its own sake. His concern was rather narrowly attached to technical improvements, and manifested no sense of the singularity of peasant life or appreciation of its diversities as expressions of human experience. Johann Heinrich Pestalozzi was perhaps the first to develop these in any clearly recognizable form, especially in his *Lienhard und Gertrud*, the famous pedagogical treatise in which Pestalozzi tried to illustrate the advantages of his step-by-step method of education through the exposure of the subjects to the concrete facts and situations of everyday life. Precisely because of the educational lessons which could be drawn from virtually every facet of the individual's daily experience, it was necessary for Pestalozzi to expose the parents and the children in *Lienhard und Gertrud* to the full range of normal village activities and experiences, from the tenderness and warmth of the home hearth to the requirements of daily work, to the intricate realm of village politics and lord-peasant relationships. Though necessarily somewhat confined by the framework of his pedagogical concerns, the picture of peasant life which emerged in Pestalozzi's story was remarkably realistic in terms both of the range of phenomena and events it covered and of the material conditions, personality types, and reactions described in it. There are deep insights into the character and motivations of people living on the margin of rural poverty in Pestalozzi's work, and both the problems and the solutions to problems of peasant life which he raises are thoroughly credible and practical. There is no romanticization of the average peasant here, but rather—and precisely herein lies its unusual contribution—a singularly objective assessment of what the peasant is, what he can be brought to be by education and unprejudiced understanding, and, above all, a gentle reminder that peasants, like all other people, are to a large extent shaped by conditions and forces which in some measure are subject to human control. It was still unusual in 1781, the year of publication of the first edition of *Lienhard und Gertrud*, to find favorable treatments of the peasant in literature; it was even more unusual, perhaps, to find a really balanced treatment which in effect clearly defined and admitted the ignorance, bad morals, superstitions, and avariciousness of the peasant, but which just as clearly demonstrated that these characteristics were neither universal nor, more important, necessary components of the peasant mentality, and that they could be overcome and supplanted by their opposites through reforms which needed not produce any dislocations in the formal class structure of society.

After Pestalozzi, and into the nineteenth century, numerous attempts were made to combine in one work the two sorts of concerns which appeared separately in Hirzel's work and that of Pestalozzi; on the one hand vocational instruction in farming techniques and other practical matters of that kind, and on the other, emphasis on the familial and social milieu of the individual as important factors in shaping his attitudes towards life and work and thus also his ability to make good use of vocational information. This combination is perhaps sufficiently illustrated in the work of Johann Evangelist Fürst, an agriculturist, director of the *Gartenbaugesellschaft* in Frauendorf, Bavaria, and editor of the *Bürger- und Bauernzeitung* from 1831 until 1845. As a response to the oppressive material need which Fürst saw everywhere around him among peasants as a consequence of the crop failures of 1816-1817, he published a two-volume work, intended as a handbook for peasants, and entitled: *Der verständige Bauer Simon Strüf, eine Familiengeschichte.* To these two volumes, after they had already gone through three editions, he added a third, in 1823, whose purpose was that of showing peasants how to make use of "the blessing of abundance," as Fürst euphemistically called the huge agricultural surpluses of the 1820s. The work was organized around the life and activities of the chief character, Simon Strüf, who appears as the model of the enlightened peasant; it was designed to cover virtually every aspect of practical farming, as well as home first aid, sanitation, recommendations for new crops, and important information about the laws of the land. The peasant Strüf kept himself informed of the best practices in agriculture by having his wife read books to him on holidays and in his spare time, and his own farming was so excellent and productive that his neighbors regularly imitated his cultivation.

As the title indicates, however, this was also to be a "family story," and Fürst therefore devoted a good deal of attention to the daily existence of the Strüf family. As in those sections of the work which dealt with agricultural cultivation and farm management, the emphasis remained on instruction. Here, Strüf's wife Theres played a major role. A model of teacher and mother, Theres not only sent her children to school diligently, but also instructed and exercised them at home in the knowledge of Christianity, reading, writing, and arithmetic. When the children were under two years of age, her prime concern was in keeping them clean and healthy; later, she taught them the value of discipline and of keeping promises; and finally she directed her efforts towards awakening in them a love for being busy at purposeful and beneficent activity.[33] In the course of his presentation of these and other ideas, buttressed by examples from the daily life of the fictional Strüf family, Fürst managed to paint a realistic picture of the essential problems of peasant life, although this "ideal" peasant family was obviously set out as a goal yet to be achieved rather than as a standard already attained.

To a degree not as apparent in either works of the kind done by Hirzel or stories such as those of Pestalozzi, Fürst attempted to appeal to an audience at two levels. Like Hirzel, he was much concerned to put specific information on agricultural improvements in the hands of peasants; but, like Pestalozzi, he was also interested in propagandizing the upper classes with the notion that a relatively small amount of agitation or encouragement on their part, chiefly in the direction of peasant education, could have the most profound results in increasing material prosperity and human happiness in rural areas. And if Fürst was not as successful as Pestalozzi in demonstrating the humanity of the peasant and his receptivity to education through the plot of the story itself,

---

[33] Johann Evangelist Fürst, *Der verständige Bauer Simon Strüf, eine Familiengeschichte*, 3 vols. (Passau and Salzburg, 1819-1823), I, 458-60.

he made up for this by presenting the reader with more or less direct statements, as in a dialogue between Karl Moll, a gentle-man-turned-peasant, and a nobleman, in which the industry, diligence, honesty, and goodheartedness of the peasantry were prominently displayed.[34]

None of the authors of the works so far mentioned, however, in spite of obvious sympathy for the peasant, was able to develop a fictional presentation of peasant life which ascribed a higher meaning to the simplicity and even rudeness of the agrarian life in terms of the ultimate values of society as a whole. The limited range of their primary purpose, which was in all cases restricted to instruction of one kind or another and their lack of awareness of the decline of an agrarian way of life as a consequence of the increasing urbanization and industrialization of the nineteenth century, tended to work against an attention to the values of peasant life itself. Hirzel and Pestalozzi, and even Fürst, could scarcely have been expected to have seen these developments, of course, because the trends which were to convert Germany into an industrial giant in the later nineteenth century were anything but apparent in the later eighteenth century, and even by 1820, the time of Fürst's publications, were by no means obvious in either social or economic terms. But by the late 1830s, critical observers of the German scene could already detect the first effects of the powerful influences which in the space of less than two generations were to sweep away most of the social traditions based upon a centuries-old agrarian constitution.

In the world of belles-lettres, one of the most anguished voices raised against the dim specter of a collectivized, industrial, deper-sonalized future was that of Karl Leberecht Immermann (1796-1840), scion of a Prussian bureaucratic family and himself an official in Prussian service. Immermann's discontent with the increasingly clear picture of the urban-oriented and mechanized society of the future found its first important expression in his work *Die Epigonen* of 1836, in which his hero represents the ideal of a rather romanticized, yet not entirely sentimentalized world in which relationships between men had not yet been reduced to a cash value and in which freedom was not merely a legal

[34] *Ibid.*, III, 220-26.

guarantee but a living principle, a thing felt with deep individual pride. Through the words of this hero, Hermann, who at the end of the book has fallen heir to a vast estate and an industrial or manufacturing community, Immermann gave vent to his own fears and dissatisfactions: "First of all," said this Hermann, speaking of his manufacturing enterprises, "the factories are to be done away with, and the fields to be restored to agriculture. These establishments for the artificial gratification of artificial wants appear to me downright ruinous and bad. The soil belongs to the plough, to sunshine and rain, which unfold the seed-corn, and to the simple industrious hand. With stormlike rapidity the present age is moving on toward a dry mechanism. We cannot check its course; but we are certainly not to blame if we hedge off a little green spot for ourselves and ours and defend this island as long as possible against the tide of the surging industrial waves."[35]

In his protest against the growth of a mechanistic society, Immermann did not turn to the idealized Christian Middle Ages with its rigidly stratified and organic hierarchical society, as dreamed up somewhat earlier by his older Romantic contemporaries. Such idealizations were to him as stupid and as pernicious, in their own way, as the slogans of the hawkers of a mass society, and fully as contemptible. But in his last novel, *Münchhausen: eine Geschichte in Arabesken* (1838-1839), and especially in "Der Oberhof," a lengthy story which forms a part of the larger novel, he did attempt to set forth a real world which he felt deserved preservation. This was, essentially, a peasant's world, whose features Immermann sought to portray as accurately and, by his standards, as objectively as possible.[36]

There is, in fact, a remarkable urgency about Immermann's insistence that the peasant world be understood *as it is,* not as it had been made over to be by poets and writers into their own desired image. In "Der Oberhof," for example, a deacon of the

---

[35] This translation is from Kuno Francke, *A History of German Literature as Determined by Social Forces* (New York, 1901), 512. The passage is from Karl Leberecht Immermann, *Die Epigonen,* Book IX, Chapter 16.

[36] It is important to emphasize that the peasants and the peasant institutions which Immermann described were Westphalian, peasants who were for the most part independent proprietors, and whose village institutions were based on their freedom of decision arising from the absence of dependence on a lord.

village church is made to correct a number of misconceptions about peasant life held by an outsider, a gentleman from the princely court. When the latter approvingly remarked that all the peasants he had seen appeared to be very genial and good-natured, the deacon quickly pointed out that they were, in fact, by no means good-natured, because they had no time for it; one could only be good-natured if one had little to do, said the cleric, and the peasant was too hard-pressed for a living to have any extra time for the development of his geniality. The peasant, on the contrary, was the very essence of practical understanding, earnestness, obstinacy, and "permissible selfishness"; but because this mixture seemed permanently to belong to him, it had something honorable about it. Like granite, which is also hard and heavy, but which holds up the very earth, the peasant class held up the civic community.[37] Similarly, when the gentleman referred to peasants as "natural men," free from the bonds of propriety, he was sharply corrected by the deacon, who pointed out that while the peasant was often out in the open air, he certainly was not a natural man: he was as dependent on tradition and class concepts and prejudices as the highest class of society, and distinctions in the village were as carefully maintained as in castles and palaces.[38]

The reason for Immermann's extreme care to set the picture straight on the nature of peasant and village life, as illustrated in the above examples, is perhaps suggested by the statement he put in the mouth of a nobleman who while on a hunt wandered into the village and spent some time there observing the peasants. Eventually he reached the conclusion that peasant life had been badly described by poets and writers, by the "pastoral-tender" as well as by the "bulbous potato-poets." The peasant world, said he, "is a sphere filled with raw nature as well as with custom and ceremony, and certainly not without poverty and elegance; only the latter lies elsewhere than it is usually sought."[39] By dispelling all idyllic and romantic visions of happy peasants merrily singing their way from one picturesque village festival

[37] Karl Leberecht Immermann, "Münchhausen: eine Geschichte in Arabesken," *Immermanns Werke*, ed. Harry Maync, 5 vols. (Leipzig and Vienna, 1906), II, 66.
[38] *Ibid.*
[39] *Ibid.*, I, 269-70.

to another, Immermann sought not merely to make the point that the peasant's life, whatever else one might think about it, was largely hard work and unpleasant work, but also, and more important in terms of his larger purpose, to focus attention on the real and genuine "elegance" of peasant life. He did this through the chief peasant character of the story, the village mayor, or *Hofschulze,* whose character and function as a stern but kind and just village patriarch are placed over against the inroads which modern state and society could make into the highly personal and simple but effective self-government of the village community.

At one level, then, Immermann's story treats of the tragic abolition of village self-government by the machinery of the modern, centralized, collectivized state, which eventually robs the *Hofschulze* of his sword of justice (represented for him in a real sword which he believed to have been given by Charlemagne) and dissolves the court in which he judged in equity a community of free peasants. But these institutions were not, after all, the basis of the "elegance" of the peasant life; they were only expressions of it. The "watchword of independence" by which these peasants maintained their self-reliance and their strength as individuals and as a community actually lay in their own unconquerable spirit, as an observer acutely pointed out to the *Hofschulze*: "You have planted the conviction that man's place is among his nearest, the plain, true, simple folk; not with strangers who will force upon him the stamp of artificiality and distortedness. . . . Your freedom, your manliness, your firm iron nature, you yourself, you sublime old man,—this is the true sword of Carolus Magnus, and the hand of theft cannot reach out for this."[40] The *Hofschulze* himself was by no means the model of a "progressive" peasant in the sense in which most agricultural reformers understood the phrase; when he was visited by a government official with the proposal that his taxes to the government be changed from grain to cash payment, a method normally much in demand among peasants, he refused, and commented further that in his opinion it would be an improvement to go back

[40] The translation is from Francke, *A History of German Literature,* 514; the passage is from Immermann, "Münchhausen," *Werke,* II, 382-83.

to the old system, whereby the tax lists were posted in the church for the ready reference of the taxpayers.[41] His opposition to many innovations normally considered forward-looking may be at least partly explained by the position he took relative to the construction of a new road by the government which was to run through village lands; having advised a group of disaffected peasants where to lodge their complaints against the project, the mayor said: "Let them [the government] build and dig what they will; but they should leave us undisturbed. If things went according to them, then we would soon be off our inheritance by reason of the common good, as it would be called."[42] The suspiciousness which found expression in these and other examples of the mayor's character and policies, a feature of the peasant mentality often damned by the upper classes, was thus actually shown to rest on the entirely laudable bases of self-reliance and the firm conviction that the liberties of individuals and of communities were best preserved by those who knew them best—the individuals and communities themselves.

Immermann was not content to express his admiration and deep feeling for the worthiness of the peasantry solely through the descriptions of the actions of the *Hofschulze* or the words he put in his mouth, although the weight of his presentation was clearly on these. Occasionally he pronounced his own judgments, as it were, through those characters in the book whose judgment, as the reader has already learned, is unerring. When the deacon solemnly makes the following estimate of the peasantry, after having spoken of the upper classes of society as distinctly inferior to the lower classes in their development, the reader has little difficulty in accepting the judgment as that of fair-mindedness itself: "This folk, like a wonder-child, continually finds pearls and precious stones, but it pays no attention to them, and remains in its frugal poverty; this folk is a giant, which can be led by the silken thread of a good word; it is pensive, innocent, loyal, valiant, and has preserved all these virtues under circumstances which have made other peoples superficial, impertinent, faithless, cowardly."[43] This statement and many others like it provide proof,

[41] Immermann, "Münchhausen," *Werke*, I, 161-62.
[42] *Ibid.*, I, 169-70.
[43] *Ibid.*, I, 238,

if any is needed, that Immermann's desire to describe the severity and rigor of peasant life in realistic terms, and to avoid all pastoral platitudes, stemmed ultimately from his conviction that one did not have to gild the peasant and his life to demonstrate their real and enduring value.

Finally, Immermann was quite conscious of the misunderstanding and contempt of the upper classes of society for the peasantry, and it is abundantly clear from his writing that for him an important part of this misunderstanding and contempt came from the inability of the upper classes to conceive of peasants as human beings, subject to the same triumphs and defeats, joys and sorrows which made up the substance of their own existence. Like Pestalozzi, therefore, but with a great deal more subtlety and literary skill, Immermann attempted to bring out in his reader a consciousness of the basic identity of human experience, in which the differences between particular situations were less important than the similarities of human responses to situations. He did this most artfully in his description of unhappiness and sorrow in various contexts within peasant life, and his own conscious effort can perhaps best be illustrated by a short preface he affixed to his description of a village tragedy. The Muse of Tragedy, Melpomene, he wrote, had two daggers: one, sharp and quick, was reserved for kings and heroes; the other, dull, rusty, and ripping, was reserved for burghers and peasants. But since there were, after all, *two* daggers, it was obvious that "the palace is not the only theater of tragedy." Why, indeed, did any particular place have to be the exclusive domain of tragedy? Was it not true that "men are not tormented by things, but by opinions about things"?[44] And if this were true, then it was human opinions which made tragedy, not the things (particular events and situations) about which opinions were held. Immermann had thus not only written a story as a vehicle for his strong views on the character and value of the peasantry, but also had legitimized peasant life as an object of true literary attention, and had fully breached one of the walls which separated the peasant from his fellow citizens in other classes.

[44] *Ibid.*, II, 299-300.

11 Summary and Conclusion

One of the most striking characteristics of German publicistic literature of the years 1770-1840 is the steadiness of the concern it showed for the agrarian problem and the extent to which those problems dominated a central place on the stage among the discussions of social issues of all kinds throughout these years. No other group of problems was more consistently discussed, and no other reforms more earnestly solicited than those which pertained to the peasant and his life and work; and no other concern found its way into more diverse types of literature. From one viewpoint, one is almost tempted to consider the constantly growing body of literature devoted to peasant problems and questions as a more or less self-contained and internally consistent publicistic campaign designed to coax a hostile or indifferent public opinion around to a recognition of the need for agrarian reform. This perspective receives apparent justification from the obvious persistence throughout the entire period of certain major reform goals and of a number of essential features in descriptions of the peasant disposition or character. Certainly the abolition of serfdom and the establishment of full proprietorship for the peasant were themes whose constant repetition could easily give an impression of coherence to almost everything written on the peasant in this period; similarly, the regular appearance in the literature of such peasant traits as piety, honesty, simple wisdom or common sense, industry, loyalty, and a number of other moral virtues almost from the outset tends to create a picture of uniformity in attitudes towards the peasant, and contributes to the impression of a monolithic body of reform writings whose central consideration was the peasant himself and the improvement of his lot.

To become preoccupied with the remarkable uniformity of agrarian reform goals and peasant characteristics in the literature of these several decades, however, is to miss the rather more striking diversity of the broader goals to which these reforms were related as means to an end. For it must be insisted that praise of the peasant and the desire to reform the circumstances of his life were never regarded as ends in themselves; they were always pointed towards and justified by their contribution to larger social ends. What is surprising, in view of the great social changes and historical events which separated the Germany of Frederick the Great from that of the *Vormärz* intellectuals, is not only the relatively static nature of reform proposals and of the picture of the peasant which went with them, but also the fact that these same proposals and this same picture were able to serve the general social ends of conceptions of society as widely different as were those of the Cameralists of eighteenth-century Prussia and the liberal intellectuals of Baden and Württemberg in the 1840s. Any consideration of the peasant and agrarian literature of this period which does not look beyond the reform proposals and the general eulogies of the peasant to the broader framework of the social concerns of which they were a part is woefully inadequate to explain the real and important consistency which throughout the period reconciled the uniformity of opinions expressed on the peasant to the diversity of personal and social situations within which these opinions were expressed.

This consistency is above all apparent in the degree to which the discussions of the peasant throughout this time revolved around the public functions which were or could be performed by him and his class. The peasant, his character, and his problems were seldom regarded in any connection other than that of their relation to other classes or to state or society; and it is this connection which raises the significance of the peasant question out of the sphere of purely agrarian problems and places it on a political level. It was with the peasant as a political man, as a citizen, and with his social contribution as such, that the agrarian writings of this entire period were chiefly concerned. This study has therefore undertaken to trace the growth of the image of the German peasant in this literature from that of a virtual social pariah to that of a folk-hero by focusing on the relationship between the political and social imperatives of German public life and the creation and development of the particular characteristics of that image. As the peasant was more and more closely implicated with the central political concerns of German national life, his stature and the honor accorded him grew steadily greater, for a constantly growing number of responsibilities were placed upon his shoulders until finally, still within the confines of this study, his participation was felt to be fundamentally and peculiarly necessary to the preservation and progress of the German nation. At this point, by the middle of the nineteenth century, the one-time serf had become, in concept, the full citizen.

It was entirely in keeping with the nature of German (and, in fact, European) social theory before the French Revolution that the beginning of a new regard for the peasant in Germany should arise from essentially statist considerations, and in fact from largely fiscal motives. From the standpoint of the absolutistic governments of eighteenth-century Germany, the individual was defined chiefly by his class, and classes in turn by the nature of their contribution to a body politic whose nature and goals were defined by the ruling prince. In this sense, the peasant shared with his admittedly more fortunate countrymen in the towns and cities the designation of *producer* of the various goods required for the maintenance of society. The peasant, in this conception, was therefore basically an economic unit, and his citizenship, if it can be spoken of in these terms, consisted in the services he rendered society as the primary producer of agricultural goods. In the late seventeenth century, and throughout the eighteenth, German bureaucracies were everywhere concerned to maximize production insofar as that would ultimately be reflected in increased income for the royal treasuries. Agriculture, and through it the peasant, benefited in a number of ways from the constant concern shown for production by the Cameralists in Germany, and this was especially true for some areas after 1763, since the financial exhaustion of the Seven Years' War gave an even more pressing inducement to governments to look after the depressed condition of the agricultural sector. In the writings of later eighteenth-century Cameralists there appeared not only numerous recommendations for technical improvements in areas such as field cultivation and animal husbandry, but also, by way of indicating the importance of such reform to the state, an emphasis on the value of the peasant's work to the state and occasionally even upon certain positive characteristics of the peasant which were allegedly responsible for his industry and which should preserve him from the contempt of the upper classes.

Physiocratic doctrine, while differing from the generally mercantilist assumptions of the Cameralists as to methods of increasing social prosperity, was in very few particulars different from them in its acceptance of a stratified social structure and a strong monarchical government. While the Physiocrats' goal was less deliberately tied to the fiscal interest of the state than that of the Cameralists, and more to the increased level of social production as such, their view of the public function of the peasant was quite similar to that of the Cameralists: his role in the state was that of a unit of economic production. It is quite true that German Physiocrats tended to be much more impatient of the impediments to thoroughgoing technical reform which they clearly recognized to be imbedded in the system of social privilege than were the Cameralists; but the latter were, after all, bureaucrats and officials in a political system to which social privilege was thought essential, and it was that system to which they were devoted more than to any reform. Both Cameralism and Physiocracy, however, by their systematic emphasis on the importance of agriculture to the economic well-being of the state made similar and significant contributions to a heightened respect for the peasant, chiefly by raising the value of his services and the importance of increasing them to the level of consciousness among those who had always merely taken him for granted.

If for these economic writers the peculiar social value of the peasant related more or less exclusively to his productive functions in a purely economic sense, there was another group to whose members the word "peasant" began to connote much more than "agricultural producer." It was this group which, from various motives, produced the first reasonably distinct picture of the peasant as a moral type, whose peculiar value lay in his preservation of virtues which were, in other classes, alas! only too subject to dissolution. It can be asserted that in general the reasons behind the creation of this conception of the peasant may be found in a series of group antagonisms which grew up around various social issues in the late eighteenth century, and which often expressed themselves, for lack of any other idiom, as moral controversies. The heightened perception and resentment of class distinctions, for example, was expressed less in protests against the objective factors which gave rise to class distinction than in mutual accusations of sin and debauchery. Philosophical disagreements frequently took the same course. And in the process of argumentation, the peasantry, perhaps the only major social group not publicly grinding an axe, began to receive compliments from everyone. Nobles inveighed against burghers as greedy money-grubbers and coupon-clippers, and suggested that the artificiality of city life was warping their sense of values; burghers anathematized the nobility as lazy parasites and arrogant ignoramuses, and piously recommended diligence and thrift as the salvation of their souls; Physiocrats damned both as haughty and unproductive; German *philosophes* cudgeled traditionalists as obscurantists, and were in turn accused of materialism, atheism, licentiousness, and worse; and Cameralists and state officials of various kinds admonished all and sundry to get to work and stop wasting their substance. Each group, seeking moral examples with which to thump its opponents, found in the peasantry the qualities it needed. Thus, for example, the damnation by Pietists and other religious figures of luxury, loose living, and the impieties produced by such a life style usually managed to involve mention of the continence, frugality, and piety of the peasant, who began to emerge as the very contrast to the overrefined and spendthrift libertine. For others, the peasant became the symbol of simplicity, hard work, honesty, sincerity, and a host of other virtues. However various the reasons, the brutish avariciousness and general lack of civilized qualities with which the peasant had been taxed in earlier years began rapidly to disappear from the literature of the 1770s and 1780s, to be replaced by the most praiseworthy moral features. As the very model of good morals, in the widest sense, the peasant was therefore indirectly put forward as the preceptor of his fellow Germans with respect to their individual and social behavior—a new role for him, which in one way or another was to be the basis for much of the future discussion of his social worth.

The quantitatively very impressive body of educational and pedagogical writings of the late eighteenth century tends to reflect and strengthen the conception of peasant "citizenship" as established in the statist-economic and moralist works. On one hand, the great emphasis on vocational education in this period is indicative both of the institutional limits and the prevailing directions of reformist thought. Few theorists departed from the assumption that reform of the peasant's life had to come within the framework of traditional social organization; and since this made social reform in any broad sense impossible, then the answer to the peasant's woes had to lie in the improvement of his standard of living through production increases which could supposedly be brought about by educating him to better utilization of his economic resources. This was, generally speaking, the state's attitude also, which was eager for increased production without the necessity for major social change. Educational theory therefore aimed at an instruction which would inculcate in the peasant a desire and an ability to get ahead in his work.

At the same time, that instruction should impress upon him that his proper role as citizen lay in the efficient performance of his work and in certain moral attitudes which expressed an essentially submissive posture towards social and political authority and privilege. An important novelty of this proposed instruction, however, was that submissiveness in the above sense was to be the result of conscious consent stemming from understanding. It was not to be the submissiveness of the slave, or much less of the dumb and bewildered beast, but that of a man who willed submission to his duty because he understood the nature and importance of his social function and the mutual interdependence of all the various groups which went to make up the society in which he lived. In its own way, therefore, pedagogical theory tended towards an emphasis upon the necessity for an increase in individual initiative among peasants in a way quite reminiscent of the imperatives of Adam Smith. Restricted though it was to the social limitations of absolutist and hierarchical regimes, it supported and itself advanced arguments which pointed towards an acceptance of the peasant as a full-fledged member of society, whose conscious and intelligent co-operation was necessary for the achievement of the goals of collective life. Furthermore, the insistence upon the educability of the peasant, which was an essential assumption of all educational writings, produced a picture of the peasant as a man equal to all other men with respect to innate intellectual capacity; and the repetition of this insight throughout the educational literature of this period undoubtedly contributed to erase from some minds an image of the peasant as a creature nearly as close to the animals as he was to man.

The reception of Adam Smith's doctrines in Germany was important, among other reasons, precisely because those doctrines appeared to demonstrate conclusively that personal freedom and effective proprietorship were essential to the maximization of wealth in the agricultural sector of the economy as in all other sectors. The effect of this demonstration is enormously important, for economic specialists both inside and outside of governments rapidly began to abandon some of the assumptions under which official economic policies in many German states had previously been conducted. One of these assumptions was that of the feasibility of substantially increasing agricultural production without the necessity of tampering with the legal position of the agricultural producer, the peasant. It now appeared that it was senseless to talk of economic progress in agriculture unless one were prepared to move in the direction of peasant emancipation. Now, governments were no less interested in increasing production from the land in the late 1780s and after than they had been before; and even though the concept of the basic function of the citizen was to remain largely restricted to the economic functions performed by the individual in his relationship to the state, it had nevertheless become necessary to modify the definition of the citizen in such a way as to include his freedom to dispose of labor and capital. One significant theoretical aspect of the citizen's tutelage to state authority was thus abolished, for as self-interest was defined within Adam Smith's economic framework, it was impossible that the state should know better than the individual citizens where their own interest lay; and, of course, it was assumed by Smith and by those who accepted his teachings that every man did have the capacity and ought to have the legal freedom to realize his self-interest. In this way, the peasant benefited from and was increasingly integrated into a new idea of social function or citizenship which presupposed both his innate ability and his external freedom to deal with property which was his own. To the extent that this idea might be implemented in actual agrarian relationships, it could provide the peasant with the opportunity to demonstrate his ability to act in his own interest as a rational creature, and to increase his standard of living; and this, in turn, could affect in a still more favorable sense the public image of what sort of a man the peasant was or could be. Smithian teachings contributed little to expand the conception of what the peasant's role in society might be; on the contrary, it tended to strengthen the Cameralist perspective on the citizen as an economic unit. But this was only because Smith's purpose for writing was involved primarily with economic questions and only secondarily with political ones. More important was the fact that the picture of the peasant which emerged from Smith's considerations was one of a rational being capable of recognizing his self-interest and of taking the initiative to satisfy its promptings.

If Smithian doctrine had modified the conception of how the peasant might make his maximum contribution to the economy of his country, there was also another view of the nature of his value to society. Just as numerous writers of various moralist persuasions had begun to find the preservation of universal moral values among the peasantry, so now the nature and importance of these values were transformed through their association with a growing reaction to foreign influence in Germany. That is, a number of writers and publicists in their attempts to account for what they had for some time already seen as a marked degeneracy of German customs and morals began to locate the primary source of corruption in the tendency of the upper classes to ape foreign and, specifically, French modes and manners in everything from literary style to profligate luxury expenditures. Moral dissolution and the various social ills it entailed were thus not really German at all, but the result of imitation of foreign example. The German in his purity as German was *not* an immoral sort, according to this interpretation. But this of course raised the problem of just what pure Germanness was, and what it meant, in moral terms. The search for an original Germanness led straight to the peasant, whose total lack of contact with foreign tastes and habits made him more than anyone else the pristine vehicle of a true and traditional German spirit, whose ancestry could be traced in a more or less direct line back to the ancient Germanic tribesman. And his morality, the essential features of which were already emerging in discussions in other contexts, thus became the ideal German national morality.

This tendency to identify the peasant with an ideal national character was given powerful support by a new insight into the cultural significance of the "folk," the common people. Johann Gottfried Herder was only the most famous of a number of philologists and literary figures who contributed to a new definition of "nation" through their emphasis on the singularity of language, and who again found in the peasant, by virtue of the unadulterated language he used and of the customs and habits which necessarily accompanied his language, the representative and preserver of pure and genuine nationality. His function was in this sense again a unique one; for the guarantee of real nationality, which lay always primarily in the preservation of the purity of language, could rest only on the shoulders of him whose spirit had not been mongrelized through exposure to and adoption of foreign languages and consequently of foreign psychologies.

Even before the French Revolution, therefore, it was possible to find, in the public literature of Germany, a number of recurrent conceptions which, taken together, suggested a singular contribution of socially important functions on the part of the peasant. He was, certainly, regarded as the chief economic support of the nation, in terms both of the gross value of the goods he produced and of the fundamental social necessity of the kinds of goods he produced (food and raw materials). He was, furthermore, a model of virtue which preserved and nurtured a nucleus of social morality which, in turn, could serve the entire nation as the exemplary alternative to degeneracy and corruption. Finally, he became a symbol of German nationality, as that term came to be defined under the impact of the search for national distinction and uniqueness in a cultural sense.

These conceptions of the role of the peasant in his society were accompanied by a number of proposals designed to make it possible for him adequately to perform the specific tasks implied by these general views of his social function. The practical reforms suggested in this time ranged from the very limited abolition of minor abuses and the mere rationalization or stream-lining of the old agrarian constitution (characteristic of official and bureaucratic circles, largely) to the thoroughgoing elimina-tion of peasant legal dependence and the establishment of free proprietary relationships (advocated chiefly by Smithian econo-mists and Physiocrats in universities and both inside and outside of government). In addition to such reforms as these, a major pedagogical reform movement emphasized the necessity for vocational instruction in order to make the peasant capable of using his time and tools to best advantage in his work. All of these groups to some extent emphasized the necessity for a greater freedom for the peasant from hindrances of one kind or another—be they legal or customary, expressed in financial or other terms. But, more than this, both Smithians and educational theorists, in particular, recognized that efficient performance of work depended not merely on the creation of externally favorable conditions of labor, but also on the desire or willingness of the individual to work, on a more or less deliberate choice to work, which should stem, as they saw it, from his recognition of the involvement of his self-interest in what he was doing. For the Smithians, property was the essential ingredient in this kind of choice; for the pedagogues, it was a moral education which taught the individual the nature of his contribution to and dependence on others.

The statist and economic view of the peasant's role in society was susceptible to a relatively easy vindication through the almost immediate benefits which technical and other agrarian reforms could bring to society through increased agricultural production; the rapidity with which at least certain aspects of such reform were recognized as desirable at all levels would appear to justify the conclusion that the new economic importance of the peasantry was therefore accepted, in general terms, without much reservation among many of the most important circles of public opinion. The conceptions of the peasantry as a reservoir of moral virtue and as the preserver of nationality, on the other hand, faced greater difficulties in achieving general acceptance. Whereas the economic view required only an intensification of the peasant's farming activity as its proof, both other views related to peasant qualities which were, for the most part, entirely passive, and which, before the 1790s at least, involved no active function. The demonstration of the practical importance of the peasant to his society in these two roles required that both somehow be made active, with observable and desirable social consequences. The opportunity for the activation of both came with the era of the French Revolution.

The decade of the 1790s and the intensified discussion of social and national problems produced by the events transpiring in a new and revolutionary France tended to promote the peasant to the novel position of an active defender of his fatherland, and to strengthen the attribution of moral qualities to him. The opponents of the revolution in Germany grasped the threat it posed to them in a number of different ways; and quite apart from their material interests, which could in some instances suffer severely from the possible extension of any revolutionary legislation to German territories, they often saw the dangers of revolution, and explained those dangers to themselves, in terms of the overthrow of certain principles of belief which together made up the ideological basis of the society they lived in and wished to preserve. For some, the revolution was militant godlessness, or atheism; for others, the triumph of greed, self-interest, and materialism; for still others, it was the conquest of an almost religiously conceived theory of duty, loyalty, and fidelity by the unholy alliance of selfishness, lust for power, and ignorance. For more than a few, after the beginnings of the "export" of the revolution from France by propaganda and military force, it also represented a final and terrible imposition of essentially foreign ideas on peoples and states to whom those ideas were at once inappropriate and repugnant. An awareness of a peculiar and characteristic set of singularly German cultural properties was greatly strengthened by the comparisons invited between a revolutionary, muscle-flexing France and the old regime of the German states.

The peasant first became involved in the complex of fear and uncertainty produced in Germany by the French Revolution through the recognition that revolutionary circumstances akin to those in France could easily be reproduced in Germany by the fusion of the objective oppressive conditions of the peasant's life and work with a knowledge on his part of the success of the revolutionary French in their struggle with the old order. The consequent recognition of the necessity for a reform of some of the worst abuses of the agrarian constitution—an attempt to "neutralize" the peasant conscience, essentially—was soon joined, however, by a more positive approach which actually sought to win the peasant masses to an active role in defense of the institutions of the old regime. The appeal to the peasant was to a considerable extent based on the acceptance of the moral image of the peasant which was already at hand from numerous writings of the 1770s and 1780s. His qualities of piety, loyalty, sincerity, and so on, were already well established in various types of public literature when they were pounced upon by opponents of the revolution to explain both to him and to themselves why he should have a stake in preserving his land from the ravages of a fundamentally impious and immoral movement which was at once revolutionary and foreign. From this, then, was created the picture of the peasant as a fusion of German national and universal moral characteristics who had as great a reason and desire as anyone to protect his fatherland from external threat, and whose sheer numbers were clearly necessary, under the conditions of the present age, to the effective defense of the country against the citizen-armies of the French.

Prussia's defeat at the hands of Napoleon in 1806-1807 fostered the rapid development of a concept of active peasant citizenship through the widespread perception that the Prussian failure was, at base, a moral one. Upper-class selfishness and lower-class indifference were fastened upon by numerous writers and officials in high places as the ultimate causes of the feeble resistance put up to Napoleon's advance. More strongly than ever, by way of contrast with the alleged self-seeking calculation of the nobility and of the middle class, the civic and social morality of the communal spirit of the peasantry was held up as the brightest hope of the nation for the future. Faced with the immediate and Herculean tasks of self-preservation and national self-assertion, it was only the *Volk*, the great and silent reservoir of national energy, which could provide the irresistible primal force to raise and rejuvenate the fallen edifice of the Prussian state. Thus the much discussed potentialities of an active role for the peasant as defender of the fatherland in the 1790s suddenly became a matter of desperate and profound concern. The agrarian reforms of the Stein-Hardenberg era, directed towards the emancipation of the peasant and his eventual transformation into a landed proprietor, were squarely based on the thought that to a unique degree the peasant possessed inbred instincts of loyalty and duty, and that these instincts could be released, strengthened, and directed towards the achievement of the common good of the entire society by allowing him to participate, through the free allocation of his own labor and his ownership of property, in the benefits and the obligations of full citizenship. The great reforms of this period, in other words, were not a product of crisis alone, but of a desperate emergency combined with a certain impression of the character of the peasant and of his social value, already at hand, which guaranteed the efficacy of these particular reforms for the desired goals. As it was felt among many economists to be necessary to awaken individual voluntarism in order to tap the full economic energies of the peasant, so it was now regarded in Prussian official circles to be necessary to awaken a similar voluntarism in order to tap the moral and political energies of the *Volk*. The similarity of the means of doing so—personal emancipation and proprietorship—should not obscure the fact that the former was designed to increase his production, while the latter aimed at political responsibility by making freedom and property the bridge between the self-interest of the individual and the welfare of the society in which he lived. The peasant was therefore not only admitted to a new rank of citizenship in theory, but was provided with the means to convert the theory into reality.

While it is scarcely possible to estimate the degree to which the Stein-Hardenberg agrarian reforms and the theory which underlay them in themselves actually contributed to strengthen the Prussian state in the years following 1807, it is in any case true that contemporaries attributed the Prussian successes against Napoleon in 1813-1814 in large measure to a popular enthusiasm which they felt to have resulted from the reforms. The Wars of Liberation therefore tended to vindicate the validity of the conception of peasant citizenship which had prompted the reforms, and discussions of Prussian and German national defense in the decades after 1815 reveal an almost uniform acceptance of the peasant in this new role. Among the most important implications of peasant emancipation and participation in the common concerns of the nation was that the peasant should in some fashion be allowed to assist in the formulation of the laws under which he was now equal to other men. The campaign for political representation for the peasant to which this gave rise was, of course, only one facet of the broader constitutionalist movement of restoration Germany, and as such fittted into the beginnings of a development towards universal suffrage which ultimately was to close completely the gap between the theoretical and political imperatives of the civic equality of the peasant with other members of his society.

In the critical period of the Napoleonic wars, the emphasis on the civic duty of the peasant had tended to become blurred with and merged into the civic duty of all other classes and descriptions of men. Freiherr vom Stein demonstrated this tendency in his own thinking about a common civic responsibility for all members of Prussian society, in which the peasantry occupied a larger place than other groups merely because of the importance of its numbers and the magnitude of the measures necessary to render it capable of fulfilling civic responsibilities as Stein defined them. The equality inherent in Stein's conception of course tended to benefit the peasant, who had not been regarded in this light before. But one must look elsewhere for the continuation of the development of the conception of the peasantry as a uniquely important social group. One of Stein's friends and associates in the liberation movement, Ernst Moritz Arndt, himself the son of a freed peasant, was in this period perhaps the most important figure in the propagation of this conception. Arndt was a strong supporter of the agrarian reforms of which Stein was the author; unlike Stein, however, who conceived of freedom and property as the framework of the education of the peasant to citizenship and the morality which underlay it, Arndt regarded these reforms as the abolition of hindrances to the active expression of those profound moral qualities which the peasant possessed as peasant. He saw the singular value of the peasantry not so much in terms of universal canons of citizenship according to the Stein model, but in its intimate connection with the land. The life and work of the peasant on his own land produced in him an awareness of freedom and a willingness to defend it—qualities missing in the burgher, whose ties to his country were always as fluid as his capital. Good citizenship was as essential to Arndt as to Stein; but for Arndt, the free peasant always made the best and most reliable citizen, partly because he was the most courageous and willing soldier, and he was therefore the *sine qua non* of any state which wished to assure itself of lasting strength and freedom.

Whatever their differences may have been, however, both Stein and Arndt were agreed that peasants must be allowed their personal freedom and, wherever possible, the opportunity to own land. They were also agreed on the necessity for eventual political representation for the peasant, so that his voice might be added to the advisory councils of the nation and enhance his sense of participation in public affairs. They were joined in their advocacy of peasant representation after 1815 by the new school of essentially bourgeois intellectual liberals, whose concepts of a constitutional state governed by laws whose origin should lie in the people themselves demanded the inclusion of the mass of the peasantry in the legislative process in one way or another. This group of political thinkers was distinguished by its rational approach to political problems, as well as by a thorough dislike of any corporatistic social distinctions. Disciples of Adam Smith in their economic theory, and generally individualistic also in their social theory, nothing was further from their minds than an inordinate praise of one social class above another. Yet by the 1830s, some of the most important leaders of the German national-liberal movement were singing special praises of the German peasantry, and had deserted some of the major tenets of the Smithian system in order to assure the continued existence of a large class of independent rural proprietors. The reasons for this, and its meaning for the evolution of a peasant image, are tied to the insights and reactions of the liberal theoreticians and publicists to the apparent social results of the agricultural depression of the 1820s and the first large-scale social dislocations of nascent German industrialism.

The freedom of the peasant to leave his land, the desirability of doing so because of a decade of abnormally low prices, and the increasing availability of various kinds of jobs in towns and cities led to what some contemporaries saw as a real exodus from the land on the part of smaller proprietors, and a noticeable increase in the number of large, entrepreneurial estates. The early warnings of Stein, Arndt, and a number of other political thinkers about the evil social effects of a proletarianized agricultural population and the growth of a propertyless class in the urban areas began to be taken seriously in an increasing number of middle-class liberal and intellectual circles as the prospects of the creation of a rootless class of wage-earners appeared to materialize. The importance of property as a foundation of social morality binding the individual to his society through the sense of responsibility inculcated by the necessities of management of property thus came to predominate over mechanistic Smithian doctrines of strict economic laissez faire. This was expressed as a rapidly increasing tendency to abandon approval of the growth of large estates, the most efficient units of production, in favor of statutory measures designed to maintain a nation of "middle-sized" farms, large enough to support the families inhabiting them, but not large enough to become truly capitalistic enterprises.

What underlay this change, then, was not only the desire to

prevent the growth of a proletariat because it was conceived as an economic problem-child, but also the desire to preserve a property ethic in a society for which universal suffrage was a growing possibility. The morality of political life, seen increasingly (and in some cases almost exclusively) as resting on ownership of property, could be maintained, in a democratized society, only if the overwhelming majority of individuals possessed property. It was therefore the morality of citizenship rather than the free play of the market which private ownership of property was to foster. In making this distinction and this choice, bourgeois liberals such as Rotteck and Welcker in effect recognized as valid some part of the criticisms which had been leveled by a number of conservative spirits after 1800 at the enlightened and rationalist conception of a society in which individual self-interest would suffice to produce and maintain free institutions and free men. Certainly they did not agree with many conservatives, who looked to spiritual bonds alone as the moral cement uniting diverse individuals in a complex society; but they did recognize that the regime of private property, embodying, as they saw it, the greatest possible opportunities for individual self-fulfillment, could have neither meaning for nor the consent of individuals who had no property and therefore no stake in this sort of society. In order, therefore, to bring their particular conception of the utility of private property as the arena for the self-fulfillment of every individual into harmony with the idea that every man should be a participant in his own governance, it was theoretically necessary for every man to possess private property.

The peasant became involved in this ideology of property ownership in several ways. It was, first of all, impossible for bourgeois liberal thinkers to conceive of the realization of a society such as they projected without the guarantee of order afforded by the overwhelming numbers of the peasant class. If a substantial portion of that class were to be harried off the land, or reduced to the status of agricultural wage-laborers, then the concept of property would become bound to an increasingly small number of urban and rural entrepreneurs and, far from serving the purpose of creating a moral bond between all members of society, would have the very opposite effect of splitting the body politic—of performing a divisive rather than an integrative function. Property, essential to the moral foundations of political consciousness, therefore had to be assured for as large a portion of the total population as possible.

If proprietorship was the fundamental element of political responsibility, however, it was not a sure-fire guarantee that all proprietors would be equally responsible; and alongside the general theory of property there grew up the notion that from a political standpoint, at least, the peasant constituted an ideal proprietor, whose nature guaranteed the integrity of the system of which he was a part. This view appears to have a number of rather confused but interrelated roots. One of these was the assumption that the average peasant proprietor was not and could scarcely become a rich man, and that he therefore would be subject to neither the avarice nor the luxurious diversions of the rich, whose vision all too often stopped at the counting house window. Selfishness, in other words, the bane of social cooperation, characterized the excessively rich as well as the propertyless poor. Then again, an emphasis in many writings on the beneficial effects of the great variety of the peasant's daily life and work, sharply opposed to the supposed one-sidedness and dull repetitiveness of urban occupations, points up more than a mere suggestion that the peasant constituted something of a political "whole man," the nature of whose existence necessarily fostered a quick intelligence, balance and maturity in judgment, and the ability to make decisions in the most varied situations. This kind of man was clearly the ideal citizen in a society whose political direction was to depend upon the integration of popular will into the processes of government; here was an individual in whom his own particular interest and the more general one of society as a whole met and blended, producing a theoretically perfect social behavior. This man, this peasant, was represented by the millions who belonged to his class; and the existence of these masses of moral individuals acted as the warranty against the failures of the automatic self-adjustment mechanisms of a society conceived in terms of a natural harmony of conflicting self-interests, whose faults were becoming all too obvious even by 1830. Once again, then, the peasant emerged from the interaction of theory and concrete circumstance as an indispensable foundation for German national life.

Throughout the various stages of evolution of the new and sympathetic image of the peasant, changing perspectives on the character and importance of the peasant for contemporary society were reflected in various kinds of historical literature, which began to include references to the past condition and significance of the peasantry as parts of regional or national German histories. In many cases, humanitarianism and reform zeal actually provoked research into peasant history in order to demonstrate the necessity, the legal validity, and the pragmatic feasibility of agrarian reform. But such writings formed actually only a kind of prologue to a more important development, a tendency to connect the history of agriculture and the agrarian population to the progress and level of happiness of civilization in general, and of the German nation in particular. A kind of "standard" peasant slowly emerged from these writings, and not surprisingly, he possessed all of the moral, military, economic, and political importance which contemporary political publicists assigned him in their tracts and papers. Although the generality of historians did not add much detail of their own to the picture of the peasant being drawn up elsewhere, they at least confirmed it, and lent to it the weight of history, which appeared to demonstrate that the qualities of the peasant just then being bruited about in Germany were not fortuitous or tied merely to the momentary fancies of contemporary publicists, but were invariably associated with the peasantry throughout history. This amounted to the confirmation of a real peasant type, which thereafter tended to dominate historical references to the peasantry. The more or less direct correlation shown by historians to exist between the freedom and vigor of the German peasantry in various periods of history and the freedom and vigor of German public life also had the effect of justifying the constantly stronger case being made by publicists throughout this period for the necessity of one or another kind of peasant participation in the public affairs of the nation.

Historical works were not the only medium of literature in which the most essential elements of a new peasant type were becoming fixed. Prose fiction, by 1840, as represented by Karl Leberecht Immermann, had begun to adopt the village and the sturdy, honest peasant as objects of artistic attention, and within a very few years had made out of them a complete genre, in which the moral steadfastness of the peasant and the simple goodness of his life played a major role. These literary themes grew slowly out of a widespread though scarcely systematic inclusion of rural motifs and agrarian social grievances in poems and short stories as early as the 1770s—part of the general agrarian reform literature of that period—and out of what may be called the "pedagogical village story," the frequent attempts to clothe instructional materials for the peasant in the garb of fictional stories set in a village milieu. Throughout the decades of this study, these belles-lettres always carried the stamp of their initial reform interest in one way or another, and Immermann's works had a no less polemical tone than any of the earlier efforts. But although the peasant stereotype which emerged from the writings of the littérateurs owed its features to social problems of immediate concern to the authors who created it, and although its origins cannot be separated from those immediate concerns, the stereotype none the less outlived them. In addition to the support given to the favorable picture of the peasant drawn up by political publicists, economists, officials, and others, belles-lettres, like historical literature, insured the continued existence of this picture beyond the periods of national crisis and the burning social issues which had originally been responsible for its birth.

By 1840, German public literature had made of the German peasant a crucial and central factor in the guarantee of the kind of life desired by virtually every major group in German society. For princes and bureaucracies, his role as primary producer and conscript warrior was indispensable to the maintenance of territorial integrity in an age to which the mass army was no longer a stranger. For German nationalists, he was the *Urgermane,* the defining element of national identity and the living link with the great German past. For the liberal constitutionalist, from left to right, he was "the people," whose singular virtues underwrote the integrity of popular participation in government. To the pious he represented an assurance that the progress of materialism and secularism would not sweep religion out of the world entirely, and that the quiet hut of the peasant remained the refuge of faith unconquered. To moralists of almost every stripe, the peasant was the font of simplicity and virtue, a rock against which the waves of decadence and degeneration would always break in vain.

For the bourgeoisie, as well, the peasant as a free proprietor had come to represent an important guarantee of property rights in general, whose interest lay with their own in resisting encroachments on property, whether on the part of government, the laboring and propertyless poor, or whomever. Even the great land-owning nobility—the Junkers of East Elbia, for example—found in the peasant the preserver of an agrarian way of life which they were concerned to defend against the inroads of commercialism and industrialism. Economically speaking, praise of the peasant and the desire to maintain a large "middle-sized" peasantry was one method of expressing opposition to the gradual transformation of land into a commodity—a process occurring everywhere in Europe under the influence of the commercial revolution. To protect the economic viability of the individual peasant farm was to protect the stability of land in general—to prevent it from becoming an object of financial speculation. The large bourgeois or noble landowner would benefit from this as surely as would the peasant himself.

As this summary indicates, the forces which led to the new concepts of the peasant's worth and significance were not all associated with "progressive" social ideas. It is certainly true that from the standpoint of political development, the recognition of the necessity for peasant participation in government is part of a general movement towards democratization of political processes which has steadily grown for nearly two centuries. And it is just as true that the idea of nationalism or national self-determination as a progressive or forward-looking force was closely involved with the growth of the new peasant image. But it would be a serious mistake to fail to note also the extent to which the peasant's new character arose from ideological reaction to the forces of social, political, and economic change which were slowly converting the agriculturally oriented and politically fragmented Germany of the eighteenth century into the politically centralized industrial giant of the late nineteenth and twentieth centuries. Whether it was secularization, foreign domination, or politically or socially revolutionary ideas which came into question, much of the service expected from this redefined peasant had to do with opposition to innovation and with preservation of the *status quo*. It therefore appears possible to suggest that the development of the image of the peasant which has been the subject of this study was in one very important sense the development of a defense mechanism against change, or against the psychological dislocations accompanying change in a critical transition period of German and indeed of western European history.

If the peasant symbolized anything in common to all the groups whose opinions made him into the creature so vastly different in 1840 from what he had been in the mid-eighteenth century, it was a bulwark against change. Each group had its own fears, its own hatreds, and its own desires, varying with the social, economic, and intellectual positions of its members. But each was able, for reasons discussed above, to find in the peasant some measure of hope that the worst could be staved off, and the best preserved. The peasant became, in this very peculiar way, a symbol of unity binding together the past and the present, and a symbol of confidence for an uncertain future. The psychological importance of such a symbol should not be underestimated: let it suffice to recall that the confusion of a prostrate and embittered Germany of the 1930s was overcome by Adolf Hitler partly through the emotional evocation of the peasant as a symbol of past and present German unity.

It would of course be a mistake to suppose that all Germans in the middle of the nineteenth century were convinced of the national salvation which the most extreme writers ascribed to the peasant's influence; but it would also be an error to deny the virtual universality of this positive picture of the peasant in the public literature of Germany by the year 1840. The writings of the period of this study had not merely modified the public image of the peasant; they had created a new peasant. No longer was he the pariah of society, but its backbone, the very essence of its claim to an active and ethical role in the progress of civilization. He was wisdom, the embodiment of all the good and essential things which tradition had to offer, and the pillar of strength in time of national crisis. Even by the end of this period, he had begun to assume the aura of the legendary—a kind of roturier Barbarossa, lost in the obscurity of his quiet village until the trumpet of danger should call him to the salvation of a desperate nation. The road up from serfdom had led beyond citizenship to sainthood.

Bibliography

PRIMARY SOURCES

Abbt, Thomas. "Vom Tode für das Vaterland" (1761), in *Deutsche Literatur: Sammlung literarischer Kunst- und Kulturdenkmäler in Entwicklungsreihen* (Reihe Aufklärung, IX) Leipzig, 1935.

Archiv der politischen Oekonomie und Polizeiwissenschaft, ed. Karl Heinrich Rau. 5 vols. Heidelberg, 1835-1843. This journal typifies the rather technical literature which began to appear in the 1830s and 1840s; the emphasis of most articles is on the use of statistics, explanation of general scientific advances in agriculture, and other similarly technical aspects of political economy.

Archiv für den Menschen und Bürger in allen Verhältnissen, ed. Johann August Schlettwein. 8 vols. Leipzig, 1780-1784. This periodical served as a primary vehicle for Physiocratic doctrines in Germany.

Arndt, Ernst Moritz. *Agrarpolitische Schriften,* ed. W. O. W. Terstegen, 2d ed. Goslar, 1942.

_____. *Arndt's Werke: Auswahl in zwölf Teilen,* ed. August Leffson and Wilhelm Steffens. 12 parts in 4 vols. Berlin, 1912.

_____. "Briefe an Franz Hegewisch," *Preussische Jahrbücher,* LVI (1885), 389-402.

_____. *Schriften für und an seine lieben Deutschen.* 4 vols. Leipzig, 1845-1855.

_____. *Über den Bauernstand und über seine Stellvertretung im Staate.* Berlin, 1815.

Aschenbrenner, Martin. *Betrachtungen über den Acker bauenden Staat.* Bamberg, Leipzig, 1816.

Athenaeum, ed. August Wilhelm Schlegel and Friedrich Schlegel. 3 vols. Berlin, 1798-1800. This work has been reproduced in facsimile, 1 vol. Stuttgart, 1960.

[Autenrieth, I. F. and others]. *Die uneingeschränkte Vertrennung der Bauern-Güter, oder Bauern-Lehen, wird in höchster*

Gegenwart Seiner Herzoglichen Durchlaucht, des regierenden Herrn Herzogs Carl, zu Wirtemberg und Töck etc. unter dem Vorsiz I. F. Autenrieth . . . öffentlich verteidiget werden, . . . 1779. Stuttgart, 1779.

Becher, Johann Joachim. *Politischer Discurs von den eigentlichen Ursachen des Auff- und Abnehmens der Staedte Laender und Republicken.* Frankfurt, 1668. One of the major works of a well-known early Cameralist.

Becker, Rudolph Z. *Noth- und Hülfs-Büchlein für Bauersleute.* 3d ed. Gotha and Leipzig, 1789. A typical example of the "household friend" type of farmer's almanac.

Berliner Abendblätter, ed. Heinrich von Kleist. Berlin, 1810-1811. This work has been reproduced in facsimile, 1 vol. Stuttgart, 1959.

Berlinische Monatsschrift, ed. F. Gedike and J. E. Biester. 28 vols. Berlin, 1783-1796.

Beyträge zur vaterländischen Historie, Geographie, Statistik und Landwirthschaft, samt einer Übersicht der schönen Literatur, ed. Lorenz Westenrieder. 7 vols. Munich, 1788-1803.

Börne, Ludwig. *Ludwig Börnes gesammelte Schriften. Vollständige Ausgabe in sechs Bänden: nebst Anhang, nachgelassene Schriften in zwei Bänden.* Introduction by Alfred Klaar. 8 vols. in 3. Leipzig, n.d.

[Buchholz, Paul Ferdinand Friedrich]. *Gemählde des gesellschaftlichen Zustandes im Königreiche Preussen, bis zum 14ten Oktober des Jahres 1806.* 2 vols. Berlin and Leipzig, 1808. Buchholz' views on the failings of the pre-1806 Prussia and his ideas concerning reforms necessary to reinvigorate the Prussian state and society found expression in these volumes.

_____. *Hermes oder über die Natur der Gesellschaft mit Blicken in die Zukunft.* Tübingen, 1810.

[_____]. *Untersuchungen über den Geburtsadel und die Möglichkeit seiner Fortdauer im neunzehnten Jahrhundert.* Berlin and Leipzig, 1807. Antiaristocratic in his sentiments, Buchholz concluded in this writing that the nineteenth century would have no place for a nobility of birth unless a basic change in that nobility's attitudes and functions took place.

Bülau, Friedrich. *Der Staat und der Landbau: Beiträge zur Agri-*

culturpolitik. Leipzig, 1834. A broad, if somewhat popularized explanation of the problems of German agriculture in the 1830s, with suggestions for improvement. The author also tries to delineate the proper role of state power in agrarian economic affairs.

——————. *Handbuch der Staatswirthschaftslehre.* Leipzig, 1835.

von Bülow-Cummerow, Ernst Gottfried Georg. *Preussen, seine Verfassung, seine Verwaltung, sein Verhältniss zu Deutschland.* 2 vols. Berlin, 1842-1843.

Bürger, Gottfried August. *Sämmtliche Werke.* 4 vols. Göttingen, 1844.

Büsch, Johann Georg. *Sämmtliche . . . vermischte Schriften.* 2d ed. 2 vols. in 1. Hamburg and Altona, 1801.

Büsching, Anton Friedrich. *Beschreibung seiner Reise von Berlin nach Kyritz in der Prignitz.* Leipzig, 1775.

Claudius, Matthias. *Matthias Claudius Werke.* Introduction by Hermann Claudius. 2 vols. Dresden, n.d.

von Clausewitz, Carl. *Politische Schriften und Briefe,* ed. Hans Rothfels. Munich, 1922.

[von Coelln, Friedrich]. *Vertraute Briefe über die innern Verhältnisse am Preussischen Hofe seit dem Tode Friedrichs II.* 6 vols. Amsterdam and Coelln, 1807-1809. Actually published at Leipzig, these "letters" are von Coelln's device for expression of a thoroughgoing criticism of the reactionary elements of the Prussian court and state.

Deutsches Magazin, ed. C. U. D. von Eggers. 20 vols. Hamburg, etc., 1791-1800. A fundamentally conservative journal, opposed to much of the innovation of Enlightenment and French Revolution.

Deutsches Museum, ed. H. C. Boie and C. W. von Dohm. 12 vols. Leipzig, 1776-1788.

Duncker, Ludwig. *Die Lehre von den Reallasten, in ihren Grundzügen.* Marburg, 1837.

Ebel, Heinrich Theophil. *Über den Ursprung der Frohnen und die Ausführbarkeit ihrer Aufhebung.* Giessen, 1823. A historical investigation of the origins of labor services and a plea for their abolition with compensation for the landlords.

Fichte, Johann Gottlieb. *Sämmtliche Werke*, ed. I. H. Fichte. 11 vols. Berlin, 1834-1846.

Fleischhauer, Johann Christian. *Die deutsche privilegirte Lehn- und Erbaristokratie, vernunftmässig und geschichtlich gewürdigt, für gebildete Deutsche aller Classen.* Neustadt an der Oder, 1831. Distinctly unfavorable to the nobility, the author said of this work that it would show clearly what to expect if the nobility all over Europe succeeded in the reaction it was then plotting.

von Forstner, Georg. *Gegenwärtiger Zustand der deutschen Landwirthschaft bey ihren dringendsten Bedürfnissen.* Tübingen, 1829. This book is an attempt to focus interest and sympathy on the agricultural class in its difficulties during the crisis of the 1820s.

——————. *Landwirthschafts-Polizey, ein Ding, das da seyn sollte—und nicht ist und Domainen-Wirthschaft, ein Ding, welches nicht seyn sollte, und doch ist.* Tübingen, 1819.

Die Franzosenzeit in deutschen Landen, 1806-1815: in Wort und Bild der Mitlebenden, ed. Friedrich Schulze. 2 vols. Leipzig, 1908.

Fulda, Friedrich Carl. *Grundsäze der ökonomisch-politischen oder Kameralwissenschaften.* Tübingen, 1816.

Fürst, Johann Evangelist. *Der verständige Bauer Simon Strüf, eine Familiengeschichte.* 3 vols. Vols. I and II, 2d ed. Passau and Salzburg, 1819. Vol. III, 1st ed. Passau, 1823.

Galletti, Johann Georg August. *Geschichte Thüringens.* 6 vols. in 3. Gotha and Dessau, 1782-1784.

Garve, Christian. *Vermischte Aufsätze.* Breslau, 1796.

von Gemmingen, Otto Heinrich Freiherr. *Der deutsche Hausvater: ein Schauspiel.* Mannheim, 1790. With regard to the peasant, this drama above all attempts to draw a respectable, even admirable, picture of the peasant's character, within the framework of an ideal lord-peasant relationship.

Gessner, Wilhelm. *Geschichtliche Entwicklung der gutsherrlichen und bäuerlichen Verhältnisse Teutschlands.* Berlin, 1820. A fairly straightforward, conservative investigation of the history of lord-peasant relationships; the author tends to be sympathetic to the peasant, but always gives full consideration to the interests of the landlords.

Gleim, Friedrich Wilhelm. *Sämmtliche Schriften von Friedrich Wilhelm Gleim* (neue verbesserte Auflage). 4 vols. Leipzig, 1802-1803.

von Goekingk, Leopold Ferdinand Günther. "Die Parforcejagd" (1771?), in *Deutsche Literatur: Sammlung literarischer Kunst- und Kulturdenkmäler in Entwicklungsreihen* (Reihe Politische Dichtung). Vol. I. Leipzig, 1930.

Görres, Joseph. *Gesammelte Schriften.* 12 vols. in 10. Cologne, 1926-1939.

Göttingisches Historisches Magazin, ed. C. Meiners and L. T. Spittler. 8 vols. Hannover, 1787-1791.

Gottsched, Johann Christoph. *Versuch einer kritischen Dichtkunst.* Leipzig, 1751.

von Grimmelshausen, Hans Jakob Christoffel. *Der abenteuerliche Simplicissimus* (1669). Bonn, 1948. An important mid-seventeenth-century source of social attitudes and of impressions of the Thirty Years' War.

Hagemann, Theodor. *Handbuch des Landwirthschaftsrechts.* Hannover, 1807.

von Halem, Gerhard Anton. *Schriften.* 7 vols. Münster and Hannover, 1803-1810.

von Haller, Albrecht. "Die Alpen" (1732), in *Deutsche Literatur: Sammlung literarischer Kunst- und Kulturdenkmäler in Entwicklungsreihen* (Reihe Aufklärung, IV). Leipzig, 1931.

Harkort, Friedrich. *Bemerkungen über die Hindernisse der Civilisation und Emancipation der untern Klassen.* Elberfeld, 1844. An unusual and interesting plea for social progress by a prominent industrialist and political liberal.

Hartleben, Theodor. *Geschäfts-Lexikon.* Vol. I. Leipzig, 1824. Not a mere series of definitions or helpful suggestions for businessmen and others, this book presents the author's forward-looking ideas for reforms in various areas of the state and the economy, together with general philosophical justifications for those ideas.

Herder, Johann Gottfried. *Sämtliche Werke,* ed. Bernhard Suphan. 33 vols. Berlin, 1877-1913. The standard edition of Herder's complete works.

Hirschfeld, Christian Cajus Lorenz. *Das Landleben* (neue Auflage). Leipzig, 1768. This book was intended as a guide to rural life for city folk who wished to vacation in the country; it contains some interesting attempts to explain the crude customs of peasant life and is in some ways an *apologia* for them.

Hirzel, H. C. *Die Wirthschaft eines philosophischen Bauers.* Zürich, 1761. Hirzel's book is an early attempt to disseminate practical and philosophical information by the use of a model, or fictional example.

Hölty, L. H. C. *Gedichte von Ludwig Heinrich Christoph Hölty: besorgt durch seine Freunde Friedrich Leopold Grafen zu Stolberg und Johann Heinrich Voss.* Hamburg, 1783.

Hufeland, Gottlieb. *Neue Grundlegung der Staatswirthschaftskunst* (erster Theil). Biesen and Wetzlar, 1807.

Hüllmann, Karl Dietrich. *Geschichte des Ursprungs der Stände in Deutschland.* 3 vols. Frankfurt an der Oder, 1806-1808.

——————. *Historische und staatswissenschaftliche Untersuchungen über die Natural-Dienste der Gutsunterthanen, nach Fränkisch-Deutscher Verfassung; und die Verwandlung derselben in Geld-Dienste.* Berlin and Stettin, 1803. This work is an excellent example of that historical research into the legal origins of social and economic institutions which aided the reformers of this period in their attempts to disprove the legality of certain traditional institutions.

Hundeshagen, Johann Christian. *Zeitbedürfnisse in politischer, administrativer und gewerblicher Beziehung oder staatswissenschaftliche Beiträge* (erstes Heft). Tübingen, 1832.

Immermann, Karl Leberecht. *Immermanns Werke.* ed. Harry Maync. 5 vols. Leipzig and Vienna, 1906.

Iselin, Isaak. *Vermischte Schriften.* 2 vols. Zürich, 1770. Insofar as his attitudes on agriculture were concerned, Iselin's inclination, as expressed with some vehemence in this work, was decidedly Physiocratic.

Jakob, Ludwig Heinrich. *Grundsätze der National-Ökonomie oder National-Wirthschaftslehre.* Halle, 1805.

Jung-Stilling, Johann Heinrich. *Sämmtliche Werke.* 12 vols. Stuttgart, 1841-1842.

von Justi, Johann Heinrich Gottlob. *Oeconomische Schriften über die wichtigsten Gegenstände der Stadt- und Landwirthschaft.* 2 vols. Berlin and Leipzig, 1760. This work is that of a dedicated Cameralist, whose views were strongly flavored with Physiocracy. In addition to his philosophical views on state economy, these volumes contain specific hints for the improvement of practical agriculture.

Kraus, Christian Jakob. *Aufsätze über staatswirthschaftliche Gegenstände,* ed. Hans von Auerswald. 5 vols. in 3. Königsberg, 1808-1811. Numerous essays by one of the most influential Smithian professors in Germany.

von Leipziger, August Wilhelm. *Geist der National-Oekonomie und Staatswirthschaft, für National-Repräsentanten, Geschäftsmänner, und die, die es werden wollen.* 2 vols. Berlin, 1813-1814.

Leipziger Magazin zur Naturgeschichte und Oekonomie, ed. Nathanael Gottfried Leske. 7 vols. Leipzig, 1781-1788. These volumes are good examples of a number of later eighteenth-century publications of agricultural and technical societies interested in the acquisition and diffusion of practical and scientific knowledge from the areas of agriculture, the crafts, and the sciences.

Leisewitz, Johann Anton. *Sämmtliche Schriften.* Braunschweig, 1838.

Leopold, Justus Ludwig Günther. *Agricola oder fassliche Darstellung des Neuesten und Gemeinnützigsten aus der gesammten Landwirthschaft.* 2 vols. Hannover, 1804-1805.

Lips, Michael Alexander. *Deutschlands National-Oekonomie.* Giessen, 1830.

—————. *Principien der Ackergesetzgebung als Grundlage eines künftigen Ackercodex für Gesezgeber und rationelle Landwirthe.* Nürnberg, 1811.

Lotz, Johann Friedrich Eusebius. *Handbuch der Staatswirthschaftslehre.* 3 vols. Erlangen, 1821-1822.

—————. *Revision der Grundbegriffe der Nationalwirthschaftslehre, in Beziehung auf Theuerung und Wohlfeilheit, und angemessene Preise und ihre Bedingungen.* 4 vols. Koburg and Leipzig, 1811-1814. A treatment of the problems of political economy from a moderate free-trade position.

Luden, Heinrich. *Geschichte des teutschen Volkes.* 12 vols. Gotha, 1825-1837.

——————. *Handbuch der Staatsweisheit oder der Politik* (erste Abtheilung). Jena, 1811.

Lueder, August Ferdinand. *Über Nationalindustrie und Staatswirthschaft.* 3 vols. Berlin, 1800-1804.

Mannert, Konrad. *Die Geschichte Bayerns.* 2 vols. Leipzig, 1826.

von der Marwitz, Friedrich August Ludwig. *Friedrich August Ludwig von der Marwitz: ein märkischer Edelmann im Zeitalter der Befreiungskriege,* ed. Friedrich Meusel. 2 vols in 3. Berlin, 1908-1913. These writings are those of the most steadfast and articulate noble opponent of the Stein-Hardenberg reforms. Many of the selections printed in these volumes did not appear in print in Marwitz' own day.

Meiners, Christoph. *Geschichte der Ungleichheit der Stände unter den vornehmsten Europäischen Völkern.* 2 vols. Hannover, 1792.

von Mohl, Robert. *Die Polizei-Wissenschaft nach den Grundsätzen des Rechtsstaates.* 3d ed. 3 vols. Tübingen, 1866. This work, originally published in 1832-1834, is an important early attempt to define the goals and functions of political administration as conditioned by the liberal and constitutional framework of the *Rechtsstaat;* the author was one of the most influential German economists of the mid-nineteenth century.

von Moser, Friedrich Carl. *Der Herr und der Diener, geschildert mit patriotischer Freyheit.* Frankfurt, 1759. An attempt to inject attitudes of mutual humility into the artificial relationships of the courts and activities of the German princes and nobility.

——————. *Doctor Leidemit.* Frankfurt, 1843. Originally published in 1783.

——————. *Gesammelte moralische und politische Schriften.* 2 vols. Frankfurt, 1763-1764.

——————. *Politische Wahrheiten.* 2 vols. Zürich, 1796.

Moser, Johann Jakob. *Von der Teutschen Unterthanen Rechten und Pflichten.* Frankfurt and Leipzig, 1774.

Möser, Justus. *Osnabrückische Geschichte.* 3d ed. 2 vols. Berlin and Stettin, 1819-1824.

——————. *Sämtliche Werke: Historisch-kritische Ausgabe in 14 Bänden,* ed. and annotated by Ludwig Schirmeyer and others. 9 vols. to date. Oldenburg and Berlin, 1943-1965. This work, when complete, will be the authoritative collection of Möser's writings. Of these volumes, IV-VII contain the *Patriotische Phantasien,* a group of essays written by Möser originally for the *Osnabrückische Intelligenzblätter,* but later also collected and published by Möser's daughter, Frau von Voigt, in three volumes in 1778, to which a fourth was added in 1786.

Müller, Adam. *Die Elemente der Staatskunst.* 3 vols. Berlin, 1809.

——————. *Vermischte Schriften über Staat, Philosophie, und Kunst* (erster Theil). 2d ed. Vienna, 1817.

von Münchhausen, Phillip Adolf Freiherr. *Über Lehnherrn und Dienstmann.* Leipzig, 1793.

Neithardt von Gneisenau, A. W. A. *Denkschriften zum Volksaufstand von 1808 und 1811,* ed. and introduced by Harald von Königswald (Kriegsgeschichtliche Bücherei, Band 10.). Berlin, 1936. Contains Gneisenau's speculations on the possibilities of popular uprisings against Napoleon's armies in Prussia.

Neue Feuerbrände, ed. Friedrich von Coelln. 6 vols. comprising 18 Hefte. Amsterdam and Coelln, 1807-1808. Actually published at Leipzig, this work, written by the Prussian official von Coelln, indicted many of the weaknesses of the Prussia of Jena and Auerstädt. It is outspokenly antinoble and proreform, and covers a multitude of topics relating to social, economic, political, and religious affairs—usually with an extremely critical tone. Many articles, though anonymous, were doubtless written by von Coelln himself.

Neues Archiv für den Menschen und Bürger in allen Verhältnissen, ed. Johann August Schlettwein. 5 vols. Leipzig, 1785-1788.

Neues Deutsches Museum, ed. H. C. Boie. 4 vols. Leipzig, 1789-1791.

Neues Göttingisches Historisches Magazin, ed. C. Meiners and L. T. Spittler. 3 vols. Hannover, 1792-1794.

Niebuhr, Barthold Georg. *Geschichte des Zeitalters der Revolution,* ed. Marcus Niebuhr. 2 vols. in 1. Hamburg, 1845.

——————. *Lebensnachrichten über Barthold Georg Niebuhr,* ed. Dora Hensler. 3 vols. Hamburg, 1838-1839. A collection of letters, memoranda, and other papers of the famous historian.

——————. *Nachgelassene Schriften B. G. Niebuhr's nichtphilo-*

sophischen Inhalts, ed. Marcus Niebuhr. Hamburg, 1842.

Novalis [Friedrich von Hardenberg]. *Novalis' Werke in vier Teilen,* ed. Hermann Friedemann. 4 parts in 2 vols. Leipzig, n.d.

Oechsle, Ferdinand Friedrich. *Beiträge zur Geschichte des Bauernkrieges in den schwäbisch-fränkischen Grenzlanden.* Heilbronn, 1830.

Oeconomische Encyclopädie, oder allgemeines System der Land-Haus- und Staats-Wirthschaft, in alphabetischer Ordnung: Aus dem Französischen übersetzt, und mit Anmerkungen und Zusätzen vermehrt, ed. Johann Georg Krünitz. Vol. III. Berlin, 1774.

[Oeder, Georg Christian]. *Bedenken über die Frage: Wie dem Bauernstande Freyheit und Eigenthum in den Ländern, wo ihm beydes fehlet, verschaffet werden könne?* Frankfurt and Leipzig, 1769. The second edition of this work, published at Altona in 1786, included the author's name.

Patriotisches Archiv für Deutschland, ed. Friedrich Carl von Moser. 12 vols. Frankfurt, Mannheim, and Leipzig, 1784-1790. Moser's journal was an essentially conservative but none the less critical review of the society of the time; it accurately reflects Moser's own belief in a society without class antagonisms, pervaded by the spirit of Christian humanitarianism, and his cordial dislike of luxury, ostentation, and imitation of things foreign.

Patriotisches Archiv für Deutschland: der Gottheit, den Fürsten, dem Vaterlande gewidmet, ed. Samuel Christian Wagener. 2 vols. in 4. Berlin, 1799. An outspokenly conservative journal, these volumes contain strongly royalist, religious, and patriotic views; a good example of antienlightened points of view on contemporary society and politics, but not of a really reactionary standpoint.

Pertz, Georg Heinrich. *Das Leben des Ministers Freiherrn vom Stein.* 2d ed. 6 vols. in 7. Berlin, 1850-1855. An old work, Pertz' volumes nevertheless retain value as a well-documented, favorable account of Stein's life and thought; they also contain some documents not found in other collections.

[Pestalozzi, Johann Heinrich]. *Figuren zu meinem A B C Buch oder zu den Anfangsgründen meines Denkens.* Basel, 1797.

—————, *Lienhard und Gertrud*. 2d ed. (?). 3 vols. Zürich and Leipzig, 1790-1792. One of Pestalozzi's most famous and influential works, these volumes contain the essence of the famous pedagogue's thought on the methods and goals of education.

von Pfister, Johann Christian. *Geschichte der Teutschen*. 5 vols. Hamburg, 1829-1835.

Politisches Journal nebst Anzeige von gelehrten und andern Sachen, ed. "von einer Gesellschaft von Gelehrten." 120 vols. Hamburg, 1781-1840. This periodical shows an especially strong emphasis on international affairs, particularly those of a political nature.

Pölitz, Karl Heinrich Ludwig. *Staatswissenschaftliche Vorlesungen für die gebildeten Stände in constitutionellen Staaten*. 2 vols. in 1. Leipzig, 1831-1832.

Posselt, Ernst Ludwig. *Geschichte der Deutschen für alle Stände*. 4 vols. Hamburg and Leipzig, 1808-1819. The fourth volume of this work was written by K. H. L. Pölitz.

Pütter, Johann Stephan. *Über den Unterschied der Stände, besonders des hohen und niedern Adels in Teutschland*. Göttingen, 1795.

Rau, Karl Heinrich. *Lehrbuch der politischen Oekonomie*. Vol. I, 7th ed. Leipzig and Heidelberg, 1863.

Riemann, Karl Friedrich. *Versuch einer Beschreibung der Reckanschen Schuleinrichtung*. Berlin and Stettin, 1781.

[Riesbeck, Johann Caspar]. *Briefe eines reisenden Franzosen über Deutschland: An seinen Bruder zu Paris*. 2 vols. n.p., n.d.

von Rochow, Friedrich Eberhard. *Sämtliche pädagogische Schriften*, ed. Fritz Jonas und Friedrich Wienecke. 4 vols. Berlin, 1907-1910.

von Rothe, A. *Der Landmann, wie er sein sollte, oder Franz Nowak, der wohlberathene Bauer*. 5th ed. Glogau, 1853. The first edition of this work was published in 1838; it is a typical instructional manual for peasants, centered around the everyday experiences of a peasant family.

von Rotteck, Carl. *Lehrbuch des Vernunftrechts und der Staatswissenschaften*. 4 vols. Stuttgart, 1829-1835. This *Lehrbuch* is an attempt to cover, briefly but methodically, the system of the political and legal sciences from the point of view of "natural law."

Sartorius, Georg. *Abhandlungen, die Elemente des National-Reichthums und die Staatswirthschaft betreffend* (erster Theil). Göttingen, 1806.

Schenck, Karl Friedrich. *Das Bedürfniss der Volks-Wirthschaft.* 2 vols. Stuttgart, 1831.

Schlettwein, Johann August. *Die in den teutschen Reichsgesetzen bestimmte weise Ordnung der Gerechtigkeit wider Aufruhr und Empörung der Unterthanen gegen ihre Obrigkeiten.* Leipzig, 1791.

Schlosser, Johann Georg. *Kleine Schriften.* 6 vols. in 3. Basel, 1780-1793.

Schmidt, Michael Ignaz. *Geschichte der Deutschen.* 22 vols. Ulm, 1785-1808. Volumes XII-XXII of this work were written by Joseph Milbiller.

Schmitthenner, Friedrich. *Lehrbuch der deutschen Geschichte.* 2d ed. Cassel, 1836.

Schubart, Christian Friedrich Daniel. *Des Patrioten: Gesammelte Schriften und Schicksale.* 8 vols. in 7. Stuttgart, 1839-1840.

Schüz, Carl Wolfgang Christoph. *Über den Einfluss der Vertheilung des Grundeigenthums auf das Volks- und Staatsleben.* Stuttgart and Tübingen, 1836. A detailed and persuasive argument for the preservation of a large proprietary peasant class.

Smith, Adam. *An Inquiry into the Nature and Causes of the Wealth of Nations,* ed. Max Lerner. New York, 1937. [Modern Library.] This is based on the fifth edition, published originally in 1789.

Spittler, Ludwig Timotheus. *Geschichte Wirtembergs unter der Regierung der Grafen und Herzöge.* Göttingen, 1783.

—————. *Vorlesungen über Politik,* ed. Karl Wächter. Stuttgart and Tübingen, 1828.

Staats-Anzeigen, ed. August Ludwig Schlözer. 18 vols. Göttingen, 1782-1793. One of the most fascinating of eighteenth-century periodicals, this is the creation of one of the most fascinating of eighteenth-century German minds, that of the irrepressible A. L. Schlözer. This series of volumes sets a model for the rational, liberal-cosmopolitan point of view of a certain number of "enlightened" German intellectuals of the time. Biting social and political criticism is characteristic of many of the articles contained in the journal.

Staats-Lexikon oder Encyclopädie der Staatswissenschaften, ed. Carl von Rotteck and Carl Welcker. 15 vols. Altona, 1834-1843. One of the early works of its kind, this creation of the liberal-minded Rotteck and Welcker serves admirably as a compendium of early nineteenth-century German national-liberal thought on many aspects of politics and social and economic affairs in Germany. It was widely read and enormously influential in its time.

vom Stein, Karl Freiherr. *Freiherr vom Stein: Briefwechsel, Denkschriften, und Aufzeichnungen,* ed. Erich Botzenhart. 7 vols. Berlin, 1931-1937. Until the recent publication of a new series of Stein's papers, this was the standard collection.

Stüve, Carl. *Über die Lasten des Grundeigenthums und Verminderung derselben in Rücksicht auf das Königreich Hannover.* Hannover, 1830.

Der teutsche Merkur, ed. C. M. Wieland and others. 131 vols. in 76. Weimar, 1773-1810.

Thaer, Albrecht. *Einleitung zur Kenntniss der englischen Landwirthschaft.* Hannover, 1798.

_____. *Leitfaden zur allgemeinen landwirthschaftlichen Gewerbslehre.* Berlin, 1815.

Voss, Johann Heinrich. *Sämtliche Gedichte.* 7 vols. Königsberg, 1802.

von Wedekind, Georg Christian Freiherr. *Über den Werth des Adels und über die Ansprüche des Zeitgeistes auf Verbesserung des Adelsinstitutes* (neue Ausgabe). 2 vols. Darmstadt, 1817. This defense of the German aristocracy, written by a man who once criticized it severely, is a relatively balanced work, by no means extreme in its point of view.

Wernher der Gartenaere. *Meier Helmbrecht,* ed. Wolfgang Schütz. Berlin, 1957.

Wichmann, Christian August. *Über die natürlichsten Mittel, die Frohn-Dienste bey Kammer- und Ritter-Güthern ohne Nachtheil der Grundherren aufzuheben.* Leipzig, 1795.

Zimmermann, Wilhelm. *Allgemeine Geschichte des grossen Bau-*

ernkrieges. 3 vols. in 2. Stuttgart, 1841-1843. A detailed survey, this work shows great sympathy for the peasant class in the Peasants' War.

Zschokke, Heinrich. *Der baierischen Geschichten.* 4 vols. Aarau, 1813-1818.

SECONDARY SOURCES

Abel, Wilhelm. *Die drei Epochen der deutschen Agrargeschichte.* 2d ed. Hannover, 1964.

——————. *Geschichte der deutschen Landwirtschaft.* Stuttgart, 1962. An excellent brief survey of German agricultural history by one of Germany's leading agrarian historians; contains fine bibliographies.

Allgemeine deutsche Biographie (herausgegeben durch die Historische Commission bei der Königlichen Akademie der Wissenschaften). 56 vols. Leipzig, 1875-1912. The standard German biographical dictionary.

Altvater, Friedrich. *Wesen und Form der deutschen Dorfgeschichte im neunzehnten Jahrhundert.* Berlin, 1930.

Anderson, Eugene N. *Nationalism and the Cultural Crisis in Prussia, 1806-1815.* New York, 1939.

Antoni, Carlo. *Der Kampf wider die Vernunft: zur Entstehungsgeschichte des deutschen Freiheitsgedankens.* Trans. from the Italian by Walter Goetz. Stuttgart, 1951.

Baumstark, Edward. *Kameralistische Encyclopädie: Handbuch der Kameralwissenschaften und ihrer Literatur.* Heidelberg and Leipzig, 1835. A uniquely valuable bibliography of Cameralistic writings to the date of publication.

Bechtel, Heinrich. *Wirtschaftsgeschichte Deutschlands.* 3 vols. Munich, 1951-1956. A rather discursive general economic history of Germany.

Biedermann, Karl. *Deutschland im achtzehnten Jahrhundert.* 2 vols. in 3. Leipzig, 1880. An old but unrivaled and still very useful and comprehensive treatment of German life in the eighteenth century.

Biographie universelle, ancienne et moderne. 85 vols. Paris, 1811-1862.

Bruford, W. H. *Culture and Society in Classical Weimar, 1775-1806.* Cambridge, 1962.

Brunner, Otto. *Adeliges Landleben und europäischer Geist: Leben und Werk Wolf Helmhards von Hohberg, 1612-1688.* Salzburg, 1949.

Bühler, Johannes. *Der deutsche Bauer im Wandel der Zeiten.* Cologne, 1938.

Büsch, Otto. *Militärsystem und Sozialleben im alten Preussen, 1713-1807: die Anfänge der sozialen Militarisierung der preussisch-deutschen Gesellschaft* (Veröffentlichungen der Berliner Historischen Commission beim Friedrich-Meinecke-Institut der Freien Universität Berlin, Band 7). Berlin, 1962. An excellent and fascinating study of the influence of military organization and mores on the structure of Prusso-German social relationships in the eighteenth century.

Carsten, Francis L. *Princes and Parliaments in Germany from the Fifteenth to the Eighteenth Century.* Oxford, 1959. This book is a well-documented study of Diets in various German states and of the relations between them and the territorial princes in the period of the growth of absolutism.

Eichler, Arthur. *Die Landbewegung des 18. Jahrhunderts und ihre Pädagogik* (Göttinger Studien zur Pädagogik, Heft 20). Langensalza, 1933.

Enslin, Theodor Christian Friedrich. *Bibliotheca Oeconomica oder Verzeichniss der in älterer und neuerer Zeit bis zur Mitte des Jahres 1840 in Deutschland und den angränzenden Ländern erschienenen Bücher über die Haus- und Landwirthschaft.* Revised 2d ed. by Wilhelm Engelmann. Leipzig, 1841. A very valuable and fairly complete bibliographical guide to agricultural literature in Germany to 1840.

Fauchier-Magnan, Adrien. *The Small German Courts in the Eighteenth Century.* London, 1958.

Flitner, Andreas. *Die politische Erziehung in Deutschland: Geschichte und Probleme, 1750-1880.* Tübingen, 1957. An excellent study of the relationship between pedagogical theory and practice and political ideologies for the period concerned.

Francke, Kuno. *A History of German Literature as Determined by Social Forces.* New York, 1901.

Freytag, Gustav. *Bilder aus der deutschen Vergangenheit.* 7th ed. 4 vols. Leipzig, 1873-1882.

Gagliardo, John G. *Enlightened Despotism.* New York, 1967.

Gerdes, Heinrich. *Geschichte des deutschen Bauernstandes.* Leipzig, 1910. A short but readable and reasonably accurate history of the German peasantry.

von der Goltz, Theodor. *Geschichte der deutschen Landwirtschaft.* 2 vols. Stuttgart and Berlin, 1902-1903.

Grathoff, Ernst. *Deutsche Bauern- und Dorfzeitungen des 18. Jahrhunderts: ein Beitrag zur Geschichte des Bauerntums, der öffentlichen Meinung und des Zeitungswesens* (Inaugural-Diss., Heidelberg, 1937). Würzburg, 1937.

von Groote, Wolfgang. *Die Entstehung des Nationalbewusstseins in Nordwestdeutschland, 1790-1830* (Göttinger Bausteine zur Geschichtswissenschaft, Band 22) Göttingen, 1955. Valuable case study in the transformation of literary cosmopolitan humanitarianism into nationalist patriotism.

Hamerow, Theodore. *Restoration, Revolution, Reaction: Economics and Politics in Germany, 1815-1871.* Princeton, 1958.

Hartung, Fritz. "Der aufgeklärte Absolutismus," *Historische Zeitschrift*, CLXXX, Heft 1 (August, 1955), 15-42. A suggestive treatment of the nature of "enlightened absolutism" by one of Germany's leading constitutional historians.

——————. *Deutsche Verfassungsgeschichte vom 15. Jahrhundert bis zur Gegenwart.* 7th ed. Stuttgart, 1950.

Hauffen, Adolf. *Geschichte des deutschen Michel.* Prague, 1918. An attempt to trace the origins and development of the use of the Archangel Michael as a German national symbol.

Haushofer, Heinz. *Die deutsche Landwirtschaft im technischen Zeitalter.* Stuttgart, 1963.

Henderson, W. O. *The State and the Industrial Revolution in Prussia, 1740-1870.* Liverpool, 1958.

Hertz, Frederick. *The Development of the German Public Mind: A Social History of German Political Sentiments, Aspirations, and Ideas.* Vol. II. London, 1962.

Janssen, Johannes. *History of the German People at the Close of the Middle Ages.* Trans. by M. A. Mitchell and A. M. Christie. 16 vols. London, 1896-1910.

Jolles, Mathys. *Das deutsche Nationalbewusstsein im Zeitalter Napoleons* (Studien zur Geschichte des Staats- und Nationalgedankens, Band 1). Frankfurt, 1936.

Kaiser, Gerhard. *Pietismus und Patriotismus im literarischen Deutschland: ein Beitrag zum Problem der Säkularisation.* Wiesbaden, 1961. A valuable contribution to the literature on the influence of Pietism on the development of patriotic-nationalistic sentiment in Germany.

Kann, Robert A. *A Study in Austrian Intellectual History: From Late Baroque to Romanticism.* New York, 1960.

Knapp, Georg Friedrich. *Die Bauernbefreiung und der Ursprung der Landarbeiter in den älteren Theilen Preussens.* 2 vols. Leipzig, 1887. An old work, which is still standard in the field.

Krieger, Leonard. *The German Idea of Freedom: History of a Political Tradition.* Boston, 1957.

Kuehnemund, Richard. *Arminius or the Rise of a National Symbol in Literature.* (University of North Carolina Studies in the Germanic Languages and Literatures, No. 8). Chapel Hill, N.C., 1953.

Lamprecht, Karl. *Deutsche Geschichte.* 1st-4th eds. 12 vols. in 16. Freiburg and Berlin, 1904-1911.

Lehmann, Max. "Das alte Preussen," *Historische Zeitschrift,* XC (1903), 385-421.

Lohre, Heinrich. *Von Percy zum Wunderhorn: Beiträge zur Geschichte der Volksliedforschung in Deutschland.* Berlin, 1902.

Lütge, Friedrich K. *Deutsche Sozial- und Wirtschaftsgeschichte.* 2d ed. Berlin, 1960.

—————. *Geschichte der deutschen Agrarverfassung.* Stuttgart, 1963. A brilliant but all too brief survey of the political, social, and legal foundations of agrarian Germany from earliest times to the mid-nineteenth century.

Martini, Fritz. *Das Bauerntum im deutschen Schrifttum: von den Anfängen bis zum 16. Jahrhundert.* Halle, 1944.

Motteck, Hans. *Wirtschaftsgeschichte Deutschlands: ein Grun-*

driss. Vol. I. Berlin, 1957. A Marxist economic history, which should be used with some care. Contains some interesting statistics and factual information, however.

Pinson, Koppel S. *Pietism as a Factor in the Rise of German Nationalism* (Columbia University Studies in History, Economics and Public Law, No. 398). New York, 1934. A pioneer ing work in the contribution of Pietism to the growth of nationalistic sentiment.

Rohr, Donald G. *The Origins of Social Liberalism in Germany.* Chicago, 1963. Rohr attempts here to refute the commonly-held opinion that no German social theorists in the three or four decades before Marx devoted much sincere attention to the rapidly growing problems of an industrializing Germany. Contains good explications of social theory of the first half of the nineteenth century.

Roscher, Wilhelm. *Geschichte der National-Oekonomik in Deutschland.* Munich, 1874.

Rössler, Helmuth, and Günther Franz. *Biographisches Wörterbuch zur deutschen Geschichte.* Munich, 1952. Contains very concise summaries of the lives of important Germans of the past.

Saalfeld, Diedrich. *Bauernwirtschaft und Gutsbetrieb in der vorindustriellen Zeit.* Stuttgart, 1960. An intensive quantitative investigation of agrarian changes in Lower Saxony from the mid-sixteenth to the beginning of the nineteenth century.

Sartorius von Waltershausen, August. *Deutsche Wirtschaftsgeschichte, 1815-1914.* Jena, 1920.

Schairer, Erich. *Christian Friedrich Daniel Schubart als politischer Journalist* (Inaugural-Diss., Tübingen). Tübingen, 1914.

Scheel, Heinrich, *Süddeutsche Jakobiner: Klassenkämpfe und republikanische Bestrebungen im deutschen Süden Ende des 18. Jahrhunderts* (Deutsche Akademie der Wissenschaften zu Berlin: Schriften des Instituts für Geschichte, Reihe I: Allgemeine und deutsche Geschichte, Band 13). Berlin, 1962. Built around the theory of class struggle in the revolutionary epoch, this tendentious work none the less contains much valuable information about liberal and republican sentiment in southern Germany in the last decade of the eighteenth century.

Schnabel, Franz. *Deutsche Geschichte im neunzehnten Jahrhundert.* Vol. II. 2d ed. Munich, 1949.

Schultze, Johanna. *Die Auseinandersetzung zwischen Adel und Bürgertum in den deutschen Zeitschriften der letzten drei Jahrzehnte des 18. Jahrhunderts, 1773-1806.* Berlin, 1925.

Shanahan, William O. *Prussian Military Reforms, 1786-1813* (Columbia University Studies in History, Economics and Public Law, No. 520). New York, 1945.

Small, Albion W. *The Cameralists: The Pioneers of German Social Polity.* Chicago and London, 1909. The standard work in English on German Cameralism; pedantic and unimaginative, but valuable.

Sommer, Louise. *Die österreichischen Kameralisten.* 2 vols. Vienna, 1920-1925.

Stulz, Percy, and Alfred Opitz. *Volksbewegungen in Kursachsen zur Zeit der Französischen Revolution.* Berlin, 1956. A Marxist interpretation of popular revolts in Electoral Saxony in the first few years of the French Revolutionary period. Well-documented and useful.

Thomas, Richard Hinton. *Liberalism, Nationalism, and the German Intellectuals, 1822-1847.* Cambridge, 1951.

Tschirch, Otto. *Geschichte der öffentlichen Meinung in Preussen vom Baseler Frieden bis zum Zusammenbruch des Staates (1795-1806).* 2 vols. Weimar, 1933-1934.

Valjavec, Fritz. *Die Entstehung der politischen Strömungen in Deutschland, 1770-1815.* Munich, 1951. A very thorough and original study of German political and social ideas in a very important period of the development of diverse ideological allegiances.

Index

Abbt, Thomas (Prussian professor): on equality of citizenship, 86-87

absolutism: opposed by Justus Möser, 78-80; and corporatism, 79-81; and new image of the peasant, 85-88; and idea of equality, 85-88; adoption of enlightened ideas by, 86; and citizenship, 86-87; and education, 92; and peasant education, 109; and origins of constitutionalism, 212

—enlightened: and egalitarianism, ix; and education, 95-96, 110-11; and Physiocrats, 96; and peasant education, 97-98; and citizenship, 110-11; and peasant citizenship, 121

Agricultural Revolution: based on Dutch and English examples, 8; influence of, on Cameralists, 34; mentioned, 31

agriculture: and reform literature, x; importance of, in Germany, 3, 30-31, 32, 38; effects of Thirty Years' War on, 3-6; reforms and improvements in, 8-11, 130-31; and Cameralism, 32-38, 286-87; and Physiocracy, 37, 39, 40; importance of, to society, 61-62, 126, 180-82, 191-92, 204-205, 219-21, 233-34, 242, 243, 259; and character of peasant life, 70-71; and peasant newspapers, 105-107; connected to patriotism, 180-82; and citizenship, 181-82; and agrarian crisis of 1820s, 218-42 *passim;* and debate over peasant farm size, 234-42, 250; and Adam Smith's doctrines, 290. *See also* peasants; reform, agrarian

amour-propre. See self-interest

armies: and state policy toward peasants, 43-44, 43n39; and political influence on peasants, 87n56; and French *levée en masse,* 177; reorganization of, in Prussia, 177-80; and the peasant in Prussia, 178, 211, 212n1; and need for peasants, 210

Arminius: as symbol of German nationality, 139-40; mentioned, 142, 202, 203

Arndt, Ernst Moritz (German writer and poet): career of, 199-200; and patriotism, 200; and Freiherr vom Stein, 200, 207-208, 210, 298; views of, on the peasant, 199-210 *passim;* on servitude, 201; and Protestantism, 201, 210n80; on the peasant as soldier, 203-204, 209-10; Gallophobia of, 200, 203; on importance of agriculture to society, 204-205; on peasant political representation, 205-206; on peasant proprietorship, 206-207; on size of peasant farms, 206-207; on life of peasants and city folk, 208; criticizes nobility, 208; and Justus Möser and F. C. von Moser, 210; and new image of peasant, 210; and peasants in Wars of Liberation, 211; criticizes industrial society, 232; on history of servitude, 257; on historical importance of peasantry, 265; on importance of peasantry to society, 298; mentioned, 218, 299

Arnim, Achim von (German writer and poet): and the folksong, 147; mentioned, 272

Auerstädt. *See* Jena and Auerstädt

Autenrieth, Jakob Friedrich (German official): on land distribution, 52

Baczko, Ludwig von (German historian): writes history of Prussia, 266

Baden: abolition of servitude in, 17, 21; Physiocracy in, 38-39

bankruptcy. *See* credit, rural

Basedow, J. B. (German educator): and peasant education, 95; philanthropic school of, 98

Battle of the Nations, 212n1

Bavaria: commutation of peasant labor services in, 17; abolition of servitude in, 20, 21

Becher, Johann Joachim (German Cameralist): attitudes of, toward peasantry, 32-33; and education, 92

Becker, Rudolph Z. (German writer and educator): on peasant litigation, 45; and peasant education, 98-99; writes peasant almanac, 107; mentioned, 166

belles-lettres: and the new image of the peasant, 271-72, 283, 303

Nassau: abolition of servitude in, 20
national character. *See* Germany,
national character of
national consciousness: in Germany,
136-50 *passim*
nationalism: and foreign influences in
Germany, 137-38, 142, 291-92, 293;
and cosmopolitanism, 142-44; and
morality of peasant life, 137; and
definition of "nation," 144-45; and
new image of the peasant, 149-50,
304; and E. M. Arndt, 202; and
moralism, 291-92
Neumark: agrarian reform in, 16
Nicolovius, Ludwig: and J. H. Pestalozzi and Freiherr vom Stein, 194
Niebuhr, Barthold Georg: criticizes liberal economic theory and legislation,
232-33; mentioned, 202, 261
nobility, noble landowners: and lack of
capital of, 5; exclusive right of land-
ownership of; 6; right of, to enter
middle-class vocations, 6; resistance
of, to agrarian reforms, 16, 19, 56,
229, 260-61; abolishes servitude in
Schleswig-Holstein, 17; absorbs peasant lands after 1815, 21; economic
liberalism of, in Prussia, 40; criticized
by writers, 44, 162-63, 167-71, 172,
175-76, 209; and peasant political
representation, 88, 214-17, 258; partition of domains of, suggested, 154;
overseers of, 160-61; and agrarian reform, 167-68, 172; and new definitions of nobility, 170-71, 175; implicated in Prussia's collapse, 176-77;
elimination of civil authority of, 185-
86; and peasant proprietorship after
1815, 213; and peasant obligations,
257, 260, 261-62; bias against in
historiography, 269
Novalis (German romantic poet): confidence of, in German culture, 148;
and the peasant, 148-49

Oeder, Georg Christian (Danish official): on civic freedom for peasants,
56
Osnabrück, Bishopric of, 45, 76, and

76n36
Pahl, Johann Gottfried (German cleric
and historian): on history of Peasants' War of 1525-1526, 264
Palatinate, Electorate of the: peasant
political representation in, 88

Patriot, Patriotismus: defined, 85n54
patriotism: and education, 95; literary,
in Germany, 141-43; and peasants,
163-66; 171-72, 180, 204-205, 243,
244, 245; and new image of the
peasant, 166; and peasant citizenship,
172-73; and common people in Prussia, 177; connected to agriculture,
180-82; and Freiherr vom Stein, 186-
87; and E. M. Arndt, 200, 201
peasants, peasantry; and citizenship, x,
xi, 86-87, 166-67, 172-73, 174, 182-
83, 185-86, 195-99 *passim,* 202, 268,
285-86, 289-90, 290-91, 295-97, 300-
301; and patriotism, x, 163-66, 171,
172, 204-205, 243, 244, 245; characteristics ascribed to, xii, 27, 28-29,
30, 36, 57, 61-90 *passim,* 110-11,
134-35, 135n27, 137, 140, 149, 164-
65, 179, 180-81, 183-84, 198, 204-
205, 210, 220-21, 238, 239, 242-45,
246-47, 249, 269, 276, 280-82 *passim,*
284, 288, 292-306 *passim;* compared
and contrasted to city folk, xii, 65-66,
178-80, 208, 249; importance of, to
German agriculture, 3, 30; inability
of, to better own condition, 3, 4, 6,
11, 132n22; effects of Thirty Years'
War on, 3-6; and proprietorship, 6,
7-8, 18-19, 20, 22, 35-36, 55, 75,
117-18, 129-30, 136, 154, 188-89,
195, 201, 206-207, 213, 215, 219,
224-25, 227-30, 233-42 *passim,* 247,
249-50, 289, 293, 296-97, 299-301;
proletarianization of, 8, 21-22, 218,
231-42 *passim,* 236, 238-41 *passim,*
247-48, 299-301; legal status of, in
Germany, 11-21 *passim;* obligations
of, to landlords, 11-14, 56, 224-26,
257, 260; land tenure of, 12-13, 14,
21, 55, 56; labor services of, 14-17
passim, 19, 21, 34, 36, 52, 54, 56,
125, 131, 133, 153, 154-57, 170, 197,
225, 257, 260, 262; in public literature of Middle Ages, 24; and advent
of printing, 25; characteristics of, 27-
28, 149; and position in literary culture, 29-30; origins of new interest
in, 30; and military policy, 43-44;
physical mistreatment of, 44; and
legal and juridical reform, 44-46; and
lawyers, 45-46; and rural beggars,
46; and rural credit, 47-50; and principle of self-interest, 52-54, 291; and
moralism, 61-90 *passim,* 242, 246-47,
292, 295; as soldiers, 62, 165-66,